WRITINGS OF
LEON TROTSKY
[1938-39]

Writings of Leon Trotsky is a collection, in twelve volumes, of pamphlets, articles, letters, and interviews written during Trotsky's third and final exile (1929-40). They include many articles translated into English for the first time. They do not include the books and pamphlets from this period that are permanently in print, nor most of the unpublished material in the Trotsky Archives at Harvard University Library. Five of the volumes cover Trotsky's residence in Turkey (1929, 1930, 1930-31, 1932, 1932-33); two in France (1933-34, 1934-35); one in Norway (1935-36); and four in Mexico (1936-37, 1937-38, 1938-39, 1939-40).

WRITINGS OF LEON TROTSKY

[1938-39]

PATHFINDER PRESS, INC.
NEW YORK

This volume is dedicated to the
memory of ROSE KARSNER (1890-1968)

Edited by Naomi Allen and George Breitman

First Edition, 1969
Second Edition, 1974

Pathfinder Press, Inc.
410 West Street
New York, N.Y. 10014

CONTENTS

*Published here in English for the first time.

PREFACE

This collection of pamphlets, articles, letters, and discussions covers the ten-month period from September 1938 to July 1939. It is another volume in the series collecting the writings of Leon Trotsky during his last exile (1929-40) which are not otherwise available in books or pamphlets permanently in print.

After his deportation from Norway, Trotsky found asylum in Mexico from January 1937 to August 1940, when he was assassinated by a Stalinist agent. In the first edition of this series these Mexican years were covered in three volumes — 1937-38, 1938-39, and 1939-40. Since then, however, a large amount of material from the Mexican period has become accessible, much of it never published before. This welcome expansion of material has made it necessary, in the second edition, to increase the number of volumes of the Mexican period from three to four, which are now designated by title as 1936-37, 1937-38, 1938-39 (the present volume), and 1939-40.

The central question of world politics in 1938-39 was the preparation for World War II. In September 1938 Hitler and Mussolini carved up Czechoslovakia with the acquiescence of the British and French governments at a conference in Munich. In March 1939 the fascists led by Franco completed their victory in the Spanish Civil War, Hitler's troops occupied Czechoslovakia, and the Stalinists, at a congress of the Communist Party of the Soviet Union, signaled their willingness to find a rapprochement with the German imperialists.

Included here are Trotsky's analyses of the Munich crisis and the light it threw on the nature of the coming war; his anticipation of the Stalin-Hitler pact (which was signed in August 1939); and his criticisms of the positions taken toward the war by the various reformist, centrist, and ultraleft tendencies in the international working class movement. (His writings about the end of the Spanish Civil War will be found

9

in *The Spanish Revolution [1931-39]* [Pathfinder Press, 1973].)

Only two weeks before the start of this volume the Fourth International, World Party of Socialist Revolution, had been founded by Trotsky's comrades at an international conference in Paris. This was the culminating step in a long process of political struggle: from 1923 to 1933 Trotsky had fought to reform the Communist International, cleanse it of Stalinism, and return it to a Leninist course; it was only after the Stalinists capitulated to fascism in Germany that Trotsky and his co-workers set out to gather the forces for a new International. Despite the extreme numerical weakness and political isolation of the Fourth International in 1938, Trotsky had no doubt about its great historic future, as several articles in this volume attest. But he also knew that it was beset by critical internal problems and contradictions and that it was his duty to try to help resolve them.

Trotsky's contributions to the life of the Fourth International and its sections were first of all political. Examples here are his March 1939 reply to "a group of Palestinian Bolshevik-Leninists" who wanted to revise the Fourth International's antiwar policy, and his proposal, raised for the first time in April 1939, that the International should advocate an independent Soviet Ukraine. But he also paid serious attention to the organizational and tactical problems of the national sections of the International, and did not hesitate to make criticisms and suggestions to them when he felt he had something useful to offer. Examples here are Trotsky's letters to the Socialist Workers Party and stenograms of discussions he held with its representatives about the SWP's newspaper, the problems facing its youth affiliate, the need to penetrate the ranks of the American Communist Party; his concern over the crisis of the French section, which was then paralyzed by a dispute over a tactical orientation toward a recently formed centrist party; and his observations on efforts being made by the International to reconstruct its Mexican section. During this time he also recorded the details of Diego Rivera's break with the Fourth International, published here for the first time.

Trotsky's major literary project at this time was his biography of Stalin (incomplete at the time of his death). The present volume shows how frequently he interrupted this historical study to respond to contemporary political events and opportunities. Under attack as the alleged force behind the

Mexican government's expropriation of foreign oil holdings, he answered the falsifications of the American press and a Republican Senator from Kansas. He brought into the open the machinations of the Mexican Stalinists, who were seeking to create the climate for his deportation or assassination. He discussed the strategy of Latin American revolutionists and the special problems of the Mexican labor movement. He condemned the efforts of the trade union and Stalinist bureaucracies to draw the workers into support for the coming war, and discussed what supporting the "democratic" imperialists meant for the colonial peoples. In two discussions with West Indian author C. L. R. James, he debated lessons from the history of the Fourth International and conclusions drawn by James in his book *World Revolution.* He was pedagogical in his criticisms of the theoretical errors of a group of radical students in Mexico and scathing in his condemnation of Stalin's revision of the Marxist theory of the state made at the congress of the CPSU.

The second edition of this volume differs from the first in the following ways:

1. Of the ninety-nine selections in this edition, more than half (fifty-three) are here published in English for the first time; they are indicated by an asterisk in the table of contents. These fifty-three include twenty-four that were written or transcribed in English but never before published, twenty-two that were published in other languages and had to be translated for this edition, and seven that to the best of our knowledge have never been published in any language before. The second edition also includes six selections from U.S. periodicals which had not yet been translated or attributed to Trotsky at the time of the first edition.

2. It covers a shorter time span (September 1938-July 1939) as compared to April 1938-August 1939 in the first edition, and therefore it does not include articles from April-September 1938 (which have been transferred to the second edition of *Writings 37-38*), and articles from July-August 1939 (which have been transferred to the second edition of *Writings 39-40*). It also does not include five articles on France from the first edition that have been transferred to *Leon Trotsky on France* (Pathfinder Press, 1974).

3. The first edition was divided into seven sections by theme. All the articles in the second edition are arranged in chronological order except for three subjects, where a number of

articles are grouped together for the convenience of readers and editors.

4. In addition, some dates mistakenly used for articles in the first edition have been corrected here, and brief passages missing from a few translations in the first edition have been restored.

Several of the articles in this volume were signed by pen names or were unsigned when first published. All of them were written in Coyoacan, a suburb of Mexico City. The date preceding each selection indicates when it was completed; if that is not known, the date when it was first published is given. Translations originally made in the 1930s and 40s have been revised to correct obvious errors and achieve uniformity in spelling of names, punctuation, style, etc. Acknowledgments about the articles and translations, and explanatory material about the persons and events mentioned in them, will be found in the section entitled "Notes and Acknowledgments." A list of 1938-39 books, pamphlets, and articles not included in this volume because they are in print and available elsewhere will be found in the section entitled "Other Writings of 1938-39."

For improvements in this second edition special thanks are due to the Harvard College Library, for its permission to examine and use material in the "open" section of the Trotsky Archives at Harvard; to James P. Cannon and Charles Curtiss, for the unpublished material they put at our disposal; and to Louis Sinclair, for the help afforded by his *Leon Trotsky: A Bibliography* (Hoover Institution Press, 1972).

The Editors
November 1973

CHRONOLOGY

—1938—

September 3 — The Fourth International is founded at a conference in Paris, a few days before Rudolf Klement, Trotsky's secretary, is found murdered by the Stalinists.

September 6-8 — The Latin American Trade Union Congress is held in Mexico.

September 12 — The Congress Against War and Fascism opens in Mexico.

September 22 — Trotsky writes "After the Collapse of Czechoslovakia, Stalin Will Seek Accord with Hitler," anticipating Stalin-Hitler pact of August 1939.

September 29-30 — Great-power conference in Munich is climaxed by signing of Munich pact, permitting Germany to partition Czechoslovakia.

October — First issue of *Clave* (Key), co-edited by Trotsky, is published in Mexico City.

October 10 — Trotsky analyzes the Munich crisis and the nature of the coming war in "A Fresh Lesson."

October 18 — Trotsky records his evaluation of the founding of the Fourth International, to be played at a New York mass meeting ten days later.

November — The International Brigades withdraw from Spain.

November 7 — Herschel Grynszpan, a 17-year-old Jewish refugee, assassinates a Nazi official in France.

November 18 — Trotsky holds a discussion about the building of a revolutionary youth group in the U.S.

December — The congress of the CGT (General Confederation of Labor) is held in Mexico.

December 9-27 — The Eighth Pan-American Conference is held in Lima.

—1939—

January 7—Diego Rivera submits his resignation from the Fourth International.

January— The Mexican section of the Fourth International is reconstituted.

February-March— Trotsky writes about the approaching end of the Spanish Civil War.

March— Trotsky moves from the Rivera house to a house on the Avenida Viena; his grandson, Sieva, arrives in Mexico. The Spanish Civil War ends with Republican forces surrendering to Franco.

March 10-21— The Eighteenth Congress of the Communist Party of the Soviet Union signals Stalin's willingness to seek an alliance with Hitler.

April— Trotsky engages in three discussions on the nature of the Afro-American struggle and two on the Fourth International and the history of the Left Opposition. Italy seizes Albania.

April 22 — Trotsky outlines the Leninist position on the Ukrainian question.

May 3 — Litvinov's replacement by Molotov as Soviet foreign minister is another sign of a shift in Soviet diplomacy away from "collective security."

May — The Mexican government severs relations with Great Britain.

May 12 — Trotsky writes "Nationalized Industry and Workers' Management."

June 10— Trotsky looks back on ten years of the Russian *Biulleten.*

June 12 — British diplomat William Strang flies to Moscow to hold negotiations with the Soviet Union.

July — British and French diplomats confer with Russians in Moscow over possible military pact.

July 1 — Trotsky writes "The Kremlin in World Politics" on the eve of the Stalin-Hitler pact and the onset of World War II.

Leon Trotsky in Mexico.

PHRASES AND REALITY [1]

September 19, 1938

These lines are written in the very midst of an ominous diplomatic muddle around the question of the Sudeten Germans. Chamberlain[2] has flown over the skies in vain hope of finding there the solution to the imperialist contradictions. Whether the war will break out now, or, what is more likely, whether the rulers of the world will succeed in putting it off for some time — not a very long time, to be sure — this question is still not definitely settled. None of these gentlemen want a war. All are afraid of its consequences. But fight they must. War they cannot avoid. Their economy, their politics, their militarism — all faces war.

Today's cables inform us that in all churches of the so-called "civilized" world public prayers are being offered up for peace. They come in time to crown a whole series of pacifist meetings, banquets, and congresses. Which of these two methods is the more efficacious, pious prayer or pacifist bleating, is not easy to decide. At any rate, only these two resources are left to the old world.

When an ignorant peasant prays, he really wants peace. When a simple worker or citizen of an oppressed country comes out against war, we can believe him — he really wants peace though only rarely does he know how to get it. But the bourgeois pray in their churches not for peace but for the maintenance and increase of their markets and colonies: if possible, peacefully (it is cheaper); if impossible — by means of arms. Similarly imperialist "pacifists" (Jouhaux, Lewis, and Co.)[3] trouble themselves not at all about peace but about gaining sympathy and support for their national imperialism.

There are three and a half million Sudeten Germans. If war breaks out, the number of dead will probably be four or five times, possibly even ten times, as much with a corresponding number of wounded, cripples, and insane; and a long wake of epidemics and other tragedies. This consideration, however,

17

is incapable of influencing in the least any of the enemy camps. For the robbers in the final analysis it is not at all a question of three and a half million Germans but of their rule over Europe and over the world.

Hitler[4] speaks of the "nation," of "race," of the unity of "blood." In reality his job is to broaden the military base of Germany before opening a struggle for rule over colonies. Here the national banner is only the fig leaf of imperialism.

The principle of "democracy" plays a similar role in the other camp. It serves the imperialists to cover up their seizures, violations, robberies and to prepare for new ones. This is very brilliantly revealed in the question of the Sudeten Germans. Democracy means the right of each nation to self-determination. But the Versailles treaty[5] concocted by the highest representatives of the most democratic governments one could find — France, Great Britain, parliamentarian Italy of yore, and, finally, the United States — basely trampled underfoot this democratic right of the Sudeten Germans, the Austrians, as well as many other national groups, Hungarians, Bulgarians, Ukrainians, etc.

For the strategic purposes of the triumphant imperialism of the Entente,[6] Messrs. Democrats, with the support of the Second International, delivered the Sudeten Germans into the possession of the young imperialists of Czechoslovakia. Meanwhile, the German Social Democracy waited with doglike submission for favors from the democracies of the Entente; waited and waited in vain. The results are known: democratic Germany, unable to stand the yoke of the Versailles treaty, threw herself in despair onto the road of fascism. It would seem that the Czechoslovakian democracy which stood under the august protection of Franco-British democracy and of the "socialist" bureaucracy of the USSR had every opportunity to show the Sudeten Germans the great advantages in reality of a democratic regime over a fascist one. If this task had been resolved, Hitler would not dare, of course, to make an attempt on the Sudetenland. His main strength lies now precisely in the fact that the Sudeten Germans themselves want unity with Germany. This desire was inspired in them by the rapacious and police regime of Czechoslovakian "democracy" which "fought" fascism by imitating its worst methods.

Superdemocratic Austria found itself until a short time ago under the tireless solicitude of the democratic Entente, which seemed to have made it its business not to let Austria live or die. It ended by Austria's throwing herself into the embrace of Hitler. On a smaller scale the same experiment was previously tried in the Saar region, which after having remained in the hands of France for fifteen years and having tried out all the benefits of imperialist democracy, by an overwhelming majority expressed a desire for unity with Germany.[7] These lessons of history are more significant than resolutions of all the pacifist congresses.

Only pitiful babblers or fascist crooks can speak of the irresistible "call of blood" in connection with the fate of the Saar, the Austrian and Sudeten Germans. The Swiss Germans, for example, do not want at all to go into slavery under Hitler, because they feel themselves masters in their country, and Hitler would think ten times before attacking them. Intolerable social and political conditions must exist for citizens of a "democratic" country to be seized by a desire for fascist power. The Germans of the Saar in France, the Austrian Germans in the Europe of Versailles, the Sudeten Germans in Czechoslovakia felt themselves citizens of third rank. "It will not be worse," they said to themselves. In Germany, at least, they will be oppressed on the same basis as the rest of the population. The masses prefer under these conditions equality in serfdom to humiliation in inequality. The temporary strength of Hitler lies in the bankruptcy of imperialist democracy.

Fascism is a form of despair in the petty-bourgeois masses, who carry away with them over the precipice a part of the proletariat as well. Despair, as is known, takes hold when all roads of salvation are cut off. The triple bankruptcy of democracy, Social Democracy, and the Comintern[8] was the prerequisite for the successes of fascism. All three have tied their fate to the fate of imperialism. All three bring nothing to the masses but despair and by this assure the triumph of fascism.

The chief aim of the Bonapartist clique of Stalin[9] during recent years has consisted in proving to the imperialist "democracies" its wise conservatism and love for order. For the sake of the longed-for alliance with imperialist democracies, the Bonapartist clique has brought the Comintern to the last stages of political prostitution. Two great "democracies," France and England, try to persuade Prague to make concessions to Hitler who is supported by Mussolini.[10] Apparently nothing is left to Prague but to yield to "friendly" advice. Of Moscow there is no mention. No one is interested in the opinion of Stalin or his Litvinov. [11] As a result of its disgusting crawling and bloody vileness in the service of imperialism, especially in Spain, [12] the Kremlin is more isolated than ever before.

What are the causes? There are two. The first lies in the fact that having definitely become a lackey of "democratic" imperialism, Stalin does not dare, however, to bring his work in the USSR to a conclusion, that is, to the restoration of private ownership of the means of production and the abolishing of the monopoly of foreign trade. And without these measures he remains in the eyes of the imperialists just a revolutionary parvenu, an untrustworthy adventurer, a bloody falsifier. The imperialist bourgeoisie does not venture to wager an important stake on Stalin.

Of course, it could utilize him for its partial and temporary aims. But here the second cause for the Kremlin's isolation looms up: in its struggle for self-preservation the unbridled Bonapartist clique has crippled the army and navy to the last degree, shaken the economy, demoralized and humiliated the country. [13] No one believes the patriotic howling of the defeatist clique. The imperialists clearly dare not risk a stake on Stalin even for episodic military aims.

In this international situation the agents of the GPU [14] cross the ocean and gather in hospitable Mexico to "fight" against war. The method is simple — to unite all the democracies against fascism. Only against fascism! "I am invited here," speaks the worthy agent of the French Bourse, Jouhaux, "for the struggle against fascism, and not imperialism at all!" Whoever fights against "democratic" imperialism, that is, for the freedom of the French colonies, is an ally of fascism, an agent of Hitler, a Trotskyite. Three hundred fifty million Indians must reconcile themselves to their slavery in order to support British democracy, the rulers of which at this very time, together with the slaveholders of "democratic" France, are delivering the Spanish people into Franco's bondage. [15] People of Latin America must tolerate with gratitude the foot of Anglo-Saxon imperialism on their neck only because this foot is dressed in a suede democratic boot. Disgrace, shame, cynicism — without end!

The democracies of the Versailles Entente helped the victory of Hitler by their vile oppression of defeated Germany. Now the lackeys of democratic imperialism of the Second and Third Internationals are helping with all their might the further strengthening of Hitler's regime. Really, what would a military bloc of imperialist democracies against Hitler mean? A new edition of the Versailles chains, even more heavy, bloody, and intolerable. Naturally, not a single German worker wants this. To throw off Hitler by revolution is one thing; to strangle Germany by an imperialist war is quite another. The howling of the "pacifist" jackals of democratic imperialism is therefore the best accompaniment to Hitler's speeches. "You see," he says to the German people, "even socialists and Communists of all enemy countries support their army and their diplomacy; if you will not rally around me, your leader, you are threatened with doom!" Stalin, the lackey of democratic imperialism, and all the lackeys of Stalin — Jouhaux, Toledano, [16] and Company — are the best aides of Hitler in deceiving, lulling, and intimidating the German workers.

The Czechoslovakian crisis revealed with remarkable clarity that fascism does not exist as an independent factor. It is only one of the tools of imperialism. "Democracy" is another of its tools. Imperialism rises above them both. It sets them in motion according to need, at times counterposing them to one another, at times amicably combining them. To fight against fascism in an alliance with imperialism is the same as to fight in an alliance with the devil against his claws or horns.

The struggle against fascism demands above all the expulsion of the agents of "democratic" imperialism from the ranks of the working class. Only the revolutionary proletariat of France, Great Britain, America, and the USSR, declaring a life-and-death struggle against their own imperialism and its agency, the Moscow bureaucracy, is capable of arousing revolutionary hopes in the hearts of the German and Italian workers, and at the same time of rallying around itself hundreds of millions of slaves and semislaves of imperialism in the entire world. In order to guarantee peace among the peoples we must overthrow imperialism under all its masks. Only the proletarian revolution can accomplish this. To prepare it, the workers and the oppressed peoples must be irreconcilably opposed to the imperialist bourgeoisie and must be rallied into a single international revolutionary army. This great liberating work is now being fulfilled only by the Fourth International. [17] That is why it is hated by fascists, by imperialist "democrats," by social patriots, and by the lackeys of the Kremlin. This is the true sign that under its banner will rally all the oppressed.

THE TOTALITARIAN
"RIGHT OF ASYLUM"[18]

September 19, 1938

The function of the journal *Futuro* is to show the readers that Lombardo Toledano has neither program nor ideas. [19] The journal achieves this task completely. In its September issue, *Futuro* declares that in "principle" Lombardo Toledano is for the right of asylum, but it does not at all consider that this right should be accorded to those for whom Lombardo Toledano does not entertain feelings of political or personal tenderness. Such are the views of these gentlemen on democracy. By freedom of the press they understand the right of the press, or rather its obligation, to praise Toledano and his boss, Stalin. By the right of asylum they understand the right of entry into Mexico for agents of the GPU. Lombardo once more discloses his basic solidarity with Hitler, who not only recognizes but even widely applies the right of asylum in relation to fascists who slipped away, earlier from Austria, now from Czechoslovakia or the United States. Toledano has approached the "ideals" of Hitler through his boss, Stalin. The October Revolution proclaimed the right of asylum for all revolutionary fighters. Now Stalin is exterminating them by tens of thousands — Germans, Hungarians, Bulgarians, Poles, Finns, etc., etc. — only because their views do not coincide with the interests of the ruling Bonapartist clique. Toledano is still not the boss in Mexico. He cannot, like his teacher and master, shoot or poison defenseless emigres. There remain means at his disposal: slander and persecution. And he uses them as widely as possible.

Toledano, of course, will repeat that we are "attacking" the CTM.[20] No reasonable worker will believe this rubbish. The CTM, as a mass organization, has every right to our respect and support. But just as a democratic state is not identical with its minister at any given time, so a trade union organization is not identical with its secretary. Toledano has the totalitarian outlook on all questions. "L'etat, c'est moi!" said Louis XIV. "Germany—that's me!" says Hitler. "The USSR—that's me!" asserts Stalin. "The CTM— that's me!" proclaims the incomparable Toledano. If this cynical gentleman came to power, he would become the worst of totalitarian tyrants to the Mexican workers and peasants. Fortunately, his personal insignificance is an earnest guarantee against this danger.

THE ASSASSINATION
OF RUDOLF KLEMENT[21]

September 20, 1938

To His Honor the examining magistrate in the case of the disappearance of Rudolf Klement:

Your Honor,

I have just learned that Mme. Jeanne Martin des Pallieres[22] has intervened in the investigation of the disappearance of Rudolf Klement on her own initiative and has cast doubt on the value of the depositions of Messrs. Pierre Naville and Jean Rous[23] on the basis of photographs of the body found at Melun.

Of course, I cannot offer an opinion as to the identity of the body and consequently on the material value of the testimony concerning it. But I see it as my regretful duty to place before the court, Your Honor, some information that may be of use to you in evaluating the conflicting testimony.

Messrs. Pierre Naville and Jean Rous were very well acquainted with Rudolf Klement. And through frequent association, discussions, and common work, they should have gotten a very exact impression of his appearance, character, and handwriting.

The situation of Mme. Jeanne Martin des Pallieres is quite different. Although she was the intimate friend of my late son, Leon Sedov,[24] she was and is a member of a political group that is extremely hostile to the organization of Leon Sedov, Rudolf Klement, and Messrs. Pierre Naville and Jean Rous. She has given rather animated expression to this hostility many times, even while Leon Sedov was still alive. Since his death, she has been mentally and morally unstable. All of the letters I have received from her as well as many of her actions give unquestionable proof of this. In addition, she did not know Rudolf Klement very well. In one of her letters to me she asked about the identity

24

of "Camille," the name Rudolf Klement used for over a year. At the same time she fostered personal resentment against this man whom she hardly knew. All of this is expressed with great passion in her letters to me.

The political group that Mme. Jeanne Martin des Pallieres belongs to had its own reasons for fostering resentment against Rudolf Klement (see their publication, *La Commune*). It has become a point of honor for this group to prove that Rudolf Klement betrayed his organization, that is, they endeavor to support the story the GPU uses to cover its crime.

Your Honor, I have but one interest in this matter: to establish the truth about the fate of the unfortunate Rudolf Klement. This interest has prompted me to place before you revelations that I would have preferred to avoid under other circumstances. I am not familiar with the body found at Melun. But I was and am familiar with Rudolf Klement, Messrs. Pierre Naville and Jean Rous, and Mme. Jeanne Martin des Pallieres, and if I had to choose between the conflicting testimony of Mme. Jeanne Martin des Pallieres, on the one hand, and that of Messrs. Pierre Naville and Jean Rous, on the other, I would place my confidence in the latter.

Your Honor, please accept my most sincere regards.

Leon Trotsky

FIGHT IMPERIALISM
TO FIGHT FASCISM[25]

September 21, 1938

The most important and the most difficult thing in politics, in my opinion, is to define on the one hand the *general* laws which determine the life-and-death struggle of all countries of the modern world; on the other hand to discover the *special combination* of these laws for each single country. Modern humanity without exception, from British workers to Ethiopian nomads, lives under the yoke of imperialism. This must not be forgotten for a single minute. But this does not at all mean that imperialism manifests itself equally in all countries. No. Some countries are the carriers of imperialism, others — its victims. This is the main dividing line between modern nations and states. From this viewpoint and only from this viewpoint should the very pressing problem of *fascism* and *democracy* be considered.

Democracy for Mexico, for instance, signifies the desire of a semicolonial country to escape from bonded dependence, to give land to the peasants, to lift the Indians to a higher level of culture, and so on. In other words, the democratic problems of Mexico have a progressive and revolutionary character. And what does democracy signify in Great Britain? The maintenance of what exists, that is, above all the maintenance of the rule of the metropolis over the colonies. The same is true in relation to France. The banner of democracy covers here the imperialist hegemony of the privileged minority over the oppressed majority.

In the same manner we cannot speak of fascism "in general." In Germany, Italy, and Japan, fascism and militarism are the weapons of a greedy, hungry, and therefore aggressive imperialism. In the Latin American countries fascism is the expression of the most slavish dependence on foreign imperialism. We must be able to discover under the political form the economic and social content.

In certain circles of the intelligentsia at present the idea of

26

the "unification of all democratic states" against fascism enjoys popularity. I consider this idea fantastic, chimerical, capable only of deceiving the masses, especially the weak and oppressed peoples. Really, can one believe for even a single moment that Chamberlain, Daladier, or Roosevelt[26] are capable of carrying on a war for the sake of the abstract principle of "democracy"? Had the British government loved democracy so, it would have given freedom to India. The same is true of France. Great Britain prefers the dictatorship of Franco in Spain to the political rule of the workers and peasants, because Franco would be a much more pliant and reliable agent of British imperialism. England and France have given Austria to Hitler without resistance although war would be inevitable if he so much as dared touch their colonies.

The conclusion is that it is impossible to fight against fascism without fighting imperialism. The colonial and semicolonial countries must fight first of all against that imperialist country which directly oppresses them, irrespective of whether it bears the mask of fascism or democracy.

In the countries of Latin America the best and surest method of struggle against fascism is the agrarian revolution. Because Mexico had made important steps on this road, the uprising of General Cedillo was left suspended in air.[27] On the contrary, the cruel defeats of the Republicans in Spain are due to the fact that the Azana government, in alliance with Stalin, suppressed the agrarian revolution and the independent movement of the workers.[28] A conservative and even more a reactionary social policy in weak and semicolonial countries means in the full sense of the word betrayal of national independence.

You will ask me how it can be explained that the Soviet government that issued from the October Revolution suppresses the revolutionary movement in Spain? The answer is simple: a new privileged bureaucratic caste, very conservative, greedy, and tyrannical, has succeeded in raising itself over the Soviets. This bureaucracy does not trust the masses but fears them. It seeks rapprochement with the ruling classes, especially with "democratic" imperialists. To prove his reliability, Stalin is ready to play the role of policeman throughout the entire world. The Stalinist bureaucracy and its agency, the Comintern, now represent the greatest danger to the independence and progress of weak and colonial peoples.

I know Cuba too little to permit myself an independent

judgment on your fatherland. You can judge better than I which of the above expressed opinions is applicable to the situation in Cuba. So far as I personally am concerned I hope that I shall be able to visit the Pearl of the Antillian islands and become more closely acquainted with your people to whom through your newspaper I send my warmest and sincerest greetings.

AFTER THE COLLAPSE OF CZECHOSLOVAKIA, STALIN WILL SEEK ACCORD WITH HITLER[29]

September 22, 1938

As a military power Czechoslovakia is disappearing from the map of Europe. The loss of three and a half million deeply hostile Germans would be an advantage in the military sense if it did not signify the loss of natural boundaries. The stanchions of the Sudeten fortress are collapsing at the sound of the fascist horn. Germany acquires not only three and a half million Germans, but also a firm boundary. If until now Czechoslovakia was considered a military bridge for the USSR into Europe, it now becomes a bridge for Hitler into the Ukraine. The international "guarantee" of the independence of the remnants of Czechoslovakia will signify immeasurably less than the same guarantee for Belgium before the world war.

The collapse of Czechoslovakia is the collapse of Stalin's international policy of the last five years. Moscow's idea of "an alliance of democracies" for a struggle against fascism is a lifeless fiction. No one wants to fight for the sake of an abstract principle of democracy: all are fighting for material interests. England and France prefer to satisfy the appetites of Hitler at the expense of Austria and Czechoslovakia rather than at the expense of their colonies.

The military alliance between France and the USSR from now on loses 75 percent of its value and can easily lose the entire 100 percent. Mussolini's old idea of a four-power pact of European powers, under the baton of Italy and Germany, has become a reality, at least until a new crisis.

The terrific blow at the international position of the USSR is the pay-off for the continuous bloody purge, which beheaded the army, disrupted the economy and revealed the weakness of the Stalinist regime. The source of the defeatist policy rests in the Kremlin. We may now expect with certainty Soviet diplomacy to attempt rapprochement with Hitler at the cost of new retreats and capitulations, which in their turn can only bring nearer the collapse of the Stalinist oligarchy.

The compromise over the corpse of Czechoslovakia does not guarantee peace in the least but only creates a more favorable basis for Hitler in the coming war. Chamberlain's flights in the sky will enter into history as a symbol of those diplomatic convulsions which divided, greedy, and impotent imperialist Europe passed through on the eve of the new slaughter which is about to drench our whole planet in blood.

ANTI-IMPERIALIST STRUGGLE IS KEY TO LIBERATION [30]

An Interview with Mateo Fossa

September 23, 1938

Fossa: In your opinion what will be the further development of the present situation in Europe?

Trotsky: It is possible that this time too diplomacy will succeed in reaching a rotten compromise. But it will not last long. War is inevitable and moreover in the very near future. One international crisis follows another. These convulsions are similar to the birth pangs of the approaching war. Each new paroxysm will bear a more severe and dangerous character. At present I do not see any force in the world that can stop the development of this process, that is, the birth of war. A horrible new slaughter is relentlessly drawing upon humanity.

Of course, timely revolutionary action by the international proletariat could paralyze the rapacious work of the imperialists. But we must look the truth straight in the face. The working masses of Europe in their overwhelming majority are under the leadership of the Second and Third Internationals. The leaders of the Amsterdam International of trade unions fully support the policy of the Second and the Third Internationals and enter together with them into so-called "People's Fronts." [31]

The policy of the "People's Front," as is shown by the example of Spain, France, and other countries, consists in subordinating the proletariat to the left wing of the bourgeoisie. But the entire bourgeoisie of the capitalist countries, the right as well as the "left," is permeated through and through with chauvinism and imperialism. The "People's Front" serves to turn the workers into cannon fodder for their imperialist bourgeoisie. Only that and nothing more.

The Second, the Third, and the Amsterdam Internationals are at present counterrevolutionary organizations whose task it is to put brakes upon and paralyze the revolutionary struggle of the proletariat against "democratic" imperialism. So long as the criminal leadership of these Internationals is not overthrown, the workers will be powerless to oppose war. This is the bitter but inescapable truth. We must know how to face it and not console ourselves with illusions and pacifist babbling. War is inevitable!

Fossa: What will be its effect on the struggle in Spain and on the international working class movement?

Trotsky: In order to understand correctly the nature of the coming events we must first of all reject the false and thoroughly erroneous theory that the coming war will be a war between fascism and "democracy." Nothing is more false and foolish than this idea. Imperialist "democracies" are divided by the contradictions of their interests in all parts of the world. Fascist Italy can easily find herself in one camp with Great Britain and France if she should lose faith in the victory of Hitler. Semifascist Poland may join one or the other of the camps depending upon the advantages offered. In the course of war the French bourgeoisie may substitute fascism for its "democracy" in order to keep its workers in submission and force them to fight "to the end." Fascist France, like "democratic" France would equally defend its colonies with weapons in hand. The new war will have a much more openly rapacious imperialist character than the war of 1914-18. Imperialists do not fight for political principles but for markets, colonies, raw materials, for hegemony over the world and its wealth.

The victory of any one of the imperialist camps would mean the definite enslavement of all humanity, the clamping of double chains on present-day colonies, and all weak and backward peoples, among them the peoples of Latin America. The victory of any one of the imperialist camps would spell slavery, wretchedness, misery, the decline of human culture.

What is the way out, you ask? Personally, I do not doubt for a moment that a new war will provoke an international revolution against the rule of the rapacious capitalist cliques over humanity. In wartime all differences between imperialist "democracy" and fascism will disappear. In all countries a merciless military dictatorship will reign. The German workers and peasants will perish just like the French and English. The modern means of destruction are so monstrous that humanity will probably not be able to endure war even a few months. Despair, indignation, hatred will push the masses of all warring countries into an uprising with weapons in hand. Victory of the world proletariat will put an end to war and will also solve the Spanish problem as well as all the current problems of Europe and other parts of the world.

Those working class "leaders" who want to chain the proletariat to the war chariot of imperialism, covered by the mask of "democracy," are now the worst enemies and the direct traitors of the toilers. We must teach the workers to hate and despise the agents of imperialism, since they poison the consciousness of the toilers; we must explain to the workers that fascism is only one of the forms of imperialism, that we must fight not against the external symptoms of the disease but against its organic causes, that is, against capitalism.

Fossa: What is the perspective for the Mexican revolution? How do you view the devaluation of money in connection with the expropriation of wealth in land and oil? 32

Trotsky: I cannot dwell on these questions in sufficient detail. The expropriation of land and of the natural wealth are for Mexico an absolutely indispensable measure of national self-defense. Without satisfying the daily needs of the peasantry none of the Latin American countries will retain their independence. The lowering of the purchasing power of money is only one of the results of the imperialist blockade against Mexico which has begun. Material privation is inevitable in struggle. Salvation is impossible without sacrifices. To capitulate before the imperialists would mean to deliver up the natural wealth of the country to despoliation, and the people — to decline and extinction. Of course, the working class organizations must see to it that the rise in the cost of living should not fall with its main weight upon the toilers.

Fossa: What can you say on the liberating struggle of the peoples of Latin America and of the problems of the future? What is your opinion of Aprismo? 33

Trotsky: I am not sufficiently acquainted with the life of the individual Latin American countries to permit myself a concrete answer on the questions you pose. It is clear to me at any rate that the internal tasks of these countries cannot be solved without a simultaneous revolutionary struggle against imperialism. The agents of the United States, England,

France (Lewis, Jouhaux, Toledano, the Stalinists) try to substitute the struggle against fascism for the struggle against
imperialism. We have observed their criminal efforts at the
recent congress against war and fascism.[34] In the countries of
Latin America the agents of "democratic" imperialism are especially dangerous, since they are more capable of fooling
the masses than the open agents of fascist bandits.

I will take the most simple and obvious example. In Brazil
there now reigns a semifascist regime that every revolutionary
can only view with hatred. Let us assume, however, that on
the morrow England enters into a military conflict with Brazil.
I ask you on whose side of the conflict will the working class
be? I will answer for myself personally — in this case I will
be on the side of "fascist" Brazil against "democratic" Great
Britain. Why? Because in the conflict between them it will not
be a question of democracy or fascism. If England should be
victorious, she will put another fascist in Rio de Janeiro and
will place double chains on Brazil. If Brazil on the contrary
should be victorious, it will give a mighty impulse to national
and democratic consciousness of the country and will lead to
the overthrow of the Vargas dictatorship.[35] The defeat of England will at the same time deliver a blow to British imperialism and will give an impulse to the revolutionary movement
of the British proletariat. Truly, one must have an empty
head to reduce world antagonisms and military conflicts to
the struggle between fascism and democracy. Under all masks
one must know how to distinguish exploiters, slave-owners,
and robbers!

In all the Latin American countries the problems of the
agrarian revolution are indissolubly connected with anti-imperialist struggle. The Stalinists are now treacherously paralyzing both one and the other. To the Kremlin the Latin American countries are just small change in its dealings with the
imperialists. Stalin says to Washington, London, and Paris,
"Recognize me as an equal partner and I will help you put
down the revolutionary movement in the colonies and semicolonies; for this I have in my service hundreds of agents
like Lombardo Toledano." Stalinism has become the leprosy
of the liberating movement.

I do not know Aprismo sufficiently to give a definite judgment. In Peru the activity of this party has an illegal character and is therefore hard to observe. The representatives of
APRA at the September congress against war and fascism in

Mexico have taken, so far as I can judge, a worthy and correct position together with the delegates from Puerto Rico. It remains only to hope that APRA does not fall prey to the Stalinists as this would paralyze the liberating struggle in Peru. I think that agreements with the Apristas for definite practical tasks are possible and desirable under the condition of full organizational independence.

Fossa: What consequences will the war have for the Latin American countries?

Trotsky: Doubtless both imperialist camps will strive to drag the Latin American countries into the whirlpool of war in order to enslave them completely afterwards. Empty "antifascist" noise only prepares the soil for agents of one of the imperialist camps. To meet the world war prepared, the revolutionary parties of Latin America must right now take an irreconcilable attitude toward all imperialist groupings. On the basis of the struggle for self-preservation the peoples of Latin America should rally closer to each other.

In the first period of war the position of the weak countries can prove very difficult. But the imperialist camps will become weaker and weaker with each passing month. Their mortal struggle with each other will permit the colonial and semicolonial countries to raise their heads. This refers, of course, also to the Latin American countries; they will be able to achieve their full liberation, if at the head of the masses stand truly revolutionary, anti-imperialist parties and trade unions. From tragic historic circumstances one cannot escape by trickery, hollow phrases, and petty lies. We must tell the masses the truth, the whole truth, and nothing but the truth.

Fossa: What in your opinion are the tasks and the methods facing the trade unions?

Trotsky: In order that the trade unions should be able to rally, educate, mobilize the proletariat for a liberating struggle they must be cleansed of the totalitarian methods of Stalinism. The trade unions should be open to workers of all political tendencies under the conditions of discipline in action. Whoever turns the trade unions into a weapon for outside aims (especially into a weapon of the Stalinist bureaucracy and "democratic" imperialism) inevitably splits the working class, weakens it, and opens the door to reaction. A full and honest democracy within the unions is the most important condition of democracy in the country.

In conclusion I ask you to transmit my fraternal greetings to the workers of Argentina. I don't doubt that they do not believe for a moment those disgusting slanders that the Stalinist agencies have spread in the entire world against me and my friends. The struggle that the Fourth International carries on against the Stalinist bureaucracy is a continuation of the great historic struggle of the oppressed against the oppressors, of the exploited against the exploiters. The international revolution will free all the oppressed, including the workers of the USSR.

PROBLEMS OF THE AMERICAN PARTY[36]

October 5, 1938

Dear Friend:

We wait here with the greatest impatience for information about the meeting in Europe. We know only that it was O.K., but no more. Without waiting for your letter, I will discuss with you some questions concerning our party (SWP).

1. The referendum seems to have been not a very happy invention.[37] The discussion seems to have produced some embarrassment in the party. This can all be overcome only by *action*. It is time, it seems to me, to show directly to the party how we have to act on this issue. I had two long discussions here with Plodkin, an organizer of the [International] Ladies Garment Workers Union, and summarized our discussion in an article which tries to put the question on its actual political level. The article is now under translation and will be sent to you simultaneously with this letter.[38] But an article is of course nothing if the party doesn't begin a serious action in the unions with the slogan that the workers should take the state into their own hands and that for this purpose they need their own independent labor party. An energetic step in this direction would surely dissipate all the misunderstandings and dissatisfactions and push the party forward.

2. In this question as in all others it is absolutely necessary to give to our propaganda-agitation a more concentrated and systematic character. It would be for example necessary to oblige all local committees to present to the National Committee[39] in one month a short report concerning their connections with the trade unions, the possibilities for work in trade unions, and especially the agitation in the trade unions for an independent labor party. The danger is that the question of the labor party will become a pure abstraction. The base for our activity is the trade unions — the question of the labor party can receive flesh and blood only insofar as we are rooted in the trade unions. A serious beginning of our

work in the trade unions led us to the slogan of a labor party. Now it is necessary to use the slogan of labor party in order to push our party more deeply into the trade unions.[40]

The answers of the local organizations should be studied and worked out in a series of articles and circular letters of the National Committee with concrete instructions, advice, and so on.

3. Very important in this respect is the attitude of the *Socialist Appeal.*[41] It is undoubtedly a very good Marxist paper, but it is as yet not a genuine instrument of political action. The connection of the paper with the real activity of the party is too loose. This looseness is determined not so much by the literary conceptions of the editorial board as by the disseminated, unconcentrated character of the activity of the whole party. It is necessary to establish for a certain time a plan for a political campaign and to subordinate to this plan the local organizations, the *Socialist Appeal,* and the *New International.*[42] It seems to us here that the labor party can be one of the items of such a campaign under the condition that the accent is put on our work in the trade unions.

4. We here were disappointed by the inexplicable passivity of our party towards the patriotic, imperialistic turn of the Communist Party.[43] The greatest hindrance for the revolutionary movement and through this the greatest hindrance for the development of our party and its success in the unions is undoubtedly Stalinism. The fight against this perfidious enemy of the proletariat should be conducted simultaneously on different levels by combined means. The investigation of the Dies Committee gave us an excellent occasion for action, but this occasion remained almost totally unexploited.[44] We should have defended energetically and ardently the right of the Communist Party to be non-American; it was our elementary democratic duty. At the same time it was necessary to unmask their perfidious turn from a non-American (internationalist) position to an American (chauvinist) one. It was absolutely necessary to arm every member of our party with quotations from the resolutions and the program of the Comintern and its first four, even six, congresses, and to oppose to these documents the recent declarations, speeches, and so on. This work should have been done in a very systematic, detailed form, with two or three articles in every issue of the *Socialist Appeal,* with more synthetic articles in the *New International,* with a special manual for our agitators including

quotations, instructions, and so on. I tried to interest the editorial board of the *Socialist Appeal* in this question, but without success. They gave something about the matter (from Olgin's articles) [45] but nothing more. I believe this grave omission could be rectified now to a certain degree. Such a concentrated and systematic campaign could be fixed for two or three months and have the greatest educational value for our own comrades, especially the youth. It is also one of the ways to prepare them for the approaching war.

5. Don't you believe that it would be timely now to create a special party committee for work among the women, with a special supplement of the *Socialist Appeal* and some articles in the *New International* illuminating the situation of worker women now under the crisis?

I will await with great interest your letter on the international meeting as well as on the state of our party as you found it upon your return.

With best greetings,

Comradely,
Hansen [Trotsky]

WHAT IS THE MEANING OF THE STRUGGLE AGAINST "TROTSKYISM"? [46]

(About Lombardo Toledano and Other GPU Agents)

October 9, 1938

In a number of letters and conversations I have been asked about the significance of the struggle now going on within the Soviet Union between Stalinists and Trotskyists, and why in other countries, especially Mexico, various leaders of the workers' movement have abandoned their work in order to develop a slander campaign against me personally, in spite of my noninvolvement in the internal affairs of this country. I appreciate these questions because they give me a chance to answer them publicly, with the greatest possible clarity and precision.

In the first place one must clearly understand that when a political struggle of great importance develops, especially one involving tens and hundreds of thousands of people, one cannot possibly explain it in terms of any "personal" motives. Not a few superficial and scheming people attribute the struggle of Trotskyists and Stalinists to motives of personal ambition. This is an absurd position to advance. Personal ambition can only motivate individual politicians; but in the Soviet Union thousands and thousands of people who are called "Trotskyists" have been executed and are still being executed. Are these people sacrificing their positions, their freedoms, their lives, and frequently the lives of their families just for the ambition of a single individual, namely Trotsky? Conversely, it is equally absurd to think that Stalinist politics can be explained in terms of Stalin's personal ambition. This struggle has long since gone beyond the borders of the Soviet

40

Union. To correctly understand the meaning of the conflict that currently divides the workers' movement all over the world, one must reject, before proceeding any further, the empty talk about personal motives and begin to deal with the historical causes that have engendered it.

The whole world is familiar, even if only in its most general outlines, with the causes and problems of the October Revolution that broke out in Russia in 1917. It was the first victorious revolution of the oppressed masses, led by the proletariat. The aim of the revolution was to abolish class exploitation and inequality, to create a new socialist society based on the collective ownership of the land, mines, and factories, and to achieve a rational and just division of the products of labor among members of society. When we were carrying out this revolution, many Social Democrats (opportunist reformists like Lewis, Jouhaux, Lombardo Toledano, Laborde, [47] etc.) told us that we couldn't succeed, that Russia was too backward a country, that communism was impossible there, etc. We answered in the following way: Of course, considered in isolation Russia is too backward and uncivilized a country to be able to build a communist society by itself. But, we added, Russia is not alone. There are more advanced capitalist countries in the world, with a more highly developed technology and culture, and a much more developed proletariat. We, the Russians, are opening up the socialist revolution; that is to say, we are taking the first bold step towards the future. But the German, French, and English workers will begin their revolutionary struggle right on our heels, will win power in those countries, and then will help us with their superior technology and culture. Under the lead of the proletariat of the more advanced countries, even the people of the backward countries (China, India, Latin America) will enter on the new socialist path. Thus we will gradually arrive at the formation of a new socialist society on a world scale.

As you know, our hopes for an early proletarian revolution in Europe did not materialize. Why not? Not because the working masses did not have the will. On the contrary, after the Great War of 1914-18, the proletariat in all the European countries initiated struggles against the imperialist bourgeoisie and showed itself to be completely disposed toward taking power. What held it back? The leaders, the conservative workers' bureaucrats, the gentlemen of the type of Lewis and Jouhaux — Lombardo Toledano's teachers.

In order to achieve its ends, the working class must create

its organizations: the unions and the political party. In this process a whole layer of bureaucrats, secretaries of unions and other organizations, deputies, journalists, etc. is raised above the level of the exploited layer. They are raised above the workers as much by their material conditions of life as by their political influence. Few of them maintain an internal connection with the working class and remain loyal to its interests. Far more labor bureaucrats begin to look towards those above them instead of those below. They begin to sidle up to the bourgeoisie, forgetting the suffering, miseries, and hopes of the laboring classes. This is the cause of many of the defeats inflicted on the working class.

In the course of history we have seen more than once that parties and organizations that have arisen out of the popular movement, have subsequently undergone a complete degeneration. That is what happened, in its day, to the Christian church which began as a movement of fishermen, of carpenters, of the oppressed, and of slaves, but which built up a powerful, rich, and cruel ecclesiastical hierarchy. This is what happened, before our very eyes, to the parties of the Second International, the so-called Social Democracy, which gradually became estranged from the real interests of the proletariat and were drawn toward the bourgeoisie. During the war, in every country, the Social Democracy defended its own national imperialism, that is to say, the interests of robber capital, selling out the interests of the workers and colonial peoples. When the revolutionary movements began in the course of the war, the Social Democracy, the party that should have led the workers toward the insurrection, in fact helped the bourgeoisie to destroy the workers' movement. The treason within its general staff paralyzed the proletariat.

This is why the hopes for a European and a world revolution after the war were never realized. The bourgeoisie maintained its hold over its wealth and power. Only in Russia, where the really revolutionary Bolshevik Party existed, did the proletariat win and create a workers' state. The Soviet Union, however, found itself isolated. Workers in the richer and more developed countries were not able to give the Soviet Union aid. As a result the Russian proletariat found itself in very difficult straits.

Had the level of technology in Russia been as high as in Germany or the United States, the socialist economy would from the start have produced everything needed to satisfy the everyday needs of the people. Under those circumstances, the Soviet bureaucracy would not have been able to play an important role, since a high level of technology would also mean a high cultural level, and the workers would never have permitted the bureaucracy to order them about. But Russia was a poor, backward country, lacking in civilization. In addition it was devastated by the years of imperialist and civil war. This is why the nationalization of the land, factories, and mines could not rapidly produce, and to this day still cannot produce, the necessary quantity of goods to satisfy the daily needs of the population, in spite of the enormous economic progress that has been made. And wherever there is a shortage of goods, a struggle for those goods inevitably develops. The bureaucracy intervenes in this struggle; arbitrating, dividing, giving to one, taking from another. Of course, in the process of doing this the bureaucracy does not forget to take care of itself. It must be remembered that in the USSR it is a matter of a bureaucracy that is not only in the party or in the unions, but also in the state apparatus. The bureaucracy has at its disposal all the nationalized property, the police, the courts, the army, and the navy.

Its control over the economy and distribution of goods has given the Soviet bureaucracy the chance to concentrate all authority in its hands, removing the laboring masses from access to power. In this way in the country of the October Revolution a new, privileged layer has risen above the masses and runs the country with methods that are almost identical to those of fascism. The workers' and peasants' soviets no longer play any role. All power is in the hands of the bureaucracy. The person who rules is the head of this bureaucracy: Stalin.

It is impossible to say that the USSR is moving towards socialist equality. In terms of its material situation, the uppermost layer of the bureaucracy lives in the same style as the big bourgeoisie in the capitalist countries. The middle layer lives more or less like the middle bourgeoisie; and finally, the workers and peasants live under much more difficult conditions than the workers and peasants of the advanced countries. This is the plain truth.

One might ask: Does this mean that the October Revolution was a mistake? Such a conclusion would be, without question, totally wrong. The revolution is not the result of the efforts of a single person or a single party. The revolution breaks out as the culmination of a historical process, when the popular masses are no longer willing to tolerate the old forms of oppression. The October Revolution has, despite everything, made possible tremendous gains. It has nationalized the means of production and, by means of the planned economy, has made possible the extremely rapid development of the productive forces. This is an enormous step forward. All of humankind has learned from this experience. The October Revolution has given the consciousness of the popular masses a tremendous push. It has awakened a spirit of independence and initiative in them. If the situation of the workers is difficult in many respects, it is nevertheless better than it was under czarism. No, the October Revolution was no "mistake." But in an isolated Russia it could not achieve its principal goal, namely, the establishment of a fraternal, socialist society. This goal remains to be achieved.

From the moment that a new parasitic layer arose on the backs of the proletariat in the USSR, the struggle of the masses has naturally been directed against the bureaucracy as the principal obstacle in the road to socialism. When the bureaucracy tries to justify its existence, it explains that socialism has already been "achieved" through its efforts. In reality, the social question is only solved for the bureaucracy, which has a life that is far from bad. "I am the state," reasons the bureaucracy. "As long as everything is going well for me, everything is in order." There is nothing surprising about the fact that the masses of people, who have not escaped from misery, harbor feelings of hostility and hatred toward this new aristocracy, which devours a large part of the fruits of their labor.

While claiming to defend the interests of socialism, the bureaucracy actually defends its own interests and smothers and relentlessly exterminates anyone who raises any criticism against the oppression and the terrible inequality that exist in the Soviet Union. The bureaucracy supports Stalin because he defends its privileged position resolutely, implacably, and with total determination. Anyone who has not understood this has not understood anything.

It is absolutely natural that the workers, who carried out three revolutions in the space of twelve years (1905-17), should be unhappy with this regime and should have tried more than once to bring the bureaucracy under control. In the Soviet Union those representatives of working class discontent who criticize and protest are called Trotskyists because their struggle corresponds to the program I defend in the press. If the bureaucracy were fighting for the interests of the people, it would be able to castigate its enemies before the masses

for real, rather than invented, crimes. But since the bureaucracy struggles only for its own interests and against those
of the people and their real friends, naturally the bureaucracy
can't speak truthfully about the causes of the innumerable
persecutions, arrests, and executions. Therefore, the bureaucracy accuses those it calls Trotskyists of monstrous crimes
which they haven't committed, and couldn't commit. In order
to shoot an opponent who defends the vital interests of the
workers, the bureaucracy simply declares him to be a "fascist agent." There are no checks whatsoever on the activities
of the bureaucracy. During the secret court proceedings, which
are carried out in the style of the Holy Inquisition, confessions
to unbelievable crimes are dragged out of the accused. Such
is the character of the Moscow trials, which have stirred the
whole world. [48] As a result of these trials it would seem that
the whole Bolshevik Old Guard, the whole generation that
developed with Lenin the supremely important struggle for
the conquest of power by the working class, was actually composed entirely of spies and bourgeois agents. Simultaneously
the major representatives of the following generation, which
bore the whole weight of the civil war on its back (1918-21),
was wiped out.

So, the October Revolution was carried out by fascists? And
the workers' and peasants' civil war was led by traitors? No!
That is a despicable slander against the revolution and Bolshevism! The basic factor in this slander is that it was precisely those Bolsheviks who had a truly revolutionary past
who were the first to protest against the new bureaucratic caste
and its monstrous privileges. The bureaucracy, mortally afraid
of the opposition, carried out a relentless struggle against
the representatives of the old Bolshevik Party and, in the end,
subjected them to almost total extermination. This is the plain
truth.

The Moscow bureaucracy maintains a huge number of agents
all over the world in order to maintain its authority abroad,
in order to make itself appear to be the representative of the
working class and the defender of socialism, and in order
to hoodwink the world working class. Toward this end it
spends tens of millions of dollars a year. Many of these secret agents are leaders of the workers' movement, trade union
officials or officials of the so-called "Communist" parties which,
in fact, no longer have anything to do with communism. The
job of these paid Kremlin agents consists of deceiving the
workers, presenting the Soviet bureaucracy's crimes as "de-

fense of socialism," slandering the advanced Russian workers who are struggling against the bureaucracy, and labeling the real defenders of the workers as "fascists." "But that is a disgusting role!" exclaims every honest worker. We also believe that it is a disgusting role.

One of the most zealous and shameless of the Moscow bureaucracy's agents is Lombardo Toledano, the secretary-general of the CTM. His contemptible activity is unfolding before everyone's eyes. He defends Stalin, Stalin's violence, his betrayals, his provocateurs, and his executioners. It is not the least bit surprising that Toledano should be the most avid enemy of Trotskyism; it is the gentleman's job!

A year and a half ago the International Commission of Inquiry began its work of reviewing the Moscow trials. 49 Toledano, along with other Stalinists, was invited to participate in this Commission: Present your accusations; bring out your evidence! Nevertheless, Toledano refused, using a false and cowardly excuse: the Commission, according to him, "was not impartial." Then why didn't the "impartial" Toledano take advantage of the opportunity to publicly demonstrate the "partiality" of the Commission? Because he doesn't have a single shred of evidence to back up the slanders he repeats at Moscow's command.

The International Commission, composed of people known throughout the world for their incorruptibility, published the results of its work in two volumes containing more than a thousand pages. All the documents were examined. Dozens of witnesses were questioned. Every lie and slander was studied under a microscope. The Commission unanimously found that all the accusations against me and against my late son Leon Sedov are malicious fabrications concocted by Stalin. What did Stalin and his agents reply? Nothing—not a single word. In spite of this, Toledano continues to present and defend Moscow's false accusations and adds new ones of his own manufacture. "But this is shameful!" any honest worker will exclaim. Absolutely true. It is disgraceful beyond description!

This February the congress of the CTM adopted a resolution against Trotsky and the "Trotskyists." The resolution repeats, word-for-word the false accusations of Prosecutor Vyshinsky, who used to be the lawyer for the oil magnates of the Caucasus before the revolution and who has long been known as a complete scoundrel. 50 How could the congress of a workers' organization possibly adopt such a disgraceful resolution? Direct responsibility for this falls in the lap of Lombardo Toledano, who in this case was not acting in his capacity as secretary of a union, but rather as an agent of Stalin's secret police, the GPU.

It hardly needs to be stated that I personally have nothing to say against Mexican workers' organizations forming an opinion about "Trotskyism" as a political tendency and making their conclusions public. But in order to do this a clear and honest examination of the question is necessary; this is an elementary requisite of workers' democracy. Before the congress it would have been necessary to submit the question of "Trotskyism" to all the unions to examine. It would have been necessary to allow supporters of "Trotskyism" the chance to express their views directly to the workers. In the congress that was preparing to judge me, moreover, the most elementary courtesy would demand that I be invited to explain myself. In reality, the machinations imposed by Moscow were prepared not only behind my back, but also behind the backs of the Mexican workers. No one knew beforehand that the questions of Trotsky and "Trotskyism" would be placed before the congress. In order to serve Stalin's ends Toledano conspired against the Mexican workers. The delegates to the congress had no informational material whatsoever available to them; they were surprised by a military-like strategem. The ignoble resolution was imposed by Toledano in the same way that Stalin, Hitler, and Goebbels[51] carry out the decisions of the "people." This method of operation indicates a "totalitarian" scorn for the working class. At the same time, Toledano demands that the Mexican government gag me and deprive me of the chance to defend myself against the slanders. This is the champion of "democracy," Lombardo the Lionhearted!

He has not been limited, however, to simply repeating the official falsehoods of Prosecutor Vyshinsky in Moscow. Toledano also employs his own imagination. Soon after my arrival in Mexico, Toledano publicly stated that I was preparing a general strike against General Cardenas's government.[52] The absurdity of this "accusation" is obvious to any reasonable person, but Toledano is not deterred by absurdity: Moscow demands zeal and obedience. The same Toledano stated in Mexico, New York, Paris, and Oslo that in the whole of Mexico I had no more than ten friends, a figure which was later reduced to five and finally to only two. If this is so, how could

I begin to organize a general strike and conspiracy? On the other hand, what happened to all my "friends" on the right — the fascists, the "brown shirts," etc.? As can be seen, the intellectual level of Toledano's accusations does not significantly differ from the level of accusations directed against the opponents of the bureaucracy in Moscow. But Toledano doesn't have his own GPU to defend him with revolvers against criticism. This should have suggested greater caution to him!

The other Mexican GPU agent, Laborde, the leader of the so-called "Communist" Party (who could believe it?) declared, at a solemn meeting last autumn, in front of a large audience that included the president of the republic, that I was secretly allied with (now pay careful attention!) General Cedillo and with Vasconselos; in order, of course, to stage a fascist coup d'etat. Laborde, compromising himself and dishonoring his party, was reduced to hurling such an idiotic accusation solely because he, like Toledano, had received orders to do this from Moscow, where they long ago lost all sense of proportion, not only as regards morality but also as regards logic and psychology. The student cannot be on a higher level than the teacher. The GPU agent cannot do as he pleases. He has to follow his boss's orders. Not to do so would immediately result in Laborde's party being deprived of Moscow's subsidy and crumbling like a house of cards.

This summer I took a trip through Mexico to learn more about the country that had offered my wife and me such generous hospitality. In Toledano's newspaper, *El Popular*, they published the news that during my trip I had met with counter-revolutionaries, and particularly with the pro-fascist Dr. Atl. [53] I stated in the press that I didn't know Dr. Atl. But my categoric denial in no way deterred Mr. Toledano from publishing notes and cartoons placing me in Dr. Atl's company. What does this signify? Toledano is a lawyer; he knows the meaning of "slander" and "false testimony." He knows that nothing discredits a person as much as the spreading of a conscious slander for personal reasons. How is it possible for him to fall so low, sacrificing his reputation as a leader of workers and as an honest person? It is likely that Toledano himself senses that a worm is eating away his conscience. But Toledano is standing on a slope. He's slipping and he can't stop himself. The GPU does not make it easy for its victims to escape its clutches.

One may object that I'm placing too much emphasis on

Toledano, but this is not true. Toledano is not an individual. He is a type. There is a multitude of carbon copies of him: a whole mercenary army trained by Moscow! By using the example of Toledano I am unmasking this army, which sows the seeds of lies and cynicism in public opinion.

Each time I feel obligated to refute the latest slanders emanating from Toledano and Laborde, these gentlemen scream that I am . . . an enemy of the Mexican Confederation of Workers. What a ridiculous charge! Lombardo and Laborde carry out their machinations under cover of the workers. When they are caught in the act, they proceed to hide behind the workers. What knaves! What heroes! . . . And what miserable sophists! How could I, a man who has spent forty-two years of his life in the service of the workers' movement, have a hostile attitude towards a proletarian organization struggling for the betterment of the lot of the workers? But the CTM is not Toledano and Toledano is not the CTM. Whether or not Toledano is a good union official is a question that must be decided by the Mexican workers themselves. But when Toledano sallies forth to defend the GPU's executioners against the best of Russia's workers, then I too must publicly rise and tell the workers of Mexico and the world: "Toledano is a treacherous liar acting in behalf of the Kremlin gang! Don't believe him!"

Toledano's methods are identical to those used in the Moscow trials. In essence both substitute detective stories for political differences: they invent monstrous concoctions to stagger the imagination of the unsophistocated; they lie and slander; they slander and lie. In Moscow they assert that I had a secret meeting with the fascist minister Hess[54] (whom I have never seen in my life and with whom, of course, I would never have any dealings). Here in Mexico they claim I had a secret meeting with this Dr. Atl, about whom I know nothing. This is the GPU school.

But in spite of these similarities, there is a difference. The GPU, after silencing every critic and making use of false witnesses, has the opportunity to drag false confessions out of the accused. If they can't do it that way, they shoot the accused in secret, without benefit of trial or court proceedings. In Mexico, Mr. Toledano still doesn't have the chance to use this kind of repression. Of course, he makes full use of the falsifications manufactured in Moscow, such as the totally dishonest and worthless film *Lenin in October,* for example, but this alone is not enough. Humanity is not composed solely of imbeciles. Not a few people are able to think. For this reason, it is easy to unmask Toledano's slanders. And we will continue this work of disclosure until the end!

I propose that a public investigation be held of Toledano's charges concerning preparations for the general strike against General Cardenas's government, concerning my "relations" with Cedillo and Vasconselos, concerning my secret discussions with Dr. Atl, etc., etc. We have here an excellent opportunity to establish the truth or falsity of the specific charges. Mr. Toledano, who is so zealous in his defense of the trials in Moscow, will do Stalin a great service if he can show the validity of the charges against me here in Mexico. I propose that an impartial commission be named to publicly investigate Toledano's accusations against me. Tell them to the judge! Accusers, present your evidence!

However, we are under no illusions. Toledano won't accept the challenge. He doesn't dare accept it. He cannot appear before an impartial commission, which would inevitably be transformed into a vehicle for the unmasking of the GPU and its agents. Evidence? What kind of evidence can the slanderer marshal? The slanderer has a lack of scruples and a disgraceful conscience. He has nothing else!

From what has already been said, every intelligent person will draw this simple conclusion: if here in Mexico, where freedom of the press and the right of asylum still exist, Stalin's agents are permitted to make such absurd and dishonorable accusations, all the while demanding that the accused not be allowed to open his mouth in his own defense, what must Stalin's agents be permitted to do in the Soviet Union itself, where all criticism, opposition, and protest are smothered in the totalitarian regime's press? In the process, and against his own wishes, Toledano has given Mexican public opinion the key to all the Moscow trials. One must say, in a general sense, that overly zealous friends are more dangerous than enemies.

My ideas are distasteful to the whole spectrum of opportunists and profiteers. I would consider it a great disgrace if my ideas were to suit these gentlemen. The oppressed cannot gain their emancipation under the leadership of the opportunists and profiteers. Let these gentlemen try to publicly attack my ideas! I belong to the Fourth International and I don't hide my colors. The Fourth International is the only world party that carries out a real struggle against imperialism, fascism, oppression, exploitation, and war. Only this young and growing organization expresses the real interests of the world proletariat. Precisely for this reason it struggles implacably against the corrupt bureaucracy of the old, patriotic Second and Third Internationals. The rabid hatred of the opportunists, adventurers, and self-satisfied profiteers toward "Trotskyism" stems from this. Where it is able to do so, the Kremlin gang assassinates our fighters (Erwin Wolf, Ignace Reiss, Leon Sedov, Rudolf Klement, and many others). [55] Where it cannot do this, it slanders them. It lacks neither money nor paid agents. Nevertheless, it is destined for a shameful collapse. Revolutionary ideas that correspond to the needs of historical development will overcome every obstacle. The slanderers will break their head against the invincible truth.

A FRESH LESSON [56]

After the Imperialist "Peace" at Munich

October 10, 1938

Twenty years after the first imperialist world war, which completely destroyed "democratic" illusions, the leaders of the Comintern are trying to prove that the capitalist world has radically altered its nature; that imperialism is no longer the decisive factor on our planet; that world antagonisms are determined not by the predatory interests of monopoly capital, but by abstract political principles, and that the new slaughter of peoples will be a defensive war on the part of innocent, peace-loving democracies against the "fascist aggressors." Human memory must indeed be very short if on the eve of a new imperialist war, the adventurists of the Third International dare to put in circulation the very ideas used by the traitors of the Second International to dupe the masses during the last war.

There is, however, more to it than mere repetition. Inasmuch as capitalism has, during the last quarter of a century, reached a very advanced stage of decay in economy as well as politics, the falsifications of the Third International assume an incomparably more obvious, cynical, and debased character than was attained by the social patriotic doctrines of the last war. The leaders of the Second International who had already lost faith in the virtues of "democratic" formulas and were verging on utter despair, seized with astonishment and a new hope upon the unexpected assistance of the Comintern. Following them, a section of the imperialist bourgeoisie cast its eyes toward the Communist patriots. Such is the chief source of the rotten and infamous policy of "People's Fronts."

Every profound crisis — whether economic, political, or military — has its positive side, in that it puts to a test all the various traditional values and formulas, laying bare the rottenness of those that served to mask "peacetime" contradictions, and thereby spurring forward the general development. The diplomatic crisis over Czechoslovakia excellently performed this progressive task. It only remains for Marxists to draw all the necessary political conclusions from the recent experience.

52

The Experience of the Last War

Let us begin with a brief backward glance. The war of 1914-18 was, as is well known, a "war for democracy." The alliance of France, Great Britain, Italy, and the United States enabled the social patriots of the Entente to keep their eyes shamefully shut to the fifth ally, czarism. After the February 1917 revolution overthrew Nicholas II,[57] the democratic front was definitely aligned. Only the incorrigible Bolsheviks could still clamor thereafter about imperialism. Was it really worth cavilling because the liberal Miliukov and the quasi-socialist Kerensky wanted to grab Galicia, Armenia, and Constantinople?[58] In the end, Miliukov and Kerensky explained that the Bolsheviks were simply the agents of Ludendorff (the "Hitler" of that day).[59]

The war ended with the complete victory for the democracies, although Soviet Russia, led by the Bolsheviks, had abandoned their holy camp. The result of that victory was the Versailles treaty, paid for, to be sure, by millions of lives, but designed to establish once and for all on this earth the reign of democracy, the free development of nations, and the peaceful collaboration of peoples on the basis of general disarmament. The League of Nations crowned the conquests of a war which was supposed to have been a war "to end all wars" — so promised Wilson and the Second International.[60]

A paradise, however, did not materialize, but something rather which very much resembled hell. The peace of Versailles suffocated Europe. Economic life was suffocated by protectionism. The war "for democracy" ushered in an epoch of the final decline of democracy. The world became more poverty-stricken and confined. One state after another took the road to a fascist or a military dictatorship. International relations grew more and more menacing. Disarmament came in the form of programs of militarism which would have seemed like a nightmare on the eve of the last war. The first clashes of new and bloody conflicts began to take place in different parts of the world. This very moment was chosen by the Comintern to abandon the last remnants of internationalism and to proclaim that the task of the new era was an alliance between the proletariat and the decaying imperialist democracies "against fascism." The greatest source of infection in the world is the heap of filth that remains of what was once the Communist International.

The Struggle For and Against
a New Partition of the World

Certain theoreticians of the Second International, like Kautsky,[61] who tried to envisage some sort of perspective, expressed a hope that the imperialists, having measured their forces in the great slaughter of the peoples, would be compelled to arrive at an agreement among themselves and to establish a peaceful rule over the world in the form of a corporation (the theory of "superimperialism"). This philistine-pacifist theory — a Social Democratic shadow of the League of Nations — tried to shut its eyes to two processes: first, the constant change in the relation of forces between the various imperialist states, with the utter impossibility of measuring these changes in practice except by force of arms; second, the liberating struggle of the proletariat in the metropolitan centers and of the colonial peoples, a struggle that is the most important factor in disrupting the equilibrium, and which by its very nature excludes the possibility of "peaceful" imperialist looting. Precisely for these reasons, the programs of disarmament remain miserable utopias.

The flagrant and ever-growing disproportion between the specific weight of France and England, not to mention Holland, Belgium, and Portugal, in world economy and the colossal dimensions of their colonial possessions are as much the source of world conflicts and of new wars as the insatiable greed of the fascist "aggressors." To put it better, the two phenomena are but two sides of the same coin. The "peaceful" English and French democracies rest on the suppression of national democratic movements of hundreds of millions in Asia and Africa for the sake of the superprofits derived from them. Conversely, Hitler and Mussolini promise to become more "moderate" if they obtain adequate colonial territory.

The United States, owing to her almost total possession of an entire continent with inexhaustible natural wealth, and owing to favorable historical conditions, has extended her sway over the world very "peacefully" and "democratically," if we disregard such trifles as the extermination of the Indians, the robbery of the choicest portions of Mexico, the crushing of Spain, the participation in the last war, and so on. This "idyllic" mode of exploitation belongs now, however, to the past. The rapid and fearful decay of American capitalism poses before it the question of life and death in a more and more obvious mili-

Munich, September 1938, moments after the Neville Chamberlain, Edouard Daladier, signing of the Munich Pact. (Left to right) Adolph Hitler, and Benito Mussolini.

tary form. From Wilson's pacifist fourteen points, Hoover's
Quaker ARA (the international philanthropic organization),
Roosevelt's reformist New Deal, the doctrine of isolation, the
laws of absolute neutrality, etc., the United States is heading
inevitably toward an imperialist explosion such as the world
has never seen. [62]

Hurled far back by the Versailles peace, Germany took the
task of "national unification" as the basis of its imperialist
program. Under this slogan, fascism, the legitimate heir of
Weimar democracy, [63] was born and grew strong. What an
irony of fate! In its period of historical rise (from the Napoleonic wars to the Versailles peace of 1871)[64] the belated German bourgeoisie proved incapable of achieving national unification through its own strength. Bismarck only half-fulfilled this
task, leaving almost intact the entire feudal and particularist
rubbish. [65] True, the revolution of 1918 abolished the German
dynasties [66] (only because the Social Democracy was powerless
to save them!), but betrayed by the Social Democracy into the
hands of the Junkers, the bankers, the bureaucracy, and the
army officers, the revolution was incapable not only of assuring
a centralized Greater German Republic, but even of centralizing
bureaucratically the Germany of the Hohenzollerns. [67] Both
these tasks fell to Hitler. The leader of fascism came forward,
in his own fashion, as the continuator of Bismarck, who in his
turn had been the executor of the bourgeois bankrupts of 1848.
But this is, in the long run, only the superficial aspect of the
process. Its social content has radically changed. From the
progressive factor that it was, the national state has long since
been transformed in advanced countries into a brake on the
development of productive forces. Ten million more Germans
within the boundaries of Germany do not alter the reactionary
nature of the national state. In their own way, the imperialists
understand this very well. For Hitler it is not at all a question
of "unifying Germany" as an independent task, but of creating
a broader European drill-ground for future world expansion.
The crisis over the Sudeten Germans, or rather over the Sudeten
mountains, was an episode on the road toward the struggle
for colonies.

A new partition of the world is on the order of the day.
The first step in the revolutionary education of the workers
must be to develop the ability to perceive beneath the official
formulas, slogans, and hypocritical phrases, the real imperialist appetites, plans, and calculations.

Imperialist Quartet Replaces the "Front of Democracies"

The lamb-like docility of European democracies is the product not of love of peace, but of weakness. The cause of weakness is not the democratic regime as such, but rather the disproportion between the economic foundations of the metropolitan centers and the colonial empires inherited from the past. To this disproportion is added the liberating struggle of the colonies which threatens, especially in time of war, to flare into a revolutionary conflagration. In these conditions, decaying "democracy" really becomes a supplementary source of weakness for the old imperialist powers.

Open reaction in France undoubtedly profits from the capitulations of the People's Front. We can expect with certainty a strengthening of French fascism, favored by the patronage of leading military circles. In England, where the conservative bourgeoisie is in power, the Labourite opposition will probably gain more in the next period than fascism. [68] But in view of the entire historic situation, the assumption of power by the Labour Party can only be an episode, or more exactly, a stage on the road to more radical changes. Neither Major Attlee nor Sir Walter Citrine will be able to cope with the malignant spirits of our epoch! [69]

Somehow, the "world front of democracies" promised by the charlatans of the "People's Fronts" found itself replaced by a four-power front of Germany, Italy, England, and France. After the Munich conference, where England and France capitulated to Hitler, with the as-always equivocal mediation of Mussolini, the heads of the four states appeared before their respective peoples as national heroes: Hitler had unified the Germans; Chamberlain and Daladier had averted war; Mussolini—helped both sides. Long live the Big Four! The petty-bourgeois fraternity which the GPU usually mobilizes for all kinds of pacifist congresses is already beginning to turn toward the new messiahs of peace. The French socialists abstained on the question of voting special powers to Daladier, the hero of capitulation. The abstention was only a transitional step from the camp of Moscow to the camp of the Big Four. The isolation of the Stalinist praetorians in the chamber of deputies and in the senate symbolized the complete isolation of the Kremlin in European politics.

But it can already be stated with certainty that the Munich quartet is as little capable of preserving peace as the "front of democracies" that was never realized. England and France threw Czechoslovakia into Hitler's maw to give him something to digest for a time and thus postpone the question of colonies. Chamberlain and Daladier made very vague and uncertain promises that a common agreement on all controversial issues would be reached. On his part, Hitler promised to present no more territorial demands *in Europe*. Thereby he has in any case indicated his intention to present territorial demands in other parts of the world. As regards Alsace-Lorraine, Schleswig, etc., Hitler is at best postponing the solution of these questions until the new world war. Should fascism conquer France in the next year or two, and the Labour Party win in England, these political changes would alter very little the arrangement of the imperialist figures on the world chessboard. Fascist France would be as little inclined as the France of the "People's Front" to yield Alsace-Lorraine to Hitler, or to share its colonies with him. The Labour Party, impregnated with the spirit of imperialism, could not mitigate the antagonism with Italy in the Mediterranean, nor check the development of the world antagonism between German and British interests. In these conditions, the four-power combination, if ever realized, will lead only to a new crisis, for which we have not long to wait. Imperialism is inevitably and irresistibly heading to a redivision of the world, corresponding to the changed relation of forces. To prevent the catastrophe, imperialism must be strangled. All other methods are fictions, illusions, lies.

The Meaning of
the Governmental Turn in Czechoslovakia

The refusal by France and Britain to defend the imperialist interests of the Czech bourgeoisie led not only to the dismemberment of Czechoslovakia but also to the collapse of its political regime. This experience revealed in a chemically pure form that Czechoslovakian democracy was not an expression of the "people's will" but simply an apparatus whereby Czech monopoly capitalism adapted itself to its patron states. No sooner did the military patronage fall away than the democratic machinery proved not only unnecessary but harmful in that it threatened to provoke needless friction with Hitler. The Czech bourgeois leaders immediately created a new apparatus of imperialist adaptation in the shape of a military dictatorship. This change of regimes was accomplished without the slightest participation of the people, without new elections, and even without any consultation of the old parliament. The president, elected by the people, the arch-"democrat" Benes,[70] summoned the ranking general of the republic to power. This summons at first had some semblance of a concession to the people, who were aroused, and who were protesting, demonstrating and demanding resistance to Hitler, arms in hand. Resistance? Here is a general as a national leader! Having performed this deed, the president withdrew. Whereupon the general, who was formerly at the head of the armed forces, and who was, so to speak, the shining sword of democracy, announced his intention, for the sake of amity with Hitler, of instituting a new state regime. And that was all!*

Generally speaking, democracy is indispensable to the bourgeoisie in the epoch of free competition. To monopoly capitalism, resting not on "free" competition but on centralized command, democracy is of no use; it is hampered and embarrassed by it. Imperialism can tolerate democracy as a necessary evil up to a certain point. But its inner urge is toward dictatorship. During the last war, twenty-two years ago, Lenin[71] wrote: "The difference between the republican-democratic and monarchic-reactionary imperialist bourgeoisie is being effaced precisely because both of them are rotting." Further, he added: "Political reaction *all along the line* is inherent in imperialism." Only hopeless idiots can believe that imperialist world antagonisms are determined by the irreconcilability between democracy and fascism. In fact, the ruling cliques of all countries look upon democracy, military dictatorship, fascism, etc., as so many different instruments for subjecting their own peoples to imperialist aims. Moreover, one of these political regimes, namely, democracy, includes within itself from the outset, in the shape, for example, of the general staff, another regime — that of military dictatorship.

---

*Immediately upon his arrival in England, the former Czechoslovakian president, Benes, declared to the press that the fate of Czechoslovakia was in "reliable hands." This dotted all the i's. All distinctions between democracy and fascism faded away when it became a question of the basic interests of capitalism. Benes, the democrat and Francophile, feels no shame in publicly recognizing General Syrovy, the profascist and Germanophile, as a "reliable" guide of Czechoslovakia's destiny. In the last analysis, they are both stewards of one and the same master.

A montage showing antiwar headlines lengthy section cut out of the Czech from newspapers of European sections paper on the left by censors in "demo-of the Fourth International. Note the cratic" Prague.

In Germany the imperialist bourgeoisie, with the active assistance of the Social Democracy, placed Field Marshal Von
Hindenburg, as a defender against fascism, in the presidential
office. [72] Hindenburg, in his turn, summoned Hitler to power,
after which the Field Marshal did not, to be sure, resign, but
died. This involves, however, merely a question of technique
and age. In essence, the overturn in Czechoslovakia repro-
duces the main features of the overturn in Germany, revealing
thereby the mainsprings of the political mechanics of imperialism. The question of the Czechoslovakian regime was no
doubt decided behind the scenes at conferences of magnates
of Czech, French, British, and German capitalism, together
with the leaders of the general staffs and of the diplomats.
The chief concern in shifting the state boundaries was to cause
as little damage as possible to the interests of the financial
oligarchy. The change in orientation from France and England
to Germany signified essentially an exchange of stocks, a new
division of military orders for the Skoda plants and so on.

Nobody, by the way, concerned himself with the position
of the Social Democracy and the ex-Communist Party, because
in Czechoslovakia they were no more capable of resistance
than were their elder brothers in Germany. Bowing before
"national necessities" these utterly corroded organizations did
everything in their power to paralyze the revolutionary resistance of the working class. After the overturn has been consummated, the financial clique will probably hold a "referendum," i.e., provide the people, driven into a blind alley,
with the precious opportunity of "approving," under the muzzle
of Syrovy's gun, the changes made without them and against
them.

Should Czechoslovakia's
"National Independence" Be Defended?

During the critical week in September, we have been informed,
voices were raised even at the left flank of socialism, holding
that in case of "single combat" between Czechoslovakia and
Germany, the proletariat would be obliged to help Czechoslovakia and save her "national independence," even in an
alliance with Benes. This hypothetical situation failed to arise.
The heroes of Czechoslovakian independence, as was to be
expected, capitulated without a struggle. It is impossible, however, in the interests of the future, not to point out here the

gross and dangerous blunder of these out-of-season theoreticians of "national independence."

Even irrespective of its international ties, Czechoslovakia
is an absolutely imperialist state. Economically, monopoly
capitalism reigns there. Politically, the Czech bourgeoisie rules
(perhaps soon we will have to say, used to rule) over several
oppressed nationalities. A war, even on the part of isolated
Czechoslovakia, would thus have been waged not for national
independence but for the preservation and, if possible, the extension of the borders of imperialist exploitation.

Even if the other imperialist states were not immediately
involved, it would be impermissible to consider a war between Czechoslovakia and Germany apart from the pattern
of European and world imperialist relations of which such a
war would have been an episode. Within a month or two,
a Czecho-German war — if the Czech bourgeoisie was desirous
and capable of fighting — would almost inevitably have involved other states. It would therefore be an error for Marxists to define their position on the basis of episodic diplomatic
and military groupings rather than on the basis of the general
character of the social forces behind this war.

We have reiterated on hundreds of occasions the irreplace-
able and invaluable thesis of Clausewitz that war is but the
continuation of politics by other means. In order to determine
in each given instance the historic and social character of a
war, we must be guided not by impressions and conjectures
but by a scientific analysis of the politics that preceded the war
and conditioned it. These politics from the very first day of
the formation of patched-up Czechoslovakia were of an imperialist character.

It may be argued that after separating the Sudeten Germans,
the Hungarians, the Poles, and, perhaps, the Slovaks, Hitler will not stop before the enslavement of the Czechs themselves, and that in this case their struggle for national independence would have every claim upon the support of the
proletariat. This means of formulating the question is nothing
but social patriotic sophistry. What paths the future development of imperialist antagonisms will follow, we do not know.
Complete destruction of Czechoslovakia is, of course, quite
possible. But it is equally possible that before this destruction
is accomplished, a European war will break out in which
Czechoslovakia may be found on the victorious side, and
participate in a new dismemberment of Germany. Is the role

of a revolutionary party then that of a nurse to "crippled" gangsters of imperialism?

It is quite obvious that the proletariat must build its policy on the basis of a *given* war, as it is, i.e., as it has been conditioned by the whole preceding course of development, and not on hypothetical speculation over the possible strategic outcome of the war. In such speculations everyone will invariably choose that variant which best corresponds to his own desires, national sympathies, and antipathies. Obviously, such a policy would be not Marxist but subjective, not internationalist but chauvinist in character.

An imperialist war, no matter in what corner it begins, will be waged not for "national independence" but for a redivision of the world in the interests of separate cliques of finance capital. This does not exclude that *in passing* the imperialist war may improve or worsen the position of this or that "nation"; or, more exactly, of one nation at the expense of another. Thus, the Versailles treaty dismembered Germany. A new peace may dismember France. Social patriots invoke precisely this possible "national" peril of the future as an argument for supporting "their" imperialist bandits of the present. Czechoslovakia does not in the least constitute an exception to this rule.

In reality all speculative arguments of this sort and raising bogies of impending national calamities for the sake of supporting this or that imperialist bourgeoisie flow from *the tacit rejection of the revolutionary perspective and a revolutionary policy*. Naturally, *if* a new war ends only in a military victory of this or that imperialist camp; *if* a war calls forth neither a revolutionary uprising nor a victory of the proletariat; *if* a new imperialist peace more terrible than that of Versailles places new chains for decades upon the people; *if* unfortunate humanity bears all this in silence and submission — then not only Czechoslovakia or Belgium but also France can be thrown back into the position of an oppressed nation (the same hypothesis may be drawn in regard to Germany). In this eventuality the further frightful decomposition of capitalism will drag all peoples backward for many decades to come. Of course if *this* perspective of passivity, capitulation, defeats, and decline comes to pass, the oppressed masses and entire peoples will be forced to climb anew, paying out their sweat and blood, retracing on their hands and knees the historic road once already traveled.

Is such a perspective excluded? *If* the proletariat suffers without end the leadership of social imperialists and communo-chauvinists; *if* the Fourth International is unable to find a way to the masses; *if* the horrors of war do not drive the workers and soldiers to rebellion; *if* the colonial peoples continue to bleed patiently in the interests of the slaveholders; then under these conditions the level of civilization will inevitably be lowered and the general retrogression and decomposition may again place national wars on the order of the day for Europe. But then we, or rather our sons, will have to determine their policy in relation to future wars on the basis of the new situation. Today we proceed not from the perspective of decline but that of revolution. We are defeatists at the expense of the imperialists and not at the expense of the proletariat. We do not link the question of the fate of the Czechs, Belgians, French, and Germans as nations with episodic shifts of military fronts during a new brawl of the imperialists, but with the uprising of the proletariat and its victory over all the imperialists. We look forward and not backward. The program of the Fourth International states that the freedom of all European nations, small and large, can be assured only within the framework of the Socialist United States of Europe.

Once Again on Democracy and Fascism

All of this does not, of course, imply that there is no difference at all between democracy and fascism, or that this difference is of no concern to the working class, as the Stalinists insisted not so very long ago. Marxists have nothing in common with such cheap political nihilism. Only, it is necessary in each given instance clearly to comprehend the actual content of this difference, and its true limits.

For the backward colonial and semicolonial countries, the struggle for democracy, including the struggle for national independence, represents a necessary and progressive stage of historical development. It is just for this reason that we deem it not only the right but also the duty of workers in these countries actively to participate in the "defense of the fatherland" against imperialism, on condition, to be sure, that they preserve the complete independence of their class organizations and conduct a ruthless struggle against the poison of chauvinism. Thus, in the conflict between Mexico and the oil kings and their executive committee, which is the democratic government of Great Britain, the class conscious proletariat of the world sides wholly with Mexico (this does not of course apply to the imperialist lackeys at the head of the British Labour Party).

As regards advanced capitalism, the latter has long since outgrown not only the old property forms but also the national state, and in consequence bourgeois democracy as well. The fundamental crisis of contemporary civilization lies precisely here. Imperialist democracy is putrefying and disintegrating. A program of "defense of democracy" for the advanced countries is a program of reaction. The only progressive task here is the preparation of the international socialist revolution. Its aim is to smash the framework of the old national state and build up the economy in accordance with geographic and technological conditions, without medieval taxes and duties.

Again, this does not imply an attitude of indifference toward the current political methods of imperialism. In all cases where the counterrevolutionary forces tend to pull *back* away from the decomposing "democratic" state and towards provincial particularism, towards monarchy, military dictatorship, fascism — the revolutionary proletariat without assuming the slightest responsibility for the "defense of democracy" (it is indefensible!) will meet these counterrevolutionary forces with armed resistance, in order, if successful, to direct its offensive against imperialist "democracy."

This policy, however, is applicable only with regard to internal conflicts, that is, in those cases where the struggle really involves the issue of a political regime, as was for instance the case in Spain. The participation of Spanish workers in the struggle against Franco was their elementary duty. But precisely and only because the workers did not succeed in time in replacing the rule of bourgeois democracy with their own rule, "democracy" was able to clear the path for fascism.

It is, however, sheer fraud and charlatanism to transfer mechanically the laws and rules of the struggle between *different* classes of *one and the same* nation over to an imperialist war, that is, the struggle waged by *one and the same class* of *different nations*. At present, after the fresh experience of Czechoslovakia, there is no necessity, it seems, to demonstrate that the imperialists are fighting one another not for political principles but for domination over the world under the cover of any principles that will serve their purpose.

Mussolini and his closest associates, so far as one can gather,

are atheists, that is, they believe neither in God nor the devil.
The king of Britain and his ministers are mired in medieval
superstitions and believe not only in the devil but in the devil's
grandmother. Yet this does not mean that a war between Italy
and England would be a war of science against religion.
Mussolini, the atheist, will do all in his power to fan the reli-
gious passions of the Mohammedans. The devout Protestant
Chamberlain will, for his part, seek assistance from the Pope,
and so on. In the calendar of human progress, a republic rates
above a monarchy. But does this signify that a war waged by
republican France, say, against monarchist Holland for colonies would be a war of a republic against a monarchy? We
shall not even dwell on the fact that in the event of a national
war waged by the bey of Tunis against France, progress would
be on the side of the barbarian monarch and not that of the
imperialist republic. Hygiene occupies an important place
in human culture. But when a murder is involved, the question
of whether the murderer washed his hands beforehand is not
of decisive importance. To substitute political or moral ab-
stractions for the actual aims of the warring imperialist camps
is not to fight for democracy, but to help the brigands disguise their robbery, pillage, and violence. This is now precisely
the main function of the Second and Third Internationals.

The International Policy
of the Bonapartist Kremlin Clique

The immediate blow fell this time on Czechoslovakia. France
and England have suffered serious injury. But the most formidable blow was suffered by the Kremlin. Its system of lies,
charlatanism, and frauds has suffered international collapse.

Having crushed the Soviet masses and broken with the policy
of international revolution, the Kremlin clique has become a
toy of imperialism. In everything essential, Stalin's diplomacy
in the last five years was only a reflection of and a supplement to Hitler's diplomacy. In 1933 Stalin strove might and
main to become Hitler's ally. But the extended hand was
spurned, inasmuch as Hitler, in search of England's friendship,
presented himself as the savior of Germany and Europe from
Bolshevism. Thereupon Stalin set himself the task of proving
to capitalist Europe that it had no need of Hitler, that Bolshevism contained no dangers within itself, that the government
of the Kremlin was a domestic animal, trained to stand up on

its haunches and beg. Thus, in moving away from Hitler, or more exactly, in being repulsed by him, Stalin gradually became a lackey and hired assassin in the service of the countries of sated imperialism.

Hence, this sudden frenzy of genuflection before gangrenous bourgeois democracy on the part of the totalitarian Kremlin gang; hence, the idiotically false idealization of the League of Nations; hence, the "People's Fronts" which strangled the Spanish revolution; hence, the substitution for the actual class struggle of declamations "against fascism." The present international function of the Soviet bureaucracy and the Comintern was revealed with especial impudence at the pacifist congress in Mexico (September 1938), where the hired agents of Moscow tried to convince the peoples of Latin America that they had to fight not against the all too real imperialism that threatened them but solely against fascism.

As was to be expected, Stalin gained neither friendship nor trust through these cheap maneuvers. The imperialists have become accustomed to appraise society not by the declarations of its "leaders," and not even by the character of its political superstructure, but by its social foundation. So long as state ownership of the means of production protected by monopoly of foreign trade is maintained in the Soviet Union, the imperialists, including the "democratic" imperialists, will continue to regard Stalin with no more confidence and incomparably less respect than feudal-monarchist Europe viewed the first Bonaparte. Surrounded by the aureole of victories and his suite of brilliant marshals, Napoleon could not escape Waterloo. Stalin has crowned the series of his capitulations, failures, and betrayals with the wholesale destruction of the marshals of the revolution. Can there be the slightest doubt about the fate awaiting him?

The only obstacle in the path of war is the fear of the property-owning classes of revolution. So long as the Communist International remained true to the principles of proletarian revolution, it represented, together with the Red Army, with which it was closely bound, the most important factor for peace. Having prostituted the Comintern, and turned it into an agency of "democratic" imperialism; having beheaded and paralyzed the military power of the Soviets, Stalin has completely untied Hitler's hands, as well as the hands of Hitler's adversaries, and pushed Europe close to war.

The Moscow falsifiers are nowadays heaping cheap curses upon their former democratic friend Benes because he "capitulated" prematurely and prevented the Red Army from crushing Hitler, regardless of France's course. This theatrical thunder only illuminates all the more glaringly the impotence and duplicity of the Kremlin. Who then compelled you to believe in Benes? Who forced you to concoct the myth of the "alliance of democracies"? And, lastly, who prevented you in the critical hours when all of Czechoslovakia was seething like a cauldron, from calling upon the proletariat of Prague to seize power and sending the Red Army to their aid? Apparently it is much more difficult to fight against fascism than to shoot and poison Old Bolsheviks. . . . From the example of Czechoslovakia, all small states and especially all colonial peoples must learn what sort of help they may expect from Stalin.

Only the overthrow of the Bonapartist Kremlin clique can make possible the regeneration of the military strength of the USSR. Only the liquidation of the ex-Comintern will clear the way for revolutionary internationalism. The struggle against war, imperialism, and fascism demands a ruthless struggle against Stalinism, splotched with crimes. Whoever defends Stalinism directly or indirectly, whoever keeps silent about its betrayals or exaggerates its military strength is the worst enemy of the revolution, of socialism, of the oppressed peoples. The sooner the Kremlin gang is overthrown by the armed offensive of the workers, the greater will be the chances for a socialist regeneration of the USSR, the closer and broader will be the perspectives of the international revolution.

The Social Basis of Opportunism

In order to understand the present role of the Social Democracy and of the ex-Comintern, it is necessary once again to recall the economic foundation upon which opportunism in the world labor movement rests.

The flowering of capitalism, which lasted, with inevitable oscillations, up to 1913, enabled the bourgeoisie on the one hand to raise slightly the living standard of certain proletarian layers, and on the other to throw rather juicy sops to the bureaucracy and aristocracy of labor, thus raising them above the masses. The trade union and parliamentary bureaucracy, whose "social problem" appeared close to a solution, was in a position to point out to the masses the beginnings of a change for the better in their own lives. This is the social basis for reformism (opportunism) as a system of *illusions* for the masses and a system of *deceit* on the part of the labor bureaucracy. The reformist optimism of the Second International reached its most luxuriant flowering in the years of the last economic boom prior to the war (1909-13). For this reason, the leaders hailed the war and depicted it to the masses as an *external* calamity that threatened the bases of growing national welfare. Hence, the policy of "defense of the fatherland," which was in actuality on the part of the masses an unconscious, and on the bureaucracy's part a conscious or semiconscious defense of the imperialist interests of their respective bourgeoisies.

The war proved in reality to be not an "external" calamity which had temporarily disrupted national progress but rather the explosion of internal contradictions of the imperialist system at a moment when further progress on the basis of this system had become practically impossible. And since the war could neither enlarge our planet nor restore youth to capitalism, it ended by accelerating and aggravating in the extreme all the processes of capitalist decay. With the decline of democracy set in the decline of the labor bureaucracy. Fascism brought the workers "only" redoubled enslavement; to the reformist bureaucracy it brought utter ruin.

The political form of democracy, even if in an extremely mutilated condition ("emergency powers," immigration laws, abandonment of the right of asylum, etc.), has been preserved among the great powers only by Great Britain, France, and the United States, the richest, traditionally the most predatory and privileged capitalist countries, which have long since concentrated in their hands a lion's share of the colonial possessions and the chief natural resources of our planet. It is not hard to find the explanation for this "natural selection." Democracy can be maintained only so long as class contradictions do not reach an explosive state. In order to mitigate social frictions the bourgeoisie has been compelled to provide feed for a broad layer of petty-bourgeois intellectuals, and the bureaucracy and aristocracy of labor. The bigger the feeding-trough the more ardent is social patriotism. The reformist feeding-trough has nowadays been preserved only in those countries which were able in the past to accumulate vast wealth, thanks to the exploitation of the world market, and their pillage of the colonies. In other words, in the condition of capitalist decay a *democratic* regime is accessible (up to a certain time) only to the most *aristocratic* bourgeoisie. The basis of social patriotism remains colonial slavery.

In countries like Italy and Germany, which have not inherited from the past vast accumulations of riches and which are deprived of the opportunity to obtain superprofits from their colonies, the bourgeoisie has destroyed the parliament, dispersed the reformist bureaucracy and placed the workers in an iron vise. To be sure, the fascist bureaucracy devours not less but more than the reformist bureaucracy; but, in return, it is not compelled to make concessions to the masses nor to issue drafts, which decaying capitalism can no longer pay. Deprived of its feeding-trough, the retired Social Democratic bureaucracy of Italy, Germany, and Austria holds high the banner of defeatism — in emigration.

The chief source of strength of the social patriotic, or more exactly, the social imperialist parties is the protection of the bourgeoisie, which through the parliament, the press, the army, and the police protects and defends the Social Democracy against all kinds of revolutionary movements and even against revolutionary criticism. In the future war, owing to the sharpening of national and international contradictions, this organic bond between the bureaucracy and the bourgeoisie will be revealed still more openly and cynically, or to put it more exactly, it is already being revealed, especially in the treacherous policy of the People's Fronts, which were absolutely inconceivable on the eve of the last war. However, the initiative for the People's Fronts originates not from the Second but from the Third International.

Communo-Chauvinism

The monstrous and rapid development of Soviet opportunism finds its explanation in causes analogous to those which, in the previous generation, led to the flowering of opportunism in capitalist countries, namely, the parasitism of the labor bureaucracy, which had successfully solved its "social question" on the basis of a rise of the productive forces in the USSR. But since the Soviet bureaucracy is incomparably more powerful than the labor bureaucracy in capitalist countries, and since the feeding-trough at its disposal is distinguished by its almost unlimited capacity, there is nothing astonishing in the fact that the Soviet variety of opportunism immediately assumed an especially perfidious and vile character.

As regards the ex-Comintern, its social basis, properly speaking, is of a twofold nature. On the one hand, it lives on the subsidies of the Kremlin, submits to the latter's commands, and, in this respect, every ex-Communist bureaucrat is the younger brother and subordinate of the Soviet bureaucrat. On the other hand, the various machines of the ex-Comintern feed from the same sources as the Social Democracy, that is, the superprofits of imperialism. The growth of the Communist parties in recent years, their infiltration into the ranks of the petty bourgeoisie, their installation in the state machinery, the trade unions, parliaments, municipalities, etc., have strengthened in the extreme their dependence on national imperialism at the expense of their traditional dependence on the Kremlin.

Ten years ago it was predicted that the theory of socialism in one country must inevitably lead to the growth of nationalist tendencies in the sections of the Comintern.[73] This prediction has become an obvious fact. But until recently, the chauvinism of the French, British, Belgian, Czechoslovak, American, and other Communist parties seemed to be, and to a certain extent was, a refracted image of the interests of Soviet diplomacy ("the defense of the USSR"). Today, we can predict with assurance the inception of a new stage. The growth of imperialist antagonisms, the obvious proximity of the war danger, and the equally obvious isolation of the USSR must unavoidably strengthen the *centrifugal nationalist tendencies* within the Comintern. Each one of its sections will begin to evolve a patriotic policy on its own account. Stalin has reconciled the Communist parties of imperialist democracies with their national bourgeoisies. This stage has now been passed. The Bonapartist procurer has played his role. Henceforth the Communo-chauvinists will have to worry about their own hides, whose interests by no means always coincide with the "defense of the USSR."

When the American Browder[74] deemed it possible to declare before a senate committee that in case of a war between the United States and the Soviet Union his party would be found on the side of its passionately beloved fatherland, he himself might have possibly considered this statement as a simple stratagem. But in reality, Browder's answer is an unmistakable symptom of a change from a "Moscow" to a "national" orientation. The "stratagem" arose out of the necessity of adaptation to imperialist "patriotism." The cynical grossness of this stratagem (the turn from the "fatherland of the toilers" to the republic of the dollar) reveals the profound extent of degeneration that has occurred and the full extent of the dependence of the sections of the Comintern on the public opinion of the bourgeoisie.

Fifteen years of uninterrupted purges, degradation, and corruption have brought the bureaucracy of the ex-Comintern to such a degree of demoralization that it has become able and anxious to openly take into its hands the banner of social patriotism. The Stalinists (we shall soon have to say, the ex-Stalinists) have not, of course, set the Thames on fire. They have simply picked up the well-worn banalities of petty-bourgeois opportunism. But in propagating them, they have injected into them the frenzy of "revolutionary" parvenus, who have turned totalitarian slander, blackmail, and murder into normal methods of "defending democracy." As for the old classic reformists, washing their hands in innocence after every embarrassing situation, they have known how to use the support of the new recruits to chauvinism.

In that imperialist country which happens to be in the same camp with the USSR during the war (if any such is found), the section of the ex-Comintern will, naturally, "defend" Moscow. This defense, however, will be of no great value, for in such a country all parties will "defend" the USSR. (In order not to compromise itself with its imperialist ally, Moscow would probably order the Communist Party not to shout too loudly, and might possibly try to dissolve it altogether.) On the contrary, in countries of the hostile camp, i.e., precisely where Moscow will be in greatest need of defenders, the ex-Communist parties will be found completely on the side of their imperialist fatherland: this course will be infinitely less dangerous and far more profitable. The ruling Moscow clique will reap the just fruits of fifteen years' prostitution of the Comintern.

The Second and Third Internationals
in Colonial Countries

The true character of the Social Democracy as a party whose policy rested and still rests on imperialist exploitation of backward peoples appears most clearly in the fact that in colonial and semicolonial countries the Second International has never had any influence. The labor bureaucracy of imperialist countries feared either consciously or semiconsciously to set in motion a movement in the colonies that might have undermined the basis of its own prosperity in the metropolitan centers.

It was otherwise with the Comintern. As a genuinely internationalist organization, it immediately threw itself upon the virgin soil of the colonies and thanks to the revolutionary program of Leninism gained important influence there. The subsequent bourgeois degeneration of the Comintern transformed its sections in colonial and semicolonial countries, especially in Latin America, into a left agency of European and American imperialism. Parallel with this, a change occurred also in the social basis of the colonial "Communist" parties. Mercilessly plundering its Asiatic and African slaves and its Latin American semislaves, foreign capitalism is at present compelled in the colonies to feed a thin layer of aristocracy — pitiful, pathetic, but still an aristocracy amid the universal poverty. Stalinism has in recent years become the party of this labor "aristocracy" as well as of the "left" section of the petty bourgeoisie, the office holders in particular. Bourgeois lawyers, journalists, teachers, etc., adapting themselves to the national revolution and exploiting the labor organizations to make careers for themselves, find in Stalinism the best possible ideology.

The revolutionary struggle against imperialism demands courage, resolution, and the spirit of self-sacrifice. Where are the petty-bourgeois heroes of the phrase to find these qualities? On the other hand, adaptation to "democratic" imperialism permits them to carve out placid and pleasant careers on the backs of the toilers. The best possible way of hiding this adaptation from the workers is provided by the slogan "defense of the USSR," i.e., friendship with the Kremlin oligarchy. This opens up an opportunity to publish newspapers without readers, arrange pompous congresses and all sorts of international publicity. This corporation of professional "friends of the Soviet Union," fake "socialists" and "Communists," who by their noisy declamation against fascism cover up their social parasitism and their subservience to the imperialists and the Kremlin oligarchy, has become a veritable plague of the labor movement in colonial and semicolonial countries. Stalinism — under all its masks — is the chief obstacle in the path of the liberating struggle of backward and oppressed peoples. The problem of colonial revolutions has henceforth become indissolubly linked with the historic mission of the Fourth International.

The International Association of Squeezed Lemons (No. 3-1/4)

The London Bureau of incurable centrists (Fenner Brockway,

Walcher, and Company), jointly with Brandler, Sneevliet, Marceau Pivert, and with the participation of "sections that have split from the so-called Fourth International," have united in view of the war danger to create — please do not smile! — the War Emergency Fund. 75 These gentlemen did not bother their heads about a "fund" of ideas. Thank heaven, they are materialists and not idealists. It is open to doubt whether this new "unification" represents a danger to imperialism. But it does perform a great service to the Fourth International, for it brings together the shallowness, the hybridity, and the inconsistency of all varieties and shades of centrism, i.e., that tendency which is in sharpest contradiction with the spirit of our epoch. Like all similar mechanical "unifications," it will become a source of new internal conflicts and splits and will fall to pieces at the very moment that the hour for action arrives.

Could it be otherwise? The organizations occupied with the heroic creation of the "Fund" did not arise on the basis of a common program, but have arrived from all the corners of the political map of centrism as the homeless splinters of old opportunist parties and factions, continuing even today to play with all the colors of the opportunist rainbow, and to evolve in different directions. All of them have steadily declined and grown weaker in recent years, with the exception of the newly split party of Marceau Pivert, for which the same unenviable fate may be predicted. In no country in the world did the London Bureau succeed in creating a new organization from young fresh elements on the basis of its own program. No revolutionary group will rally to this banner which has neither a past nor a future. In the colonial countries the London Bureau does not possess even a shadow of influence. It may be regarded as a law that the "revolutionary" organization which in our imperialist epoch is incapable of sinking its roots into the colonies is doomed to vegetate miserably.

Each of these outlived groups holds together by force of inertia and not by the strength of ideas. The one organization with a more serious revolutionary past in this quarter, the POUM, has to date proved incapable of courageously revising its centrist policy, which was one of the main reasons for the collapse of the Spanish revolution. 76 The remaining members of the group are even less capable of criticism and self-criticism. The spirit of senile dilettantism hovers over this whole enterprise.

Assuredly not a few "remnants" had gathered in the beginning around the banner of the Fourth International. But the enormous work of selection, cleansing, and reeducation was accomplished here on the basis of a scientific theory and a clear program. This work, the meaning and importance of which philistines have never understood, has gone on and is still going on in an atmosphere of free, open, and patient discussion. Whoever has failed to pass this test has proved in action his organic inability to contribute anything to the building of a revolutionary International. It is these winnowed, worn, and rejected "remnants" that have been incorporated today into the "Fund" of international centrism. This fact alone places on the entire enterprise a stamp of hopeless disability.

In a lucid moment Marceau Pivert declared a few years ago that any tendency in the working class conducting a struggle against "Trotskyism" thereby characterizes itself as a reactionary tendency. This did not, we notice, prevent Pivert, as a congenital centrist whose words are always contrary to his deeds, from joining the London Bureau, which seeks to create a physiognomy of its own by convulsively shying away from "Trotskyism."

It is not hard, however, to forecast that the bourgeoisie, the reformists, and the Stalinists will continue to label these creators of the "Fund" as — "Trotskyists" or "semi-Trotskyists." This will be done in part out of ignorance but chiefly in order to compel them to excuse, justify, and demarcate themselves. And they will actually vow, with might and main, that they are not at all Trotskyists, and that if they should happen to try to roar like lions, then like their forerunner, Bottom the weaver, they succeed in "roaring" like sucking doves. We know them: they are no fledglings. The Fenner Brockways, the Walchers, the Brandlers, the Sneevliets, the Piverts, as well as the rejected elements of the Fourth International, have managed in the course of many long years — for some, decades — to evince their hopeless eclecticism in theory and their sterility in practice. They are less cynical than the Stalinists and a trifle to the left of the left Social Democrats — that is all that can be said for them. That is why in the list of the Internationals they must therefore be entered as number three and one-eighth or three and one-quarter. With a "fund" or without one, they will enter into history as an association of squeezed lemons. When the great masses, under the blows of the war, are set in revolutionary motion, they will not bother to inquire about the address of the London Bureau.

Perspectives

All the forces and mainsprings of the last war are again
being set in motion but in an incomparably more violent and
open form. The movement follows well-worn grooves and consequently proceeds at a swifter pace. Nobody believes at present,
as they did on the eve of 1914, in the inviolability of frontiers
or the stability of regimes. This is an enormous advantage
to the revolutionary party. If on the eve of the last war, the
sections of the Second International themselves did not know
as yet what their conduct would be on the morrow, and adopted
superrevolutionary resolutions; if the left elements only gradually freed themselves from the pacifist swamp and groped
for their road, then today *all the starting positions have been
occupied with precision prior to the war.* Nobody expects an
internationalist policy from the Social Democratic parties, which
themselves do not promise anything but the "defense of the
fatherland." The departure of the Czech social patriots from
the Second International is the beginning of the latter's official
disintegration along national lines. The policy of the Third
International is fixed in advance almost as distinctly; the prognosis in this case is only slightly complicated by an element
of adventurism. If the German and Italian Social Democrats
and ex-Communists will be platonic defeatists, it is only because
Hitler and Mussolini forbid them to be patriots. But wherever
the bourgeoisie still continues to feed the labor bureaucracy,
the Social Democrats and ex-Communists will be found completely on the side of their general staffs, and, what is more,
the first fiddle of chauvinism will be in the hands of the musi-
cians of the Stalin school. Not only the fiddle, but also the
revolver aimed at the revolutionary workers.

At the beginning of the last war, Jean Jaures was assassinated, and at the end of the war, Karl Liebknecht and Rosa
Luxemburg. [77] In France the assassination of the leader of
the French Socialist Party did not deter other leaders from
entering the government of imperialist war. In Germany the
murder of two great revolutionists was accomplished with the
direct participation of the Social Democratic government. The
actual murderer in France was an obscure petty-bourgeois
chauvinist, while in Germany counterrevolutionary officers did
the killing. The situation today even in this respect is incomparably clearer. The work of exterminating the internationalists
has already commenced on a world scale prior to the outbreak

of the war. Imperialism no longer has to depend on a "happy accident." In the Stalinist Mafia it has a ready-made international agency for the systematic extermination of revolutionists. Jaures, Liebknecht, Luxemburg enjoyed world fame as socialist leaders. Rudolf Klement was a young and as yet little known revolutionist. Nevertheless the assassination of Klement because he was the secretary of the Fourth International is of profound symbolic significance. Through its Stalinist gangsters imperialism indicates beforehand from what side mortal danger will threaten it in time of war.

The imperialists are not mistaken. If they succeeded, after the last war, in maintaining themselves everywhere except in Russia, it was only because of the absence of revolutionary parties. Freeing themselves with difficulty from the web of the old ideology, with its fetishism of "unity," most of the oppositional elements in the Social Democracy did not go further than pacifism. In critical moments such groupings proved more capable of checking the revolutionary mass movement than of heading it. In this sense, it is no exaggeration to say that the "unity" of the parties of the Second International saved the European bourgeoisie.

At present, sections of the Fourth International exist in thirty countries. True, they are only the vanguard of the vanguard. But if today, prior to the war, we had mass revolutionary organizations, then revolution and not war would be on the order of the day. We lack this, of course, and we hold no illusions on this score. But the position of the revolutionary vanguard is far more favorable today than it was twenty-five years ago. The main conquest is that before the war there already exist in all the most important countries of the world tested cadres, numbering hundreds and thousands of revolutionists in growing numbers, welded together by the unity of a doctrine, and tested in the school of cruelest persecutions by the imperialist bourgeoisie, the Social Democracy, and, in particular, the Stalinist Mafia. The Second, the Third, and the Amsterdam Internationals cannot at present convene their congresses, because they are paralyzed by their dependence on imperialism and because they are torn asunder by "national" contradictions. On the contrary, the sections of the Fourth International, despite their extremely meager resources, the difficulties of obtaining visas, the murder of their secretary and the hail of repressions, were able in the most critical moment to convene their international congress and adopt unan-

imous decisions in which the tasks of the present titanic struggle
are formulated precisely and concretely, on the basis of all
historic experience.

These precious cadres will not be swerved from their road
by any wave of chauvinism, nor intimidated by Stalinist
Mausers and knives. The Fourth International will enter the
next war as a tightly welded unit, whose sections will be able
to follow one and the same policy, irrespective of the boundaries and trenches dividing them. It is quite possible that at
the beginning of the war, when the blind instinct of self-preservation combined with chauvinist propaganda will push the
popular masses towards their governments, the sections of
the Fourth International will find themselves isolated. They
will know how to withstand national hypnosis and the epi-
demic of patriotism. In the principles of internationalism they
will find a bulwark against the herd panic below, and the
terror from above. They will view with contempt the oscillations
and vacillations of philistine "democracy." On the other hand,
they will listen closely to the most oppressed sections of the
population and to the army pouring out its blood. Each new
day of war will work in our favor. Mankind has become poorer
than it was twenty-five years ago, while the means of destruction have become infinitely more powerful. In the very first
months of the war, therefore, a stormy reaction against the
fumes of chauvinism will set in among the working masses.
The first victims of this reaction, along with fascism, will be
the parties of the Second and Third Internationals. Their collapse will be the indispensable condition for an avowed revolutionary movement, which will find for its crystallization no
axis other than the Fourth International. Its tempered cadres
will lead the toilers to the great offensive.

TO OUR FRIENDS AND READERS[78]

October 11, 1938

The first issue of *Clave* has met an unmistakably warm response by the advanced workers and revolutionary intellectuals of Mexico. All revolutionaries — that is, real revolutionaries and not charlatans or self-serving intriguers — have been waiting for the appearance of a Marxist journal.

The events of the present epoch are complex and of far-reaching significance. Mexico and Latin America as a whole cannot be considered apart from the maelstrom of world events. In Spain, Marxist literature is suppressed not only under Franco, but under Stalin-Negrin as well.[79] Of all the Spanish-speaking countries, Mexico is virtually the only one where the necessary freedom exists for the dissemination of the Marxist word. This international situation assigns a leading role to Mexican Marxists not just with respect to Latin America, but with respect to Spain itself, as well as the growing Spanish emigration to all the countries of the Old and New World. Great opportunities imply great obligations. History has assigned serious responsibilities to Mexican Marxists.

The so-called "Communist" Party of Mexico suffers from the same degeneration as the other sections of the Comintern. It has been decisively transformed from the party of the proletarian vanguard into the party of the conservative petty bourgeoisie. One part of the petty bourgeoisie, as everyone knows, looks to the Pope in Rome for its salvation; another more adventurous part looks to the Fuehrer in Moscow. The theoretical value of Stalinism is not superior to the theoretical value of Catholicism. It is not without purpose that a recent encyclical from Moscow calls for the fraternization of the Stalinists with the Catholics. It is not without purpose that the mindless paper put out by the Stalinists changed its name from *Machete,* which was known to have a compromising past, to the respectable name, *Voz de Mexico,* which at one time was the name of the paper of the Catholic reaction.

The literature that Lombardo Toledano publishes on behalf of the CTM (but not in its interests) is not much better than the "Catholic-Communist" literature put out by Laborde and Company. Marxism is a scientific doctrine and at the same time a guide for action. In order to apply this doctrine correctly, one must study events conscientiously from the moment of their appearance and in the course of their development.

In our epoch the scientific study of the various tendencies of world imperialism is particularly important. This is now the historical factor with the greatest weight, the one that determines the destiny of both the advanced and the underdeveloped peoples, the one that is leading to the hurling of human civilization into the abyss of a new war. The Lombardo Toledano gang is ignorant of even the ABCs of Marxism and does not feel the slightest necessity to familiarize itself with it. These gentlemen set themselves the task of using Marxist formulations from here and there to hide from the workers the nakedness of their ambitions, appetites, and intrigues. This sort of literature compromises the very name of Marxism and poisons progressive public opinion.

Under these conditions a real *Marxist forum* is doubly necessary and important. It is necessary to restore the real face of scientific socialism. All thinking revolutionaries received the first issue of our magazine as a breath of fresh air in an atmosphere polluted by pseudo-Marxist imitations and falsifications. The sympathetic welcome accorded us by our friends and readers strengthens us and redoubles our confidence in following the road we have taken.

Many readers have complained about the poor typographical features of our publication; they have complained about the inconvenient format, excessively small print, etc. We recognize that these complaints are fully justified. The principal reason for the technical defects in *Clave* is the insufficiency of our funds. We receive no subsidies from either the Pope in Rome or the one in Moscow, or in general from any secret source. Unlike certain pseudo-Marxist publications, we can give our readers an accounting of every penny we have spent. (Unfortunately we have but little to spend.) Our funds are provided by the editors and their friends. With the firm conviction that the number of our friends will increase endlessly, we request, or, rather, we implore them to lend us their moral and material support. Under these circumstances, we will succeed not only in enlarging the contents of our magazine but in considerably improving its typographical aspect as well.

Friends of *Clave,* you have the floor!

THE PROBLEM
OF THE NEW INTERNATIONAL[80]

October 11, 1938

The bankruptcy of the Second and Third Internationals as organizations of the international proletariat is undisputed among real Marxists. The ex-Communist International, following in the footsteps of the Social Democracy, has transformed itself from an instrument of the emancipation of the workers and the exploited into an instrument of "democratic" imperialism. At this time, the problem of the new international is the most important problem facing the vanguard of the world proletariat.

In this issue of *Clave,* we are reprinting various documents that relate to the recent world conference of the Fourth International or reflect the activity of some of its sections. We hope these documents will provoke a lively exchange of ideas among Mexican Marxists and among Spanish-speaking Marxists in general. The new International cannot be created by means of encyclicals. Every step forward must come as the result of scientific investigation, open criticism, and collective consideration.

In the first issue of *Clave* we reproduced draft theses on the problem of development in Latin America. These draft theses were prepared by Comrade Diego Rivera[81] (a fact that was not mentioned). The draft on Mexican problems is also his. The editors, who are in general agreement with these theses, entreat their readers to give careful consideration to both drafts.

Clave is not published for entertainment, nor to provide light reading. Marxism is a scientific doctrine. Mastering it requires constant, serious thinking. We recommend that advanced workers read the articles in our magazine in their meetings; groups that are less advanced should invite teachers. The reading of each article should provoke an exchange of opinions. Conclusions, critical observations, questions, and proposals can be communicated to the editors in written or verbal form. We give our assurance beforehand that the editors will give all comments their attentive consideration.

TASKS OF THE TRADE UNION MOVEMENT IN LATIN AMERICA[82]

October 11, 1938

In Mexico from September 6 to 8 there was a congress of trade union representatives from several Latin American countries resulting in the founding of a so-called "Confederation of Latin American Workers."[83] We, the undersigned, consider it our duty to declare to the workers of Latin America and the whole world that this congress, prepared behind the backs of the masses, was stacked one-sidedly for purposes that have nothing to do with the interests of the Latin American proletariat, but which, on the contrary, are fundamentally hostile to these interests. The "confederation" created at this congress represents not the unification of the organized proletariat of our continent but a political faction closely linked with the Moscow oligarchy.

From Mexico alone the following were neither invited nor admitted to this congress: the Casa del Pueblo, the CROM, and the CGT.[84] Comrade Mateo Fossa, who had arrived from Buenos Aires with a mandate from twenty-four independent Argentine trade unions, was not admitted to the congress simply because he was an opponent of Stalinism. We could point to trade union organizations in every Latin American country which from the outset were deliberately kept out of the pre-congress preparations, so as not to disrupt its political homogeneity, i.e., its total subordination to Stalinism.

The majority of the delegates at the trade union congress also took part in the congress against war and fascism, where they had the opportunity to fully disclose their political silhouette. They all voted for hollow resolutions on the struggle against fascism but decisively repudiated (except for the representatives from Puerto Rico and Peru) the struggle against imperialism. This policy fully · characterizes the Moscow bureaucracy, which in view of the threats from Hitler is seeking the trust and friendship of the imperialist democracies: France, Great Britain, and the United States. The working masses of

Latin America, who see fascism as their mortal enemy, cannot, however, for even an instant give up the irreconcilable revolutionary struggle against imperialism, even an imperialism concealed behind a mask of democracy. That is why the proletariat and the peoples of Latin America can have no aims in common with the Stalinist bureaucracy! We can never forget or close our eyes to the fact that in the name of friendship with the French and English bourgeoisie, the Stalinist bureaucracy strangled the revolutionary movement of the Spanish workers and peasants!

"Democratic" imperialism, which is infinitely stronger in Latin America than fascist imperialism, endeavors — and not without success — by means of bribery, doles, and privileges to establish its own political agents in our countries, not only within the bourgeoisie, the bourgeois bureaucracy, and the petty-bourgeois intelligentsia, but in the upper strata of the working class as well. Such corrupted elements from the labor bureaucracy or labor "aristocracy" often entertain not proletarian or revolutionary but slavish and servile feelings toward their imperialist protectors. The agents of the Kremlin oligarchy exploit these feelings in order to reconcile the Latin American proletariat with the "democratic" slaveholders.

To this must be added the fact that in Mexico where the unions, unfortunately, are directly dependent on the state, posts in the union bureaucracy are frequently filled from the ranks of the bourgeois intelligentsia, attorneys, engineers, etc. — by people who have nothing in common with the working class and who seek only to use the trade union organizations in the interests of their own personal material well-being or their political careers. In an effort to conceal their crudely egotistical politics from the workers, these bourgeois careerists usually come forward as "antifascists" and "friends of the USSR," while in reality they are agents of Anglo-Saxon imperialism.

So as to keep the trade unions in the hands of their faction, they ferociously trample on workers' democracy and stifle any voice of criticism, acting as outright gangsters toward organizations that fight for the revolutionary independence of the proletariat from the bourgeois state and from foreign imperialism. By thus splitting the trade union movement and greatly embittering the struggle among its various tendencies, Stalin's agents weaken the proletariat, corrupt it, undermine democracy in our country, and in fact clear the road for fascism. The Mexican attorney Lombardo Toledano, elected as secretary of the Latin American Federation which he himself organized, is the leader most responsible for this criminal policy.

We, the undersigned, are ardent and devoted supporters of the unification of the Latin American proletariat as well as of the closest possible ties between it and the proletariat of the United States of North America. But this task, as is evident from what has been stated, still remains totally undone. The factional political organization that was formed in September is not an aid but an obstacle on the road to its completion.

We are firmly convinced that the genuine unification of the Latin American proletariat can and will be achieved on the basis of the principles listed below:

1. The full independence of the trade union movement from its own bourgeois government as well as from foreign imperialism, fascist or "democratic";

2. A revolutionary class-struggle program;

3. Purging the trade union movement of petty-bourgeois careerists who are alien to the working class;

4. The unification in every country of all working class unions on the basis of workers' democracy, i.e., that struggle of ideas within the union conducted freely and in a fraternal way, with the minority strictly submitting to the majority and with iron discipline in action;

5. The honest preparation of a Latin American congress of trade unions with the active participation of the mass of the workers themselves, that is, with an unrestricted and serious discussion of the tasks of the Latin American proletariat and its methods of struggle.

Our proletariat must step out in solid ranks into the arena of history in order to take the fate of Latin America into its hands and make its future secure. The unified proletariat will attract to its side the tens of millions of Indo-American peasants, eliminate the hostile borders dividing us, and unite the two dozen republics and colonial possessions under the banner of a Workers' and Peasants' United States of Latin America.

We present this program for the discussion of all workers' organizations of our continent. Revolutionary workers of Latin America, you have the floor!

THE FOUNDING
OF THE FOURTH INTERNATIONAL[85]

October 18, 1938

I hope that this time my voice will reach you and that I will be permitted in this way to participate in your double celebration. Both events — the tenth anniversary of our American organization as well as the foundation congress of the Fourth International — deserve the attention of the workers incomparably more than the warlike gestures of the totalitarian chiefs, the diplomatic intrigues, or the pacifist congresses.

Both events will enter history as important milestones. No one has now the right to doubt that.

It is necessary to remark that the birth of the American group of Bolshevik-Leninists, thanks to the courageous initiative of Comrades Cannon, Shachtman, and Abern,[86] didn't stand alone. It approximately coincided with the beginning of the systematic international work of the Left Opposition. It is true that the Left Opposition arose in Russia in 1923, but regular work on an international scale began with the Sixth Congress of the Comintern.[87]

Without a personal meeting we reached an agreement with the American pioneers of the Fourth International, before all, on the criticism of the program of the Communist International. Then, in 1928, began that collective work which after ten years led to the elaboration of our own program recently adopted by our international conference. We have the right to say that the work of this decade was not only persistent and patient, but also honest. The Bolshevik-Leninists, the international pioneers, our comrades across the world, searched the way of the revolution as genuine Marxists, not in their feelings and wishes, but in the analysis of the objective march of events. Above all were we guided by the preoccupation not to deceive others nor ourselves. We searched seriously and honestly. And some important things were found by us. The events confirmed

85

our analysis as well as our prognosis. Nobody can deny it. Now it is necessary that we remain true to ourselves and to our program. It is not easy to do so. The tasks are tremendous, the enemies — innumerable. We have the right to spend our time and our attention on the jubilee celebration only insofar as from the lessons of the past we can prepare ourselves for the future.

Dear friends, we are not a party like other parties. Our ambition is not only to have more members, more papers, more money in the treasury, more deputies. All that is necessary, but only as a means. Our aim is the full material and spiritual liberation of the toilers and exploited through the socialist revolution. Nobody will prepare it and nobody will guide it but ourselves. The old Internationals — the Second, the Third, that of Amsterdam, we will add to them also the London Bureau — are rotten through and through.

The great events which rush upon mankind will not leave of these outlived organizations one stone upon another. Only the Fourth International looks with confidence at the future. It is the World Party of Socialist Revolution! There never was a greater task on the earth. Upon every one of us rests a tremendous historical responsibility.

Our party demands each of us, totally and completely. Let the philistines hunt their own individuality in empty space. For a revolutionary to give himself entirely to the party signifies finding himself.

Yes, our party takes each one of us wholly. But in return it gives to every one of us the highest happiness: the consciousness that one participates in the building of a better future, that one carries on his shoulders a particle of the fate of mankind, and that one's life will not have been lived in vain.

The fidelity to the cause of the toilers requires from us the highest devotion to our international party. The party, of course, can also be mistaken. By common effort we will correct its mistakes. In its ranks can penetrate unworthy elements. By common effort we will eliminate them. New thousands who will enter its ranks tomorrow will probably be deprived of necessary education. By common effort we will elevate their revolutionary level. But we will never forget that our party is now the greatest lever of history. Separated from this lever, every one of us is nothing. With this lever in hand, we are all.

We aren't a party like other parties. It is not in vain that the imperialist reaction persecutes us madly, following furiously at our heels. The assassins at its services are the agents of the Moscow Bonapartistic clique. Our young International already knows many victims. In the Soviet Union they number by thousands. In Spain by dozens. In other countries by units. With gratitude and love we remember them all in these moments. Their spirits continue to fight in our ranks.

The hangmen think in their obtuseness and cynicism that it is possible to frighten us. They err! Under blows we become stronger. The bestial politics of Stalin are only politics of despair. It is possible to kill individual soldiers of our army, but not to frighten them. Friends, we will repeat again in this day of celebration . . . *it is not possible to frighten us.*

Ten years were necessary for the Kremlin clique in order to strangle the Bolshevik Party and to transform the first workers' state into a sinister caricature. Ten years were necessary for the Third International in order to stamp into the mire their own program and to transform themselves into a stinking cadaver. Ten years! Only ten years! Permit me to finish with a prediction: During the next ten years the program of the Fourth International will become the guide of millions and these revolutionary millions will know how to storm earth and heaven.

Long live the Socialist Workers Party of the United States!
Long live the Fourth International!

TO THE EDITORS OF BIULLETEN OPPOZITSII, LUTTE OUVRIERE, AND QUATRIEME INTERNATIONALE[88]

October 22, 1938

Dear Comrades,

All the articles I write for the workers' press are intended, in France, for your three publications. No other publication may reprint my articles without your permission. I do not doubt that you will gladly give that permission to every honest organ of the workers' press that wishes to reprint my articles so as to acquaint their readers with them. But I protest firmly against the reprinting of my articles by organs which use them for ends directly opposed to those for which they were written. Thus, *La Commune*,[89] with which you are acquainted, systematically reprints my articles not only without my permission but even against my direct prohibition. *La Commune* is a publication devoid of any ideological foundation whatsoever, of any principled standard. It reprints my articles not to make use of the ideas in them, but only to use them to conceal the lack of any ideas of their own and to confuse the reader. In connection with the tragic fate of Rudolf Klement the truly adventurist physiognomy of *La Commune* was fully exposed. They are not allies and not honest opponents but cursed foes of the Fourth International, who stop at nothing to cause it harm.

I utterly refuse to give *La Commune* a single line written by me. The same applies to *La Verite*,[90] whose very name is stolen. I request you, if they reprint my articles again, to bring to court for literary theft the publishers of *La Commune* and *La Verite*. These gentlemen must be talked to in the language they understand.

With comradely greetings,
L. Trotsky

A FALSE VIEW [91]

October 22, 1938

We have received from one of our readers a letter in which he complains that in spite of the approaching war we continue, as he puts it, to occupy ourselves with the exposure of Stalin. This letter was written at the very height of the Czechoslovak crisis. But if this constitutes the psychological explanation for the letter, it is in no way a political justification for it.

The war will be, of course, a tremendous catastrophe. But it is, nonetheless, a continuation of the prewar policy of the imperialists. The war cannot be fought against except by continuing and developing the prewar revolutionary policy. We have not and cannot have any other means or levers to counteract the war but the revolutionary organization of the proletarian vanguard. The main hindrance to the unification and education of this vanguard is at the present time the so-called Comintern. The struggle for a new revolutionary organization capable of resisting the war cannot, therefore, consist in anything but the struggle against the poison that Stalinism is introducing into the workers' movement. Whoever, under the pretext of the danger of war, recommends stopping the war against Stalinism is in fact deserting the revolutionary tasks, covering himself with loud phrases about world catastrophe. We have nothing in common with this fundamentally false view.

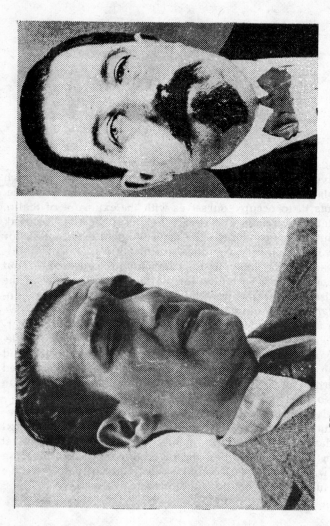

Vicente Lombardo Toledano (left) and Leon Jouhaux.

TWO AGENTS
OF "DEMOCRATIC" IMPERIALISM[92]

October 22, 1938

At the pacifist congress in Mexico, the inimitable Leon Jouhaux exclaimed: "We have come together for a struggle against fascism, not against imperialism." This meant: we must prevent Hitler from seizing French colonies, but we may not interfere with the French slaveholders as they "peacefully" prey upon their own colonial slaves. After France and England capitulated to Hitler, Jouhaux found a new, fresh, and sure means for salvation: to convene an international conference . . . for disarmament. "Even Hitler is not excluded," adds this incomparable anarcho-imperialist. Unfortunately, Jouhaux is very much like the clever rabbit who suggests to the wolf that they go to the dentist together to get their fangs removed.

This, then, is the shameful finale to Moscow's many long years of pacifist campaigning! How many tens of millions of dollars did all these banquets, congresses, parades, trips for Leon Jouhaux, and pastoral letters by Romain Rolland cost the Russian workers?

Toledano in *Futuro* began politely and carefully to dissociate himself from Jouhaux — after the Mexican supporters of the Fourth International, to Toledano's surprise, published Lenin's comments on Jouhaux (it was a surprise to Toledano because he has no understanding of either Lenin or Marx).[93] Perhaps Toledano would now deign to answer some questions clearly and precisely for the workers: Just what and whom does he agree with? What and whom does he disagree with? Does he approve of Stalin's politics? What, in general, is his program?

We guarantee in advance: Toledano will not answer any of these questions. Why? There is nothing he could say. Like Andersen's emperor, he has no clothes.

AMERICAN PROSPECTS [94]

October 24, 1938

Dear Friend:

Thank you very much for your letters, especially for the important report upon the congress. As yet I have not received anything except your report; not one letter, not one document.

I am sending you a long article on the international situation, etc., also the recording of a speech of fifteen minutes.[95] I was very busy and accomplished the whole story with the speech very hastily. Upon another occasion I promise to do better. Now I am again absolutely absorbed by the book,[96] at least for six weeks. Then possibly I shall devote a week more to party questions.

Concerning the documents, please guard them with complete security. When the complete archives come I will ask Glenner to put them in order,[97] but now it is not necessary that he lose his time for this partial work.

I am very glad that you appreciate optimistically the party situation and I hope with you that everything will go ahead satisfactorily. It seems that the conjuncture is improving. During the last two months I have not followed the economic life of the States closely and cannot judge if this improvement is more or less durable. In any case even a short economic improvement is a plus for our party. We are too weak for an immediate critical situation. We can and will use even a short postponement of the denouement. On the other hand, the mitigation of the crisis will be favorable for the party treasury and will permit you to establish your own printing shop, which is an elementary requisite for serious work.

Warmest greetings from Natalia and me to you and Rose.

Yours fraternally,
L. Trotsky

A FEW WORDS ON ANDRE BRETON[98]

October 27, 1938

A few words on Breton. I do not believe that we can demand that he make his literary magazine into a magazine of the bloc.[99] He represents the surrealist school. We don't bear the slightest responsibility for him. In the domain of art, which takes precedence for him, he naturally has the most absolute right to do as he wishes. It is not for us to get involved in artistic tendencies, but to unite them as they are against the totalitarian attacks on art. Any attempt on our part to subordinate artistic tendencies as such to political interests could only compromise us in the eyes of true artists.

LETTER TO ANDRE BRETON[100]

October 27, 1938

Dear Comrade Breton,
    The purpose of this letter is to clarify a point which could give rise to deplorable misunderstandings. In one of my letters to *Partisan Review* I advise having a critical, expectant, and . . . "eclectic" attitude toward the different artistic tendencies. The last will seem strange to you, because generally I am hardly the partisan of eclecticism. But it is worth discerning the sense of this counsel. *Partisan Review* is not the review of an artistic school. It is a Marxist review devoted to the problems of art. It must maintain toward the different artistic schools a critical and friendly attitude. But each artistic school must be faithful to itself. That is why it would be absurd to propose, for example, to the surrealists, the advice that they become eclectic. Each artistic tendency has the absolute right to dispose of itself. This is, moreover, the sense of your manifesto.[101]

My best regards,
Leon Trotsky

"PEACE IN OUR TIME"?[102]

November 4, 1938

Chamberlain has proclaimed the formula that the Munich agreement inaugurated "peace in our time." Never before, if you please, has major policy been so empirical, so blind, never has it been so content to simply "live for today," never has it been so quickly satisfied with ephemeral results, never so much as now. The explanation for this is that those who guide the world's destiny, especially that of Europe, are afraid to face what tomorrow will bring. Every soothing formula, however empty it may be, fulfills a ready and grateful demand. "Peace in our time"? It seems, then, that all the disputes and convulsions of European politics were caused by nothing more than the patchwork existence of Czechoslovakia or the absence of cordial talks between the German and English rulers. In truth, it is almost frightening to observe the credulity and passivity of a public opinion that can be served up with such sugary banalities from the most authoritative rostrums!

Let's go back to the ABC's. The essence of the present world crisis is conditioned by two fundamental circumstances. First, the classic capitalism of free trade has transformed itself into monopoly capitalism and has long since outgrown the boundaries of the nation state. Hence, the pursuit of foreign markets for goods and capital, the struggle for sources of raw materials, and crowning all this, the colonial policy. The second historical factor is the unevenness of the economic, political, and military development of the different countries. The development of the old mother countries of capital, like England and France, has come to a halt. The upstarts, like Germany, the United States, and Japan, have moved a long way forward. As a result of this radical and feverish alteration in the relationship of forces, it is necessary ever more frequently to revise the map of the world. The Munich agreement changed nothing in these basic conditions.

The last war was begun by Germany with the slogan: "The world has been divided up? Then it must be redivided." The twenty years which passed after the war revealed with new force the disparity between the specific weight of the main European states and their share in the world's plunder, based on the Versailles treaty. Naive public opinion was surprised by the weakness the European democracies displayed during the recent crisis; the international prestige of fascism has undoubtedly risen. This, however, had nothing to do with "democracy" per se, but with the specific economic weight of England, and especially France, in the world economy. The present economic foundations of these two "democracies" has absolutely no correspondence with the size and wealth of their colonial empires. On the other hand, the dynamic of the German economy, temporarily paralyzed by the Versailles peace, has been reestablished and it is again beginning to loosen and knock down boundary markers. We are not talking specifically about Italy since war and peace are not in Italy's hands. Until Hitler came to power, Mussolini was quiet as a mouse. In the struggle for world supremacy, he is doomed henceforth to the role of a satellite.

England and France fear every earthshaking tremor since they have nothing to gain and everything to lose. Hence their panicky willingness to concede. But partial concessions secure only short breathing spells, without eliminating or weakening the fundamental source of the conflicts. As a result of the Munich agreement Germany's European base has widened; her opponents' base has narrowed. If one takes Chamberlain's words seriously, it turns out that the weakening of the democracies and the strengthening of the fascist states opens up an "era of peace." The head of the Conservative government clearly did not mean to say this. However, just what he did mean to say is not completely clear, apparently even to himself.

It would be possible to speak with some justification of "peace in our time" if German capitalism's demands for raw materials and markets were satisfied by the incorporation of Germany's "blood brothers" or by the increased influence of Germany in Central and South-Eastern Europe. But in fact the incorporation of the Saar region, Austria, and the Sudetenland only kindles the aggressive tendencies of the German economy. German imperialism must look for the resolution of its internal contradictions in the world arena. It is no accident, therefore, that General Von Epp,[103] the future minister of the future colonies, immediately after the opening of the "era of peace," on Hitler's instructions, raised the demand for the return to

Germany of its former colonial possessions. Chamberlain intends, as several voices affirm, to make a "symbolic" gesture, namely to return to Germany not *all* — oh, of course not! — but *some* of her former possessions and to satisfy Hitler's ambitions by restoring Germany to the ranks of the colonial powers.

All this has a ring of childishness, if not mockery. Germany had insignificant colonies before the world war; but it became so cramped within its old borders that it sought to break out onto the real arena of world exploitation by means of war. Therefore, returning its old overseas possessions will not resolve even one of the problems of German capitalism. Hitler needs Hohenzollern's old patches of colonial territory only as strong points in the struggle for "real" colonies, i.e., for a redivision of the world. But this redivision cannot be carried out in any way short of the liquidation of the British and French empires.

In the process, the second- and third-rate colonial powers will be eliminated. The destructive law of concentration is applied in the very same measure to petty slaveholding states as to petty capitalists within states. It is quite probable, therefore, that the next four-power agreement will be achieved at the expense of the colonies of Holland, Belgium, Spain, and Portugal. But this, again, would only mean a short breathing space.

What then? In no way can the tempo at which Germany is presenting its demands be called slow and patient. Even if England and France decided to liquidate themselves in installments, this would only give the German offensive new strength. Moreover, the United States could not remain a passive observer of such an obvious upsetting of the "balance of forces" in the world. The North American colossus in no way relishes the prospect of finding itself face to face with a Germany which is the mistress of world colonies and the major shipping routes. That is why it will use all its strength to urge England and France not toward compliance but toward resistance. And meanwhile Tokyo's Prince Konoye has proclaimed the need to "revise all treaties in the interest of justice," i.e., in the interest of Japan.[104] The Pacific Ocean hardly promises to be a fount of peace during the next ten years.

In the good old days, it was only England that thought in terms of continents. And she thought slowly: in terms of centuries. In the present epoch, all the imperialist states have learned to think in such terms. And the timetable is no longer laid out in centuries, but in decades, or even years. This is the real character of our epoch, which after the Munich meeting remains an epoch of unbridled, frenzied, and violent imperialism. Until the peoples subdue it, it will more and more frequently recarve our bloody planet.

The state of the German economy requires Hitler to exercise his military strength as soon as possible. On the other hand, the army requires postponement, since it is not yet ready for war; it is a new army, in which not everything is yet coordinated or adjusted to the proper proportions. But the contradiction between these two requirements can be measured in terms not of decades but of a year or maybe two, possibly even months. The mobilizations that Hitler carried out so demonstratively during the Czechoslovakian crisis had the aim of testing the ruling classes of England and France. From Hitler's point of view, the test was a marvelous success. The sources of restraint upon him, none too sturdy to begin with, were decisively weakened. Opposition from the German generals and the leaders of the German economy was undermined, and a decisive step toward war was taken.

Hitler will not be able to repeat his bluff a second time. But he will undoubtedly exploit the effect of this ever-so-successful experiment to produce the opposite result. In a new crisis, when he mobilizes, he will try to give the impression that he is simply making a threat, giving the outward appearance of a new bluff, and then, in fact, will fall upon his opponents with the combined strength of all his armies.

Meanwhile, the diplomatic gentlemen are once again warming up the notion of an arms limitation agreement. The pacifists (in accordance with their fundamental profession as social imperialists), those such as Jouhaux and Company, come trailing along behind the diplomats, calling for total disarmament. It was not without reason that the Russian poet said:

> We treasure deceit that uplifts us
> More than thousands of burdensome truths.[105]

However, these worthy gentlemen are deceiving not themselves so much as the people.

The war of 1914-18 was termed by statesmen the "war to end all wars," as a sop to the peoples of the world. Since then the phrase has acquired a certain ironic ring. There can be no doubt that soon that same bitter note of irony will attach itself to Chamberlain's phrase of "peace in our time" as well. For our part, we look to the future with eyes wide open. Europe is heading toward war, and with it all of humanity.

KARL KAUTSKY[106]

November 8, 1938

The death of Karl Kautsky has passed unnoticed. To the young generation this name says comparatively little. Yet there was a time when Kautsky was in the true sense of the word the teacher who instructed the international proletarian vanguard. To be sure, his influence in the Anglo-Saxon countries, especially also in France, was less considerable; but that is explained by the feeble influence of Marxism in general in these countries. On the other hand, in Germany, in Austria, in Russia, and in the other Slavic countries, Kautsky became an indisputable Marxian authority. The attempts of the present historiography of the Comintern to present things as if Lenin, almost in his youth, had seen in Kautsky an opportunist and had declared war against him, are radically false. Almost up to the time of the world war, Lenin considered Kautsky as the genuine continuator of the cause of Marx and Engels.[107]

This anomaly was explained by the character of the epoch, which was an era of capitalist ascension, of democracy, of adaptation of the proletariat. The revolutionary side of Marxism had changed into an indefinite, in any case, a distant perspective. The struggle for reforms and propaganda was on the order of the day. Kautsky occupied himself with commenting upon and justifying the policy of reform from the point of view of the revolutionary perspective. It was taken for granted that with the change of the objective conditions, Kautsky would know how to arm the party with other methods. That was not the case. The appearance of an epoch of great crises and of great shocks revealed the fundamentally reformist character of the Social Democracy and of its theoretician Kautsky. Lenin broke resolutely with Kautsky at the beginning of the war. After the October Revolution he published a merciless book on the "renegade Kautsky." As for Marxism, Kautsky, from the beginning of the war, behaved incontestably like a renegade. But as for himself, he was only half a renegade from his past, so to speak: when the problems of the class struggle were posed in all their acuteness, Kautsky found himself constrained to draw the final conclusions of his organic opportunism.

Kautsky undoubtedly leaves behind numerous works of value in the field of Marxian theory, which he applied successfully in the most variegated domains. His analytical thought was distinguished by an exceptional force. But it was not the universal creative intelligence of Marx, of Engels, or of Lenin: all his life Kautsky was, at bottom, a talented commentator. His character, like his thought, lacked audacity and sweep, without which revolutionary politics is impossible. From the very first cannon-shot, he occupied an ill-defined pacifist position; then he became one of the leaders of the Independent Social Democratic Party [108] which tried to create a Two-and-one-Half International; then, with the debris of the Independent Party he returned under the wing of the Social Democracy. Kautsky understood nothing of the October Revolution, showed the petty-bourgeois savant's fright before it, and devoted to it not a few works imbued with a spirit of fierce hostility. His works in the last quarter of a century are characterized by a complete theoretical and political decline.

The foundering of the German and Austrian Social Democracy was also the foundering of all the reformist conceptions of Kautsky. To be sure, he still continued to affirm to the last that he had hopes of a "better future," of a "regeneration" of democracy, etc.; this passive optimism was only the inertia of a laborious and in its way honest long life, but it contained no independent perspective. We remember Kautsky as our former teacher to whom we once owed a good deal, but who separated himself from the proletarian revolution and from whom, consequently, we had to separate ourselves.

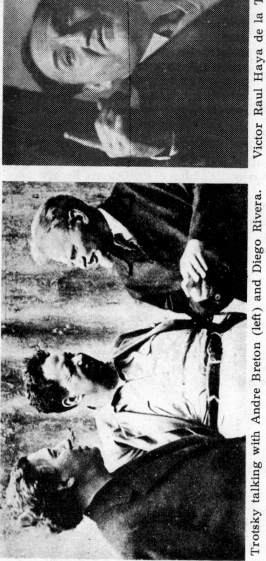

Victor Raul Haya de la Torre.

Trotsky talking with Andre Breton (left) and Diego Rivera.

HAYA DE LA TORRE AND DEMOCRACY[109]

A Program of Militant Struggle
or of Adaptation to American Imperialism?

November 9, 1938

The August 1938 number of the Argentine review *Claridad* publishes a letter on the Peruvian situation by Haya de la Torre. We won't apply either a Marxian or socialist criterion to this document; Haya de la Torre wrote the letter as a democrat and we shall consider it from that angle, primarily from the democratic point of view. A good democrat is better than a bad socialist, but precisely from this point of view, the letter of Haya de la Torre has great limitations.

It seems that Haya de la Torre limits the dangers that threaten Latin America only to Italy, Germany, and Japan. He does not consider imperialism in general but only one of its varieties, fascism. He declares categorically: "In case of aggression, we all certainly think that the United States — the guardian of our liberty — will defend us." Could it be irony? Of course not. Speaking of the possibility of encroachment upon the Latin American continent by the fascist "aggressors," the author declares: "As long as the United States is strong and alert, those dangers are not immediate but . . . they are dangers." It is not possible to speak with greater clarity. The APRA leader searches for a powerful protector.

The United States only exists as a "guardian of liberty" for Haya de la Torre; we see in that country the most immediate danger and, in a historical sense, the most threatening. By this we don't mean to say that the governments of the Latin American countries should not take advantage of the antagonisms between the various imperialist countries and groups of countries in order to defend themselves. But the tactical utilization of such antagonisms on certain occasions, according to the concrete circumstances, is one thing; to base a strategical calculation upon the idea that the United States is a permanent defender is something else. We consider this opportunist position not only erroneous but also profoundly dangerous because it creates a false perspective and hinders what is the real task, the revolutionary education of the people.

In what sense can one qualify the United States as "the guardian of the liberty" of those very people it exploits? Only in the sense that Washington is ready to "defend" the Latin American countries from *European or Japanese* domination. But every such act of "defense" would imply the complete reduction to slavery of the country "defended" by the United States. The example of Brazil demonstrates that the higher "guardians" are not at all interested in "liberty." The relations between Washington and Rio de Janeiro have not become worse but indeed have improved after the coup d'etat in Brazil. The reason is that Washington considers the Vargas dictatorship a more docile and sure tool of American imperialist interests than revolutionary democracy. This basically is the position of the White House in regard to the whole southern continent.

Can it be that Haya de la Torre simply proceeds from the premise that the imperialist domination of the United States is a "lesser evil"? But one must say openly in this case: democratic politics demands clarity. Moreover, until when will this evil be the lesser? To ignore this problem is to risk too much on chance. The United States is ruled by the same historical laws dominating the European capitalist centers. The "democracy" of the United States at the present time is nothing more than one expression of its imperialism. Due to the frightful decay of North American capitalism, democracy will not hinder the "guardians" of liberty from displaying in the near future an extremely aggressive imperialist policy, directed especially against the countries of Latin America. This must be pointed out clearly, precisely, and firmly and this perspective must be placed at the base of the revolutionary program.

Strange as it may seem, some of the APRA leaders declare that an alliance of the APRA and, in general, of the Latin American national revolutionary parties with the revolutionary proletariat of the United States and other imperialist countries hasn't any practical meaning because the workers of those countries "are not interested" in the condition of the colonial and semicolonial countries. We consider this point of view suicidal in the full sense of the word. While imperialism endures, the colonial peoples will not be able to liberate themselves and the oppressed peoples will not be able to defeat the imperialist bourgeoisie except by allying themselves with the international proletariat. One cannot fail to see that on this fundamental question the position of the most opportunist leaders of the APRA is supported by Haya de la Torre's letter. It is self-evident that one who considers the North American imperialist bourgeoisie the "guardian" of the colonial peoples' liberty cannot seek an alliance with the North American workers. The underestimation of the role of the international proletariat on the colonial question arises inevitably out of the effort *not to frighten the "democratic" imperialist bourgeoisie*, above all, the bourgeoisie of the United States. It is very clear that whoever hopes to find an ally in Roosevelt cannot become an ally of the international proletarian vanguard. This is the fundamental line of demarcation between the policy of revolutionary struggle and the unprincipled policy of adaptation.

Haya de la Torre insists on the necessity for the unification of the Latin American countries and finishes his letter with this formula — "We, the representatives of the United Provinces of South America." In itself this idea is absolutely correct. The struggle for the United States of Latin America is inseparable from the struggle for the national independence of each one of the Latin American countries. However, it is necessary to respond clearly and precisely to this question: Which roads can lead to unification? One can conclude from the extremely vague formulas of Haya de la Torre that he hopes to convince the present governments of Latin America that they should unite voluntarily . . . under the "guardianship" of the United States. In reality, only through the revolutionary movement of the popular masses against imperialism, including its "democratic" variety, is it possible to attain that great end. It is a difficult road, we admit, but there isn't any other.

We note further that this letter of a programmatic character does not say a single word about the Soviet Union. Does Haya de la Torre consider the USSR the defender of colonial and semicolonial countries, their friend and ally, or does he agree with us that under the present regime, the Soviet Union represents a very great danger for the weak and backward peoples whose independence is far from complete. The silence of Haya de la Torre is also determined in this case by openly opportunist considerations. It appears that de la Torre wants to hold the USSR in "reserve" in case the United States will not support him. But he who desires many friends will lose the few he has.

These are the ideas that come to our mind after reading the APRA leader's letter; although we limit ourselves to purely democratic criteria. Are our conclusions erroneous? We shall listen with pleasure to the answers of the APRA representatives. We only want their replies to be more precise, more concrete, and less evasive and diplomatic than Haya de la Torre's letter.

IN DEFENSE OF ASYLUM[110]

A Reply to Toledano

November 10, 1938

In his speech at the Palace of Fine Arts on November 8, Toledano declared: ". . . Something that I have never affirmed, because I am not crack-brained, is that Trotsky had proposed a general strike during the petroleum conflict. . . ." It is to be presumed that the report of the speech in *El Popular* has been edited by the orator himself with the necessary care. It is not possible to desire anything more categorical than the refutation cited above: "because I am not crack-brained"!!! Nevertheless we shall try to check what Mr. Toledano says.

In the newspapers of May 31, 1937 (*El Universal,* first section, page 8; *Excelsior,* first section, page 4; *El Nacional,* first section, page 6; *La Prensa,* page 6), in the report of Toledano's speech at a meeting held May 30, 1937, in the Theater of the People, it was stated: "We are not going to follow those who label themselves of the extreme left and wish to carry us into a general strike in the republic. We are not going to follow Trotsky, who represents the counterrevolution. The general strike is against the government."

In these four newspapers we encounter the same phrase. It is clear that the text has a character that, if not official, is at least not less than authoritative. Neither the discourse as a whole nor the phrase that interests us have ever been disavowed by Mr. Toledano.

In the same newspaper is printed my declaration of June 26, 1937, in which I said: "Mr. Toledano, in a series of public declarations, attributes to me various acts of intervention in the internal life of Mexico (particularly, for example, a call for . . . a general strike). In such statements there is not one word of truth."

Yet after this, Mr. Toledano did not publish a single rectification of his speech. We had to wait a year and a half for Toledano to find it necessary in a new speech to declare that he is not "crack-brained" and that he had not made such

statements. He is not correct this time either. The facts and
the texts speak in another manner. The refutations of Mr.
Toledano, as we see, are distinguished by the same exactitude as his affirmations. But minus times minus equals plus.

Mr. Toledano does not want an investigation of his accusations made by an impartial commission. In place of this, he
has begun to refute them himself. Personally, I do not have
any objection to these methods, and accept with gratitude the
testimony that the only ones able to accuse me of wishing to
provoke a general strike against the government of General
Cardenas — according to Mr. Toledano — are the crack-brained.
I add only that the other accusations launched against me
have the same value.

TERRORISM AND THE MURDERS
OF RASPUTIN AND NICHOLAS II[111]

November 14, 1938

You ask what role I personally played in the assassination of Rasputin and the execution of Nicholas II. I doubt that this question, which already belongs to history, can interest the press; it deals with times that are long past.

As for the assassination of Rasputin, I had absolutely nothing to do with it. Rasputin was murdered on December 30, 1916. At that moment, I was on board the ship that was carrying my wife and me from Spain to the United States. This geographical separation alone proves that I had no hand in this matter.

But there are also serious political reasons. The Russian Marxists had nothing in common with individual terror; they were the organizers of the revolutionary mass movement. In fact, the assassination of Rasputin was carried out by elements around the imperial court. Direct participants in the assassination included the deputy to the Duma, the ultrareactionary monarchist Purishkevich, Prince Yusupov, who had ties with the czar's family, and other such persons; it seems that one of the Grand Dukes, Dimitri Pavlovich, took part directly in the assassination.

The purpose of the conspirators was to save the monarchy, by ridding it of a "bad counselor." Our purpose was to do away with the monarchy and all its counselors. We never busied ourselves with the adventures of individual assassinations, but rather with the task of preparing the revolution. As is known, the assassination of Rasputin did not save the monarchy; the revolution followed it only two months later.

The execution of the czar was an entirely different matter. Nicholas II had already been arrested by the Provisional Government; he was first held in Petrograd and then sent to Tobolsk. But Tobolsk is a small city with no industry and no proletariat, and it was not a sufficiently secure residence for the czar; the counterrevolutionaries could be expected to make an attempt to rescue him in order to put him at the head of the White Guards.[112] The Soviet authorities transported the czar from Tobolsk to Ekaterinburg (in the Urals), an important industrial center. There it was possible to be certain that the czar's guard was adequate.

The imperial family lived in a private house and enjoyed certain liberties. There was a proposal to organize a public trial of the czar and czarina, but it never came to anything. Meanwhile, the development of the civil war decided otherwise.

The White Guards surrounded Ekaterinburg and from one moment to the next might have been able to descend upon the city. Their chief purpose was to liberate the imperial family. Under these conditions, the local Soviet decided to execute the czar and his family.

At this moment I personally was at another part of the front and, strange as it seems, I didn't hear about the execution for more than a week, if not even longer. Amid the turbulence of events, the fact of the execution didn't produce much of an impression upon me. I never bothered to find out "how" it had happened. I must add that special interest in the affairs of royalty or former royalty contains a certain measure of servile instincts. During the civil war, which was provoked exclusively by the Russian capitalists and rural landowners, with the collaboration of foreign imperialism, hundreds of thousands of people perished. If among them could be counted the members of the Romanov dynasty, it was impossible not to see that as a partial payment for all the crimes of the czarist monarchy. The Mexican people, who dealt harshly with Maximilian's imperial state, have a tradition in this respect that leaves nothing to be desired.[113]

THE TWENTY-FIRST ANNIVERSARY[114]

November 14, 1938

The February Revolution was brought about by workers and soldiers, i.e., peasants under arms. The mortal blow at czarism was struck by the workers of St. Petersburg. But they themselves did not yet know that the blow was mortal. It often happens that the oppressed cannot enjoy the fruits of their victory because they do not realize its significance. The power which the masses in revolt were unable to grasp fell into the hands of a coalition of liberals, Mensheviks, and "Social Revolutionaries," i.e., of the bourgeoisie and petty bourgeoisie. [115] It was a classical "Popular Front" of that period.

Stalin wrote and said, "The Provisional Government must be supported, because. . . ." Lenin arrived from abroad and declared, "The least support for the Provisional Government is a betrayal."[116] Stalin said at the March Conference of the Bolsheviks, "We must unite with the party of Tseretelli (Mensheviks)."[117] Lenin declared, "Any thought of unity with the Menshevik defensists is a betrayal."[118]

The real Bolshevik policy started after the arrival of Lenin (April 4, 1917), with his irreconcilable opposition to the February "Popular Front." The point of this opposition was to unite all the oppressed and exploited against the "democratic" imperialist bourgeoisie supported by the Mensheviks and "Social Revolutionaries" (social patriots). Lenin sought the unity of the revolutionary masses on the basis of class struggle, and not the unity of "socialist" phrasemongers with the liberal capitalists to deceive the masses. Anyone who did not understand the difference between these two forms of "unity" had to be swept out of the workers' movement with a broom.

In the critical months of the revolution, the parties of the "Popular Front," the liberals, Mensheviks, and "Social Revolutionaries," squeezed by the revolutionary masses, found no other means of defense but the vilest slander against the Bolsheviks. Accusations of relations with the German general staff, connections with the Black Hundreds[119] and the pogromists (the fascists of the day), rained down as from a horn of plenty. The present riff-raff in the Kremlin and its international agents have invented nothing; they have only developed to gigantic proportions the base slander of Miliukov, Kerensky, and Tseretelli.

The October Revolution was the victory of Bolshevism, i.e., of the party of the workers and poorest peasants over the "Popular Front," i.e., the parties of the liberal bourgeoisie, the Mensheviks and the "Social Revolutionaries," who were indissolubly linked with the "democratic" imperialism of the Entente.

Now, every philistine who considers himself a "friend of the USSR" calls the February coalition of 1917 "counterrevolutionary." But the Cadets,[120] Mensheviks, and "Social Revolutionaries" were counterrevolutionary only in relation to the Bolshevist, i.e., socialist, revolution, but not in relation to the monarchy, not in relation to the fascism of the day or the dictatorship of the generals. If you translate the political concepts of that time into contemporary ones, then you have to say that Lombardo Toledano is at best a caricature of Kerensky, and Laborde stands considerably further from Marxism than the Mensheviks did in the February Revolution.

The Kerenskys of the whole world were irreconcilable foes of the October Revolution. Its friends were the revolutionary workers of the whole world. At that time, paid friends did not yet exist. It was not possible to make a career out of friendship with the USSR. It was possible to travel to the USSR only illegally. Some people who attempted it perished by the shot of a border guard or drowned in the sea trying to sail across at night in a small boat. They were *real* friends!

To make Lombardo Toledano and his like into paid "friends" of the USSR it was necessary for the Soviet bureaucracy to oppress the masses and seize in its own hands power and control over all the riches of the country; it was necessary, in other words, for the proletarian revolution to be replaced by the Thermidorean reaction.[121] In France the Thermidorean careerists who enriched themselves out of the revolution hated the honest Jacobins. And the present bureaucracy and its foreign friends hate genuine proletarian revolutionaries. To justify their hatred to the masses these careerists are forced to slander those who remain faithful to the program of the October Revolution. The Soviet bureaucracy pays for slander with support, publicity, and often with 24-carat gold. As a result it turns out that Trotsky, Zinoviev, Kamenev, Rykov, Bukharin, Radek, Pyatakov, Sokolnikov, Serebryakov, Smirnov — all comrades-in-arms of Lenin — Tukhachevsky, Yegorov, Bluecher, Muralov, Yakir, Mrachkovsky, Uborevich, Gamarnik — all heroes of the civil war — are traitors [122] ; and the faithful defenders of the October Revolution turn out to be the Moscow prosecutor Vyshinsky and the Mexican lawyer Toledano.

On the eve of the twenty-first anniversary, Soviet policy, both internal and external, and the policy of the Comintern, have revealed all their rottenness and falseness. Inside the country complete extermination of the Bolshevik Party has been necessary, and completely shameless deification of the leader to support the unstable regime of bureaucratic dictatorship. In external policy — after a series of pointless and humiliating capitulations — the USSR is more isolated than it has ever been. Finally, the international policy of "People's Fronts" has led to the ruin of the Spanish revolution and has brought France close to fascism. [123] The Comintern stands before the international proletariat as a wretched, despised bankrupt.

As was to be expected, Moscow is trying to execute a new about-face. At the grandiose but completely forced demonstration of November 7 on Red Square, foreign journalists and diplomats were surprised when they heard long-forgotten cries in favor of world revolution. Stalin wants to terrorize his enemies with shouts. After having failed to do anything with crude cunning, he is trying to take the imperialists by fright. A miserable attempt by a disgraced schemer! For a revolutionary policy there must be revolutionary parties. There are none. It was not easy to transform the young sections of the Comintern, by means of bureaucratic pressure, deceit, slander, violence, bribery, and murder, into repellent cliques of out-and-out careerists. But this work has been accomplished in full. In fifteen years a revolutionary organization can be turned into a heap of muck. Such a heap of muck cannot be turned into the gold of revolution by mere wishing. After the "third period" of ultraleft grimaces [124] we were faced with the spectacle of the "fourth period": shameful groveling before "democratic" imperialism. The attempt to create now a fifth period — of belated revolutionary gestures and bluff — will finish as an even crueler fiasco. The terrible dictator will soon begin to look like a back-garden scarecrow.

On the road of the Soviet bureaucracy and the Comintern

there is no way out and not a ray of hope. The advanced workers must put an end to the Soviet bureaucracy and the Comintern. Only an uprising of the Soviet proletariat against the base tyranny of the new parasites can save what is still left over in the foundations of the society from the conquests of October. Only a proletarian revolution in the advanced capitalist countries can help the workers of Russia to construct a genuine socialist society on the foundations laid by October. In this sense and in this sense only, we defend the October Revolution from imperialism, fascist and democratic, from the Stalin bureaucracy, and from its hired "friends."

A CONTRIBUTION
TO CENTRIST LITERATURE[125]

November 15, 1938

Rodrigo Garcia Trevino, *The Munich Pact and the Third International* (A Lecture and Four Articles), Publications of the Marxist Students Society of the National School of Economics (Mexico, 1938, 66 pp.).

This pamphlet is published by the Marxist Students Society. As its name implies, the society has set itself the task of studying Marxism. One could not but praise such a laudable goal in these days of complete prostitution of Marxist doctrine — if the society approached its task with the necessary seriousness. Unfortunately the preface of the pamphlet, written and signed by all the members of the society, does not give any proof of this seriousness.

It would be wrong to pick a quarrel with young people who have not yet managed to familiarize themselves with the ABCs of Marxism if they themselves took into account the state of their knowledge. At a certain age, ignorance is natural and can be overcome through study. But the problem arises when presumption is added to ignorance, when instead of diligently educating oneself, one desires to educate others. Unfortunately, however, this is the character of the editors' preface. Let us point out the principal errors; it would be impossible to enumerate them *all*.

The preface attempts to establish a relationship between the development of revolutionary theory and the different stages of development of bourgeois society. The intention is completely praiseworthy, but in order to realize it, it is necessary to know the history of bourgeois society and the history of ideologies. Our authors are acquainted with neither. They begin by stating that in the middle of the last century, the bourgeoisie "consolidated its political power on a world scale and opened up the stage of imperialism," and that it was at this point that the works of Marx and Engels appeared in the realm of doctrine and politics. This is all wrong, from beginning to end. In the middle of the last century the bourgeoisie was still far removed from "political power on a world scale." Let us not forget that the *Communist Manifesto* was written on the *eve* of the 1848 revolution. [126] After the defeat of this revolution the German bourgeoisie remained nationally dispersed, under the oppression of numerous dynasties. Bourgeois Italy was neither free nor unified. In the United States the bourgeoisie had yet to go through the Civil War to achieve unification of the (bourgeois) national state. In Russia absolutism and serfdom were completely dominant, etc., etc.

Furthermore, to say that the epoch of *imperialism* opened up in the middle of the last century, is to have not the slightest notion about either the past century or imperialism. Imperialism is the economic and political system (both domestic and foreign) of *monopoly* (finance) capital. In the middle of the past century only "liberal" capitalism existed, i.e., capitalism based on free competition, which at that time was still just tending toward the creation of democratic political forms. The trusts, the unions, the combines, were formed largely beginning in the thirties of the last century and progressively conquered a dominant position. Imperialist politics, in the scientific sense of the word, began at the turn of the present century. Had the authors read Lenin's well-known little book on imperialism,[127] they would not have made such frightful errors. Just the same, they invoke Lenin. What sense does all of this make?

This is, however, just the beginning of a series of sad misunderstandings. Citing, apparently from some secondary source, Lenin's statement that imperialism is "the highest stage of capitalism," our authors attempt to complete and expand upon Lenin. " . . . Our generation," they write, "interpreting Lenin, can in turn establish as a point of doctrine that fascism is the highest phase, the highest degree, of imperialism, the highest stage of the bourgeois regime." Reading these pretentious lines makes our hair stand on end. "Our generation" should study before giving lessons. Imperialism is the highest stage of capitalism in the objective economic sense: imperialism brought the forces of production to the ultimate level of development conceivable on the basis of private property forms and closed the road to their further development. In doing this it opened up the era of capitalist decay. Moreover, having centralized production, imperialism created the most important economic precondition for a *socialist* economy. Thus the characterization of imperialism as the highest stage of capitalism rests on the dialectic of the development of the productive forces and has a strictly scientific character.

The analogous conclusion that our authors attempt to draw, that "fascism is the highest stage of imperialism," has absolutely no economic content. Fascism is above all the political regime that crowns the regime of economic decay. Arising from the decline of the productive forces, fascism opens up no further possibilities for their development. Imperialism was a historical necessity. Marx *predicted* the rule of monopoly. It was impossible to predict fascism, because it is not determined by economic necessity in the dialectical (rather than the mechanical) sense of the word. Once the proletariat had found itself incapable, for various historical reasons, of seizing power in time and taking hold of the economy in order to reconstruct it along socialist lines, decaying capitalism was only able to continue its existence by substituting fascist dictatorship for bourgeois democracy. Since imperialism appeared as the *most advanced* form of capitalism, fascism was a *step backward*, a political setback, the beginning of society's descent into barbarism.

Our authors are completely mistaken when they try to prove their discovery (that "fascism is the last stage of imperialism") by citing Marx's words that no society disappears from the historical scene before it has exhausted all of its productive potential. For it is precisely the case that imperialism had already exhausted its creative potential by the eve of the last world war. Bourgeois society has not disappeared *in good time*, for no society that outlives its time has disappeared *by itself*. The revolutionary class must overthrow it. The Second International and then the Third International *prevented* this from being done. Fascism follows from this and from this alone. The present crisis of human civilization is the result of the crisis of proletarian leadership. The revolutionary class does not yet have a party that can assure by its leadership the resolution of the fundamental problem of our epoch: the conquest of power by the international proletariat.

*   *   *

From the fact that imperialism has attained its "ultimate" (?!) stage, fascism, our authors draw the conclusion that a renewal of revolutionary doctrine is necessary. They take this task upon themselves. They propose to start with a critique of the doctrine of the Third International. It seems that they are completely unaware of the enormous volume of critical work on this subject that the international Bolshevik-Leninist faction has produced during the last fifteen years, especially since the Chinese revolution (1925-27). [128] The authors of the preface treat the sole Marxist tendency of our epoch with an impertinence and light-mindedness that are totally inadmissible. Here is what they say about the Fourth International: "In our opinion, on international questions it [the Fourth International] has without doubt made mistakes — let us call them that — that have robbed it of its militancy as a vanguard group." That is all. Such an appreciation can arise only in minds infected with the microbe of Stalinism. The Fourth International is the only organization that has provided a Marxist analysis of all the events and processes of the previous historical period: the Thermidorean degeneration of the USSR, the Chinese revolution, Pilsudski's coup d'etat in Poland, Hitler's coup d'etat in Germany, the defeat of the Austrian Social Democracy, the "third period" line of the Comintern, the People's Front, the Spanish revolution, etc. [129] What do our authors know about all of this? Apparently, absolutely nothing. To demonstrate the bankruptcy of the Fourth International, they cite . . . the panegyrics Trotsky addressed to Cabrera and De la Fuente.

The Cabrera episode consisted of the fact that this intelligent conservative lawyer saw through the falsifications of the Moscow trials, while certain imbeciles on the "left" took them for good coin. Trotsky drew the attention of public opinion to Cabrera's absolutely correct *juridical* analysis. [130] Nothing more! It would be absurd to view this as some sort of *political* solidarity. Up till now, our "Marxist" students have said nothing, absolutely nothing, about the Moscow trials, which claimed the party of Lenin as their victim. Isn't it shameful under these conditions to hide behind Cabrera? Stalinism has consciously created this sort of bogeyman for frightening small children. Cabrera! Oh, horrible! However, from a Marxist point of view the difference between Cabrera and Toledano is not very great. Both of them maintain themselves on the terrain of bourgeois society and both of them carry its traits. Toledano is more harmful and more dangerous, because he hides behind the mask of socialism.

As for De la Fuente, we have no idea what they are talking about. Won't our impertinent authors explain this to us?

In any case there is nothing more light-minded and shame-

ful than evaluating the historical role of an organization that
has suffered thousands of victims on the basis of a journalistic
episode of the second order. Basically the authors of the preface
adopt the tone of Stalinism. The crux of the matter is this:
they promise to submit all doctrines to an "independent" critique,
but in fact they bow to the rotten, nauseating milieu of the
Stalinist bureaucracy. In order to legitimize their pitiable Marxist exercises, they consider it opportune to attack Trotskyism.
It should be said, moreover, that this "method" of reassuring
oneself is characteristic of all the petty-bourgeois intellectuals of
our time.

*   *   *

As for Trevino's contribution (the lecture and the articles),
his positive trait is his effort to wrench himself from the toils
of Stalinism, and Toledanoism, which represents the worst
form of Stalinism, the worst because it is the most superficial,
the most insubstantial, the most blustering and vacuous form
of Stalinism. The misfortune is that Trevino thinks and writes
as if history began with him. Marxists approach all phenomena,
including ideas, in the context of their development. To say:
"Return to Lenin!" or "Return to Marx!" is saying very little.
It is impossible now to return to Marx while leaving Lenin
aside, that is to say, while closing one's eyes to the enormous
amount of work carried out under Lenin's leadership in applying, explaining, and developing Marxism.

Since Lenin ceased to play an active role fifteen years have
already passed — a whole historic period, crammed with great
world events! During this time "Leninism," in the formal sense
of the word, has divided into two wings: Stalinism, the official
ideology and practice of the parasitic Soviet bureaucracy, and
revolutionary Marxism, which its adversaries call "Trotskyism."
All world events have passed through these two theoretical
"filters." Trevino, however, feels that it is his right — the right
of a subjectivist and not of a Marxist — to ignore the real ideological development that is expressed in the implacable battle
of these two tendencies. He himself, without knowing it, feeds
on the debris scattered by our critique, but after a long delay.
Of course, it is not simply a question of the delay itself: after
a certain time lag the whole young generation must pass
through the school of the Fourth International. That is not
the problem. The problem is that Trevino tries to adapt his
critique to the official "doctrine" of Stalinism. He tries to make

his revolutionary ideas into friendly "remarks" on common-places and on pacifist and social-imperialist banalities. He wants to convince the Comintern of his good intentions and of the advantages of diluted Marxism (centrism) over outright opportunism. But the task of the revolutionary is not to re-educate the Stalinist bureaucracy (they are a hopeless case!) but to educate the workers in the spirit of intransigent defiance towards the bureaucracy.

We will not go into a detailed evaluation of Trevino's pam-phlet here, because we would have to comment on every page and every line. Trevino is wrong even when he is right. By this we mean to say that even the various correct observations (and there are some that are not bad) are put in an incorrect framework, an imprecise perspective, because the author re-mains basically a centrist. It is impossible to live with this position. It is Trevino's immediate duty to undertake a radical revision of his political baggage, comparing his hybrid correc-tions of Stalinism to the clear and precise formulations of the Fourth International. This is the only way that he will be able to get out of the impasse of centrism.

When Trevino enumerates the occasional errors of the Fourth International discovered here and there in his effort to evaluate the movement as a whole, and when he arrives at the mon-strous conclusion that this movement plays a "counterrevolu-tionary" role, he is trying basically to adapt himself to his former allies and comrades. Fearfully he looks behind him and sees the Bonapartists of the Kremlin. He takes on a pro-tective coloration. His various critical remarks on certain epi-sodes of a secondary nature involving certain sections of the Fourth International may be well taken or not (in general they are wrong). But it is the very manner in which he ap-proaches the question that is false. The task and the obligation of a serious Marxist is to discern what is basic, fundamental, to see things in their entirety, and to base his judgments on this. We are afraid, however, that the problem is not simply that Trevino is little acquainted with the literature of the Fourth International. Dilettantism, superficiality, and a lack of pre-occupation with theory are at present widespread in the ranks of intellectuals, even among those who consider themselves "Marxists." This is a result of the oppression of world reaction, Stalinism included. But it is impossible to take a step forward without returning to the tradition of scientific Marxist con-sciousness.

When Lombardo Toledano, with the grace befitting him, asks where and when the representatives of the Fourth International have written anything on fascism, we can only shrug our shoulders with pity. The Fourth International emerged and grew from the fight against fascism. From 1929 on we predicted the victory of Hitler if the Comintern continued on its "third period" course. The Bolshevik-Leninists wrote a great number of articles, pamphlets, and books on this subject in various languages. If Toledano knows nothing of this, that is in the order of things. But Trevino? Is it possible that he insists on speaking of something he knows nothing about?

In 1933 we publicly declared: if the victory of Hitler, assured by the Kremlin's political orientation, teaches the Comintern nothing, this will mean that the Comintern is dead.[131] And since the Comintern learned nothing from Hitler's victory, we drew the proper conclusions: we founded the Fourth International. The petty-bourgeois pseudo-Marxists, who are good for nothing even as democrats, imagine that the struggle against fascism consists of declamatory speeches at meetings and conferences. The real struggle against fascism is inseparable from the class struggle of the proletariat against the foundations of capitalist society. Fascism is not an inevitable economic stage. But it is not a mere "accident." It is the result of the inability of the degenerated and completely rotten parties of the proletariat to assure the victory of socialism. Consequently the struggle against fascism is, above all, the struggle for a new revolutionary leadership for the international proletariat. That is the historical significance of the work of the Fourth International. It is only from this point of view that this work can be understood and evaluated!

The theoretical side of Marxism is indissolubly linked to its active side. In this epoch of unbridled reaction, aggravated by the decay of what not long ago was the Comintern, it is only possible to be a Marxist if one has an unshakable will, political and ideological courage, and the ability to swim against the stream. We sincerely hope that Trevino has these qualities. If he can put an end to indecision and vacillation, he will have the opportunity to render important services to the cause of revolutionary Marxism.

TOWARD A REVOLUTIONARY
YOUTH ORGANIZATION [132]

November 18, 1938

Trotsky: I believe nobody can propose a concrete program and method in order to conquer the youth in this critical situation in the world and the United States. We don't have precedents. We don't have experience of this kind and we must experiment in this field. The fact that during the last year the youth organization lost almost more than a third is not a terrible catastrophe but it shows that the organization has not as yet found the necessary methods and that it must be very inventive in the future and not accuse the center every time for not giving directives. I believe this mentality is dangerous. It can be said that every people has the government which it deserves. It can be repeated about the party or the youth organization. The National Committee can only summarize the experience of the local groups. I believe it very important that the local committees of the party at least in the first period do more for the local organization of youth than the center in New York because the local conditions are the same and the adult comrades can observe the youth and without pretending to dictate to them can give good advice. I repeat, we do not have a definite program, a definite method. We must not close the doors to different propositions and in this respect we must be open.

But from a general point of view we can trace some general lines. We have proposed and now accepted at the International Congress a Transitional Program, [133] which replaces the old minimal program of the Social Democracy and the empiricism of our national sections which from time to time invented a slogan without having a general perspective and general combination of slogans conducting to the socialist revolution. The difference between the minimal program and the Transitional Program is that the Transitional Program is an introduction to the socialist revolution. Such an introduction is necessary

everywhere, especially in the United States; because the workers are charged with very bad conservative traditions, etc.,
and we must begin where these traditions finish and indicate
the road for the socialist revolution.

But the situation with the youth is different in that the youth
from one side doesn't have such heavy traditions, from the
other side their situation is more terrible, more acute. I speak
of the proletarian youth but the bourgeois youth also is in
a terrible situation. This critical situation of the young generation and the absence of tradition, of trade union education, of democratic elections, adherence to one party or another
party — these factors transformed the youth as we saw in the
European experience into cannon fodder for the fascists. What
does this fact show? That the youth asks for a radical solution. I believe that is a very important fact — the most important fact, that youth which is socially transformed into
pariahs, which cannot have any attachment to the regime
either socially or politically, which is more audacious by the
very nature of youth, and which has no conservative traditions, this youth waits for a radical leadership. Who will give
this leadership to the youth? We or the fascists? Yesterday
I proposed semihypothetically, semiseriously, to give to the
organization the name "Legion of the Socialist Revolution."
I believe I did not find the necessary support. Now I repeat
with more insistence. "Legion of the Socialist Revolution." It is
a program. We say to the youth, "We will overthrow the existing society. We will create a new society. That is our aim."
That doesn't mean we will exclude a transitional program.
Youth is in a different strata, different situations. The mood
of the same young worker changes. One time he is very radical, another time a bit opportunistic. In some way we must
approach him, even the approach of giving a dance. But I
believe that the Stalinists and fascists will dance better than
we. They are richer than we and have more advantages. Our
advantages are not in the field of the dance. It is in the field
of socialist revolution. Better, we *are* the "Legion of the Socialist Revolution." Nobody can imitate us. No other party can
proclaim it.

The question of legality arises. Many will say, yes, such
a party can immediately fall under the law which persecutes
under the guise of non-American activity. Yes, we must take
this into consideration and combine legal and illegal work
in this field and give to the revolutionary perspective and
even to the revolutionary party a very adroit explanation in

this sense: that democracy is very good; but Hague, German
Nazism, Italian fascism. [134] We must defend ourselves. We saw
in Europe that as soon as the workers approached the goal,
immediately big business armed the fascists. We must be ready
to launch a struggle against the reaction. We must prepare
ourselves for a revolution. Juridically we must prepare it not
as a direct revolution against democracy but as a fight against
the bad people who make it impossible for us to use the democracy for our liberation. But I repeat that is only a secondary point of view. The most important is that we are the
"Legion of the Socialist Revolution."

This is not a definite proposition but I believe in this respect
that we might call it also the "Legion of Lenin, Liebknecht,
Luxemburg," the three "L's." That would not be too bad for
our emblem. It can form three "L's." Perhaps it is too personal. It would be necessary to explain to everybody. The
"Legion of the Socialist Revolution"—I find it better. I am
sure also that Luxemburg, Liebknecht, and Lenin would also
find it better. Of course, such an organization should have
auxiliary organizations of different kinds.

Now the resolution speaks about idealism and enthusiasm
against cynicism. I am not sure if it is genuine cynicism. It
is often the imitated cynicism of a young man who fights for
independence, who fights against the tutelage of the apparatus,
etc. Possibly there are genuine cynics but if you would provoke these idealistic tendencies you must begin with these and
give it in the name of the organization itself. To a young
worker, to the unemployed, to a Negro, to the persecuted
Jew, give him the feeling that as the persecuted, he is a member
of the "Legion of the Socialist Revolution." I believe it is a very
good feeling. You should express it. Why not? The first thing
is a clear opinion, a very sharp expression of revolutionary
aim.

The second thing is democracy. I believe democracy is very
important in the organization. Why? Because democracy is
perishing everywhere in the States, in the trade unions, in the
old revolutionary parties. Only we can permit genuine honest democracy so that a young worker, a young student can
feel he has the possibility of expressing his opinion openly
without being immediately subjected to persecution. Ironical
statements from someone in authority is also persecution. We
can attract new members to the youth as to the party only by
genuine intelligent democracy. Everybody is tired of the lack
of democracy. This question is tied with the relationship be-

tween the party and the youth. It is clear that the youth cannot replace the party or duplicate the party. But that does not
mean that we have the technical possibility of prohibiting the
youth from trying to replace the party in every case where the
youth think they find the party following a bad line. We cannot establish with one blow or with one resolution the authority
of the party. We cannot create the authority for the party with
one resolution. If the young comrades have two, three, five,
or ten experiences proving to them that the party is more
wise, more experienced, then they will become more cautious in
their opposition to the party and more moderate in the forms
of this opposition. Anyone who speaks in a tone of contempt
to the party will immediately feel around himself a vacuum
and irony of contempt and it will educate the people. But if
we approach the young comrades with a general conception
such as this: "Boys and girls, you acted very well against
the Socialist Party because it was a bad party; 135 but we
are a good party. Don't forget it. You must not oppose us."
How can you convince them with such a general conception?
It is very dangerous. "You believe it is a good party, but we
don't believe it!"

"Yes, we are against vanguardism insofar as it is directed
against us."

Then they will answer, "You are bureaucrats, no more, no
less." It is very dangerous. Theoretically it is correct like the
question of discipline. Iron discipline, steel discipline, is absolutely necessary, but if the apparatus of the young party
begins by demanding such iron discipline on the first day
it can lose the party. It is necessary to educate confidence in
the leadership of the party and the party in general because
the leadership is only an expression of the party.

We can fail now in two directions. One in the direction of
centralization; the other in the direction of democracy. I believe now we should exaggerate the democracy and be very,
very patient with centralism in this transitional time. We must
educate these people to understand the necessity of centralism.
I am not sure that these losses were not to a certain degree
due to the centralist impatience or lack of indulgence toward
elements who had had no experience at all, who have had
only the bad experience of the Socialist Party, who would
breathe freely and who don't know themselves what they wish.
They answer, "Now you say you will strangle us by genuine
revolutionary Bolshevik methods." He is afraid and he says,
"No, I will get out of the party." No, I am for democracy

which can form the base for centralism, but centralism in a vacuum cannot create a democracy, it can only destroy what exists.

I believe a census of the party and youth is absolutely necessary to know what we have because the term "workers" is also very elastic; especially we must know how they are divided, by jobs, by unions, by localities, by districts, etc., and if we have a diagram before us the National Committee can act with more clarity and more feeling for opportunity.

If you have such a tendency as that of students believing they are more proper for the revolution, I am in favor of proposing every such member as a candidate. It is possible also that it would be good to introduce candidacy as a probationary period, also demotion from full membership to candidacy, especially for lack of courage, for lack of devotion. If it is clear to everybody that a member did not accomplish his obligation, especially if it is not for the first time but for the second or third time then say to this member, "You must choose, my friend, between abandoning the organization or becoming a candidate." I believe that such a candidacy can last for six months; but he can win membership again if he gains for the organization at least two young workers during the period.

I believe we should give to all students this task and this obligation that during six months they must find their place in the workers' movement; if not, they will be transformed one after the other into candidates in order to let them understand that it is a proletarian party of class struggle and not of intellectual discussions. Here we can be less indulgent in this respect.

Concerning the relations between the party and the youth. I do not know your plans about the new National Committee as you discussed it, but in order to make clear my opinion, I propose that if you have to choose a new National Committee of nineteen members do not introduce more than seven party members, less than one-half. The party members are party members. If they work in the youth we cannot give them the right to vote in the youth against the decisions of the National Committee. Of course the National Committee of the party should not commit the mistake of adopting obligatory resolutions too early, especially concerning the youth, but if such a resolution is adopted with the full understanding of the party they must vote in the sense of the party. It is absolutely clear that it is their duty to convince the other twelve and to

win them for this decision. If they are defeated, the decision
remains. The party cannot simply change a decision.

I also have something to say on semimilitary organization.
It is good on paper but to organize it is not so easy. It is
connected with the question of discipline, devotion, and so
on, and so forth. The principle is correct but possibly you
should proceed gradually here in the sense that you create
a genuine military group through a youth militia and that
nobody is obliged immediately to adhere to the youth militia
and uniform and discipline. I am sure it is absolutely clear,
they will be the best in learning because they have the spirit
of fighters. They will become the model members of the organization and through them you can educate the others.

The uniform — it is also a question of money. Now the students are reluctant, but if it is accepted it is more easy for the
students to have a uniform than for the workers. I don't know
the American mores but a young unemployed worker can
say, "That is not for me." If he sees the magnificent young
boys well dressed and singing, etc., he can consider himself
apart as a poor boy considers the cadet. It is a very important
question. If it would be possible to give such a uniform to
every boy who wishes to belong it might be different, but it
can very well be that some workers can say, "If I enter, I
will be in an inferior position." It must be considered from
every point of view. An insignia is very good, a tie, an arm
band, etc. It is not expensive. But a uniform, I find nothing
about the material question, the money; that is a question I
would like to have answered.

I would correct what I said yesterday about conspirative
methods. It is not quite correct about the youth. I was told
[said] yesterday that I could be understood to oppose conspirative methods in regard to correspondence, danger from
the GPU, etc. I underlined one sphere, that is, our activity
inside the Communist Party, inside the Communist youth, with
the fascists. It is very important but not exclusive. We cannot
invite our small youth to enter immediately into a fight with
the joint forces of the state, fascists, GPU, etc. Nobody proposes it. But what is very necessary for a future fight is to
know our enemies very well. And know them not only theoretically — that is necessary it seems to me — but also concretely. This study in your resolution is mentioned only in
passing. The uniform occupies too large a place. We must
underline the necessity of this — to fight such powerful forces
it is necessary to know them from the point of view of scien-

tific socialism. We must know them practically, where they are located, where are the headquarters of the Stalinists, of the Nazis, and so on. If you came into a new city, one question should be, "Show me your map, please, your general staff, with circles and pins of your town, city, of your county, of your state, of your friends and forces. For the military education it is very important. You should penetrate into every organization of the enemy and obtain exact numbers as far as possible, clippings from their papers which give an understanding of the character of their forces, aims, etc. It is the work of the general staff of the army. It should be accomplished by every local committee of the youth organization.

I would also change — *Challenge* is not bad, but possibly *Revolution* is better. 136 But it is a secondary question. All our European sections, Belgian, France, etc., use *Revolution*.

Question: On the question of having the word "Revolution" as part of the name of the organization, don't you think that might serve as one excuse for deporting foreign-born members?

Gould: I don't know the legal aspect, but every organization with foreign connections must give the government its files, names, and is subject to thorough investigation.

I am happy that the question of the new youth organization was discussed from the point of view that we have no fixed views on the basis of past traditions, that our whole problem now is one of experimentation, of learning from the relatively modest experiences we have had in the past. But I don't think that I can agree that there is too much of a tendency to direct criticism at the center in the youth organization. That, comrades, is precisely the criticism of all of our locals and rank-and-file comrades. It is a fault that we all bear together, but it is a fact. The experience with this resolution testifies to the validity of that fact. Our whole point of view must be to give encouragement to the initiative of the locals; and the resolution stresses that at length; initiative, more autonomy to the local units. But without initiative from the center, the locals found it impossible to effect the change they all felt was needed and it was only with the directives from the center that they began to function. If one could have witnessed the functioning of the center for the past year one would not hesitate in criticizing it sharply.

Unless they criticize, we are going to witness a repetition of the experience of the past.

On the name of the organization, again, I do not think that I can agree with it. I don't have a definitive opinion on it, but I will certainly give it much more consideration. But I don't think that the name "Legion of the Socialist Revolution" would be attractive to the American youth. I don't think it will convey to them what we want to convey. It will convey a program, but it will immediately be colored with qualities which American youth will consider foreign. That is my impression; that is my opinion. I think we must find a name which also represents a program, which characterizes the revolutionary character of our movement, the boldness, the determination of that movement; but it must be a name which will be acceptable to the youth. However, I will propose this name at the convention and we will let the delegates decide on it. We will let the delegates discuss it and decide upon it, not as my own, but as one of the names suggested, unless, of course, I agree with it. It is best to let the delegates discuss and decide the question. Also, I agree with Comrade Trotsky that the Stalinists and fascists can dance better than us and outdo us in the wearing apparel, because they have much greater resources and the resolution makes that point well. What they can not give to the youth, what only we can give to the youth is the revolutionary program and the struggle for the revolutionary program which will win the youth. Other aspects are external expressions of the fighting character of the organization.

Now on the question of the National Committee composed of not more than seven comrades who are members of the party. As Comrade Crux says himself, again theoretically that is as it should be; but institute that method today, that procedure tomorrow, and you will have no leadership, because all the advanced cadres are members of the party. You ask any comrade here from any section who the leaders of the youth are; they are members of the party. That is because the youth organization is not ideal, but the most advanced members are members of the party. Likewise there is a provision in the resolution that all members of the youth organization past the age of twenty-one shall be sent out of the youth organization into the party. Ideologically that is correct and eventually it will be carried out. Put it into practice tomorrow and I don't think that it will be fruitful to the organization. It must be done gradually, and the same is true about the National Committee.

The question of the money for the uniform is a very important point. Incidentally, the resolution does not call for a complete uniform with breeches, boots, etc., but a very simple uniform: shirt, tie, cap, etc., which is not only accessible, but is accepted very enthusiastically by the youth and is within the reach financially of the average youth, blue shirt, red tie — the tie, 10¢; the shirt between 50¢ and $1.00; the hat, 15¢ or 20¢. But we have always had the custom insofar as our experience is concerned that where a comrade is incapable of purchasing them himself, the organization collectively purchases them. From a monetary point of view it is entirely realistic.

And finally the question of education. True, the resolution glances right over it. Not only on this but on all questions. You have the program of action, which goes into great detail on the ways in which this resolution will be carried into effect, suggesting concrete ways and means of carrying it into effect. Our youth organization needs education very badly. And one of the most important sections of the program of action is the section on education as I indicated. And the future organization proposes to give it to them.

Trotsky: "We are not a youth organization; we are a party organization." Then I propose that we remove the party bureaucrats from the National Committee and call fresh elements of youth to the National Committee. "No! No! No! That is dangerous. The possibility of the youth's directing themselves, that is dangerous." That is bureaucratism. Bureaucratism is lack of confidence in the limited understanding of the masses. I assure you that the National Committee is the highest university of the organization. It is very important. If seven are good teachers and from the party, then the seven will be the best and the twelve will be good people. They will be accessible to good arguments and by the next convention you will eliminate half of them. It will become clear that they are not apt. But the other six members will develop very well and will replace the eliminated party members. I believe in general that with the education and development of the organization in this respect we must make a very brutal turn at the next convention. I would propose only five party members and fourteen rank and file of the youth organization, and I assure you it would be excellent. But I can make a concession and repeat my proposition, seven and twelve.

What is the present relationship between these party members and the youth? In this relationship there is no elasticity, none at all. The National Committee decides what the youth shall do. In this connection the National Committee of the youth is also a link between the National Committee of the party and the rank and file of the youth. There you have the second party. A young edition of the party in an independent organization of the youth. If there are twelve, the majority, you are sure that they represent better the spirit of youth than the principles of Marxism; but if you are not capable of winning them for your decision, then the decision is bad, or the decision comes too early for this organization and then you must postpone it. It is better to postpone than to rule by bureaucratic decision. It is a very, very important proposition, more important than all the others. In discussion once with other comrades, I mentioned the fact that in our fight under illegality against czarism, every time after the arrest of the leadership, every one of them in prison was absolutely sure every time that everything was lost. But every time the organization was better than before, because the young were good and capable, but oppressed a bit by the authority of the illegal committee because nobody can control it. I am sure that our most important problem is the renewal of the organization from the sources of the youth.

Yes, the proposition of the name. If you have a better name, a proletarian name, a revolutionary name, it can provoke enthusiasm — but not the socialist revolution. I believe the revotion is attractive to the youth. "Legion of the Socialist Revolution" makes a good name. Comrade Gould promises to propose it at the convention, but not as someone who proposes a good name. But I want you to propose it not as a bad one but as a good one.

On conspirative work, I believe even in the trade unions, even in Minneapolis, a turn can come where the reformists are in the majority and expel our comrades from the trade unions. We must have comrades who don't act openly, but act secretly and will remain in case of expulsion. It is absolutely necessary.

On education, one important phase is to habituate the comrades to be exact in everything. To come on time to meetings, to give exact numbers about the composition, etc., and without exaggeration, because very often where enthusiasm and activity are lacking, they find expression of the enthusiasm in the exaggeration of numbers, activities, etc. It is also a part of Marxist and Bolshevik education.

THE INDIVIDUAL IN HISTORY [137]

1938

I have come to the necessity of clarifying a theoretical question which also has a great political importance. It essentially involves the relation between the political or historical personality and the "milieu." To go straight to the heart of the problem, I would like to mention Souvarine's book on Stalin, [138] in which the author accuses the heads of the Left Opposition, myself included, of various errors, omissions, blunders, etc., beginning with 1923.

I do not at all wish to deny that there were many mistakes, unskillful acts, and even stupidities. Nevertheless, what is important, from the theoretical as well as the political viewpoint, is the relation, or rather the disproportion, between these "errors" and their consequences. It is precisely in this disproportion that the reactionary character of the new historical stage expressed itself.

We made not a few mistakes in 1917 and in the following years. But the sweep of the revolution filled up these gaps and repaired the errors, often with our aid, sometimes even without our direct participation. But for this period the historians, including Souvarine, are indulgent because the struggle ended in victory. During the second half of 1917 and the following years, it was the turn of the liberals and Mensheviks to commit errors, omissions, blunders, etc.

I would like to illustrate this historical "law" once again with the example of the Great French Revolution in which, thanks to the remoteness in time, the relations between the actors and their milieus appear much more clear-cut and crystallized.

At a certain moment in the revolution the Girondin leaders entirely lost their sense of direction. [139] Despite their popularity, their intelligence, they could commit nothing but errors and inept acts. They seemed to participate actively in their own downfall. Later it was the turn of Danton and his friends. [140]

Historians and biographers never stop wondering at the confused, passive, and puerile attitude of Danton in the last months of his life. The same thing for Robespierre and his associates:[141] disorientation, passivity, and incoherence at the most critical moment.

The explanation is obvious. Each of these groupings had at a given moment exhausted its political possibilities and could no longer move forward against the overpowering reality: internal economic conditions, international pressure, the new currents that these generated among the masses, etc. Under these conditions, each step began to produce results contrary to those that were hoped for.

But political abstention was hardly more favorable. The stages of the revolution and counterrevolution succeeded one another at an accelerated pace, the contradictions between the protagonists of a certain program and the changed situation acquired an unexpected and extremely acute character. That gives the historian the possibility of displaying his retrospective wisdom by enumerating and cataloguing the mistakes, omissions, ineptness. But, unfortunately, these historians abstain from indicating the right road which would have been able to lead a moderate to victory in a period of revolutionary upswing, or on the contrary, to indicate a reasonable and triumphant revolutionary policy in a Thermidorean period.

STALIN VS. STALIN[142]

November 19, 1938

Lying is socially determined. It reflects the contradictions between individuals and classes. It is required wherever it is necessary to hide, soften, or smooth over a contradiction. Wherever social contradictions have a long history, lying takes on a character of equilibrium, tradition, and respectability. In the present epoch of unprecedented exacerbation in the struggle between classes and nations, however, lying takes on a stormy, tense, and explosive character. Moreover, the lie now has the rotary press, radio, and cinema at its disposal. In the worldwide chorus of lies, the Kremlin does not occupy the back row.

The fascists, of course, lie a great deal. In Germany, there is a special official in charge of falsifications: Goebbels. Nor does Mussolini's apparatus remain idle. But the lies of fascism have, so to speak, a static character; in fact, they verge on monotony. This is explained by the fact that the day-to-day politics of the fascist bureaucrats do not contradict their abstract formulations in such a shocking way as the ever-growing gulf between the program of the Soviet bureaucracy and its real politics. In the USSR, social contradictions of a new sort have sprung up before the eyes of a generation that is still living. A powerful parasitic caste has elevated itself above the masses. Its very existence is a challenge to all the principles in whose name the October Revolution was made. That is why this "Communist" (!) caste finds itself forced to lie more than any ruling class in human history.

The official lies of the Soviet bureaucracy change from year to year, reflecting the different stages of its rise. The successive layers of lies have created an extraordinary chaos in the official ideology. Yesterday the bureaucracy said something different from the day before, and today it says something different from yesterday. The Soviet libraries have become the source of a terrible infection. Students, teachers, and professors doing research with old newspapers and magazines discover at each step that within short intervals the same leader has expressed completely opposite opinions on the same subject—not only on questions of theory but also on questions of concrete fact. In other words, that he has lied according to the varying needs of the moment.

This is why the need to rearrange the lies, reconcile the falsifications, and codify the frauds became pressing. After long work, they published a *History of the Communist Party* in Moscow this year.[143] It was edited by the Central Committee, or more precisely, by Stalin himself. This "history" contains neither references, nor citations, nor documents; it is the product of pure bureaucratic inspiration. To refute just the principal falsifications contained in this incredible book would take several thousand pages. We will try to give the reader an idea of the extent of the falsification by taking a single example (although the clearest one): the question of the leadership of the October insurrection. We challenge the "friends of the USSR" in advance to refute so much as one of our citations, or one of our dates, or one single sentence from one of our citations, or even one single word from one of our sentences.

Who led the October Revolution? The new "history" answers this question in a completely categorical way: "the party center, headed by Comrade Stalin, . . had practical direction of the whole uprising." It is remarkable, however, that no one knew anything about this center until 1924. Nowhere, neither in the newspapers, nor in memoirs, nor in the official proceedings, will you find any mention of the activity of the party center "with Stalin at its head." The legend of the "party center" only began to be fabricated in 1924 and attained its definitive development last year with the creation of a feature film, *Lenin in October.*

Did anyone take part in the leadership, apart from Stalin? "Comrades Voroshilov, Molotov, Dzerzhinsky, Ordzhonikidze, Kirov, Kaganovich, Kuibyshev, Frunze, Yaroslavsky, and others,"[144] says the "history," "received special assignments from the party in the leadership of the insurrection in different areas." Later on they add to the list Zhdanov and . . . Yezhov.[145] There you have the complete list of Stalin's general staff. There were, he avows, no other leaders. That is what Stalin's "history" says.

Let's take a look at the first edition of Lenin's *Collected Works,* published by the party's Central Committee while

Lenin was still alive. On the subject of the October insurrection, in a special note on Trotsky, it says the following: "*After the Petrograd Soviet came over to the Bolsheviks, Trotsky was elected its president: and in this capacity he organized and led the insurrection of October 25.*" Not a word on the "party center." Not a word on Stalin. These lines were written when the entire history of the October Revolution was still completely fresh, when the main participants were still alive, when the documents, the minutes, and the newspapers were available to everyone. While Lenin was alive no one, including Stalin himself, ever questioned this characterization of the leadership of the October insurrection, which was repeated in thousands of regional newspapers, in the official collections of documents, and in the school books of that day.

"A Revolutionary Military Committee created alongside the Petrograd Soviet became the legal leadership of the insurrection," says the "history." It simply forgets to add that the president of the Revolutionary Military Committee was Trotsky, and not Stalin. "Smolny . . . became the headquarters of the revolution, and the military orders were issued from there," says the "history." It simply forgets to add that Stalin never worked at Smolny, never became a part of the Revolutionary Military Committee, and took no part whatsoever in the military leadership, but was on the editorial board of a newspaper and only appeared at Smolny after the decisive victory of the insurrection.

From the wide range of testimony on the question that interests us, let us choose one example, the most convincing in the present case: the testimony of Stalin himself. At the time of the first anniversary of the revolution, he devoted a feature article in the Moscow *Pravda* to the October insurrection and its leaders. The secret aim of the article was to tell the party that the October insurrection had been led not only by Trotsky, but *also* by the Central Committee. However, Stalin could not yet permit himself open falsification. Here is what he wrote on the leadership of the insurrection: "*All the work of the practical organization of the insurrection was carried out under the immediate leadership of the president of the Petrograd Soviet, Comrade Trotsky. One can say with certainty that the party owes the rapid passage of the garrison to the side of the Soviet and the success of the work of the Revolutionary Military Committee above all and especially to Comrade Trotsky.* Comrades Antonov and Podvoiski[146] were the principal aides of Comrade Trotsky." These lines, which we cite word for word, were written by Stalin, not twenty years after the insurrection, but one year. In this article, one specifically dealing with the leadership of the insurrection, there is not a word on the so-called party center. On the other hand, it cites a number of persons who have completely disappeared from the official "history."

It was only in 1924, after Lenin's death, at a time when people had already forgotten a number of things, that Stalin for the first time declared out loud that the task of the historians was to destroy "the legend (!) of the special role of Trotsky in the October insurrection." "It is necessary to say," he declared publicly, "that Trotsky did not play and could not have played any special role in the October insurrection." But how can Stalin reconcile this new version with his own article of 1918? Very simply: he forbids anyone to cite his old article. Every attempt to refer to it in the Soviet press has provoked the most serious consequences for the unfortunate author. In the public libraries of the world capitals, however, it is not difficult to find the November 7, 1918, issue of *Pravda,* which represents a refutation of Stalin and his school of falsification, furnished by none other than himself.

I have on my desk dozens, if not hundreds, of documents that refute each falsification of the Stalinist "history." But this is enough for the moment. Let us just add that shortly before her death, the famous revolutionary Rosa Luxemburg wrote: "Lenin and Trotsky and their friends have been the first who have provided the example for the world proletariat. Today they still remain the only ones who can shout with Hutten: 'I dared!'"[147] There are no falsifications that can change this fact, even if they have rotary presses and the most powerful radio stations at their disposal.

REPLY TO
FATHER COUGHLIN'S CHARGES[148]

November 28, 1938

The name Jacob Schiff means nothing to me. Is Mr. Schiff in the United States?

In 1917 I was in the States from January to March. After the outbreak of the revolution I held meetings. There were collections of money for the return of the exiles to Russia. I, personally, had nothing to do with this money. I do not know whether among the contributors there was anyone by the name of Jacob Schiff or not; but this is only a theoretical possibility. I, personally, never received money from Jacob Schiff.

In order to avoid any possible misunderstanding, I must add that if some gentleman who was unknown to me had transmitted five or ten dollars through me for the exiles, I could have forgotten it. However, if it had been 100 or 500 dollars, I could not forget it, because at that time such a sum was a great deal in my eyes. If Mr. Coughlin indicated an important sum then it must be a pure invention.

FOR AN INDEPENDENT
YOUTH MOVEMENT[149]

November 30, 1938

Dear Friend:

I am a bit disquieted about my correspondence with Europe and especially with France. The comrades working on the Russian *Biulleten* complain that my correspondence arrives after a great delay, which makes the regular publication of the *Biulleten* very difficult. I send most things from here by airmail, but it is essential then that the letters be sent immediately on the fastest and most direct ship. It can be done only by someone who follows very closely the itinerary and who understands the importance of the matter.

If I am not mistaken, the matter is now in the hands of Comrade Isaacs,[150] who is busy with too many things and therefore can hardly accomplish this technical work with the necessary efficiency. Would it not be possible to find a comrade whose time is less occupied and arrange the matter?

I wait with a great deal of interest for the news of the youth conference.[151] It seems to me that the youth is guided a bit too firmly; that they do not feel their independence and their right not only to obey, but also to make their own errors and stupidities, not leaving this prerogative to us older ones. I guess that the overly firm direction does not give sufficient encouragement for personal and local initiative and this is one of the reasons for the losses in the youth during the past year. It is my opinion that in the various directing bodies of the youth, national as well as local, there should not be more than one-third party members. These comrades should impose party decisions not by arithmetical predominance, but by discussion and conviction. We will never have a good youth movement if we deprive it of the possibility of independent development.

My warmest greetings to you both.

Comradely yours,
Leon Trotsky

ON THE MURDER
OF RUDOLF KLEMENT[152]

December 1, 1938

I have received a letter from Rudolf Klement's aunt, who lives in one of the countries of Latin America, asking whether I know anything about her missing nephew. She states that Rudolf's mother, who lives in Germany, is in a state of utter despair, torn by the lack of any word about his fate. In the heart of the unhappy mother the hope arose that Rudolf might have succeeded in escaping danger and that he was hiding perhaps at my home. Alas, nothing remains to me but to destroy her last hopes.

The letter of Rudolf's aunt is a further proof of the GPU's crime. If Rudolf had in fact voluntarily abandoned Paris, as the GPU with the help of its agents of various kinds would like us to believe, he would not of course have left his mother in ignorance and the latter would not have had any reason to appeal to me through her sister in Latin America. Rudolf Klement was murdered by the agents of Stalin.

OPEN LETTER TO SENATOR ALLEN 153

December 2, 1938

Dear Sir:

On July 27 you paid me the honor of calling on me in Coyoacan. I had not sought this honor. I must confess I even tried to avoid it. But you were persistent. Because it turned out that I had no free time before your departure from Mexico, you joined a tour of the Committee on Cultural Relations with Latin America.154 Thus, among the friends of Mexico one of its active enemies unexpectedly appeared.

I will venture to say that the figure of Senator Allen did stand out quite sharply at our modest gathering on Avenida Londres. By his every remark, by the expression on his face, and by the intonation of his voice it was obvious that this man was fully insured against the slightest capacity to sympathize with the needs of oppressed classes and people and that he was thoroughly imbued with the interests of the upper echelons of capitalist society and with the imperialists' hatred for any liberation movement.

You took part in a general discussion, Senator. After your return to the States, you submitted articles to a number of newspapers dealing with your visit to Mexico and with me in particular. On November 22 you returned to the topic in your address to the annual dinner of the New York Chamber of Commerce. You are pursuing your goal with an undeniable tenacity. What is your goal? We will begin with the article.

According to your words, you found that my yard was soggy — it was the rainy season — but my remarks were all too dry. Far be it from me to take issue with these appraisals. But you went further. You have tried tendentiously to distort the fact that I spoke to you in the presence of forty people. This I cannot allow you to do. Ironically, you mention that the questions put to me by the tour members concerned the "hair-splitting of Marxist doctrine." "Not one of the questions concerned Mexico," you added significantly.

This is absolutely true: beforehand I had asked the tour leader, Dr. Hubert Herring, not to include Mexican politics as a topic for discussion. This, of course, was in no way because I hoped by this to conceal, as you imply, some sort of "conspiracy" on my part; but only because I did not want to give my enemies grounds for additional insinuations (there are enough of those as it is). But you, Mr. Senator, fear-lessly took the bull by the horns and posed the question for the sake of which, according to your own words, you had paid me the visit, namely: "Mr. Trotsky, what is your evalua-tion of the new Communist leader, President Cardenas, com-pared with the Communist leaders in Russia?" to which I al-legedly answered: "He is actually more progressive than some of them."

Allow me to say, Mr. Senator, that this is not true. If you had asked me such a question in the presence of forty in-telligent and thoughtful people, very likely they would all have burst into jovial laughter, and I would undoubtedly have joined them. But you did not compromise yourself by ask-ing such a question. And I gave you no such answer.

The fact is that in the discussion I simply tried to restore to the word "communism" its genuine meaning. At the present time, reactionaries and imperialists call everything that does not please them "communism" (sometimes "Trotskyism"). On the other hand, the Moscow bureaucracy calls everything that serves its interests communism. In passing, by way of ex-ample, I remarked: although Stalin bears the title Communist, in reality he is carrying out reactionary policies; the Mexi-can government, which is not in the least Communist, is carry-ing out progressive policies. This was the only reference I made to that subject. Your attempt to attribute to me a char-acterization of the Mexican government as "Communist" is false and fatuous, although it may possibly have been use-ful for your purposes.

Colonial and semicolonial countries or countries of colonial origin are late in passing through the state of national-demo-cratic, not "Communist," development. History, it is true, does not repeat itself. Mexico entered into the democratic revolu-tion in a different epoch and under different conditions than the first-born of history. But as a historical analogy it can, nevertheless, be said that Mexico is passing through the same stage of development that the States passed through, for ex-ample, beginning with the Revolutionary War and ending with the Civil War against slavery and secession. During that three-quarters of a century the North American nation was in process of formation on bourgeois-democratic foundations. The emancipation of the Negroes, i.e., the expropriation of the slaveholders, was considered and proclaimed by all the Allens of that time to be in defiance of divine prophecy and —

incomparably worse—a violation of property rights, i.e., communism and anarchism. However, from the scientific point of view, it is indisputable that the Civil War led by Lincoln was not the beginning of the Communist revolution but only the completion of the bourgeois-democratic one.

However, a scientific historical analysis is the last thing that interests you, Senator. You called on me, as is obvious from your words, in order to find in my remarks something that you could use in your campaign against the Mexican government. Because you found nothing that was suitable, you indulged in fabrications. Hand in hand with the *Daily News*, you are developing the idea that I am the one who inspired the measures for the expropriation of property owned by foreigners and am preparing—the reconstruction of Mexico on Communist principles. You write explicitly about a "Trotskyist Communist state!"

During your stay in this country you could have easily found out from your co-thinkers (you yourself mention "secret" meetings with them) how far I stand apart from Mexican politics. But this does not stop you. As proof that Mexico is being transformed into a "Trotskyist state," you cite the growing influence of the Mexican trade unions and the individual role of Lombardo Toledano, winding up your article (*Herald Tribune*, October 29) with the following remarkable words: "Toledano spent some time in Russia and is a follower of Trotsky."

Toledano, a follower of Trotsky—that's the limit! Every literate person in Mexico and many of the same in other countries will be convulsed with heartfelt laughter when they read this sentence—just as I was and just as my friends were when I showed them this sentence. General Cardenas as a "new Communist leader," Trotsky as the inspiration for Mexican policies, Toledano as a follower of Trotsky—and we might add further, Senator Allen as an authority on Mexico!

You, Mr. Senator, made an appearance at my home as a spy for petroleum capital. We will not ask ourselves how worthy of respect this role is in general. Our standards and yours are much too different. However, there are different categories of spies. Some gather the necessary information precisely, carefully, in their opinion "conscientiously," and report it to the boss. You proceed in a different way. You dream up information when you don't have enough. What you are is a *negligent* spy!

You advance the theory of my sinister role in the internal

life of Mexico with a threefold end in mind: first, to stir up
the imperialist circles of the United States against the Mexican
government for allegedly being "Communist"; second, to strike
the chord of national sensibility in Mexico with your non-
sensical legend about the influence of a foreign immigrant on
the country's policies; third, to make my personal situation
in Mexico more difficult. As an arrogant imperialist to the
marrow of your bones, you proceed from the unspoken assumption that Mexico is not capable of resolving its own
problems without foreign aid. You are bitterly mistaken,
Senator!

The political leaders in the bourgeois countries during the
revolutionary epoch were, as a general rule, incomparably
superior to the present-day leaders. In the oldest of the civilized countries Oliver Cromwell[155] has been replaced by the
present-day Neville Chamberlain: this says everything.

On the contrary, the backward and oppressed countries that
have to struggle for their independence are much more capable
of putting forth outstanding political leaders. You yourself,
Mr. Senator, evidently believe you have been called upon to
lead the Latin American countries. Yet your articles and
speeches reveal such a limited horizon, such self-seeking and
reactionary narrow-mindedness that they nearly call for con-
dolences.

At the beginning of your banquet, Bishop William
Manning[156] prayed for the Most High to grant all the members of the Chamber of Commerce sympathy for the persecuted and deliverance from racist prejudices (*New York Times*,
November 23). Meanwhile, I am asking myself: Is it conceivable that you would write an article registering such flip-
pant charges with respect to Canada, for example? I answer,
no; it would be impossible. You would be more careful, more
attentive, and therefore more conscientious. But you believe
that it is fully admissible to string together a series of ab-
surdities with respect to Mexico. What is the reason for this
difference between your attitude toward Mexico and your attitude toward Canada? I dare say it is the racist arrogance
of an imperialist. Bishop Manning's prayer has obviously
not helped you, Senator!

The reactionaries think that revolutions are artificially provoked by revolutionaries. This is a monstrous blunder! The
exploited classes and oppressed peoples are pushed onto the
road to revolution by slaveholders like Mr. Allen. These gentlemen are undermining the existing order of things with great
success.

VICTOR SERGE
AND THE FOURTH INTERNATIONAL[157]
December 2, 1938

Several friends have asked us what Victor Serge's relationship is to the Fourth International. We are obliged to reply that it is the relationship of an opponent. Ever since his appearance outside the Soviet Union Victor Serge has done nothing but change positions. There is no other way to define his political position than "changeability." Not on one single question has he presented clear or distinct proposals, rebuttals, or arguments. He has invariably, though, supported those who have moved away from the Fourth International, whether toward the right or the left.

Surprising everyone, Victor Serge declared in an official letter that he was joining the POUM, without ever having attempted to reply to our criticism of the POUM as a centrist organization that has played a miserable role in the Spanish revolution. Victor Serge flirted with the Spanish anarcho-syndicalists in spite of their treacherous role in the Spanish revolution. Behind the scenes, he supported that ill-fated hero of "left" trade unionism, Sneevliet, without ever deciding to openly defend the Dutch opportunist's unprincipled politics. Simultaneously Victor Serge repeated on several occasions that his differences with us were of a "secondary" character. To the direct question of why he did not then collaborate with the Fourth International rather than with its rabid opponents, Victor Serge never came up with an answer. All this, taken together, deprived his own "politics" of any consistency whatsoever and turned it into a series of personal combinations, if not intrigues.

If Victor Serge still speaks, even now, of his "sympathies" for the Fourth International, it is in no other sense than Vereecken, Molinier, Sneevliet, Maslow, etc., do the same,[158] having in mind not the real International, but a mythical one, created by their imagination in their own likeness and form, and necessary to them only as a cover for their opportunist or adventurist politics. With this nonexistent International our actually functioning International has nothing in common, and neither the Russian section nor the International as a whole takes any responsibility for the politics of Victor Serge.

PROBLEMS OF THE MEXICAN SECTION[159]

December 5, 1938

In his statement Galicia says that he is "abiding by" the decision of the Fourth International. But this only means that he either failed to understand this decision or he is being hypocritical, or he is combining his lack of understanding with hypocrisy. The decision of the Fourth International calls for a complete, radical change of policy. If Galicia understood the need for a new course, he would not have written his absurd and criminal declaration.

Like all petty-bourgeois individualists of anarchist bent, Galicia is making an appeal for *democracy*. He is demanding that the International guarantee complete freedom for his individuality. He completely forgets about *centralism*. But for the revolutionist, democracy is only one element of organization; the other no less important element is centralism, since without centralism revolutionary activity is impossible. *Democracy* guarantees *freedom to discuss: centralism* guarantees *unity in action*. Petty-bourgeois windbags restrict themselves to criticism, protests, and conversations. This is why they make an appeal for democracy, unlimited and absolute, ignoring the rights of centralism.

Where is the violation of democracy with respect to Galicia? Over a long period of time Galicia and his group defied the fundamental principles of the Fourth International regarding the trade unions. If the International is guilty of anything it is excessive patience. When it became clear to Galicia that the International could no longer tolerate a policy of petty-bourgeois dilettantism and intrigue, Galicia *disbanded* the section of the Fourth International! No more, no less! To disband a revolutionary organization signifies a shameful capitulation to opponents and enemies; it signifies the betrayal of our banner. What did the International do in this instance? It dispatched a delegation of three authoritative and internationally respected North American comrades to Mexico to examine the matter firsthand and try to persuade the members of the Mexican section of the need to change their policy. When Galicia saw that despite his criminal activities the Fourth International was still willing to place some moral confidence in him, on credit, Galicia quickly proclaimed the Mexican League "reconstituted." By so doing he again showed that for him the organization is not an instrument for the class struggle but an instrument for his personal combinations; i.e., he laid bare his nature as a petty-bourgeois adventurist.

Representatives from twelve sections gathered at the international congress. The facts on the internal struggle of the Mexican League had been well known to them for a long time from our press. For them these facts contained nothing new. As has already been said, Galicia is only repeating in a caricatured form the activities of Vereecken, Molinier, Eiffel, and those like them.[160] The congress had before it all Galicia's documents and the report from the delegation of the Socialist Workers Party of the United States. What the congress was faced with was no mystery. The best representatives of the Fourth International brought forth their opinion on the basis of this material. "This is bureaucratism!" Galicia shouts.

Why bureaucratism? By what other course could a judgment be rendered under the circumstances? Or is Galicia in fact claiming that generally the International should not dare to examine the problems of the Mexican movement? The charge of bureaucratism is in this instance the slander of a sectarian clique that is concerned with neither Marxism, nor the collective experience of the Fourth International, nor the authority of its international congresses.

Galicia is trying to present matters in such a way as to claim that he is trying to conduct a revolutionary policy but the "bureaucracy" of the Fourth International is hindering him in these efforts; that this bureaucracy wants to blunt the class struggle in Mexico; that this bureaucracy is applying strangulation methods in pursuit of that goal, trampling on "democracy," not listening to Galicia and his friends, and so on and so forth. All this is false from beginning to end. By his entire conduct, Galicia has revealed that he is not a revolutionary, since a revolutionary is first and foremost a *person of action.* Galicia has not the slightest understanding of action, he does not attempt to take action, but on the contrary, refrains from participating in any serious struggle. During meetings which the Stalinists and Toledanoists arrange for the struggle against so-called "Trotskyism," Galicia is always conspicuous by his absence. In fact, why subject oneself to the risk of an open struggle? Why bother to organize groups of activists, to defend the organization, to protest, and to make one's existence known? It is much simpler to remain on the sidelines and attack the "bureaucrats" of the Fourth International. Sectarian intrigue always goes hand in hand with political passivity. This is again borne out by the example of Galicia and his group.

Galicia asserts that the Fourth International is allegedly attempting to force him to function in an alliance with the bourgeoisie and government of Mexico. This is a repetition of Eiffel's vile slander. "Revolutionaries" of Eiffel's type are distinguished mainly by their *abstention* from revolutionary struggle. They lead a parasitic existence. They always have a thousand explanations and arguments for abstention and passivity. Their political life consists of smearing revolutionaries who are taking part in the class struggle. Galicia belongs to this school.

But let us suppose for a moment that on the basis of some special circumstances the International should decide to apply more "peaceful," more "cautious" methods in Mexico in the interest of the international struggle as a whole. How should Mexican revolutionaries act in this case? They would have to decide whether the International's directive, dictated by a concern over the general interests of the movement, was right or wrong, i.e., whether this directive serves the end that had been posed. But Galicia and his group are not even trying to explain why the International is "imposing" on them a policy that they consider to be opportunist. Or are they trying to say, like Eiffel, Oehler, and Company, [161] that our International is opportunist in general? No, they say that the International is making an inadmissible exception in Mexico's case. However, they do not analyze this "exception"; they do not say whether it was really prompted by international concerns or not. In other words, *they are not trying to take an international point of view.* Even on this question they remain petty-bourgeois nationalists and not internationalist Marxists.

Is it true that the International is prescribing different methods of struggle for Mexico? Is it calling for an alliance with the bourgeoisie and the government? No, this is a lie from beginning to end, a lie thought up not by Galicia, but by

Eiffel, Oehler, and similar plotters and sectarians. The trouble is that Galicia does not understand what the class struggle against the bourgeoisie and the government means. He believes that in order to fulfill your duty as a Marxist it is perfectly sufficient to once every month or two publish a shallow newspaper in which you rail against the government. To date, this has been the sum total of his r-r-revolutionary activity. Yet in Mexico, more than anywhere, the struggle against the bourgeoisie and its government consists above all in *freeing the trade unions from dependence on the government.* The trade unions in Mexico formally embrace the entire proletariat. The essence of Marxism is to provide the leadership for the class struggle of the proletariat. The class struggle demands the independence of the proletariat from the bourgeoisie. Consequently, the class struggle in Mexico must be directed toward winning the independence of the trade unions from the bourgeois state. This demands of Marxists *a concentration of all efforts inside the trade unions against the Stalinists and Toledanoists.* Everything else is trifles, chatter, intrigue, petty-bourgeois betrayal, and self-deception. And Galicia is no beginner at this kind of betrayal and self-deception.

Work in the trade unions means work in the *proletarian* unions. Of course, participation in the teachers' union is necessary; but this is an organization of the petty-bourgeois intelligentsia and is not capable of playing an independent role. Those who do not play a systematic role in the work of the *proletarian* trade unions are dead weight for the Fourth International.

When Galicia enigmatically insinuates that he was prevented from carrying out a revolutionary policy against the bourgeoisie, he apparently has in mind his pathetic experience of "struggle" against high prices. As is well known, Galicia issued an absurd poster with a call for a "general strike," "sabotage," and "direct action," without explaining how he thought a general strike would be organized, without having the slightest influence on the trade unions, and without explaining what "sabotage" means or precisely what sort of "direct action" he was calling for. As far as the workers were concerned, the entire appeal bore a resemblance to a provocation. But considering that he had not the slightest influence and was not even concerned about his lack of influence, the provocation was not tragic but comical. For Galicia the matter comes down not to involving one or another section of the masses in active struggle but to shouting some ultraleft phrases that have no connection with the real life of the class. A blend of sectarianism, adventurism, and cynicism is extremely typical of a certain category of petty-bourgeois pseudorevolutionaries. But what has this to do with Marxism? What has this to do with the Fourth International?

To date, there is not one key question on which Galicia has presented his own theses, countertheses, or amendments. With his own brand of ideological parasitism he confines himself to picking up rumors and gossip here and there, translating into Spanish ultraleft articles against the Fourth International from all corners of the world, entering into dealings with enemies of the Fourth International, taking no direct responsibility for anything or anyone, but simply playing the role of an offended disrupter. Does this type really have anything in common with a revolutionary fighter?

Galicia's crude and unjustified attacks on Diego Rivera form a necessary part of his petty-bourgeois politics. The fact that an artist of world importance belongs fully and completely to our own movement is of enormous value to us. It is well known that Marx valued highly the fact that the German poet Freiligrath was a member of the International,[162] although Freiligrath neither by his revolutionary commitment nor by his artistic talents could compare with Rivera. The same thing could be said about the attitude Lenin had toward Gorky,[163] who in revolutionary attitude always represented a vague blur. Marx and Lenin proceeded from the fact that Freiligrath and Gorky, with their artistic creativity, rendered great service to the cause of the proletariat, and by their support for the party enhanced its world authority. All the more should we appreciate Diego Rivera's participation in the Fourth International! It would be ridiculous and criminal to assign to a great artist perfunctory, day-to-day work, tearing him away from artistic creation; it is still more criminal to cover up the mistakes of one's own organization by constant personal attacks on Rivera. This fully characterizes the envious, plotting, petty-bourgeois psychology of Galicia and those like him.

Who is supporting Galicia in the international arena? Molinier, who reprints Galicia's documents and gives his own to Galicia for reprinting in turn; Vereecken, who gets Galicia's support on all his declarations; Oehler, who encourages Galicia and Company, slapping them on the back in a friendly

manner and counseling them to go all the way, i.e., to openly
break with the International. What camp does Galicia belong
to in the last analysis? To the camp of the Fourth International or to the camp of its enemies? Galicia makes statements
about "abiding" by the decision evidently for the sole purpose
of remaining inside the Fourth International and pursuing
his disruptive politics.

Galicia finds it possible to suggest that the congress of the
Fourth International was guided by some sort of behind-the-
scenes or personal considerations. The majority of our organizations lead an illegal or semilegal existence entailing extraordinary sacrifices and demanding, therefore, an extraordinary
level of idealism and heroism. And now it appears that these
organizations sent their delegates in order to condemn Galicia
on the basis of some sort of ignoble considerations. Is it possible for his own nature to be more clearly betrayed? Is not
Galicia showing that he is simply an exasperated petty bourgeois?

Galicia takes the liberty of likening the Fourth International
to the Stalinist International. In fact, Galicia himself is a legitimate product of Stalin's International. Bureaucrats or aspir-
ing bureaucrats-to-be can as a general rule be divided into
the satisfied and the dissatisfied. The former apply the most
rabid repression in order to preserve their posts. The latter
conceal their wounded ambition with frenzied left-wing phraseology. One type shifts into the other as easily as a poacher
becomes a gendarme. If Galicia finds it possible to suspect
the congress of the Fourth International of unworthy motives,
what is it in general that is binding him to this organization?

What conclusions flow from what has been stated here? Galicia
has obviously failed to understand the purpose of the decisions
of our international congress, just as he has obviously failed
to understand the purpose and spirit of the Fourth International. It is not surprising that he has failed to understand
the significance of his own mistakes. He is continuing and
accentuating these mistakes. He is ignoring our International
in the name of solidarity with all the centrist and ultraleft
cliques. This is why, in our view, the decision concerning him
at the international congress is today already inadequate. It
must be supplemented. It is impossible to admit Galicia into
the organization on the basis of his obviously false "recognition" of the congress' decisions. These decisions make the

old politics of Galicia and his group no longer permissible. Galicia may be given another half year to deliberate, while he remains outside the threshold of the Mexican section of the Fourth International. If during this half year Galicia comes to understand that the Fourth International is a revolutionary organization based on definite principles of action and not a discussion club created for petty-bourgeois intellectuals, he will again find a way into the organization. Otherwise, he will forever remain beyond the threshold. As regards the other members of Galicia's group, they can join the organization only on the basis of a real — and not a diplomatic — recognition of the congress' decisions. Otherwise, the organization will be built without them. Such is our proposal.

A REVOLUTIONARY NAME
FOR A REVOLUTIONARY YOUTH GROUP[164]

December 10, 1938

Dear Friends:

I am told that the proposition of naming the youth organization the "Legion of the Socialist Revolution" met with opposition from the point of view that the American worker does not "like" anything that smacks of revolution, illegal action, hostility to democracy, etc. These arguments are incomparably more important than the question of the name itself.

It is an old historic experience that one who does not find it opportune to carry his political name openly does not possess the courage necessary to defend his ideas openly, for the name is not an accidental thing but is a condensation of the ideas. It was for that reason that Marx and Engels called themselves Communists and never liked the name Social Democrats. It was for the same reason that Lenin changed the dirty shirt of Social Democracy and adopted the name Communist, as more intransigent and militant. Now we must again throw off the names that have been compromised and choose a new one. We must find this name not through adaptation to the prejudices of the masses, but on the contrary, we most oppose these prejudices by a name adequate to the new historic tasks.

The above-mentioned argument is incorrect in its theoretical, political, and psychological aspects. The conservative mentality of a large stratum of workers is an inheritance of the past and an integral part of "Americanism" (of Hoover's as well as of Roosevelt's pattern). The new economic situation is in absolute opposition to this mentality. Which should we consider decisive: traditional stupidity or the objective revolutionary facts? Look at Mr. Hague on the other side of the barricades. He is not afraid to trample the traditional "democracy" underfoot. He proclaims, "I am the law." From the traditional point of view it seems to be very imprudent, provocative, unreasonable; but no, it is absolutely correct from the point of view of the capitalist class. Only by this procedure can a militant, reactionary party be formed which will be adequate for the objective situation.

Do we not have at least as much courage as those on the other side of the barricades?

The crisis of American capitalism has a very rapid tempo. People who are frightened by the militant name today will understand its meaning tomorrow. The political name is not for a day or a year, but for a historic period.

Our youth organization has only 700 members. In the States there are certainly tens and hundreds of thousands of young boys and girls who are thoroughly disgusted by the society which deprives them of the possibility of working. If our name is not understandable or "agreeable" to the backward millions, it can become very attractive to tens of thousands of active elements. We are a vanguard party. During the time in which we are assimilating the thousands and tens of thousands, the millions will learn the real meaning of the name from the economic blows to which they are subjected.

A colorless name passes unremarked and this is the worst thing in politics, particularly for revolutionists. The political atmosphere is now extremely confused. In a public meeting, when everybody is speaking and no one can hear the other, the chairman should bring his gavel down on the desk with a heavy blow. The name of the party should now resound with such a blow on the desk.

The youth organization can and should have auxiliary organizations with various purposes and different names, but the leading political body should have a definite and open revolutionary character and a corresponding banner and name.

From the first information it also seems to me that the danger does not lie in the fact that the youth wishes to be a second party, but rather in the fact that the first party dominates the youth too directly and too firmly by organizational means. The party cadres in the youth naturally make a high level of discussion in the conventions and in the National Committee, but this high level is an expression of the negative side of the situation. How can you educate the youth without a certain amount of confusion, errors, and internal fights which have not been infiltrated by the "old gentlemen," but arise from the natural development of the youth themselves. I now have the impression that well-educated party members inside the youth organization think, speak, discuss, and decide in the name of the youth, and this might be one of the reasons for our having lost people in the last year. The youth does not have the right to be too wise or too mature, or better, it has the right to be youth. This side of the question is much more important than that of colors, rituals, etc. The worst thing that could happen to us would be to establish a division of labor within the youth organization: the young rank and file play with colors and trumpets and the selected cadres attend to the politics.

Comradely yours,
Joe Hansen [Trotsky]

FOR A SYSTEMATIC
POLITICAL CAMPAIGN[165]

December 12, 1938

Dear Friends:

It would be well to begin the bi-weekly *Socialist Appeal* with a detailed investigation throughout the country of the fascist, semifascist, and reactionary organizations in general. Possibly the Stalinists have already tried to do something of the kind. However, the situation changes, the old organizations disappear, and new ones arise. In any case, it would be an excellent job for our local organizations, particularly the youth.

Of course, it would be good to involve not only our party branches, but also the local trade unions, sympathetic organizations, and so on. We must instill in the vanguard of the proletariat an understanding of the growing threat of fascism. It is the best weapon with which to demolish the prejudices of Americanism: "democracy," "legality," etc.

With a bi-weekly the question of a systematic political campaign will become even more important than now.

Comradely,

Hansen [Trotsky]

A POLITICAL DIALOGUE[166]

December 20, 1938

(This conversation takes place in Paris. It could for that matter also take place in Brussels. *A* is one of those "socialists" who can only stand on their feet when they have some power to lean on. *A* is a "friend of the Soviet Union" and is naturally a supporter of the People's Front. The author finds it rather difficult to characterize *B*, for *B* is his friend and co-thinker.)

A. But you cannot deny that the fascists use your criticisms. All the reactionaries shout for joy when you unmask the USSR. Obviously, I do not believe all these slanders about your friendship with the fascists, your collaboration with the Nazis, etc. That's only for fools. Subjectively no doubt you maintain a revolutionary point of view. It is not, however, the subjective intentions that matter in politics, but the objective consequences. The right uses your criticisms against your will. In that sense, then, one can say that you are in an objective bloc with the reactionaries.

B. Thanks very much for your brilliant objectivity. But you have discovered, my friend, an America that was discovered long ago. Even the *Communist Manifesto* told us that feudal reaction tried to exploit for its own use the socialist criticisms directed against the liberal bourgeoisie. That is why the liberals and the "democrats" have always, and invariably, accused the socialists of an alliance with reaction. Honest, but—how shall we put it?—somehow limited gentlemen have spoken of an "objective" alliance, of "actual" collaboration. Real crooks, on the other hand, have accused the revolutionaries of having made a direct agreement with the reactionaries, spreading rumors that the socialists work with foreign money, etc. Truly, my friend, you have not invented gunpowder.

A. One can answer your analogy with two decisive objections. First, that so far as bourgeois democracy is concerned. . . .

B. You mean imperialist bourgeois democracy?

A. Yes, I mean bourgeois democracy, which—we cannot deny this—is at the moment in deadly danger. It is one thing to expose the imperfections of bourgeois democracy when it is strong and healthy, but to undermine it from the left at the very moment when the fascists want to overthrow it from the right, that means . . .

B. You don't have to go on; I know this tune only too well.

A. I beg your pardon, I haven't finished yet. My second objection comes down to this: It is not merely a question of bourgeois democracy this time. After all, there is the USSR, which you used to recognize as a workers' state and which you apparently still recognize as such. Complete isolation threatens this state. You reveal only the defects of the USSR, and consequently this lowers the prestige of the first workers' state in the eyes of the workers of the world, and thus objectively you are helping fascism.

B. Thanks again for your objectivity. In other words what you mean to say is that one must only criticize "democracy" when criticism constitutes no danger for it. According to you, socialists are to shut up precisely when decaying *imperialist* bourgeois democracy (not just "bourgeois democracy" in general!) has proven in practice its complete inability to cope with the tasks posed by history (and this inability is precisely the reason why "democracy" crumbles so easily under the blows of reaction). You are reducing socialism to the role of a "critical" ornament upon the architecture of bourgeois democracy. You will not acknowledge to socialism the role of *heir* to democracy. What it boils down to is that you are a very frightened conservative democrat, that's all. And your "socialist" phraseology is nothing but a cheap ornament upon your conservatism.

A. Well, what about the USSR, which undoubtedly *is* the heir of democracy and constitutes the embryo of the new society? Mind you, I do not deny that there are errors and deficiencies in the USSR. To err is human. Imperfections are inevitable. But it is not by accident that all of world reaction attacks the USSR. . . .

B. Aren't you at all uneasy repeating such banalities? Yes, in spite of the Kremlin's voluntary but useless crawling upon its belly, world reaction continues its struggle against the USSR. Why? Because the USSR has, up to the present, maintained the nationalization of the means of production and the monopoly of foreign trade. We revolutionaries attack the *bureaucracy* of the USSR precisely because its parasitic policy and suppression of the workers undermine the nationalization of the means of production and the monopoly of foreign trade, which are the basic components of socialist construction. Here you see the tiny, the very tiny difference between us and reaction. World imperialism calls upon the oligarchy of the Kremlin to carry its work to a conclusion and, having introduced military ranks (distinctions, decorations), privileges, domestic servants, prostitution, punishment for abortions, etc., to also introduce private property in the means of production. We, on the other hand, call on the workers of the USSR to overthrow the Kremlin oligarchy and to build a true Soviet democracy as the necessary prerequisite for building socialism.

A. But you cannot deny that the USSR, despite all its imperfections, constitutes progress?

B. Only the superficial tourist, whom the hosts of Moscow have favored with their hospitality, can regard the USSR as a single unit. There are in the USSR, besides extremely progressive tendencies, also malignantly reactionary ones. One must know how to differentiate between the two and to defend one against the other. The never-ending purges show, even to the blind, the power and tension of the new antagonisms. The most fundamental of these social contradictions is the one between the betrayed masses and the new aristocratic caste which is preparing the restoration of a class society. That is why I cannot be "for the USSR" in general. I am for the working masses who created the USSR and against the bureaucracy which has usurped the gains of the revolution.

A. But do you mean to say that you demand the immediate introduction of complete equality in the USSR? But even Marx. . . .

B. For goodness sake, don't use these worn-out phrases of Stalin's hirelings. I assure you, I too have read that in the first stage of socialism there cannot yet be complete equality and that that is the task of communism. But that is not the question at all. The point is that during the last several years, as the bureaucracy has become more and more omnipotent, inequality has *grown* by enormous dimensions. It is not the static situation, but the dynamics, the general direction of development, that is of decisive importance. The inequality in the USSR, far from adjusting itself, sharpens and grows daily and hourly. The growth of this social inequality can only be stopped by revolutionary measures against the new aristocracy. That alone determines our position.

A. Yes, but the imperialist reactionaries use your criticisms as a whole. Therefore it follows, doesn't it, that they also use them against the gains of the revolution?

B. Of course they *try* to make use of them. In political struggle every class tries to make use of the contradictions in the ranks of its opponents. Two examples: Lenin, who, as you might have heard, was never for unity just for the sake of unity, tried to separate the Bolsheviks from Mensheviks. As we have since found out from czarist archives, the police department, with the help of its provocateurs, further deepened the split between the Bolsheviks and the Mensheviks. After the February revolution of 1917 the Mensheviks continually insisted that the aims and methods of Lenin coincided with those of the czarist police. What a cheap argument! The police hoped that the splitting of the Social Democrats would weaken them. Lenin, on the other hand, was convinced that the split with the Mensheviks would enable the Bolsheviks to develop a truly revolutionary policy and to capture the masses. Who was right?

Second example: Wilhelm II and his General Ludendorff tried during the war to use Lenin for their own purposes and put a train at his disposal for his return to Russia.[167] The Russian Cadets and Kerensky called Lenin nothing else but an agent of German imperialism. And it can be said for them that they certainly used more convincing, or at least less stupid, arguments in their favor than their imitators of today are employing. And what was the result? After the defeat of Germany, Ludendorff admitted — read his memoirs — that in his estimation of Lenin he had made the biggest mistake of his life. The German army, according to Ludendorff's admission, was destroyed, not by the armies of the Entente, but by the Bolsheviks through the October Revolution.

A. Well, what about the military security of the USSR? What about the danger of weakening its defenses?

B. You'd better keep quiet about that! Stalin, having broken with the earlier Spartan simplicity of the Red Army, had crowned the officer corps with five marshals. But he could not bribe the commanding staff that way. So he decided to destroy it. Four of the five marshals — precisely the ones who had some ability — were shot, and with them the flower of the military command. A hierarchy of personal spies of Stalin was created over the army. It has been shaken to its very core. The USSR has been weakened. This weakening of the army goes on. Parasitic tourists can sit back and enjoy the military displays on the Red Square. It remains the duty of a serious revolutionary to state quite frankly and openly: Stalin is preparing the defeat of the USSR.

A. And what are your conclusions then?

B. It is very simple. The petty pickpockets of politics believe that a great historical problem can be solved by cheap claptrap, cunning, intrigue behind the scenes, deception of the masses. The ranks of the international labor bureaucracy are teeming with such pickpockets. I believe, however, that social problems can only be solved by a working class that knows the truth. Socialist education means *to tell the masses the truth.* Truth most often has a bitter taste and the "friends of the Soviet Union" like sweets. But those who like sweets represent the element of reaction and not of progress. We shall continue to tell the masses the truth. We have got to prepare for the future, and revolutionary politics is farsighted politics.

ANSWERS TO THE LIES
OF THE NEW YORK DAILY NEWS[168]
December 28, 1938

Q: The *News*, in an editorial published October 29, 1938, said in part that "Trotsky is a friend and adviser of Cardenas," and that therefore you were behind the expropriation of petroleum properties in Mexico. Your counsel, Mr. Albert Goldman,[169] has demanded that the *News* retract the editorial. Will you please state your personal views as to the truth or falsity of the *News*'s allegations?

It has been frequently implied in the daily press of the United States, probably because the Cardenas government gave you asylum, that you were the inspiration of many of President Cardenas's policies; also that he has frequently consulted you, especially as regards his agrarian policy and the taking over of industry by the government for the benefit of the workers. Is that true?

A: Since your editorial office has engaged itself by telegraph to reproduce my answers integrally, I willingly answer your questions. The editors of the *Daily News* have expressed themselves in their articles on Mexico, its government, and my alleged participation in Mexican politics with a laudable frankness that would appear as brutality. I shall strive to avoid brutality, however, without damaging frankness.

The affirmation of the *Daily News* (October 29, 1938) that Trotsky is "a friend and counselor of Cardenas" is absolutely false. I have never had the honor of meeting General Cardenas or speaking with him. I have had no relations through writing with him, except the ones concerning the right of asylum. I have not been and I am not now in any relationship, direct or indirect, with any other members of the government.

I have not engaged, and I do not now engage, in any political activity connected with the internal life of the country, if we do not consider my unmasking the slanders spread against me here by Stalin's agents. Finally, the program of the Fourth International, which I support, is very far from the program of the Mexican government.

It is not difficult, on the other hand, to understand that the Mexican government, preoccupied with the national prestige of its country, would never seek counsel from a foreign immigrant. I learned of the agrarian and other measures of the Mexican government through the newspapers, exactly like the majority of other citizens.

On the basis of what data did your paper arrive at its conclusion? Evidently on the basis of the simple fact that the government of General Cardenas accorded me the right of asylum. Is it not monstrous? In 1916, I was expelled from Europe as a result of my struggle against the imperialist war, and I found asylum in the United States. Without any passport, without any visa, without any absurd and humiliating formalities! Your immigration authorities were interested that I did not have trachoma but were absolutely unconcerned about my ideas.

Yet twenty-two years ago, my ideas, I venture to assure you, were as bad as now. At that time, it did not occur to anyone to draw the conclusion that President Wilson had given me the right of asylum in order to utilize my "counsels." You will object, perhaps, that this was in the remote past, when the United States had not yet been emancipated from the vestiges of barbarism; and that the present flowering of civilization began only after the great emancipatory "war for democracy."

I will not discuss that. Democratic civilization has now reached, it seems, such a flowering that the mere fact of the Mexican government's granting me the right of asylum immediately provokes the hypothesis: this government evidently sympathizes with Trotsky's conceptions. Permit me, nevertheless, to point out that granting the right of asylum to one's followers is still not democracy; this is done by Hitler, by Mussolini, by Stalin. This was done in the past by the Russian czar and the Turkish sultan.

The principle of the right of asylum, if we consider it seriously, supposes hospitality also towards political adversaries. I permit myself to think that the government of General Cardenas accorded me hospitality not through sympathy for my political conceptions, but through respect for its own.

Q: Mr. Henry J. Allen, former governor of Kansas, visited Mexico in the fall of 1938. He attended a seminar of American tourists at your Mexico City residence. He later wrote in part, "All through Latin America in the last few weeks Cardenas has sent emissaries preaching the rewards of confiscation. . . . It is easy to guess who taught him this — Trotsky.

. . . Lombardo Toledano, who went to Russia to study the Soviet system and who is a follower of Trotsky" . . . etc. Mr. Allen repeated the gist of these charges recently in New York City. Please state the truth or falsity of these charges.

A: I have answered Mr. Allen's insinuations in the Mexican weekly *Hoy* and you have the opportunity to utilize my answer completely. In Mr. Allen's articles and speeches, so far as they concern my life and activity in Mexico, there is not a word of truth.

You yourselves quote in your question Mr. Allen's assertion that Lombardo Toledano, secretary of the union organizations, is my "follower." In Mexico this sentence is capable of provoking only a Homeric laugh, perhaps not very flattering to the reputation of the ex-governor of Kansas. It is enough to say that my curious "follower" systematically repeats in his speeches and articles that I am preparing . . . the overthrow of the government of General Cardenas. What basis does he have for such affirmations? The same as your paper. What is his aim? To secure my deliverance into the hands of the GPU.

I proposed to Mr. Toledano that an impartial commission be created for public verification of his declarations. Toledano, of course, evaded reply. I am ready to send the same proposition to the address of ex-governor Allen. He, too, of course, will evade reply. Toledano and Allen are not identical, but symmetrical, at least, in the sense that they find themselves at the same distance from the meridian of exactitude.

Q: Your counsel, Mr. Albert Goldman, according to a story in the Mexico City newspaper *Excelsior,* is quoted as saying that the instigator of "these editorials published in the *Daily News* (my paper) is a foreign correspondent living here, who has connections with the Communists in the United States and in Mexico." Inasmuch as Mr. Goldman has publicly made that charge against the *News,* may I have the name of the "foreign correspondent"?

A: Yes, I have information that the person who informed the *Daily News* about my alleged "participation" in the government policy of Mexico is a member of the Communist Party of the United States. You know how difficult it is in such cases to present judicial evidence even if the facts are indisputable. For your editorial office, it will not be difficult, however, to verify the exactness of this information.

Two groups exist, both interested in making the insinuations which have been repeated in your newspaper in a series of articles: on the one hand are the capitalists, discontented with the Mexican government and desirous of presenting its measures as alien "communism"; on the other hand is the GPU, which would compromise my right of asylum in Mexico. The combining of efforts by these two groups is absolutely possible: they are also not identical but symmetrical.

Q: It has been publicly stated in New York City that your stay in Mexico City is being financed by a group of anti-Stalinists in New York City. Please state the truth or falsity of that assertion.

A: The source of my income is my literary work. And only that! But it is absolutely true that my friends in the United States as well as in other countries come with devotion to Mexico in order to help me in my work and to protect me against possible attempts at assassination. They do that on their own initiative, voluntarily sacrificing their time and their means or the means of their friends. They did so when I was in Turkey, in France, and in Norway. They did it then and they do it now not for me personally, but for the ideas which I represent. It is evident that these ideas have an attractive force.

Q: Is the Rome-Berlin-Tokyo "axis" a threat to world peace?

A: Of course, the Berlin-Rome-Tokyo "axis" is a menace to peace. But it is only one side of the war danger. To make war, at least two sides are necessary. Contemporary wars arise from the irreconcilability of imperialist interests.

On the same rails of our planet, several trains are headed toward each other loaded with greed and hate. Of course, they must collide. Which engineer will be more "guilty," which less, this fact has no importance. Guilty is the regime of imperialism which concentrates the riches of the nations and of humanity into the hands of a few monopolists. It is necessary to put an end to this regime of monopoly; it is necessary to expropriate the expropriators.

P.S. — Now, after receiving the issue of your paper dated December 10, I must make this addition to what I have said already.

When the *Daily News* affirms that I was the inspirer of the expropriation measures of the Mexican government, there is no slander in that. It is simply false. But your paper has now launched a second report, which, while a *lie,* represents at the same time a *slander.* The *Daily News* affirms that Mexican oil is sent to the German government on my counsel, and that moreover, my aim is to cause Stalin damage.

The *Daily News* here in its own name launches the version which passed like a yellow thread through all the Moscow trials. The International Commission of Inquiry under the leadership of Dr. John Dewey declared that the Moscow accusations were frame-ups. The editorials of your newspaper are not capable of converting an unmasked frame-up into truth.

To whom the Mexican government sells oil is its own affair. I have nothing to say about that. I will add only that the "democracies" have a simple means of concentrating Mexican oil in their hands; they need only buy it. Insofar as Great Britain, for example, boycotts Mexican oil, it obliges the Mexican government to sell oil to Germany, Italy, or Japan. Chamberlain's government apparently has more at heart the interests of the oil magnates than the interests of national defense, not to speak of the interests of "democracy."

But this is still not all. When the masters of destiny in the great democracies give Hitler a present of Czechoslovakia for his birthday and *then* manifest discontent toward the Mexican government which sells its oil to whoever wishes to buy, it is impossible not to say that here hypocrisy surpasses all admissible bounds and thus becomes stupid and ridiculous.

But I am preoccupied now with another aspect of the matter. The affirmation that thanks to Mexican oil, I want to help Hitler gain victory over Stalin is not only a lie, but also a slander. The USSR and Stalin are not the same thing. I am an adversary of Stalin but not of the USSR. The task of overthrowing the reactionary parasitic dictatorship of the Stalinist oligarchy is the task of the Russian workers and peasants. They cannot transfer this task to Hitler. Hitler is only the perfidious agent of German imperialism. Hitler's victory would signify frightful economic, political, and national slavery for all the people of the USSR and above all the restoration of the rights of private capital.

Or perhaps you think that I advocate expropriation of oil resources only for Mexico? No, to defend the nationalization of the means of production realized by the October Revolution — against Hitler as against all other imperialists — I consider this the elementary duty of every socialist, beginning with myself.

LENIN AND IMPERIALIST WAR [170]

December 30, 1938

"It has always been the case in history," Lenin wrote in 1916, "that after the death of revolutionary leaders popular among the oppressed classes, their enemies try to assume their names in order to deceive the oppressed classes." With no one has history performed this operation so cruelly as with Lenin himself. The present official doctrine of the Kremlin and the policies of the Comintern on the question of imperialism and war ride roughshod over all the conclusions that Lenin came to and brought the party to from 1914 through 1918.

With the outbreak of the war in August 1914 the first question which arose was this: Should the socialists of imperialist countries assume the "defense of the fatherland"? The issue was not whether or not individual socialists should fulfill the obligations of soldiers — there was no other alternative; desertion is not a revolutionary policy. The issue was: Should socialist parties support the war politically? vote for the war budget? renounce the struggle against the government and agitate for the "defense of the fatherland"? Lenin's answer was: No! the party must not do so, it has no right to do so, not because *war* is involved but because this is a *reactionary* war, because this is a dog fight between the slave owners for the redivision of the world.

The formation of national states on the European continent occupied an entire epoch which began approximately with the Great French Revolution and concluded with the Franco-Prussian War of 1870-71. During these dramatic decades the wars were predominantly of a national character. War waged for the creation or defense of national states necessary for the development of productive forces and of culture possessed during this period a profoundly progressive historical character. Revolutionists not only could but were obliged to support national wars politically.

From 1871 to 1914 European capitalism, on the foundation

of national states, not only flowered but outlived itself by becoming transformed into monopoly or imperialist capitalism. "Imperialism is that stage of capitalism when the latter, after fulfilling everything in its power, begins to decline." The cause for decline lies in this, that the productive forces are fettered by the framework of private property as well as by the boundaries of the national state. Imperialism seeks to divide and redivide the world. In place of national wars there come imperialist wars. They are utterly reactionary in character and are an expression of the impasse, stagnation, and decay of monopoly capital.

The world, however, still remains very heterogeneous. The coercive imperialism of advanced nations is able to exist only because backward nations, oppressed nationalities, colonial and semicolonial countries, remain on our planet. The struggle of the oppressed peoples for national unification and national independence is doubly progressive because, on the one side, this prepares more favorable conditions for their own development, while, on the other side, this deals blows to imperialism. That, in particular, is the reason why, in the struggle between a civilized, imperialist, democratic republic and a backward, barbaric monarchy in a colonial country, the socialists are completely on the side of the oppressed country notwithstanding its monarchy and against the oppressor country notwithstanding its "democracy."

Imperialism camouflages its own peculiar aims — seizure of colonies, markets, sources of raw material, spheres of influence — with such ideas as "safeguarding peace against the aggressors," "defense of the fatherland," "defense of democracy," etc. These ideas are false through and through. It is the duty of every socialist not to support them but, on the contrary, to unmask them before the people. "The question of which group delivered the first military blow or first declared war," wrote Lenin in March 1915, "has no importance whatever in determining the tactics of socialists. Phrases about the defense of the fatherland, repelling invasion by the enemy, conducting a defensive war, etc., are on both sides a complete deception of the people." "For decades," explained Lenin, "three bandits (the bourgeoisie and governments of England, Russia, and France) armed themselves to despoil Germany. Is it surprising that the two bandits (Germany and Austria-Hungary) launched an attack before the three bandits succeeded in obtaining the new knives they had ordered?"

The objective historical meaning of the war is of decisive importance for the proletariat: What class is conducting it? and for the sake of what? This is decisive, and not the subterfuges of diplomacy by means of which the enemy can always be successfully portrayed to the people as an aggressor. Just as false are the references by imperialists to the slogans of democracy and culture. ". . . The German bourgeoisie . . . deceives the working class and the toiling masses by vowing that the war is being waged for the sake of . . . freedom and culture, for the sake of freeing the peoples oppressed by czarism. The English and French bourgeoisies . . . deceive the working class and the toiling masses by vowing that they are waging war . . . against German militarism and despotism." A political superstructure of one kind or another cannot change the reactionary economic foundation of imperialism. On the contrary, it is the foundation that subordinates the superstructure to itself. "In our day . . . it is silly even to think of a progressive bourgeoisie, a progressive bourgeois movement. All bourgeois 'democracy' . . . has become reactionary." This appraisal of imperialist "democracy" constitutes the cornerstone of the entire Leninist conception.

Since war is waged by both imperialist camps not for the defense of the fatherland or democracy but for the redivision of the world and colonial enslavement, a socialist has no right to prefer one bandit camp to another. Absolutely in vain is any attempt to "determine, from the standpoint of the international proletariat, whether the defeat of one of the two warring groups of nations would be a lesser evil for socialism." In the very first days of September 1914, Lenin was already characterizing the content of the war for each of the imperialist countries and for all the groupings as follows: "The struggle for markets and for plundering foreign lands, the eagerness to head off the revolutionary movement of the proletariat and to crush democracy within each country, the urge to deceive, divide, and crush the proletarians of all countries, to incite the wage slaves of one nation against the wage slaves of another nation for the profits of the bourgeoisie — that is the only real content and meaning of the war." How far removed is all this from the current doctrine of Stalin, Dimitrov, and Co.![171]

The policy of "national unity" during wartime means, even more than in peacetime, support for reaction and the perpetuation of imperialist barbarism. Denying such support — the elementary duty of a socialist — is, however, only the negative or passive side of internationalism. This alone is not enough. The task of the party of the proletariat is "comprehensive propaganda, applying to both the army and the theater of war, for a socialist revolution and the need to direct the weapons not against our brothers, the wage slaves of other countries, but against the reactionary and bourgeois governments and parties of all countries. There is an absolute need for the organization of illegal cells and groups in the armies of all countries for such propaganda in all languages. The struggle against the chauvinism and 'patriotism' of the philistines and the bourgeoisie of all countries without exception is relentless."

But a revolutionary struggle in time of war can lead to the defeat of one's own government. This conclusion did not frighten Lenin. "In every country the struggle against one's own government, which is conducting an *imperialist* war, must not stop short of revolutionary agitation for the defeat of that country." This is precisely what the line of the so-called theory of "defeatism" involves. Unscrupulous enemies have tried to interpret this to mean that Lenin supposedly approved of collaboration with foreign imperialism in order to defeat national reaction. In fact, what he was talking about was a parallel struggle by the workers of each country against their own imperialism, as their primary and most immediate enemy. "For us, the Russians, from the standpoint of the interests of the working masses and the working class of Russia," Lenin wrote to Shlyapnikov[172] in October 1914, "there cannot be the slightest doubt — there can be absolutely no doubt of any kind — that the lesser evil would be the defeat of czarism now, without delay, in the present war."

It is impossible to fight against imperialist war by sighing for peace after the fashion of the pacifists. "One of the ways of fooling the working class is pacifism and the abstract propaganda of peace. Under capitalism, especially in its imperialist stage, wars are inevitable." A peace concluded by imperialists would only be a breathing spell before a new war. Only a revolutionary mass struggle against war and against imperialism which breeds war can secure a real peace. "Without a number of revolutions the so-called democratic peace is a middle class utopia."

The struggle against the narcotic and debilitating illusions of pacifism enters as the most important element into Lenin's doctrine. He rejected with especial hostility the demand for "disarmament as obviously utopian under capitalism."

"The oppressed class that does not try to learn how to use arms and try to have them in its possession — such an oppressed class would deserve to be treated as no more than slaves." And further: "Our slogan must be: The arming of the proletariat in order to defeat, expropriate, and disarm the bourgeoisie. . . . Only after the proletariat has disarmed the bourgeoisie can it consign all weapons to the scrap heap without betraying its world-historical mission." This leads to the conclusion that Lenin draws in dozens of articles: "The slogan 'peace' is wrong. The slogan must be to turn the national war into a civil war."

Most of the labor parties in the advanced capitalist countries turned out on the side of their respective bourgeoisies during the war. Lenin named this tendency as *social chauvinism*: socialism in words, chauvinism in deeds. The betrayal of internationalism did not fall from the skies but came as an inevitable continuation and development of the policies of reformist adaptation. "The ideological-political content of opportunism and of social chauvinism is one and the same: class collaboration instead of class struggle, support of one's 'own' government when it is in difficulties instead of utilizing these difficulties for the revolution."

The period of capitalist prosperity immediately prior to the last war — from 1909 to 1913 — tied the upper layers of the proletariat very closely with imperialism. From the superprofits obtained by the imperialist bourgeoisie from colonies and from backward countries in general, juicy crumbs fell to the lot of the labor aristocracy and the labor bureaucracy. In consequence, their patriotism was dictated by direct self-interest in the policies of imperialism. During the war, which laid bare all social relations, "the opportunists and chauvinists were invested with a gigantic power because of their alliance with the bourgeoisie, with the government and with the general staffs."

The intermediate and perhaps the widest tendency in socialism is the so-called center (Kautsky et al.) who vacillated in peace time between reformism and Marxism and who, while continuing to cover themselves with broad pacifist phrases, became almost without exception the captives of social chauvinists. So far as the masses were concerned they were caught completely off guard and duped by their own apparatus, which had been created by them in the course of decades. After giving a sociological and political appraisal of the labor bureaucracy of the Second International, Lenin did not halt midway. "Unity with opportunists is the alliance of workers with their 'own' national bourgeoisie and signifies a split in the ranks of the international revolutionary working class." Hence flows the conclusion that internationalists must break with the social chauvinists. "It is impossible to fulfill the tasks of socialism at the present time, it is impossible to achieve a genuine international fusion of workers without decisively breaking with opportunism . . ." as well as with centrism, "this bourgeois tendency in socialism." The very name of the party must be changed. "Isn't it better to cast aside the name of 'Social Democrats,' which has been smeared and degraded, and to return to the old Marxist name of Communists?" It is time to break with the Second International and to build the Third.

* * *

What has changed in the twenty-odd years that have since elapsed? Imperialism has assumed an even more violent and oppressive character. Its most consistent expression is fascism. Imperialist democracies have fallen several rungs lower and are themselves evolving into fascism naturally and organically. Colonial oppression becomes all the more intolerable the sharper is the awakening and eagerness of oppressed nationalities for national independence. In other words, all those traits which were lodged in the foundation of Lenin's theory of imperialist war have now assumed a far sharper and more graphic character.

To be sure, communo-chauvinists refer to the existence of the USSR, which supposedly introduces a complete overturn into the politics of the international proletariat. To this one can make the following brief reply: Before the USSR arose, there existed oppressed nations, colonies, etc., whose struggle also merited support. If revolutionary and progressive movements beyond the boundaries of one's own country could be supported by supporting one's own imperialist bourgeoisie then the policy of social patriotism was in principle correct. There was no reason, then, for the founding of the Third International. This is one side of the case, but there is also another. The USSR has now been in existence for twenty-two years. For seventeen years the principles of Lenin remained in force. Communo-chauvinist policies took shape only four-five years ago. The argument from the existence of the USSR is therefore only a false cover.

If a quarter of a century ago Lenin branded as social chau-

vinism and as social treachery the desertion of socialists to
the side of their nationalist imperialism under the pretext of
defending culture and democracy, then from the standpoint
of Lenin's principles the very same policy today is all the
more criminal. It is not difficult to guess how Lenin would
have designated the present-day leaders of the Comintern who
have revived all the sophistries of the Second International
under the conditions of an even more profound decomposition of capitalist civilization.

There is a pernicious paradox in this, that the wretched
epigones of the Comintern, who have turned its banner into a
dirty rag with which to wipe away the tracks of the Kremlin
oligarchy, call those "renegades" who have remained true to
the teachings of the founder of the Communist International.
Lenin was right: The ruling classes not only persecute great
revolutionists during their lifetime but revenge themselves upon
them after they are dead by measures even more refined, trying to turn them into icons whose mission is to preserve "law
and order." No one is, of course, under compulsion to take
his stand on the ground of Lenin's teachings. But we, his
disciples, will permit no one to make mockery of these teachings and to transform them into their very opposite!

TO THE PILLORY![173]

On the Last Congress of the CGT

December 31, 1938

If anyone still had even the slightest illusion regarding the character of the leadership of the General Confederation of Labor, the last congress of this organization would have dispelled it. If anyone, even yesterday, might have hoped that the leadership of the CGT was capable of evolving in a progressive direction, today we have to bury those hopes. Ramirez[174] and his cronies have shown, with laudable frankness, the depth of their degeneracy and their fall. The political vocabulary does not contain appropriate terms to characterize the present political physiognomy of this gang.

Faced with the approaching election campaign,[175] and the plots and searching for sinecures that go along with it, the leaders of the CGT have suddenly dropped their "anarchist" and "internationalist" masks to unite with the bourgeois nationalist state. On the pretext of fighting Stalinism, they turn a proletarian organization over to the worst bourgeois reaction in the service of foreign imperialism. For the petroleum magnates and other capitalists, Ramirez is now nothing more than a second-rate agent. No one has done or could have done greater service to Lombardo Toledano and to the whole agency of Stalinism in general than the CGT gang.

The great majority of working class members of this organization, obviously, have not the slightest idea of the traitorous intrigue which has been carried out behind their backs. The workers are merely victims of the personal and factional machinations of the "leaders." This makes even more criminal and shameful the reactionary turn that reached its peak at the last congress of the CGT and has opened an era of real and shameless political prostitution.

The slanderers of the Stalinist camp are circulating the rumor that the Fourth International and its sympathizing groups are soliciting a political bloc with the leadership of the

171

CGT. We reject this slander like all the rest, with an understandable disgust. The elementary duty of the revolutionary Marxist consists in carrying out systematic work in the mass proletarian organizations and above all in the trade unions. This duty includes the CTM, the CGT, and trade unions in general. But systematic work inside the unions, and education of the rank and file in the spirit of revolutionary Marxism, are as remote from a policy of adventurous blocs with corrupt union officials as the heavens are from the earth. If you give the devil your finger, you risk your whole hand. But there is not a single revolutionary Marxist who would give even a fingernail, let alone a whole finger, to the gang currently leading the CGT. An implacable struggle against it, in full sight of the working class, is a basic revolutionary duty. Ramirez and his friends should be pilloried forever by the proletarian vanguard!

*   *   *

The Toledano-Laborde gang organizes physical persecutions of the CGT: attacks on its headquarters and its meetings, technical sabotage, radio broadcasts, etc. This type of gangsterism, given currency in the world workers' movement by Stalin, has nothing in common with a real struggle against reaction; it is nothing more than a normal method used by the various groups within the labor aristocracy to work things out among themselves. The task of revolutionary politics is not to mechanically stop a trade union leader from speaking, but to teach the masses to distrust reactionary leaders and to get rid of them.

It is impossible not to point out once again that the Stalinists, imitating their master, employ ever more insolently and openly for their own ends all sorts of "totalitarian" repressions; however, since they are not in power in Mexico, they are obliged to limit themselves to the struggle within the working class movement. Totalitarian methods used in a *bourgeois* state, that is, in a society based on private property, are nothing other than *fascism*. In this sense, the actions of Toledano-Laborde open the road to fascist dictatorship. All restrictions on democratic rights in a bourgeois society in the last analysis bear down with all their weight on the working class. The true precursors of fascism in Mexico are not only Ramirez, the agent of open reaction, but also the Stalinists Laborde and Toledano. Nevertheless, it should not be presumed that they will find absolution under the fascist dictatorship they are preparing. No, in the event of a fascist victory, they will find themselves in a concentration camp . . . if they don't flee in time. Once in the concentration camps, they will probably understand at last the meaning of the warnings we repeatedly gave them.

Trotsky in 1939.

ONE MORE LESSON
ON THE LIMA CONFERENCE[176]

December 31, 1938

The laborious production of the so-called Lima solidarity resolution had just been completed as this issue of *Clave* went to press. We thus find ourselves unable to give a detailed analysis of the Pan-American Conference at this point, but we will do so in the next issue. For the time being, we will limit ourselves to hastily expressing some summary conclusions, which are, however, unshakable and at the same time instructive.

Latin America is an absolutely indispensable point of support for the worldwide aggression of the United States. At this point, it is a question not of the White House defending the American democracies, but of its defending Latin America as such, for the United States. The alignment of Latin American countries with respect to the United States has nothing to do with the line separating democracy from fascism. It is geographic and strategic considerations, as well as commercial interests, and not politics, that have determined the attitude of each country towards the pious and hypocritical demands of Cordell Hull,[177] who has the support of some of the most brutal dictatorships and the opposition of countries which are approaching "democracy."

It is clear that Roosevelt's policy, that is, imperialism with a friendly smile, has failed — a fairly natural complement to the failure of the New Deal in the internal politics of the United States. The conclusion which must be drawn — which is already being drawn by American capital — is quite clear: nothing significant can be gained through concessions to the workers, internally, nor through concessions to the "barbarians," in the realm of foreign politics. The formidable armaments program of the United States throws into eloquent relief the diplomatic defeat of Cordell Hull in Lima.

For the new continent as well, an iron era is beginning. No more pacifist illusions or mirages. Only by means of revolutionary struggle can the Latin American peoples, as well as the proletariat of the United States, secure their emancipation.

TO THE READERS OF CLAVE[178]

January 1939

Our magazine is not intended to be easy reading. Marxist theory is a guide for action. We want readers who will *study* Marxism, who will *learn to think* in a Marxist manner, in order to *act* like proletarian revolutionaries.

The problems that face the world working class at the present time are extremely complex. We try to give the simplest and clearest answers possible to these questions. However, it is impossible for the average worker to understand many of the articles in our magazine. To overcome this difficulty, it is necessary to establish *study groups* to study *Clave*. Proletarian revolutionaries take a serious attitude toward all problems and above all toward the problem of their own theorectical education. Each article must be submitted to a thorough discussion. Any doubts or objections that arise must be precisely formulated and brought to the attention of the editors of the magazine. Constant communication between the editors and the readers is the fundamental precondition for a correct orientation of the magazine and for its close ties with the class struggle of the proletariat.

At the same time we hope that our readers will supply material assistance. We have already said that the editors have no special funds at their disposal. If you need *Clave*, friends and readers, show it by your actions: send in subscriptions, give the magazine wide circulation, solicit subscribers, broaden the base of *Clave!*

CLAVE
AND THE ELECTION CAMPAIGN[179]

January 1939

Some of our readers have asked about the position of our magazine on the presidential election campaign. We reply: Our magazine does not take part in electoral campaigns. Naturally, this is not due to an anarchist prejudice against participation in politics. More than once we have seen where this prejudice leads — in France, in Spain, and in Mexico itself. No. We are for the fullest participation of the workers in politics. But we are for *independent* participation. At the present time in Mexico there is no workers' party, no trade union that is in the process of developing independent class politics and that is able to launch an independent candidate. Under these conditions, our only possible course of action is to limit ourselves to Marxist propaganda and to the preparation of a future independent party of the Mexican proletariat.

A PROPOSED BIOGRAPHY [180]

January 21, 1939

Dear Friend,

Van showed me your letter. Allow me to give you a bit of advice. The book about me would be much better written after I have settled my affairs in this the best of all worlds. Not that I fear that I myself will change, but rather that others may change and retract what they have written in their articles. In any case, my most sincere thanks for your indispensable efforts.

I would be most happy to remain in permanent contact with you.

Best regards,
Leon Trotsky

JOUHAUX AND TOLEDANO[181]

January 30, 1939

The inimitable Leon Jouhaux has sent a telegram to the inimitable Lombardo Toledano. The wire poses a menacing question: Is it true that the government of Mexico is preparing to grant oil concessions to Japan and other fascist countries? This would mean strengthening the military power of the fascists and would lead to international catastrophes; it would mean peaceful cities in flames, huge numbers of victims, etc. In the tone of a schoolboy caught misbehaving Toledano replied: "No, no, Mexico will never grant such concessions!" Quite recently the same Toledano exclaimed: "No, Mexico will *never* give its oil to the fascists. England *cannot* survive without Mexican oil," etc. These gentlemen think that they can solve vital economic problems with hollow declarations! If Lombardo had even a little, let us not say revolutionary sentiment, but just a sense of national dignity (and the citizens of an oppressed country should have a certain amount of national dignity) he would have replied to Jouhaux with the point of his boot.

Jouhaux is a direct agent of French and British imperialism. France, following Britain's lead, is boycotting Mexican oil in order to support imperialist property-holders against a semicolonial country. France and England use their air forces to suppress the liberation movements in their colonies. How, under these circumstances, does Jouhaux dare to open his mouth?

The struggle against fascist atrocities, and imperialist atrocities in general, especially the fight against the bombing of peaceful cities, can and should only be conducted by honorable workers and peasants who have not taken part in similar criminal acts either directly or indirectly. But Jouhaux — a dog on an imperialist leash — how does he dare declare himself Mexico's mentor and moral guardian? It is because he knows whom he is dealing with. He doesn't look upon Toledano as a representative of the working masses of an oppressed country, but as an agent of the French "People's Front" (alas, deceased!), that is to say, as a stand-by agent for "democratic" imperialism. And Jouhaux is not mistaken.

STALIN, SKOBLIN, AND COMPANY [182]

January 30, 1939

On October 31, 1931, the German newspaper *Rote Fahne* [Red Flag], the central organ of the late Communist Party, unexpectedly published a report that the White Guard General Turkul,[183] at that time operating in the Balkans, was preparing a terrorist attempt on Trotsky, Gorky, and Litvinov. By the contents of this report, by its tone, and finally by its anonymity, it was completely evident that the information came from the very depths of the GPU. The Soviet press did not breathe a word about this warning, and this still more underlined the highly official source of the information in the German Comintern newspaper. L. D. Trotsky was at that time in exile in Constantinople; Blumkin had already been shot for connections with Trotsky.[184] The question naturally arose: what goal was the GPU pursuing in making this printed warning? Gorky and Litvinov were under the protection of the GPU and did not need any printed warning. That their names had been added only as a cover was obvious to any thinking person even then.

The French and German Bolshevik-Leninists contacted the USSR embassies in France and Germany with written declarations something like this: "If you are reporting a planned attempt on Trotsky, that means you know who is planning it, and where and how it is being planned. We demand from you a united front against White Guard terrorists. We suggest collaboration to work out means of defense." There was no answer. Nor did our French and German comrades expect one. They only needed confirmation of the fact that in making its warning the GPU only wanted to ensure its alibi in advance, and not at all to prevent a terrorist act. The French and German comrades then took their own measures: the guard at Prinkipo was considerably reinforced.

Not long ago, during the Plevitskaya trial,[185] this whole

179

episode floated to the surface again. Commissioner of judicial
police Roche, according to the newspaper accounts, testified
as follows: "Turkul was once a brave general. . . . In documents there are indications that at one time he was planning
an attempt on Trotsky. . . . General Turkul was displeased
not only with Leon Trotsky. He was also dissatisfied with
General Miller."[186] Gorky and Litvinov were not mentioned
by Roche. Commissioner of judicial police Pigue testified:
"Larionov was entrusted with making an attempt on Trotsky.
But General Turkul blabbed. And there wasn't any money.
They abandoned the project. (Sounds of amazement.)" Not
a word about Gorky and Litvinov. Both the commissioners —
freemasons and "friends of the USSR" — are giving testimony
in the interests of the GPU. They are trying to draw attention
away from the Kremlin. Hence Roche's far-fetched remark
that Turkul was dissatisfied with Miller (that is, Turkul could
have kidnapped him). Hence also the remark of Pigue, thrown
out as it were in passing, that Turkul's conspiracy failed because
of his free talking (that is, Skoblin didn't take part), and for
lack of money (that is, Moscow was not financing him). It
must also be added that the French police, informed in time
about the conspiracy, did not warn Trotsky at all; they preferred to preserve a benevolent neutrality toward the GPU
and the principle of noninterference in the internal affairs of
the "brave general" Turkul.

Now, however, the real nature of these "internal affairs" have
inconveniently leaked out into the open. Skoblin was carrying
out secret work inside the White Guard military organization.
In this work he was connected with Turkul, in his capacity
as a White terrorist. Skoblin was carrying out secret work in
the service of the GPU. In this work he was connected through
Yagoda with the Kremlin.[187] Stalin knew about the attempt
being planned because . . . he prepared it himself, through
Skoblin. It was a ticklish business. At that time Stalin did not
yet have the fully finished reputation of Cain, which now ab-
solves him from the necessity of taking precautionary measures.
He still had traces of revolutionary "prejudices." He understood
that the murder of Trotsky would inevitably be ascribed to him.
And so, in *Rote Fahne* it was said straight out that it was
Turkul's intention not only to carry out the assassination
but also to "lay the blame for the murder on the Soviet government." That is why, at the same time as supporting the
"brave general" Turkul through Skoblin, Stalin prepared an

alibi for himself. That was the purpose of the warning (which in fact did not warn about anything). The mechanics of the whole business was clear to us even then. In No. 27 of the *Biulleten* (March 1932) was printed the declaration from all the sections of the International Left Opposition saying, among other things: *"Stalin is in an actual united front with General Turkul, the organizer of a terrorist act against Trotsky.* No alibi in the form of disclosures printed in a German newspaper, but concealed from the people of the USSR . . . will refute or weaken our accusation. . . ."[188]

Why did Turkul's attempt not take place? Most probably the White Guards did not want to fall under the Mausers of the Bolshevik-Leninists. In any case it was precisely from that time that Stalin came to the conclusion that it was impossible to reconcile "public opinion" to the murder of Trotsky and other Bolshevik-Leninists without the help of an elaborate fraud. He started to prepare the Moscow trials. This specimen, obtuse for all his cunning, seriously imagined that it was possible to deceive the whole world. In fact, he deceived only those to whose advantage it was to be deceived. . . . The Plevitskaya trial raised another corner of the veil over the prehistory of the Moscow trials. The coming years, or possibly even months, will bring the revelations of all the remaining mysteries. Cain-Djugashvili will stand before world public opinion and before history the way nature and the Thermidorean reaction made him. His name will become a byword for the uttermost limits of human baseness.

IGNORANCE IS NOT
A REVOLUTIONARY INSTRUMENT [189]

January 30, 1939

We published in No. 3 of our review an article by Diego Rivera that dealt with a programmatic letter written by Haya de la Torre [see p. 101]. Comrade Rivera's article, as all our readers were able to see, took under consideration extremely important problems and, moreover, was written in an extremely serene manner. However, one of the APRA journalists, a certin Guillermo Vegas Leon,[190] responded with an article that can only be described as impudent and vile. Mr. Vegas Leon, under the guise of replying to the principal questions that were presented, uses personal insinuations and believes that it is possible to attack Diego Rivera as a man and artist.

Is it necessary to defend Rivera against stupid and filthy attacks? Vegas Leon, with comical scorn in each line, calls Comrade Rivera "painter," as if this word carries in itself a frightful condemnation. Senor Vegas Leon, in order to add to the weight of his irony, the irony of an impotent philistine, should have spoken of a "great painter": if it is an evil to be a painter, it is incomparably worse to be a gifted master. Imitating Lombardo Toledano and other bourgeois "socialists," Vegas Leon accuses Rivera of selling his paintings to the bourgeoisie. But who can buy paintings in capitalist society if not the bourgeoisie? The overwhelming majority of artists, dependent upon the bourgeoisie because of social conditions, are united ideologically to the bourgeoisie. Rivera represents an exceptional case because he maintains complete moral independence from the bourgeoisie. Precisely for this reason, he has the right to be respected by every socialist worker and sincere democrat. But Vegas Leon does not fall into either one of these categories.

Vegas Leon becomes indignant because Rivera treats Haya de la Torre like a democrat. Vegas Leon sees insult and slander in this fact. Haya de la Torre "is not a democrat but a revolutionist," he exclaims. It is absolutely impossible to understand what this opposition means. On the one hand, the democrat can oppose the partisan of monarchy or fascist dictatorship; on the other hand, and in a different way, he can oppose the socialist. But to oppose the democrat to the revolutionary means almost the same thing as opposing a redhead to a lawyer. The democrat in France and the United States cannot, naturally, be a revolutionist; he is for the maintenance of the existing system; he is a conservative. But the democrat of a backward country, who finds himself under the double oppression of imperialism and police dictatorship, as is the case in Peru, cannot but be a revolutionist if he is a serious and logical democrat. This is precisely the idea that Diego Rivera develops. Diego Rivera reproaches Haya de la Torre for his position as a defender of democracy and not because he doesn't appear to be a socialist in his programmatic letter. Rivera takes this position, conditionally, and tries to demonstrate, in our opinion successfully, that Haya de la Torre appears to be an *illogical* democrat. This is what Leon should have answered.

Haya de la Torre calls the United States the "guardian of our liberty" and promises to address himself to the guardian in case of a fascist danger (Benavides is not a danger?) [191] "in search of aid." Comrade Rivera justly condemns this idealization of North American imperialism. What is Vegas Leon's answer? He replies with insults, invokes quotations from Lenin, cites other statements by de la Torre . . . and more insults. But he doesn't explain in this manner why the Aprista leader, instead of exposing the true role of that country, considered it possible on the eve of the Lima conference to present the United States—as Toledano did in *Futuro*—as a philanthropic hen who protects the Latin American chicks (including the tender little chickie Benavides) from the vulture across the ocean. Such an amendment to reality is doubly inadmissible when written by a democrat of an oppressed country.

Revolutionary Marxists can conclude practical agreements with democrats, but precisely with those who are *revolutionary,* that is to say, with those who rely on the masses and not on the protecting hen. APRA is not a socialist organization in the eyes of the Marxist because it is not a class organization of the revolutionary proletariat. APRA is an organization of bourgeois democracy in a backward, semicolonial country. Due to its social type, historical objectives, and to a considerable degree, ideology, it falls into the same class as the Russian populists (Social Revolutionaries) and the Chinese Kuomintang.[192] The Russian populists were much richer in doctrine and "socialist" phraseology than APRA. However, that did not hinder them from playing the role of petty-bourgeois democrats, even worse, *backward* petty-bourgeois democrats, who did not have the strength to carry out purely democratic tasks in spite of the spirit of sacrifice and heroism of their best combatants. The "Social Revolutionaries" issued a revolutionary agrarian program but, as is the case with petty-bourgeois parties, they were prisoners of the liberal bourgeoisie—this good hen who protects her little ones—and they betrayed the peasants at the decisive moment during the 1917 revolution. It is impossible to forget that historical example. A democrat who sows confidence in imperialist "guardians" can only bring bitter illusions to oppressed peoples.

Comrade Rivera affirms in his theses, as well as in his article, that oppressed peoples can attain their complete and definitive emancipation only by means of the revolutionary overthrow of imperialism and that this task can be achieved only by the world proletariat in alliance with the colonial peoples. Senor Vegas Leon pours out a torrent of offensive objections and a few arguments of the same character on this idea. Putting the insults to one side, we shall try to locate the basis of his argumentation. The proletariat of the imperialist countries, he says, hasn't the slightest interest in the struggle of the colonial countries, and, consequently, the latter must pursue their own course. To consider that the fate of the backward countries is dependent upon the struggle of the proletariat of the advanced countries, no matter to how small a degree, is . . . "defeatism." We will not consider the absurdity of this viewpoint: Vegas Leon gives an example to prove the validity of his ideas: Mexico expropriated the petroleum enterprises. Isn't that a step towards the emancipation of the country from its imperialist dependence? Nevertheless, that measure was taken without the least participation of the American and English proletariat. This recent example demonstrates, according to Vegas Leon, that semicolonial and colonial peoples can attain complete emancipation independently of the international proletariat's attitude.

All this reasoning reveals that the APRA publicist does not

understand the ABC of the question that is of fundamental importance for his party, i.e., the interrelation between the imperialist and the semicolonial countries. It is absolutely true that Mexico has taken a step forward towards economic emancipation by expropriating the petroleum interests. But Vegas Leon closes his eyes to the fact that Mexico as a seller of petroleum products has now fallen — and it was inevitable — under the dependence of other imperialist countries. What forms does this new dependence assume or can it assume? History has not yet spoken the final word on this subject.

On the other hand, can it be affirmed that the concrete act — the expropriation of the petroleum enterprises — is definitely assured? Unfortunately, it is impossible to say so. Military or even purely economic pressure from abroad, together with an unfavorable international relationship of forces for Mexico, that is, defeats and retreats of the world proletariat, *may* force this country to take a step backward. It would be a hollow fanfaronade to deny such a possibility. Only lamentable utopians can represent the future of Mexico, as well as any other colonial or semicolonial country, as one of a constant accumulation of reforms and conquests until complete and definite emancipation has arrived. Likewise, the Social Democrats, those classical opportunists, expected for a long time that they would succeed in transforming capitalist society by means of a continuous series of social reforms and attain the complete emancipation of the entire proletariat. In reality, the road of social reforms was only possible up to a certain point, when the dominant classes, frightened by the danger, launched a counteroffensive. The struggle can only be decided by revolution or counterrevolution. The accumulation of democratic reforms in a number of countries has not led to socialism but to fascism, which has liquidated all the social and political conquests of the past. The same dialectic law is applicable to the liberation struggle of oppressed peoples. Definite conquests that will aid the struggle for their further independence can be gained in a relatively peaceful manner under certain favorable conditions. But this by no means signifies that similar partial conquests will continue without interruption, until complete independence is achieved. After granting a number of secondary concessions in India, British imperialism is determined not only to put a final end to reforms but to turn the wheel back. India can only be liberated by the joint and

open revolutionary struggle of the workers, peasants, and
the English proletariat.

This is one of the question's aspects. But there is also another. Why has the Mexican government successfully carried
out the expropriation, at least for the time being? Thanks,
above all, to the antagonism between the United States and
England. There was no fear of an active, immediate intervention upon the part of England. But this is a small matter.
The Mexican government also considered unlikely military
intervention by its northern neighbor when expropriation was
decreed. On what basis did those calculations rest? On the
present orientation of the White House: the "New Deal" in national affairs was accompanied by the "Good Neighbor" policy
in foreign relations.[193]

Vegas Leon evidently does not understand that the present
policy of the White House is determined by the profound crisis of North American capitalism and the *growth of radical
tendencies in the working class*. These new tendencies have
found their clearest expression until now in the form of the
CIO.[194] Senor Vegas Leon complains that the CIO does not
interest itself in the fate of Peru. This probably means that
the CIO treasury has refused to finance APRA. On our part,
we are not in the least inclined to close our eyes to the fact
that the political consciousness of the CIO leaders is not superior to that of the left wing of Roosevelt's conservative party and, one can add, it falls below that miserable level in
certain respects. Nevertheless, the existence of the CIO reflects
an enormous leap in the thoughts and sentiments of the North
American workers.

The influential section of the bourgeoisie whose representative
is Roosevelt says (or said yesterday): "It is impossible to
govern by the old methods; it is necessary to achieve an agreement; it is necessary to grant partial concessions in order
to safeguard that which is fundamental, i.e., private ownership of the means of production." This precisely is the meaning of the New Deal. Roosevelt extends the same policy to
international relations, above all, to Latin America: to give
in where secondary questions are involved in order not to
lose on the important ones.

Precisely, this international political relationship has made
possible the expropriation of petroleum in Mexico without military intervention or an economic blockade. In other words, a
peaceful step on the road to economic emancipation was

possible thanks to a more active and aggressive policy on the part of large layers of the North American proletariat. As one can see, the issue is not whether Lewis and Co. "sympathize" or "do not sympathize" with the APRA or the Peruvian people. Those gentlemen do not see beyond the tip of their noses and don't sympathize with anyone except themselves.

Furthermore, the extent to which the American workers today understand their struggle for emancipation to be tied up with the struggle of the oppressed peoples is not the issue involved. Although the situation when viewed from this angle may be very lamentable, it remains an indisputable and, moreover, extremely important fact that the intensification of the class struggle in the United States has extraordinarily facilitated the expropriation of the petroleum enterprises by the Mexican government. Mr. Vegas Leon, as a typical petty bourgeois, cannot understand in the least this internal logic of the class struggle, this interrelation of internal and external factors.

It would be radically erroneous to draw the conclusion from what has been said that the policy of the United States will continue to unfold in the same direction in the future without interruption, thus opening ever greater possibilities for peaceful emancipation to the Latin American people. On the contrary, it can be predicted with full certainty that the "New Deal" and "Good Neighbor" policy, which didn't solve any question or satisfy anyone, will only arouse the needs and aggressive spirit of the North American proletariat and Latin American peoples. The intensification of the class struggle engendered the "New Deal"; a further intensification of the class struggle will kill the "New Deal," giving rise and preponderance within the ranks of the bourgeoisie to the most reactionary, aggressive, and fascist tendencies. The "Good Neighbor" policy will inevitably be replaced, and probably in the very near future, by the policy of the "threatening fist" which might be raised first of all against Mexico. Only the blind or petty-bourgeois phraseologists of the Lombardo Toledano or Vegas Leon type can close their eyes to those perspectives. A year sooner or later, the question will be presented in a very acute form: Who is master on this continent? The imperialists of the United States or the working masses who people all the nations of America?

This question, by its very essence, can only be resolved by an open conflict of forces, that is to say by revolution, or more exactly, a series of revolutions. In those struggles against imperialism will participate, on the one hand, the American proletariat, in the interests of its own defense; and on the other hand, the Latin American peoples, who are struggling for their emancipation, and who *precisely for that reason* will support the struggle of the American proletariat.

It can be clearly deduced from what has been said that we far from recommend to the Latin American people that they passively await the revolution in the United States or that the North American workers fold their arms until the Latin American peoples' moment of victory arrives. He who waits passively gets nothing. It is necessary to continue the struggle without interruption, to extend and deepen it, in harmony with the actually existing historical conditions. But at the same time, one must comprehend the reciprocal relation between the two principal currents of the contemporary struggle against imperialism. By merging at a certain stage, definite triumph can be assured.

Naturally, this doesn't mean to say that Lewis and Green will become outstanding advocates of the Socialist Federation of the American continent.195 No, they will remain in the camp of imperialism until the very end. It also will not mean that the *whole* proletariat will learn to see that in the liberation of the Latin American peoples lies its own emancipation. Nor will the entire Latin American people comprehend that a community of interests exists between them and the American working class. But the very fact that a parallel struggle goes on will signify that an objective alliance exists between them; perhaps not a formal alliance, but, indeed, a very active one. The sooner the American proletarian *vanguard* in North, Central, and South America understands the necessity for a closer revolutionary collaboration in the struggle against the common enemy, the more tangible and fruitful that alliance will be. To clarify, illustrate, and organize that struggle — herein lies one of the most important tasks of the Fourth International.

*   *   *

The example developed by us demonstrates sufficiently Mr. Vegas Leon's general theoretical and political level. Is it worth the trouble after this to tarry over all his assertions? We will only consider two of the most important.

Leon attributes to us the idea that the USSR is an imperialist country. Naturally, nothing resembling it is found in

Rivera's article. We only said that the Soviet bureaucracy, in the struggle to maintain power, has transformed itself during the last few years into an agent of "democratic" imperialism. In order to gain the sympathies of the latter, it is willing to perpetrate every sort of betrayal at the expense of the working class and oppressed peoples. The attitude of the Stalinists at the pacifist congress in Mexico (September 1938) revealed completely their betrayal of the colonial and semicolonial peoples. Precisely for that reason, the *left* Apristas were in sharp opposition to the Stalinist majority at the congress. Is Vegas Leon in agreement with this or not? When this gentleman, assuming an air of importance, declares (differently than us?) that he is not an "enemy of the USSR," we can only shrug our shoulders with contempt. What does the USSR mean to Vegas Leon? A geographical notion or a social phenomenon? If he takes "Soviet" society under consideration, he must understand that that society is completely contradictory. It is impossible to be a friend of the *people* of the USSR without being an enemy of the "Soviet" *bureaucracy*. All the pseudo-"friends" of the Kremlin, as L.D. Trotsky has demonstrated more than once, are *perfidious enemies of the struggle for emancipation carried on by the workers and peasants of Soviet Russia.*

Vegas Leon evidently accuses us of "dividing the forces of republican Spain" in its struggle against fascism. Once again he reveals by this his reactionary stupidity. Revolutionary Marxists have demonstrated since the very beginning of the Spanish revolution, and above all, after the start of the open Civil War, that victory is only possible with a socialist program: give land immediately to the peasants, expropriate the banks and trusts, allow the workers to emancipate themselves from capitalist exploitation. The Spanish revolution would have been invincible with these conditions. But the lawyers and lackeys of the landed proprietors, bankers, capitalists, and clergy answered: "No, you are destroying unity!" Every revolutionary movement of the workers and peasants was implacably smashed in the name of "unity" of the exploited with the exploiters. All true revolutionary socialists and anarchists were victims of slander, prison, extermination. Moreover, the principal part was played by the Stalinist GPU. "No, you are destroying unity"—between the victims and the hangmen! We now see the results of that treacherous policy. The deceived workers and peasants have turned their backs upon the republicans and have fallen into despair, apathy, and in-

difference. *This is exactly what has assured victory to Franco.*
Those who now repeat after the fall of Barcelona that the
"Trotskyists" preach division of Republican Spain, demonstrate
by this alone that they are agents of the Spanish landed proprietors, bankers, capitalists, and clergy. This alone is enough
to force us to say openly to the Peruvian workers: Do not
believe individuals of Vegas Leon's type; they are conservative
petty bourgeois who do not understand the logic of the class
struggle, and consequently are absolutely incapable of leading
you in your struggle for national and social emancipation; they
can bring you nothing but defeats!

We believe that enough has been said. Vegas Leon's insults and insinuations are not arguments. Shamelessness does
not excuse ignorance. And ignorance is not an instrument
of the revolution.

FOR GRYNSZPAN[196]

Against Fascist Pogrom Gangs and Stalinist Scoundrels

February 1939

It is clear to anyone even slightly acquainted with political history that the policy of the fascist gangsters directly and sometimes deliberately provokes terrorist acts. What is most astonishing is that so far there has been only one Grynszpan. Undoubtedly the number of such acts will increase.

We Marxists consider the tactic of individual terror inexpedient in the tasks of the liberating struggle of the proletariat as well as oppressed nationalities. A single isolated hero cannot replace the masses. But we understand only too clearly the inevitability of such convulsive acts of despair and vengeance. All our emotions, all our sympathies are with the self-sacrificing avengers even though they have been unable to discover the correct road. Our sympathy becomes intensified because Grynszpan is not a political militant but an inexperienced youth, almost a boy, whose only counselor was a feeling of indignation. To tear Grynszpan out of the hands of capitalist justice, which is capable of chopping off his head to further serve capitalist diplomacy, is the elementary, immediate task of the international working class!

All the more revolting in its police stupidity and inexpressible violence is the campaign now being conducted against Grynszpan by command of the Kremlin in the international Stalinist press. They attempt to depict him as an agent of the Nazis or an agent of Trotskyists in alliance with the Nazis. Lumping into one heap the provocateur and his victim, the Stalinists ascribe to Grynszpan the intention of creating a favorable pretext for Hitler's pogrom measures. What can one say of these venal "journalists" who no longer have any vestiges of shame? Since the beginning of the socialist movement the bourgeoisie has at all times attributed all violent demonstrations of indignation, particularly terrorist acts, to the degenerating influence of Marxism. The Stalinists have inherited, here as elsewhere, the filthiest tradition of reaction. The Fourth International may, justifiably, be proud that the reactionary scum, including the Stalinists, now automatically links with the Fourth International every bold action and protest, every indignant outburst, every blow at the executioners.

It was so, similarly, with the International of Marx in its time. We are bound, naturally, by ties of open moral solidarity to Grynszpan and not to his "democratic" jailers, or the Stalinist slanderers, who need Grynszpan's corpse to prop up, even if only partially and indirectly, the verdicts of Moscow justice. Kremlin diplomacy, degenerated to its marrow, attempts at the same time to utilize this "happy" incident to renew their machinations for an international agreement among various governments, including that of Hitler and Mussolini, for a mutual extradition of terrorists. Beware, masters of fraud! The application of such a law will necessitate the immediate deliverance of Stalin to at least a dozen foreign governments.

The Stalinists shriek in the ears of the police that Grynszpan attended "meetings of Trotskyites." That, unfortunately, is not true. For had he walked into the milieu of the Fourth International he would have discovered a different and more effective outlet for his revolutionary energy. People come cheap who are capable only of fulminating against injustice and bestiality. But those who, like Grynszpan, are able to act as well as conceive, sacrificing their own lives if need be, are the precious leaven of mankind.

In the moral sense, although not for his mode of action, Grynszpan may serve as an example for every young revolutionist. Our open moral solidarity with Grynszpan gives us an added right to say to all the other would-be Grynszpans, to all those capable of self-sacrifice in the struggle against despotism and bestiality: *Seek another road!* Not the lone avenger but only a great revolutionary mass movement can free the oppressed, a movement that will leave no remnant of the entire structure of class exploitation, national oppression, and racial persecution. The unprecedented crimes of fascism create a yearning for vengeance that is wholly justifiable. But so monstrous is the scope of their crimes, that this yearning cannot be satisfied by the assassination of isolated fascist bureaucrats. For that it is necessary to set in motion millions, tens and hundreds of millions of the oppressed throughout the whole world and lead them in the assault upon the strongholds of the old society. Only the overthrow of all forms of slavery, only the complete destruction of fascism, only the people sitting in merciless judgment over the contemporary bandits and gangsters can provide real satisfaction to the indignation of the people. This is precisely the task that the Fourth International has set itself. It will cleanse the labor movement of the plague of Stalinism. It will rally in its ranks the heroic generation of the youth. It will cut a path to a worthier and a more humane future.

INTELLECTUAL EX-RADICALS
AND WORLD REACTION[197]

February 17, 1939

During the last decade the older generation of the radical intelligentsia has been greatly influenced by Stalinism. Today the turn away from Stalinism in the advanced countries, at any rate, has been reaching ever wider proportions. Some are sincerely disappointed in their illusions while others are simply aware that the ship is in dangerous straits and are in a hurry to leave it. It would be naive to expect that the "disillusioned" should turn to Marxism with which, in the nature of things, they were never acquainted. For most intellectuals their departure from Stalinism signifies a complete break with the revolution and a passive reconciliation with nationalistic democracy. These "disillusioned" provide a unique culture medium for the bacilli of skepticism and pessimism.

They say: "It is impossible to do anything at the present time. Europe will fall wholly under the sway of fascism anyway, and the bourgeoisie in the United States is far too powerful. The revolutionary roads lead nowhere. We must adapt ourselves to the democratic regime; we must defend it against all attacks. There is no future for the Fourth International, at all events, not for the next two or three decades . . ." and so forth and so on.

The ranks of the disillusioned include not only Stalinists but also the temporary fellow-travelers of Bolshevism. Victor Serge — to cite an instance — has recently announced that Bolshevism is passing through a crisis that presages in turn the "crisis of Marxism." In his theoretical innocence, Serge imagines himself the first to have made this discovery. Yet, in every epoch of reaction, scores and hundreds of unstable revolutionists have risen to announce the "crisis of Marxism" — the final, the crucial, the mortal crisis.

That the old Bolshevik Party has spent itself, has degenerated and perished — that much is beyond controversy. But the ruin of a given historical party, which had for a certain period based itself upon the Marxian doctrine, does not at all signify the ruination of that doctrine. The defeat of an army does not invalidate the fundamental precepts of strategy. Should an artilleryman fire wide of the mark, that would by no means invalidate ballistics, that is, the algebra of artillery. If the army of the proletariat suffers a defeat, or if its party degenerates, then this does not at all invalidate Marxism, which is the algebra of revolution. That Victor Serge himself is passing through a "crisis," i. e., has become hopelessly confused like thousands of other intellectuals — is clear enough. But Victor Serge in crisis is not the crisis of Marxism.

In any case, no serious revolutionist would think of using intellectuals in confusion, Stalinists in disillusion, and skeptics in dejection as a yardstick with which to measure the march of history. World reaction has unquestionably assumed monstrous proportions nowadays. But thereby it has prepared the soil for the greatest revolutionary crisis. Fascism may perhaps seize upon the whole of Europe. But it will be unable to maintain itself there not only for a "thousand years," as Hitler dreams, but even for a decade. The fascistization of Europe means the monstrous aggravation of class and international contradictions.

It is absurd, unscientific, unhistorical to think that reaction will continue to unfold at the same gradual pace at which it has been accumulating hitherto. Reaction signifies this, that the social contradictions are mechanically suppressed. At a certain stage, an explosion is inevitable. World reaction will be overthrown by the greatest catastrophe in world history, or, more correctly, by a series of revolutionary catastrophes. The coming war, which is now being awaited by everyone within the nearest future, will signify the crash of all illusions. Not only the illusions of reformism, pacifism, and democratism but also the illusions of fascism. Only one beacon will rise above the blood-drenched chaos — the beacon of Marxism.

Hegel was fond of saying: all that is rational is real. [198] This means: every idea that corresponds to objective needs of development attains triumph and victory. No intellectually honest individual can deny that the analysis and prognosis made by the Bolshevik-Leninists (Fourth Internationalists) during the past fifteen years have met and still meet with confirmation in the events of our time. It is precisely in this certainty of their correctness that the basic sections of the Fourth International are strong and immutable. The catastrophes of European and world capitalism which are hovering over mankind will clear the path before the steeled cadres of the revolutionary Marxists.

Let the disillusioned ones bury their own dead. The working class is not a corpse. As hitherto, society rests upon it. It needs a new leadership. It will find this nowhere but in the Fourth International. All that is rational is real. Social Democracy and Stalinocracy even today represent stupendous fictions. But the Fourth International is an impregnable reality.

KRUPSKAYA'S DEATH[199]

March 4, 1939

In addition to being Lenin's wife — which, by the way, was not accidental — Krupskaya was an outstanding personality in her devotion to the cause, her energy, and her purity of character. She was unquestionably a woman of intelligence. It is not astonishing, however, that while remaining side by side with Lenin, her political thinking did not receive an independent development. On far too many occasions, she had had the opportunity to convince herself of his correctness, and she became accustomed to trust her great companion and leader. After Lenin's death Krupskaya's life took an extremely tragic turn. It was as if she were paying for the happiness that had fallen to her lot.

Lenin's illness and death — and this again was not accidental — coincided with the breaking point of the revolution, and the beginning of Thermidor. Krupskaya became confused. Her revolutionary instinct came into conflict with her spirit of discipline. She made an attempt to oppose the Stalinist clique, and in 1926 found herself for a brief interval in the ranks of the Opposition. Frightened by the prospect of split, she broke away. Having lost confidence in herself, she completely lost her bearings, and the ruling clique did everything in their power to break her morally. On the surface she was treated with respect, or rather with semihonors. But within the apparatus itself she was systematically discredited, blackened, and subjected to indignities, while in the ranks of the Young Communists the most absurd and gross scandal was being spread about her.

Stalin always lived in fear of a protest on her part. She knew far too much. She knew the history of the party. She knew the place that Stalin occupied in this history. All of the latter-day historiography which assigned to Stalin a place alongside of Lenin could not but appear revolting and insulting to her. Stalin feared Krupskaya just as he feared Gorky.

Krupskaya was surrounded by an iron ring of the GPU. Her old friends disappeared one by one; those who delayed in dying were murdered either openly or secretly. Every step she took was supervised. Her articles appeared in the press only after interminable, insufferable, and degrading negotiations between the censors and the author. She was forced to adopt emendations in her text, either to exalt Stalin or to rehabilitate the GPU. It is obvious that a whole number of the vilest insertions of this type were made against Krupskaya's will, and even without her knowledge. What recourse was there for the unfortunate crushed woman? Completely isolated, a heavy stone weighing upon her heart, uncertain what to do, in the toils of sickness, she dragged on her burdensome existence.

To all appearances, Stalin has lost the inclination to stage sensational trials, which have already succeeded in exposing him before the whole world as the dirtiest, the most criminal, and most repulsive figure in history. Nevertheless, it is by no means excluded that some sort of new trial will be staged, wherein new defendants will relate how Kremlin physicians under the leadership of Yagoda and Beria[200] took measures to expedite Krupskaya's demise. . . . But with or without the aid of physicians, the regime that Stalin had created for her undoubtedly cut short her life.

Nothing can be further from our mind than to blame Nadezhda Konstantinovna for not having been resolute enough to break openly with the bureaucracy. Political minds far more independent than hers vacillated, tried to play hide and seek with history — and perished. Krupskaya was to the highest degree endowed with a feeling of responsibility. Personally she was courageous enough. What she lacked was mental courage. With profound sorrow we bid farewell to the loyal companion of Lenin, to an irreproachable revolutionist and one of the most tragic figures in revolutionary history.

THE BETRAYERS OF INDIA[201]

March 4, 1939

In this issue we are printing an article by Stanley[202] on the political situation in India. The article very cogently lays bare the oppressive policy that British "democracy" pursues in order to bar democracy in India. The population of England is 40 million; the population of India 370 million. In order to maintain democracy in an imperialist nation of 40 million, a nation of 370 million must be stifled. Such is the essence of imperialist democracy.

Only a victorious revolution can liberate India. The Indian bourgeoisie, closely tied to British capital, fears revolution. The Indian bourgeois intelligentsia fears its own bourgeoisie. Instead of preparing for a popular revolution, these gentlemen constantly advocate the same old "Popular Front," i.e., a union of the frightened liberals with the frightened democrats of various hues. In this work, the Stalinists, of course, are in the forefront. In order to put a brake on the revolutionary movement of the masses against the direct and immediate enemy — *British imperialism* — these gentlemen conduct agitation against — the danger from Japan. With such methods they hope to win the sympathy of the British slaveholders for democracy in India, and at the same time for — Stalin, who is dreaming of an alliance with the British bourgeoisie. The colonial peoples are small change in the Bonapartist oligarchy's reckonings with the imperialist democracies.

WHAT LIES BEHIND STALIN BID FOR AGREEMENT WITH HITLER?[203]

March 6, 1939

In recent months, the newspapers have printed a good deal concerning secret negotiations between Berlin and Moscow. It has been rumored that a political and even a military agreement in the guise of an economic treaty is in preparation. It is difficult to judge as yet just what is correct in these communications. At all events, there are quite unmistakable symptoms that testify to the fact that some sort of negotiations have been and are going on. In any case, the outcome of these secret negotiations, at the present stage, depends not upon Stalin's loyalty to the principles of democracy or upon Hitler's fealty to the banner of "anti-Marxism" but rather upon the international conjuncture. An agreement between Stalin and Hitler, if attained — and there is nothing impossible in that — could astonish only the most hopeless simpletons from among all the varieties of democratic "fronts" and pacifist "leagues."

We shall not dwell here on the question of how probable is an agreement between Stalin and Hitler, or, to put it more correctly, between Hitler and Stalin in the *immediate* future. This question would require a detailed analysis of the international situation in all its possible variants. But even if this were done, the answer would still have to be rigidly qualified, inasmuch as the players themselves could hardly state today with complete certainty just where the play will lead them. But even before the rapprochement between Moscow and Berlin has been factually attained, it has become a factor in international politics, for all the diplomatic centers of Europe and the world are now taking this *possibility* into account. Let us, too, briefly consider this possibility.

An agreement with an imperialist nation — regardless of whether it is fascist or democratic — is an agreement with slave-owners and exploiters. A temporary agreement of such a nature may, of course, be rendered compulsory by circumstances. It is impossible to state once and for all time that agreements with imperialists are impermissible under any and all conditions, just as it is impossible to tell a trade union that it has no right under any conditions to conclude a compromise with the boss. "Irreconcilability" of such a nature would be sheerly verbal.

So long as the workers' state remains isolated, episodic agreements with the imperialists to one extent or another are inevitable. But we must clearly understand that the question reduces itself to profiting from the antagonisms between two gangs of imperialist powers, and nothing more. There cannot even be talk of disguising such agreements by means of common idealistic slogans, for example, the common "defense of democracy"—slogans which involve nothing but the most infamous deceit of the workers. It is essential that the workers in capitalist countries not be bound in their class struggle against their own bourgeoisie by the empiric agreements entered into by the workers' state. This fundamental rule was rigorously observed during the first period of the existence of the Soviet Republic.

However, the question of whether agreements between a workers' state and an imperialist state, including a fascist one, are in general permissible, and if so, just under what conditions—this question, in its abstract form, has lost all meaning today. In question is not a workers' state, in general, but a degenerated and putrefying workers' state. The nature of an agreement, its aims and its limits, depend directly upon those who conclude such an agreement. Lenin's government might have been compelled in Brest-Litovsk.204 to conclude a temporary agreement with Hohenzollern—in order to save the revolution. Stalin's government is capable of entering into agreements only in the interests of the ruling Kremlin clique and only to the detriment of the interests of the international working class.

The agreements between the Kremlin and the "democracies" meant for the respective sections of the Communist International the renunciation of the class struggle, the strangulation of revolutionary organizations, the support of social patriotism, and in consequence the destruction of the Spanish revolution and sabotage of the class struggle of the French proletariat.

The agreement with Chiang Kai-shek signified the immediate liquidation of the revolutionary peasant movement, the renunciation by the Communist Party of its last vestiges of independence and the official replacement of Marxism by Sun Yat-senism.[205] The semi-agreement with Poland signified the destruction of the Polish Communist Party and the annihilation of its leadership.[206] Every agreement of the Kremlin clique with a foreign bourgeoisie is immediately directed against the proletariat of that country with which the agreement is made, as well as against the proletariat of the USSR. The Bonapartist gang in the Kremlin cannot survive except by weakening, demoralizing, and crushing the proletariat everywhere within its reach.

In Great Britain the Comintern is nowadays conducting agitation in favor of creating a "People's Front" with the participation of the liberals. At first glance such a policy appears to be absolutely incomprehensible. The Labour Party represents a mighty organization. One could easily understand an urge on the part of the social patriotic Comintern to draw closer to it. But the liberals represent an utterly compromised and politically second-rate force. Moreover they are split into several groups. In the struggle to maintain their influence the Labourites naturally reject any idea of a bloc with the liberals, so as not to infect themselves with a gangrenous poison. They are defending themselves rather energetically—by means of expulsions—against the idea of a "People's Front."

Why then doesn't the Comintern confine itself to fighting for a collaboration with the Labourites? Why does it instead invariably demand the inclusion of the liberal shadows of the past into the united front? The crux of the matter lies in this, that the policy of the Labour Party is far too radical for the Kremlin. An alliance between the Communists and the Labourites might assume some shade of anti-imperialism and would thereby render more difficult a rapprochement between Moscow and London. The presence of liberals in the "People's Front" signifies a direct and an immediate censorship exercised by imperialism over the actions of the Labour Party. Under the cover of such a censorship Stalin would be able to render all the necessary services to British imperialism.

The fundamental trait of Stalin's international policy in recent years has been this: that he *trades* in the working class movement just as he trades in oil, manganese, and other goods. In this statement there is not an iota of exaggeration. Stalin looks upon the sections of the Comintern in various countries and upon the liberation struggle of the oppressed nations as so much small change in deals with imperialist powers.

When he requires the aid of France, he subjects the French proletariat to the Radical bourgeoisie.[207] When he has to support China against Japan, he subjects the Chinese proletariat to the Kuomintang. What would he do in the event of an agreement with Hitler? Hitler, to be sure, does not particularly require Stalin's assistance to strangle the German Communist Party. The insignificant state in which the latter finds itself has moreover been assured by its entire preceding policy. But it is very likely that Stalin would agree to cut off all subsidies for illegal work in Germany. This is one of the most minor concessions that he would have to make and he would be quite willing to make it.

One should also assume that the noisy, hysterical, and hollow campaign against fascism that the Comintern has been conducting for the last few years will be slyly squelched. It is noteworthy that on February 20, when our American section mobilized considerable masses of workers to fight against the American Nazis,[208] the Stalinists refused pointblank to participate in the counterdemonstration, which had nationwide repercussions, and did everything in their power to minimize its importance, thereby giving aid to the American followers of Hitler. What is there behind this truly treacherous policy? Is it only conservative stupidity and hatred of the Fourth International? Or is there also something new: for example, the latest instruction from Moscow — recommending to Messrs. "Antifascists" that they muzzle themselves so as not to interfere with the negotiations between Moscow and Berlin diplomats? This supposition is by no means far-fetched. The next few weeks will bring their verification.

We can state one thing with certainty. The agreement between Stalin and Hitler would essentially alter nothing in the counterrevolutionary function of the Kremlin oligarchy. It would only serve to lay bare this function, make it stand out more glaringly and hasten the collapse of illusions and falsifications. Our political task does not consist in "saving" Stalin from the embraces of Hitler but in overthrowing both of them.

ONCE AGAIN
ON THE "CRISIS OF MARXISM"[209]

March 7, 1939

In the good old days, when people referred to the crisis of Marxism they had in mind some specific proposition of Marx which had allegedly failed to withstand the test of facts: namely, the theory of the sharpening of the class struggle; the so-called "theory of impoverishment," and the so-called theory of "catastrophic collapse" of capitalism. These three principal points served as the target for bourgeois and reformist criticism. Today it is simply impossible to engage in a controversy over these issues. Who will undertake to prove that social contradictions are not sharpening but rather softening? In the United States, Mr. Ickes, the secretary of the interior, and other high dignitaries are compelled to speak openly in their speeches about the fact that "sixty families" control the economic life of the nation;[210] on the other hand, the number of unemployed oscillates between ten millions in years of "prosperity" and twenty millions in years of crisis. Those lines in *Capital* in which Marx speaks of the polarization of capitalist society, the accumulation of wealth at one pole and of poverty at the other—these lines, which have been indicted as "demogogic," now simply prove to be a picture of reality.

The old liberal democratic conception of a gradual and universal rise of prosperity, culture, peace, and liberty has suffered decisive and irreparable shipwreck. In its wake, there has been bankrupted the social reformist conception, which represented in essence only an adaptation of the ideas of liberalism to the existing working class conditions. All these theories and methods had their roots in the epoch of industrial capitalism, the epoch of free trade and competition, that is to say, in the past beyond recall, a time when capitalism was still a relatively progressive system. Capitalism today is reactionary. It cannot be cured. It must be removed.

There is hardly a blockhead remaining who seriously believes—all the Blums do not believe,[211] they lie—that the monstrous sharpening of social contradictions can be overcome by means of parliamentary legislation. Marx has been proved correct in every — yes, every — element of his analysis, as well as in his "catastrophic" prognosis. In what then consists the "crisis" of Marxism? Present-day critics do not even bother to frame articulately the question itself.

It will be recorded in the annals of history that capitalism, before sinking into the grave, made a tremendous effort at self-preservation over a protracted historical period. The bourgeoisie does not want to die. It has transformed all the energy inherited by it from the past into a violent convulsion of reaction. This is precisely the period in which we are living.

Force not only conquers but, in its own way, it "convinces." The onset of reaction not only wrecks parties physically, but also decomposes people morally. Many Radical gentlemen have their hearts in their shoes. Their fright in the face of reaction they translate into the language of immaterial and universal criticism. "Something must be wrong with old theories and methods!" "Marx was mistaken. . . ." "Lenin failed to foresee. . . ." Some even go further. "The revolutionary method has proved itself bankrupt." "The October Revolution has led to the most vicious dictatorship of the bureaucracy." But the Great French Revolution also terminated with the restoration of the monarchy. Generally speaking, the universe is poorly built: youth leads to age, birth to death; "all things that are born must perish."

These gentlemen forget with remarkable ease that man has been cutting his path from a semi-simian condition to a harmonious society without any guide; that the task is a difficult one; that for every step or two forward there follows half a step, a step, and sometimes even two steps back. They forget that the path is strewn with the greatest obstacles and that no one has invented or could have invented a secret method whereby an uninterrupted rise on the escalator of history would be rendered secure. Sad to say, Messrs. Rationalists were not invited to a consultation when man was in process of creation and when the conditions of man's development were first taking shape. But generally speaking, this matter is beyond repair. . . .

For argument's sake, let us grant that all previous revolutionary history and, if you please, all history in general is nothing but a chain of mistakes. But what to do about present-day reality? What about the colossal army of permanently unemployed, the pauperized farmers, the general decline of economic levels, the approaching war? The skeptical wiseacres promise us that sometime in the future they will catalogue all the banana peels on which the great revolutionary movements of the past have slipped. But will these gentlemen tell us what to do today, right now?

We would wait in vain for an answer. The terrified rationalists are disarming themselves in the face of reaction, renouncing scientific social thought, surrendering not only material but also moral positions, and depriving themselves of any claim to revolutionary vengeance in the future. Yet the conditions which have prepared the present wave of reaction are extremely unstable, contradictory, and ephemeral, and they prepare the ground for a new offensive by the proletariat. The leadership of this offensive will justly belong to those whom the rationalists call dogmatists and sectarians. Because "dogmatists" and "sectarians" refuse to renounce the scientific method so long as nobody, absolutely nobody, has proposed anything superior in its place.

A STEP TOWARD SOCIAL PATRIOTISM[212]

On the Position of the Fourth International Against War and Fascism

March 7, 1939

Our Palestinian friends have made an obvious and extremely dangerous concession to the social patriots, even though their point of departure is opposed to that of social patriotism. We shall indicate only those points which are in our opinion the most erroneous in the document "Isn't It a Mistake?"

We maintain that in the quarter of a century that has elapsed since the outbreak of the last war, imperialism has come to rule even more despotically over the world; its hand weighs more heavily on events during peacetime as well as wartime; and finally, under all of its political masks it has assumed an even more reactionary character. In consequence, all the fundamental rules of proletarian "defeatist" policy in relation to imperialist war retain their full force today. This is our point of departure, and all the conclusions that follow are determined by it.

As regards this point of departure, the authors of the document hold a different position. They differentiate qualitatively between the coming war and the last war and, what is more, in two respects. In the last war only imperialist countries presumably participated: the role of Serbia, they say, was far too insignificant to place its stamp on the war (they forget about the colonies and China). In the coming war, they write, one of the participants will certainly be the USSR, a far more sizable factor than Serbia. On reading these lines, the reader tends to conclude that the subsequent reasoning of the authors of the letter will revolve precisely around the participation of the USSR in the war. But the authors drop this idea very quickly, or to put it more correctly, it is relegated to the background by another, namely, the world menace of fascism. Monarchist reaction in the last war, they state, was not of an aggressive

207

historical character, it was rather a vestige, whereas fascism nowadays represents a direct and immediate threat to the whole civilized world. The struggle is therefore the task of the international proletariat as a whole in peacetime as well as wartime. It is only natural if we become suspiciously wary: such a narrowing down of revolutionary tasks — replacing imperialism by one of its political masks, that of fascism — is a patent concession to the Comintern, a patent indulgence of social patriots of the "democratic" countries.

Let us first of all establish that the two new historical factors which presumably dictate a change in policy during wartime — namely, the USSR and fascism — need not necessarily operate in one and the same direction. The possibility is not at all excluded that Stalin and Hitler, or Stalin and Mussolini, may be found in one and the same camp during a war, or at all events, that Stalin may buy a brief, unstable neutrality at the price of an agreement with the fascist governments, or one of them. For some unknown reason, this variant drops out completely from the field of vision of our authors. Yet they state justly that our principled position must arm us for any possible variant.

However, as we have already stated, the question of the USSR does not play any real role in the entire trend of reasoning of our Palestinian comrades. They focus their attention on *fascism,* as the immediate threat to the world working class and the oppressed nationalities. They hold that a "defeatist" policy is not applicable in those countries which may be at war with fascist countries. Again, such reasoning oversimplifies the problem, for it depicts the case as if the fascist countries will necessarily be found on one side of the trenches while the democratic or semidemocratic are on the other. In point of fact, there is absolutely no guarantee for this "convenient" grouping. Italy and Germany may, in the coming war as in the last, be found in opposing camps. This is by no means excluded. What are we to do in that case? Indeed, it is becoming increasingly difficult to classify countries in accordance with purely political features: Where would we assign Poland, Rumania, present-day Czechoslovakia, and a number of other second-rate and third-rate powers?

The main tendency of the authors of this document is apparently the following: to hold that "defeatism" is obligatory for the leading fascist countries (Germany, Italy), whereas it is necessary to renounce defeatism in countries which are even of doubtful democratic virtue, but which are at war with the leading fascist countries. That is approximately how the main idea of the document may be worded. In this form, too, it remains false, and an obvious lapse into social patriotism.

Let us recall that all the leaders of the German Social Democracy in emigration are "defeatists" in their own fashion. Hitler has deprived them of their sources of influence and income. The progressive nature of this "democratic," "antifascist" defeatism is exactly zero. It is bound up not with revolutionary struggle but with pinning hopes on the "liberating" role of French or some other imperialism. The authors of the document, obviously against their own will, have taken, alas, a step in this very direction.

In the first place, they have, in our opinion, given far too nebulous, and especially far too equivocal a definition of "defeatism" as of some special and independent system of actions aimed to bring about defeat. That is not so. Defeatism is the class policy of the proletariat, which even during a war sees the main enemy at home, within its particular imperialist country. Patriotism, on the other hand, is a policy that locates the main enemy outside one's own country. The idea of defeatism signifies in reality the following: conducting an irreconcilable revolutionary struggle against one's own bourgeoisie as the main enemy, without being deterred by the fact that this struggle may result in the defeat of one's own government; *given a revolutionary movement* the defeat of one's own government is a *lesser evil.* Lenin did not say, nor did he wish to say, anything else. There cannot even be talk of any other kind of "aid" to defeat. Should revolutionary defeatism be renounced in relation to nonfascist countries? Herein is the crux of the question; upon this issue, revolutionary internationalism stands or falls.

For instance, should the 360,000,000 Indians renounce any attempt to utilize the war for their own liberation? The uprising of Indians in the midst of a war would undoubtedly aid strongly in the defeat of Great Britain. Furthermore, in the event of an Indian uprising (despite all "theses") should the British workers support them? Or, on the contrary, are they duty-bound to pacify the Indians, and lull them to sleep — for the sake of a victorious struggle of British imperialism "against fascism"? Which way for us?

"Victory over Germany or Italy is at present (on the morrow the case may be different) tantamount to the downfall of fascism." Our attention is first of all struck by the qualifica-

tion "at present (on the morrow the case may be different)."
The authors do not elucidate just what they mean to say by
this. But they do in any case indicate that—even from their
own viewpoint—their position is episodic, unstable, and uncertain in character; it may already prove useless on the "morrow." They do not take sufficiently into account the fact that
in the epoch of decaying capitalism shifts and semishifts of political regimes occur quite suddenly and frequently without
altering the social foundation, without checking capitalist decline. On which of these two processes must our policy be
based in such a fundamental question as war: on the shifts
of political regimes, or on the social foundation of imperialism common to all political regimes and unfailingly uniting
them against the revolutionary proletariat? The fundamental
strategic question is our attitude toward war, which it is impermissible to subordinate to episodic tactical considerations
and speculations.

But even from the purely episodic standpoint, the above-
cited idea of the document is incorrect. A victory over the
armies of Hitler and Mussolini implies in itself only the military defeat of Germany and Italy, and not at all the collapse
of fascism. Our authors admit that fascism is the inevitable
product of decaying capitalism, insofar as the proletariat does
not replace bourgeois democracy in time. Just how is a military victory of decaying democracies over Germany and Italy
capable of liquidating fascism, even if only for a limited period? If there were any grounds for believing that a new victory of the familiar and slightly senile Entente (minus Italy)
can work such miraculous results, i.e., those counter to socio-
historical laws, then it is necessary not only to "desire" this
victory but to do everything in our power to bring it about.
Then the Anglo-French social patriots would be correct. As
a matter of fact they are far less correct today than they were
twenty-five years ago, or to put it more correctly, they are
playing today an infinitely more reactionary and infamous
role.

If there are chances (and there indubitably are) that the
defeat of Germany and Italy—provided there is a revolutionary movement—may lead to the collapse of fascism, then,
on the other hand, there are more proximate and immediate
chances that the victory of France may deal the final blow to
corroded democracy, especially if this victory is gained with
the political support of the French proletariat. The entrench-

ment of French and British imperialism, the victory of French military-fascist reaction, the strengthening of the rule of Great Britain over India and other colonies, will in turn provide support for blackest reaction in Germany and Italy. In the event of victory, France and England will do everything to save Hitler and Mussolini, and stave off "chaos." The proletarian revolution can of course rectify all this. But the revolution must be helped and not hindered. It is impossible to help revolution in Germany otherwise than by applying in action the principles of revolutionary internationalism in the countries warring against her.

The authors of the document come out flatly against abstract pacifism, and in this they are of course correct. But they are absolutely wrong in thinking that the proletariat can solve great historical tasks by means of wars that are led not by themselves but by their mortal enemies, the imperialist governments. One may construe the document as follows: during the crisis over Czechoslovakia our French or English comrades should have demanded the military intervention of their own bourgeoisie, and thereby assumed responsibility for the war — not for war in general, and of course not for a revolutionary war, but for the given imperialist war. The document cites Trotsky's words to the effect that Moscow should have taken the initiative in crushing Hitler as far back as 1933, before he became a terrible danger (*Biulleten Oppozitsii,* March 21, 1933).[213] But these words merely mean that such should have been the behavior of a real revolutionary government of a workers' state. But is it permissible to issue the same demand to a government of an imperialist state?

Assuredly, we do not assume any responsibility for the regime they call the regime of peace. The slogan "Everything for Peace!" is not our slogan, and none of our sections raises it. But we can no more assume responsibility for *their* war than we do for *their* peace. The more resolute, firm, and irreconcilable our position is on this question all the better will the masses understand us, if not at the beginning then during the war.

"Could the proletariat of Czechoslovakia have struggled against its government and the latter's capitulatory policy by slogans of peace and defeatism?" A very concrete question is posed here in a very abstract form. There was no room for "defeatism" because there was no war (and it is not accidental that no war ensued). In the critical twenty-four hours of universal confusion and indignation, the Czechoslovak proletariat had the full opportunity of overthrowing the "capitulatory" government and seizing power. For this only a revolutionary leadership was required. Naturally, after seizing power, the proletariat would have offered desperate resistance to Hitler and would have indubitably evoked a mighty reaction in the working masses of France and other countries. Let us not speculate on what the further course of events might have been. In any case the situation today would have been infinitely more favorable to the world working class. Yes, we are not pacifists; we are for revolutionary war. But the Czech working class did not have the slightest right to entrust the leadership of a war "against fascism" to Messrs. Capitalists who, within a few days, so safely changed their coloration and became themselves fascists and quasifascists. Transformations and recolorations of this kind on the part of the ruling classes will be on the order of the day in wartime in all "democracies." That is why the proletariat would ruin itself if it were to determine its main line of policy by the formal and unstable labels of "for fascism" and "against fascism."

We consider as erroneous to the core the idea of the document that of the three conditions for "defeatist" policy enumerated by Lenin, the third is presumably lacking nowadays, namely, "the possibility of giving mutual support to revolutionary movements in all warring countries." Here the authors are obviously hypnotized by the reported omnipotence of the totalitarian regime. As a matter of fact, the immobility of the German and Italian workers is determined not at all by the omnipotence of the fascist police but by the absence of a program, the loss of faith in old programs and old slogans, and the prostitution of the Second and Third Internationals. Only in this political atmosphere of disillusionment and decline can the police apparatus work those "miracles" which, sad to say, have produced an excessive impression also on the minds of some of our comrades.

It is naturally easier to begin the struggle in those countries where the workers' organizations have not yet been destroyed. But the struggle must be begun against the main enemy who remains, as hitherto, at home. Is it conceivable that the advanced workers of France will say to the workers of Germany: "Inasmuch as you are in the toils of fascism and cannot emancipate yourselves we will help our government to smash your Hitler, i.e., strangle Germany with the noose of a new Versailles treaty and then . . . then we shall build socialism together with you." To this the Germans can well reply: "Pardon us, but we have already heard this song from the social patriots during the last war and know very well how it all ended. . . ." No, in this way we shall not help the German workers to rouse themselves from their stupor. We must show them in action that revolutionary politics consists in a simultaneous struggle against the respective imperialist governments in all the warring countries. This "simultaneity" must not of course be taken mechanically. Revolutionary successes, wherever they may originally erupt, would raise the spirit of protest and uprisings in all countries. Hohenzollern militarism was overthrown completely by the October Revolution. For Hitler and Mussolini the success of a socialist revolution in any one of the advanced countries of the world is infinitely more terrible than the combined armaments of all the imperialist "democracies."

The policy that attempts to place upon the proletariat the insoluble task of warding off all dangers engendered by the bourgeoisie and its policy of war is vain, false, mortally dangerous. "But fascism might be victorious!" "But the USSR is menaced!" "But Hitler's invasion would signify the slaughter of workers!" And so on, without end. Of course, the dangers are many, very many. It is impossible not only to ward them all off, but even to foresee all of them. Should the proletariat attempt at the expense of the clarity and irreconcilability of its fundamental policy to chase after each episodic danger separately, it will unfailingly prove itself bankrupt. In time of war, the frontiers will be altered, military victories and defeats will alternate with each other, political regimes will shift. The workers will be able to profit to the full from this monstrous chaos only if they occupy themselves not by acting as supervisors of the historical process but by engaging in the class struggle. Only the growth of their international offensive will put an end not alone to episodic "dangers" but also to their main source: class society.

"LEARN TO WORK
IN THE STALIN MANNER"[214]

(Reflections from On High, at the Lower Levels)

March 7, 1939

All citizens of the Soviet Union are today studying, as is their duty, the Stalinist *History of the CPSU,* the unique codification of lies and frame-ups. Among the students are of course to be found thousands of thinking representatives of the youth who are trained in handling facts and checking history by documents. Many of them doubtless ask those official leaders whom they have least cause to fear: "But why do we find that the assertions in this 'history' are refuted at every step by the newspapers and periodicals of the corresponding period?" The instructor, a finger upon his lips, replies significantly: "One must learn to work in the Stalinist manner." This means, one must learn how to lie expediently, or at least wink one's eyes at the totalitarian lie.

We are struck with a peculiar kind of astonishment by the revelations of Vyshinsky and other Stalinist overlords on the subject of illegal persecutions, fake investigations, forced confessions, etc. The Soviet press, especially *Pravda,* Stalin's own and almost chaste daughter; waxes indignant. It is an unheard-of thing, that in our fatherland, secretaries, investigating magistrates, prosecutors, and judges should be guided by base personal considerations in persecuting honest citizens, placing false accusations against them or extorting false testimony from them! And all this on the road from socialism to communism! Incredible!

"Let us work in the Stalinist manner," chants daily the almost virginal *Pravda*, and after her the rest of the press. "Yes, indeed. Yes, indeed!" echo all the local big and little satraps. And following in Stalin's footsteps they promptly liquidate anyone who dares criticize them or cross their path or simply cast upon them the reproachful glance of an honest man. The measures of the Kremlin clique inevitably become the measures of local cliques. "We too must work in the Stalinist manner," say in self-justification all the petty cheats who encounter the same sort of difficulties as their sublime patron.

And this is where Vyshinsky comes into his own. In his sternest circular letter he explains: "Thou shalt not poach upon the prerogative of Stalin. The right of political frame-ups is his monopolistic privilege, for he is the Leader and Father of the Peoples." The circular letter is very eloquent but can hardly prove effective. The Bonapartist regime, perhaps the most Bonapartist of all Bonapartist regimes in history, requires a numerically large hierarchy of swindlers and frame-up artists. The legal sphere, the military and historical "sciences," the sphere of statistics, all spheres that bear directly or indirectly upon the interests of the ruling oligarchy — and which one does not? — each one needs its own Yagoda, its own Yezhov, its own Vyshinsky, its own Beria, and a whole detachment of storm troopers at their disposal. In the nature of things, honest and devoted people are to be found everywhere, in science, in technology, in economic institutions, in the army and even within the bureaucratic apparatus. But they are the ones who are dangerous. It is against them that it is necessary to select specialized slickers, 100 percent Stalinists, a hierarchy of flotsam and jetsam. These people are strung together with lies, frame-ups, and deceit. They have no ideal higher than their own personal interests. How can one expect and demand of people for whom the frame-up serves as a legal and technical aid in their official capacity that they should not apply the frame-up for their personal aims? That would be against all laws of nature.

It is here that one of the tiny "lapses" of the Bonapartist system reveals itself. State power has been centralized but frame-ups have been decentralized. Yet the decentralization of frame-ups carries with it the greatest dangers. The petty provincial secretary or prosecutor demonstrates by his mode of action that he has completely penetrated into Stalin's state secrets and knows how "enemies of the people" are manufactured and how confessions are extorted. The democratization of the frame-up signifies the direct exposure of Stalin. "Oho, so that's how it's done!" finally guesses the least discerning average citizen.

It goes without saying that Vyshinsky-Krechinsky is splendid when he comes to the fore as the standard-bearer of state morals. Who else is qualified if not he? Nevertheless, his efforts are in vain. Bonapartism is a regime personalized through and through. All functionaries strive to have haircuts like Stalin and "to work like Stalin." That is why frame-ups have become the all-permeating element of official life. In the end, his own frame-up will choke Stalin.

STALIN'S CAPITULATION[215]

March 11, 1939

First reports on Stalin's speech at the current Moscow congress of the so-called Communist Party of the Soviet Union show that Stalin has hastened to draw conclusions from the Spanish events, as far as he is concerned, in the direction of a new turn toward reaction.

In Spain Stalin suffered a defeat less direct, but no less profound, than that of Azana and Negrin. It is a question, moreover, of something infinitely greater than a purely military defeat or even of a lost war. The whole policy of the "Republicans" was determined by Moscow. The relations that the Republican government established with the workers and peasants were nothing but the translation into wartime language of the relations existing between the Kremlin oligarchy and the peoples of the Soviet Union. The methods of the Azana-Negrin government were nothing but a concentrate of the methods of the Moscow GPU. The fundamental tendency of this policy consisted in substituting the bureaucracy for the people, and the political police for the bureaucracy.

Thanks to the war conditions, the tendencies of Moscow Bonapartism not only assumed their supreme expression in Spain, but also found themselves rapidly put to the test. Hence the importance of the Spanish events from the international, and especially the Soviet, point of view. Stalin is incapable of struggle, and when he is forced to struggle, he is incapable of producing anything but defeats.

In his speech to the congress, Stalin openly shattered the idea of the "alliance of the democracies to resist the fascist aggressors." The instigators of an international war are now neither Mussolini nor Hitler but the two principal democracies of Europe, Great Britain and France, who, according to the speaker, want to draw Germany and the USSR into conflict under the guise of a German attack on the Ukraine. Fascism? That has nothing to do with it. There can be no question, according to Stalin's words, of an attack by Hitler on the Ukraine, and there is not the slightest basis for a military conflict with Hitler.

The abandonment of the policy of "alliance of the democracies" is supplemented at once with a humiliating cringing before Hitler and a hurried polishing of his boots. Such is Stalin!

In Czechoslovakia the capitulation of the "democracies" before fascism found expression in a change of government. In the USSR, thanks to the manifold advantages of the totalitarian regime, Stalin is his own Benes and his own General Syrovy. He replaces the "principles" of his policy precisely in order not to find himself replaced. The Bonapartist clique wants to live and govern. Everything else is for it a question of "technique."

In reality, the political methods of Stalin are in no way distinguished from the methods of Hitler. But in the sphere of international politics, the difference in results is obvious. In a brief space of time Hitler has recovered the Saar territory, overthrown the Treaty of Versailles, placed his grasp on Austria and the Sudetenland, subjected Czechoslovakia to his domination and a number of other second-rate and third-rate powers to his influence.

During the same years, Stalin met only defeats and humiliations on the international arena (China, Czechoslovakia, Spain). To look for the explanation of this difference in the personal qualities of Hitler and Stalin would be much too superficial. Hitler is indubitably cleverer and more audacious than Stalin. However, that is not decisive. The decisive things are the general social conditions of the two countries.

It is now the fashion in superficial radical circles to lump the regimes of Germany and the USSR together. This is meaningless. In Germany, despite all the state "regulations," there exists a regime of private property in the means of production. In the Soviet Union industry is nationalized and agriculture collectivized. We know all the social deformities which the bureaucracy has brought forth in the land of the October Revolution. But there remains the fact of a planned economy on the basis of the state ownership and collectivization of the means of production. This statified economy has its own laws which accommodate themselves less and less to the despotism, the ignorance, and the thievery of the Stalinist bureaucracy.

Monopoly capitalism throughout the entire world, and particularly in Germany, finds itself in a crisis that has no way out. Fascism itself is an expression of this crisis. But within the framework of monopoly capitalism, the regime of Hitler is the only possible one for Germany. The enigma of Hitler's success is explained by the fact that through his police regime he gives highest expression to the tendencies of imperialism. On the contrary, the regime of Stalin has entered into irreducible contradiction with the tendencies of dying bourgeois society.

Hitler will soon reach his apogee, if he has not already done so, only to plunge thereafter into the abyss. But this moment has not yet arrived. Hitler continues to exploit the dynamic strength of an imperialism struggling for its existence. On the other hand, the contradictions between the Bonapartist regime of Stalin and the needs of economy and culture have reached an intolerably acute stage. The struggle of the Kremlin for its self-preservation only deepens and aggravates the contradictions, leading to an incessant civil war at home and, on the international arena, defeats that are the consequences of that civil war.

What is Stalin's speech? Is it a link in the chain of a new policy in process of formation, basing itself on preliminary agreements already concluded with Hitler? Or is it only a trial balloon, a unilateral offer of heart and hand? Most likely the reality is closer to the second variant than to the first. As a victor, Hitler is in no hurry to determine his friendships and enmities once and for all. On the contrary, it is to his utmost interest that the Soviet Union and the Western democracies accuse each other of "provoking war." By his offensive Hitler has, in any case, already gained this much: Stalin, who only yesterday was almost the Alexander Nevski of the Western democracies,[216] is today turning his eyes toward Berlin and humbly confesses the mistakes made.

What is the lesson? During the last three years Stalin called all the companions of Lenin agents of Hitler. He exterminated the flower of the general staff. He shot, discharged, and deported about 30,000 officers — all under the same charge of being agents of Hitler or his allies. After having dismembered the party and decapitated the army, now Stalin is openly posing his own candidacy for the role of . . . principal agent of Hitler. Let the hacks of the Comintern lie and get out of this how they can. The facts are so clear, so convincing that no one will succeed any longer in deceiving the public opinion of the international working class with charlatan phrases. Before Stalin falls, the Comintern will be in pieces. It will not be necessary to wait for years before both these things come to pass.

P. S. — After Hitler's entry into Prague rumors spread of a return by Stalin into the circle of the democracies. It is impossible to consider this excluded. But neither is it excluded that Hitler entered Prague with proof of Stalin's estrangement from the "democracies" in his hands. Hitler's abandonment to Hungary of the Carpatho-Ukraine, which did not belong to him, is a fairly demonstrative renunciation of plans for a Greater Ukraine. Whether this will be for any length of time is another question.

In any case, one must consider it likely that Stalin knew in advance the fate of the Carpatho-Ukraine, and that is why he denied with such assurance the existence of any danger from Hitler to the Soviet Ukraine. The creation of a common frontier between Poland and Hungary can also be interpreted as a manifestation of Hitler's "goodwill" toward the USSR. Whether this will be for long is still another question.

At the present pace of development of world antagonisms, the situation can change radically tomorrow. But today it would seem that Stalin is preparing to play with Hitler.

Mexican President Lazaro Cardenas, as depicted in a contemporary mural in the Labor Department building in Mexico City. The legend begins: "The nation is not a simple explosion of enthusiasm, but rather and above all the sharing of the wealth of an area."

ON MEXICO'S SECOND SIX YEAR PLAN[217]

March 14, 1939

A Program, Not a Plan

We are not dealing here with a "plan" in the true sense of the word. In a society where private property prevails, it is impossible for the government to direct economic life according to a "plan." The document contains algebraic formulas but no arithmetic facts. In other words, it is a general program for governmental activity and not, strictly speaking, a plan.

Unfortunately, the authors of the plan do not take into account the limits of governmental activity in a society where the means of production, including the land, are not nationalized. They have apparently taken the Five Year Plans of the USSR as a model and often use the same phraseology, without taking into account the fundamental differences in social structures. It is for this reason, as we shall see later, that the algebraic formulas are often a means for passing over the most burning questions of Mexican life while taking solace in perspectives borrowed from the reports and official statements of the USSR.

Reform of the State Machinery

The document starts off, in paragraph two, with a proposal for instituting "a technical body subordinate to the president" to carry out the Six Year Plan. This proposal, despite its rather secondary, administrative nature, seems to contain a fundamental error. Governmental action in carrying out the plan cannot develop within the scope of governmental action pure and simple. Superimposing on the government a "technical body," whose task is neither more nor less than transforming the entire national economy, would mean creating a "supergovernment" alongside the regular government, i.e., administrative chaos.

A more realistic proposal, based on the experience of various countries during the war as well as on the experience of the USSR, would be to create a limited government committee composed of the heads of the ministries most directly involved in the plan and placed under the direction of the president or his immediate representative. In this case, general governmental activity along with the activity that concerns the plan would be concentrated in the same hands, and useless repetition — this bureaucratic scourge — would be minimized as far as possible.

Paragraph three proposes "functional participation of the organized sectors of the country's population" in various organs of the government. This formulation is extremely vague and allows all sorts of possible interpretations. We hasten to point out first of all that this proposal threatens to incorporate a bureaucratic hierarchy of the unions, etc., without precise delimitation, into the bureaucratic hierarchy of the state (nearly impossible to accomplish in practice) thereby restraining the regular activity of the organs of state and creating an almost insurmountable state of confusion.

Mexico's Foreign Policy

In this most important domain, the plan rests on generalities. It doesn't name a single country, and even within the realm of generalities it points to a line of conduct that should be considered fundamentally wrong.

In the name of "democracy and liberty," the plan proposes to improve the relations Mexico currently has with "Latin American nations and those nations on all continents that have a democratic form of government." We immediately run into an obvious contradiction. For the Americas the policy is to enter into friendly relations will all nations, whatever the nature of their internal regimes, while for the other continents the prescription is for friendly relations exclusively with the so-called "democratic" countries. The plan does not indicate how to develop increasingly friendly relations with "democratic" England, which treats Mexico like a fief for its oil interests. Is it necessary to beg London's pardon and immediately reestablish diplomatic relations in the name of "democracy and liberty"? Moreover, in the struggle developing at the present time between the "democratic" mother country of 45 million inhabitants and India, deprived of democracy but with a population of 370 million people, to which side should Mexico extend its positive friendship in order to solidly reinforce its world position? The organic weakness of the plan lies in dissolving the opposition between oppressor and oppressed nations into the abstract concept of democracy. This division is far more profound and bears far more weight than the division of the slaveholders' camp into democratic and fascist nations.

The expropriation of the oil companies and the resolute attitude of the Mexican government toward England have greatly diminished "sympathy" toward Mexico in that capitalist "democracy"; but at the same time, these acts have enormously elevated Mexico's prestige in India and in all the colonies and oppressed nations. The only conclusion to draw is that a semicolonial country should not allow itself to be fooled by the democratic form of its actual or potential oppressors.

Mexico cannot safeguard and develop its independence and assure its future in any other way than *by taking advantage of the antagonisms and conflicts between the imperialist slaveholders* without identifying with one side or the other, and by assuring itself of the esteem and support of the enslaved nations and the oppressed masses in general.

Agrarian Reform

This part of the program, the most important part for Mexican life, is based not on an analysis of the needs of the country, but rather on some general formula borrowed from the vocabulary of the USSR and very badly adapted to national realities.

Paragraph eight states: "Restitutions, grants, and extensions of land to the peasant communities will proceed at a rate not slower than that of the years 1935-38." At the same time, point (c) of paragraph thirteen states: "Organization of the collective exploitation of all common public lands" for the next six years. These two dimensions of the program are not at all coordinated. They are simply superimposed, one upon the other.

What is the main question in Mexico today? Agrarian reform, or the *democratic agrarian revolution;* that is, the life of the peasants is characterized by a massive accumulation of the holdovers of feudal property forms and the relations and traditions of slavery. It is necessary to courageously and definitively liquidate these holdovers from medieval barbarism with the aid of the peasants themselves. The large parasitic or semiparasitic landed proprietors, the economic and political domination of the landowners over the peasants, forced agricultural labor,

the quasi-patriarchal sharecropping system, which is fundamentally equivalent to slavery — these are the things that must
be definitively liquidated in the shortest possible time. Now,
the program does not even call for the completion of this task,
which is essential to the democratic revolution, within the next
six years; but at the same time it does call for the complete
collectivation of the common lands in the same period of time.
This is a complete inconsistency, which can lead to the most
dire consequences, economic, social, and political.

"Complete Collectivization"

A. Collectivization means the replacement of small-scale rural
agriculture by large-scale agriculture. This change is only advantageous if highly developed technology adequate to the
tasks of large-scale agriculture exists. This means that the proposed rate of collectivization should be adapted to the development of industry, of production of farm machinery, fertilizer,
etc.

B. But technology alone is not sufficient. The peasants themselves must accept collectivization, that is, they must understand the advantages on the basis of their own experience or
that of others.

C. Finally, the human material, or at least a large part of
it, must be educated and prepared for the economic and technical management of the common lands.

The plan itself says in paragraph fifteen that it is necessary
to count on "peasants who are properly educated" and calls
for the creation of a sufficient number of schools, especially
agricultural schools. If we allow that such schools will be
established in sufficient number during the next six years, it
is clear that the necessary personnel will not be ready till quite
some time later. Collectivizing ignorance and misery by means
of state compulsion would not mean advancing agriculture,
but rather would inevitably lead to forcing the peasants into
the camp of the reaction.

The agrarian revolution must be completed within six years
in order for the country to be in a position to advance toward
the goal of collectivization on this foundation, very carefully,
without compulsion, and with a very sympathetic attitude toward
the peasantry.

The Example of the USSR

The USSR went through not only a bourgeois democratic revolution, but a proletarian revolution as well. The Russian peasants, although very poor, were not as poor as the Mexican peasants. Soviet industry was considerably more developed. Nevertheless, after the nationalization of the land, i.e., the complete agrarian democratic revolution, for many long years the collectivized sector of agriculture formed only a tiny percentage of the agricultural economy in relation to the individual peasant economy. It is true that twelve years after the abolition of the latifundia, etc., the ruling bureaucracy passed over to "complete collectivization" for reasons that we do not need to go into here. The results are well known. Agricultural production fell off by half, the peasants revolted, tens of millions died as the result of terrible famines. The bureaucracy was forced to partially reestablish private agriculture. Nationalized industry had to produce hundreds of thousands of tractors and farm machines for the kolkhozes to begin making progress. Imitating these methods in Mexico would mean heading for disaster. It is necessary to complete the democratic revolution by giving the land, all the land, to the peasants. On the basis of this established conquest the peasants must be given an unlimited period to reflect, compare, experiment with different methods of agriculture. They must be aided, technically and financially, but not compelled. In short, it is necessary to finish the work of Emiliano Zapata[218] and not to superimpose on him the methods of Joseph Stalin.

Agricultural Credit

The entire agrarian part of the program is deformed by a false perspective that tries to take the third or fourth step before the first step is completed. This deformation of perspective is particularly flagrant with regard to the question of credit. Paragraph sixteen, point (d) calls for all agricultural credit to be extended to the common lands "abandoning the aim of maintaining the economy of small agricultural property." That the state should accord financial privileges to voluntary collectives goes without saying. But proportions must be maintained. The collective enterprises must be kept viable, but the small individual farms must continue

to survive and grow as well during the historical period necessary to accomplish "complete collectivization"; and this period
may entail several decades.

If methods of compulsion are used, this will only produce
collectives that exist at state expense, while lowering the general level of agriculture and impoverishing the country.

The Industrialization of the Country

In this area the program becomes extremely vague and
abstract. In order to collectivize the common lands in six
years an enormous outlay for the production of farm machinery, fertilizer, railroads, and industry in general would be necessary. And all of this immediately, because a certain technological development, at least on an elementary level, should
precede collectivization and not follow it. Where will the necessary means come from? The plan is silent on this point
except for a few sentences about the advantages of domestic
loans over foreign loans. But the country is poor. It needs
foreign capital. This thorny problem is treated only to the
extent that the program does not insist on the cancellation
of the foreign debt. And that is all.

It is true that the realization of the democratic agrarian
revolution, i.e., handing over all the arable land to the peasantry, would increase the capacity of the domestic market
in a relatively short time; but despite all that, the rate of industrialization would be very slow. Considerable international
capital is seeking areas of investment at the present time, even
where only a modest (but sure) return is possible. Turning
one's back on foreign capital and speaking of collectivization and industrialization is mere intoxication with words.

The reactionaries are wrong when they say that the expropriation of the oil companies has made the influx of new
capital impossible. The government defends the vital resources
of the country, but at the same time it can grant industrial
concessions, above all in the form of mixed corporations,
i.e., enterprises in which the government participates (holding 10 percent, 25 percent, 51 percent of the stock, according
to the circumstances) and writes into the contracts the option
of buying out the rest of the stock after a certain period of
time. This government participation would have the advantage of educating native technical and administrative personnel in collaboration with the best engineers and organizers

of other countries. The period fixed in the contract before the optional buying out of the enterprise would create the necessary confidence among capital investors. The rate of industrialization would be accelerated.

State Capitalism

The authors of the program wish to completely construct state capitalism within a period of six years. But nationalizing existing enterprises is one thing; creating new ones with limited means on virgin soil is another.

History knows only one example of an industry created under state supervision — the USSR. But,

a) a socialist revolution was necessary;

b) the industrial heritage of the past played an important role,

c) the public debt was canceled (1.5 billion pesos a year).

Despite all these advantages the industrial reconstruction of the country was begun with the granting of concessions. Lenin accorded great importance to these concessions for the economic development of the country and for the technical and administrative education of Soviet personnel. There has been no socialist revolution in Mexico. The international situation does not even allow the cancellation of the public debt. The country, we repeat, is poor. Under such conditions it would be almost suicidal to close the doors to foreign capital.

To construct state capitalism, capital is necessary.

The Unions

Paragraph ninety-six speaks quite correctly about the necessity to "protect the working class more effectively than is the case today." It would only be necessary to add: "It is necessary to protect the working class not only against the excesses of capitalist exploitation but against the abuses of the labor bureaucracy as well."

The program has a lot to say about democracy and the workers' organizations, which are the essential base of this democracy. This would be absolutely correct if the unions were themselves democratic and not totalitarian. A democratic regime in the union should assure the workers control over their own bureaucracy and thus eliminate the most flagrant abuses. The strictest accountability of the unions should be a public affair.

*   *   *

These notes may seem embued with a very moderate, almost conservative spirit in comparison to the high-flown, but, alas, empty, formulations of the program. We believe, however, that our point of view is more realistic and at the same time more revolutionary. The central point of the program is the agrarian question. It is a thousand times easier to preach total collectivization in a vacuum than to carry out with an iron hand the total elimination of feudal remnants in the countryside. This cleansing operation would truly be an excellent program for the next six years. The peasantry would understand such a program, set down in ten lines, and accept it much more warmly than this vague and verbose translation of the official documents of the Kremlin.

A PROPOSAL FROM SHANGHAI[219]

March 18, 1939

Comrade F.'s proposition seems to me to be correct if there is no possibility of Comrade C.'s leaving his state with the official authorization of the government. A "friendly" pressure on the Chinese authorities might possibly have the desired results; but if that fails the governmental supervisions would become firmer and thus diminish his possibilities of leaving China. That is why I propose to prepare two ways simultaneously, namely:

(1) Create immediately in New York a nonpublic commission for the purpose of studying the possibilities of C.'s departure from China as quickly as possible without any official interference; to collect money immediately for this purpose, and so on. (2) At the same time begin a campaign of "friendly" pressure on the Chinese authorities through liberals, radicals, and prominent figures of our own movement.

For example, some Mexican intellectuals with names (Diego Rivera, Juan O'Gorman, [220] and others) could visit the Chinese ambassador here and introduce a written petition somewhat as follows:

"We, the undersigned, and many of our friends, are sincere and zealous friends of China in her struggle for liberation against Japanese imperialism. We are personally interested in the fate of C., whom we know as an honest man and a sincere patriot.

"We do not adhere to the Stalinist camp. On the other hand, we understand the reasons for cooperation between the Chinese government and Moscow. This cooperation creates a very difficult situation for C., making it impossible for him even to wage a public fight in favor of China. We learned of this situation through a trustworthy foreign correspondent, a sincere friend of China.

"Permit us to insist before the Chinese authorities, that if Mr. C. comes abroad, he can be very useful in an international campaign of the left elements, especially the workers, against the oppression of Japanese imperialism. The military situation in the Far East indicates that the great fight will last a long time, with ups and downs. A systematic and insistent mobilization of international public opinion is necessary. In such a campaign, the role of the independent left elements can be of the greatest value to the Chinese people. The official Communist parties are known as the instruments of Moscow. Their influence is therefore limited. Mr. C. is known as an independent Chinese revolutionist. With his knowledge and help we could surely render important services to such an international campaign.

"We do not wish to conceal another thought which disquiets us. In various countries the Moscow GPU seeks to exterminate all those left elements which have a critical attitude toward the methods of the Kremlin. We know from authoritative sources that Mr. C. is on the blacklist of the GPU. On one pretext or another he can be assassinated on Chinese territory and the GPU would then try to place the responsibility for such a crime on the Chinese authorities. We feel certain that in the United States Mr. C.'s life could be better safeguarded from a possible attempt against it by the GPU.

"These are the reasons, Mr. Ambassador, which prompt us to interfere in this affair with feelings of sincerest sympathy for your people in their heroic fight against the imperialist invasion."

An analogous, but not necessarily identical, letter should be drawn up in the States and signed by appropriate personalities — and also in England and France.

A document of this kind would be a warning to the Chinese authorities, although a far from absolute guarantee for C.'s life. Such a document cannot be prejudicial to C.'s situation in China, especially if no time is lost and preparations for the other version are made.

Comradely yours,
V. T. O'Brien [Trotsky]

ONLY REVOLUTION CAN END WAR[221]

March 18, 1939

Q: Is a world war inevitable? If so, will it mean the end of the capitalist system?

A: Yes a world war is inevitable, if a revolution does not forestall it. The inevitability of the war flows first from the incurable crisis of the capitalist system; second from the fact that the present partition of our planet, that is to say, above all, of the colonies, no longer corresponds to the economic specific weight of the imperialist states. Looking for an escape out of the mortal crisis, the parvenu states aspire, and cannot fail to aspire, to new partitioning of the world. Only children at the breast and professional "pacifists" to whom even the experience of the unfortunate League of Nations has taught nothing, can suppose that a more "equitable" repartition of the territorial surface can be realized around the green tables of democracy.

If the Spanish revolution had been victorious, it would have given a powerful impulse to the revolutionary movement in France and in other countries of Europe. In this case it would have been possible to hope confidently that the victorious socialist movement would forestall the imperialist war, making it useless and impossible. But the socialist proletariat of Spain was strangled by the coalition of Stalin-Azana-Caballero-Negrin-Garcia Oliver,[222] even before it was definitely crushed by Franco's bands. The defeat of the Spanish revolution postponed a revolutionary perspective for the imperialist war. Only the blind cannot see that!

Of course, the more energetically and the more audaciously the advanced workers fight in all countries against militarism and imperialism now, in spite of the unfavorable conditions, the more quickly they will be able to stop the war when it

has started, the greater will be the hopes for the salvation
of our civilization from destruction.

Yes, I do not doubt that the new world war will provoke
with absolute inevitability the world revolution and the collapse of the capitalist system. The imperialist governments
of all countries are doing all that is possible to accelerate
this collapse. It is only necessary that the world proletariat
be not again taken unawares by the great events.

The task that the Fourth International puts before itself,
I note in passing, is precisely the revolutionary preparation
of the vanguard. This is exactly why it names itself the World
Party of Socialist Revolution.

Q: Is not the world too afraid of Hitler?

A: The democratic governments look upon Hitler, who succeeded in "liquidating" the social question, with admiration
and fear. The working class, which during one and a half
centuries periodically shook the civilized countries of Europe
by its revolts, is suddenly reduced to complete silence in Italy
and Germany. The official politicians attribute this "success"
to the internal, quasimystical properties of fascism and National Socialism. In reality the strength of Hitler is not in
himself, or in his contemptible philosophy, but in the terrible
deception of the working masses, in their confusion and in
their lassitude.

During many decades the proletariat of Germany built up
a trade union organization and a Social Democratic party.
Abreast of the strong Social Democracy appeared later a powerful Communist Party. And all these organizations, which
rose upon the shoulders of the proletariat, were in the critical
moment a zero, and crumbled away before the offensive of
Hitler. They did not find in themselves the courage to call
the masses to struggle, as they themselves were completely
degenerated and bourgeoisified, and had lost the habit of
thinking about struggle.

The masses pass through such catastrophes heavily and
slowly. It is incorrect to say that the German proletariat has
reconciled itself with Hitler! But it no longer believes in the
old parties, in the old slogans, and at the same time it has
not yet found a new way. This and only this explains the
strong-arm omnipotence of fascism. It will continue until the
masses have dressed their wounds, have regenerated them-

selves, and have once more lifted their heads. I think we can expect that in not a long time.

The fear Great Britain and France have for Hitler and Mussolini explains itself by the fact that the world position of these two colony-holding countries, as has already been said, no longer corresponds with their economic specific weight. The war can bring nothing to them, but can take a great deal from them. It is natural that they attempt to postpone the moment of a new partitioning of the world and that they toss a bone, like Spain and Czechoslovakia, to Mussolini and Hitler.

The struggle is for colonial possessions, for the domination of the world. The attempt to represent this brawl of interests and appetites as a struggle between "democracy" and "fascism" can only dupe the working class. Chamberlain will give all the democracies in the world (there are not many left) for a tenth part of India.

The strength of Hitler (at the same time also his weakness) consists in the fact that under the pressure of the helpless position of German capitalism, he is ready to resort to the most extreme means, using blackmail and bluff in passing, at the risk of leading to war. Hitler has fully realized the fear of the old colony-holders before any disturbance and has played on this fear, if not with a very great heart, at least with indubitable success.

Q: Should the "democracies" and the USSR unite to crush Hitler?

A: I do not feel that it is my mission to give counsel to imperialist governments, even if they call themselves democratic, or to the Bonapartist clique of the Kremlin, even if it calls itself socialist. I can only give counsel to the workers. My counsel to them is not to believe for a single instant that the war of the two imperialist camps can bring anything else but oppression and reaction in both camps. It will be the war of the slave-owners who cover themselves with various masks: "democracy," "civilization," on the one hand, "race," "honor," on the other. Only the overthrow of all slave-owners can once and for all put an end to war and open an epoch of true civilization.

Q: Does Hitler represent a great danger for the democracies?

A: The "democracies" themselves represent a much greater danger for themselves. The regime of bourgeois democracy appeared on the basis of liberal capitalism, that is to say, free competition. That epoch is now far in the past. The present monopoly capitalism, which has decomposed and degraded the petty and middle bourgeoisie, has thus undermined the ground under bourgeois democracy. Fascism is the product of this development. It does not come at all "from without." In Italy and Germany fascism conquered without foreign intervention. Bourgeois democracy is dead not only in Europe but also in America.

If it is not liquidated in time by socialist revolution, fascism will inevitably conquer in France, England, and the United States, with the aid of Mussolini and Hitler or without this aid. But fascism is only a respite. Capitalism is condemned. Nothing will save it from collapse. The more resolute and audacious the policy of the proletariat, the less the socialist revolution will provoke sacrifice, the sooner mankind will enter upon a new road.

My opinion about the civil war in Spain? I have expressed myself on this subject in the press many times.

The Spanish revolution was socialist in its essence: the workers attempted several times to overthrow the bourgeoisie, to seize the factories; the peasants wanted to take the land. The "People's Front," led by the Stalinists, strangled the socialist revolution in the name of an outlived bourgeois democracy. Hence the disappointment, the hopelessness, the discouragement of the masses of workers and peasants, the demoralization of the Republican army, and as a result, the military collapse.

To invoke the treacherous policy of England and France explains nothing. Of course the "democratic" imperialists were with the Spanish reaction with all their hearts and helped Franco as much as possible. It was so and will always be so. The British were naturally on the side of the Spanish bourgeoisie, which passed entirely to the side of Franco. However, in the beginning Chamberlain did not believe in the victory of Franco, and feared to compromise himself by a premature revelation of his sympathies. France, as ever, executed the will of the French bourgeoisie. The Soviet government played the role of hangman toward the revolutionary Spanish workers, in order to demonstrate its trustworthiness and loyalty to London and Paris. The fundamental cause of the defeat of a powerful and heroic revolution is the treacherous antisocialist policy of the so-called "People's Front." If the peasants had seized the land and the workers the factories, Franco never would have been able to wrest this victory from their hands!

Q: Can the regime of Franco maintain itself?

A: Not, of course, for a thousand years, as the boasting National Socialism of Germany promises. But Franco will maintain himself for a certain time, thanks to the same conditions as Hitler. After great efforts and sacrifices, after terrible defeats, in spite of these sacrifices, the Spanish working class must be disappointed to the bottom of their hearts in the old parties: Socialists, Anarchists, "Communists," who by their common forces, under the banner of the "People's Front," strangled the socialist revolution. The Spanish workers will now pass inevitably through a period of discouragement before they begin slowly and stubbornly to look for a new road. The period during which the masses lie prostrate will coincide precisely with the time of Franco's domination.

You ask how serious a menace Japan is to the USSR, England, and the United States. Japan is not capable of a war on a great scale, partly for economic reasons, but above all for social reasons. Not having emancipated itself up to now from the heritage of feudalism, Japan represents the reservoir of a gigantic revolutionary explosion. In many respects it calls to mind the czarist empire on the eve of 1905.[223]

Japan's leading circles attempt to escape from the internal contradictions by the seizure and pillage of China. But the internal contradictions make external success on a great scale unfeasible. To seize strategical positions in China is one thing; to subdue China is another. Japan would never dare to challenge the Soviet Union, if there were not a glaring antagonism, evident to everyone, between the leading clique of the Kremlin and the Soviet people. The regime of Stalin, which is weakening the USSR, can make a Soviet-Japanese war possible.

I cannot believe for a single instant in the victory of Japan. I think that the most indubitable results of the war would be the collapse of the medieval regime of the Mikado and of the Bonapartist regime of Stalin.

On my life in Mexico I can communicate very little. On the part of the authorities I have met with nothing but kindness. I am absolutely apart from Mexican political life, but I follow the efforts of the Mexican people to conquer a complete and true independence with ardent sympathy.

I am finishing a book on Stalin, which will appear this year in the United States, England, and other countries. The book is a political biography of Stalin and has as its objective an explanation of how a second- or third-rank revolutionary can appear at the head of the country when the Thermidorean reaction begins. The book will show, in particular, how and why the former Bolshevik Stalin is now completely ripe for an alliance with Hitler.

OUR WORK IN THE COMMUNIST PARTY[224]

March 20, 1939

The discussion was opened with the reading of the following excerpts from two letters:

Letter from Trotsky:

"I see again from your letter, as from my discussion with two women comrades who came here from New York, that there exists a very poor state of affairs as regards the work of our party inside the Communist Party. There are no connections at all and there is a certain fatalism in this respect. 'We are too weak. We do not have enough manpower to begin a systematic action. Etc.'

"I find it absolutely false, dangerous, almost to say, criminal. It is my opinion that we must register all the comrades who came from the Communist Party within the last two or three years, those who have personal connections with the Stalinists, and so on. Organize small discussions with them, not of a general, but of a practical, even an individual character. Elaborate some very concrete plans and re-discuss the matter after a week or so. On the basis of such a preparatory work a commission can be crystallized for this purpose.

"The end of the Spanish tragedy, the truth about the activities of the Stalinists in Spain, and such articles as the excellent correspondence from Terence Phelan in Paris,[225] will inevitably create some disintegration in the Stalinist ranks. We must be present to observe these processes and to utilize the opportunities presented. It is the most important task of the party in this period."

Letter to Trotsky:

"I read your letter with a good deal of attention and discussed its contents with several comrades. There are some attempts being made about the CP, but they are local in character and far, far from being handled organizationally as the

first task of the party. A comrade of very militant and intelligent character considered your suggestions very good and
thought they could lead to success. Other comrades higher
in the party were not so confident.

"Their doubts take the following line: The membership of
the CP as a whole is not more than a year or a year and
a half old. These members came into the party not for the
struggle to achieve communism but in order to better fight
for capitalist democracy. The experience of our comrades in
contact with CP rank-and-file members in many parts of the
country shows that these CPers speak an entirely different
language from ours. When we talk politics with them, they
simply do not know what we are talking about. In line with
this I have learned from a very close friend of mine in California, an artist sympathetic to us but not a party member,
that the CP is making an intensive drive among university
circles in California and making some success solely on a
platform of fighting for democracy. The members they are
gaining are people I knew in college as liberals, believers in
democracy who thought even the *Nation* very radical [226] —
and they have not changed one whit in their beliefs. The CP
has moved over to them. In addition, the activity of the CP
members is on an incredibly low level. They are not trained
the least bit in the class struggle but are merely being roped
to the war machine. If these people leave the CP as they have
in the past by the thousands, they do not come to us, but become apathetic or material for the fascists. Work in the CP
is extremely difficult because the membership is atomized —
the opposite pole to the centralization of the leadership — there
are no possibilities for members to meet together and discuss
on any scale larger than a single small branch or unit.

"All the comrades agree that we know too little about the
composition and happenings within the CP and agreed that
we could do much more. I proposed work on a national scale
be instituted of an organizational nature, and one of the higher
comrades wondered how I would like to do that kind of work.
Naturally the problem of breaking up this organization and
initially of discovering what goes on within it, interests me
keenly, but there are many comrades far better fitted for this
work than I.

"Yes, there is some skepticism among some of the people.
When I argue that a split is inevitable in the CP and that it
cannot but help educate to a degree the people who stay even
a short time in its ranks — even the *Daily Worker* uses the

socialist background to some degree[227] — they agree that there is a contradiction in their ideology but cannot see gains for us. · "One curious observation—some of the people who were among the foremost militants in the third period are now devout followers of Roosevelt in the CP. They listen to his speeches over the radio as if God himself were speaking out of a rock. They are not cynical; they really are followers of Roosevelt. What can be done with people like that?"

Trotsky: It seems to me that these two letters are a sufficient introduction and that possibly the comrades will express their opinions about the possibility of work within the Stalinist party.

O'Brien: I could add a little on the relations of our members to the Stalinists from my experiences while I was in New York on the *Appeal.* From the field we had complaints whenever we printed articles against the Stalinists. Comrades would write to us that now we were trying to build a mass party and that we should make our paper a paper for the masses, not with our faces turned constantly toward the Stalinist party. To them, a turn towards the workers meant a turn away from the Stalinist party. Yet whenever the same comrades would write for the *Appeal,* the realities of the party's work demanded that they write against the Stalinists. Other comrades who complained about attacks on the CP, when asked for concrete suggestions, could only suggest further attacks!

Their objections, it seems to me, were based on the quantity of the anti-Stalinist material. Certainly a review of the *Socialist Appeal* will show that 60 percent of the articles are against the Communist Party. But the work seems too diffuse, it is shooting into the sky. What is needed is a concrete plan and a consistent approach to the Stalinists.

As I listened to this letter with its analysis of the CP membership, it seems that our approach must take that analysis into consideration. It must deal with fundamentals — if the CP membership is interested only in "preserving democracy" we must deal with the question in that aspect. If we are serious in our desire to influence the *present* membership of the CP, we must be willing to attempt the task of educating them to a revolutionary viewpoint. We cannot attempt to speak to the *new* Stalinist rank and file from a revolutionary premise. Nor can we expect them to be familiar with the history of the Comintern.

I would suggest for the present a definite column, to be conducted by some person specifically for that job, in the paper once or twice a week if necessary, to hit on two or three fundamental points and hammer away at them each week. Our anti-Stalinist campaign, although concrete on a local scale, on a national scale is incomprehensible to the CP rank and file. Coupled with the press, of course, we must do organizational work within the CP so that we can both reap a benefit from, and direct and guide, the press.

Lankin: I believe that the only way we can really find out what is going on in the CP is to actually send people in for a certain period and give them special tasks to do — qualified people. I believe, and it has been my opinion for a long time, that so far as actually gaining members is concerned, our gains from this organization can only be small. There are few revolutionary elements in the CP. Almost all those people who joined before Hitler came to power, went through the third period, and now accept the new line, are absolutely worthless. They are dishonest and degenerate. No one can accept the third period and now the new line and do it honestly. The new people, who joined after the third period, are not revolutionists, but for them there is a certain amount of hope. Among these people there are a certain number of workers who came in, not on a revolutionary line, but because it was their first contact with the radical movement and because they were interested in "maintaining democracy." Many of them came from the trade unions. We could win some of these elements with our work in the Stalinist party. But we must send in qualified people to remain only for a certain length of time.

Guy: I agree with what Comrade Lankin has to say, but in order to be able to send people in, they must be entirely unknown and qualified comrades who can do the work we want done and that is going to be very difficult to find.

Cornell: What Comrade Guy says is quite correct — it is very difficult to send qualified comrades, or for that matter any of our comrades, into the CP. Our people are known, they are articulate, and the mere fact of being Trotskyists has given them something of a reputation. Even though they may be sent to another locality, halfway across the country, the Stalinists also move about and it would not take long to discover them. Even with considerable sacrifice, their activity in the CP is shortlived. You may suggest that we can leave within the CP those people whom we are winning over. This too presents difficulties. The change does not take place overnight, but develops over a considerable period. As their doubts and questionings increase, they expose themselves more and more, until they become known as Trotskyists even before they actually face the fact themselves. They expose themselves even before they come to us. If, through some fortunate combination of circumstances, this should not be the case, they are not usually trained to carry on such careful work nor do they have the political background. If left in the CP they would be far more likely to become demoralized and leave the movement entirely than to bring new members to us.

Finding people to send in is a difficult task, but obviously it must be done, and together with it the very essential work of careful and alert planning and direction.

O'Brien: At the time of Comrade Gould's visit here, we discussed the project of circulating a mimeographed bulletin or paper within the CP itself. Have you heard of anything being done along that line?

Trotsky: Nothing is being done, as we see from the letter just read. And some comrades believe that it is not possible to do anything or to win many comrades. It is also the opinion expressed by Comrade Lankin. We have two tasks that are connected, but at the same time must be considered separately. One task is to compromise, smash, crush the CP as an obstacle for our movement. If we win out, many will come to us. But now the Communist Party is the most important obstacle. The first obstacle was the Socialist Party — weaker than the Communist Party. We tried to pass through this obstacle, and met with some success. Now the Socialist Party, as an obstacle, does not exist for us. The Old Guard is a petty-bourgeois, semiliberal organization without direct influence in the workers' movement. And the Norman Thomas section is dying.[228] The task resolves itself on the CP. What Comrade O'Brien tells us of the objections of many comrades — do not make direct polemics among the CPers, better approach the CP in a constructive manner — this signifies an anonymous approach. They hope in this way to avoid the friction and the blows. It shows that in this form we can see some fear before the public opinion of the Stalinists. It signifies that the Stalinists are strong and we are weak. This objection shows that the Stalinists are now the next and most important obstacle in our way. And we cannot answer, as some comrades do, that sociologically they are made up not of proletarian elements primarily, but that what proletarian elements they have are demoralized and we cannot win them. It is not what Comrade Lankin says, because he proposes some action within the party. The comrades in the letter say they are skeptical about the work in general. The first task is to compromise this party in the eyes of the workers. The second is to win as many as possible from the ranks of the party.

In his speech before the eighteenth congress of the CPSU Manuilsky said that the American Communist Party had a membership of 20,000 and now has 90,000.[229] I am not sure that it is correct, but it is possible that they now have around this number. How many workers? I do not know.

In this letter, as in our discussion with comrades, we hear that the Stalinists' growth is due to the petty-bourgeois elements. It is almost certain that the great majority are petty-bourgeois elements, but I ask our comrades about the influence in the trade unions. In the CIO they are very influential. Where does their influence in the trade unions come from — is it from the rank and file or from the top? We know that the Lovestoneites have influence through the top, by personal connections, etc.[230] How is it with the Stalinists — is it based on the nuclei of members, or through the top leadership? I do not know the answer. Do they have organized nuclei in the trade unions? Are they numerous? Do they have meetings and accept instructions from the party? It is only hypothetical that the influence of the Stalinists comes in a double way — to a certain degree from a direct influence of a strata of workers, and to a greater degree through the apparatus. They have a powerful apparatus, with educated fakers who are very useful to other fakers less educated. The combination is quite natural. But at the same time, does not this bureaucratic apparatus have a base in the rank and file? They must have some base in the masses. If it is so, it proves that among the 90,000 there are many thousands of workers and sufficient influential workers.

Have we a map of the trade unions and a map of the influence of the Stalinists in the trade unions? We must have such a map with statistics, characteristics, etc., of all the trade unions, nationally and locally. We cannot fight a foe without a previous reconnaissance. We must penetrate, we must have more posts in the trade unions, we must penetrate into the Communist Party. The trade unions are more or less democratic and we are better able to work there. We must generalize, analyze, summarize, concretize all the information we have and create a map of the trade unions and the influence of the Stalinists, because the trade union movement is the most important field for us. Here the Stalinists come into direct conflict with the interests of the trade unions. We have seen it in the auto union and in others. And as Comrade O'Brien says, our criticism is correct, but it is too abstract. It cannot reach the rank-and-file worker in the trade union. Our criticism is based upon our general conceptions, but not upon the worker's own experience. We cannot do this because we do not have the information, because we do nothing in order to have it. Let us suppose for a moment that the whole influence of the Stalinists in the trade unions comes not through the workers but only through their apparatus composed of the petty-bourgeois elements and bureaucrats. It is absolutely exaggerated — impossible — but for the moment we will accept this view, which confirms the opinion that we cannot win many members; but even in this case, we must approach the workers in general in the trade unions in order to split and compromise this apparatus. It is not homogeneous. It is composed of Jimmy Higginses,[231] bureaucrats, and fakers. The CP also has Jimmy Higginses who are honest and devoted.

Comrade Lankin says that people who passed through the third period experience and now the new orientation are absolutely demoralized and unworthy. The bureaucrats yes, but the workers no — not even the majority. In the third period they had a series of defeats and they felt the necessity of changing the policy. It was the same in France. Then the Comintern proposed a new way. The leaders told them that this was a maneuver. These workers were not educated and they had a very confused conception of the value of a maneuver. They knew that the Bolsheviks had used maneuvers with success. It got worse through the years. They became more and more involved and could not find a way out. They passed through a moral crisis. A worker who is awakened by an organization is thankful to it and it is not easy to break with it, particularly if he cannot find a new road. We consider him as lost too prematurely. It is not correct.

I repeat that there must be an opposition to the bureaucracy at the top. The top is omnipotent and the modest functionaries must feel that it is not a comradely organization. It is one line of friction in the organization itself. We must find in the bureau the woman who cleans the floors, and those a bit higher, and begin with them.

On the other side are political contradictions in the apparatus, the leading and semi-leading elements are of two kinds. The leaders — part of them — have the "cosmopolitan" education of Stalinist culture and are ready to betray anything for it. They are the active, influential, and absolutely vicious minority of the apparatus. But there are others. In this large party it is inevitable that there should be new ones — Yankees — not "international" rascals. They are honest Yankees. They are devoted to Roosevelt, democracy, etc. If the Soviet Union marches together with the United States then these two parts of the bureaucracy can remain together with a sort of friendship. It will reflect the friendship of Roosevelt and Stalin, and will be reflected in the Communist Party itself. But if the politics of Roosevelt and the Soviet Union are in opposition, we will have friction in the apparatus itself. Possibly it is going on now, but we know nothing about it. If, at the proper moment, we can put a clear question to the members, or in a review, then we can project a split, if we know what is going on.

I believe that we should organize a census of all party comrades who have connections or knowledge about the people or proceedings in the CP or the nuclei in the trade unions. Locally and nationally. Then convoke them and discuss what they know and the material they have. Give them two or three days or a week to complete the information, because in most cases they will have abandoned their relationships. They can establish them again. Then convoke these comrades again and discuss concrete plans. They are advised to see a certain person, or to send a brother or a sister to see him. Elementary and practical means of approach are elaborated. By and by an organization can be established, which must do work of two kinds: one, very delicate and illegal work which must be organized only from the top, locally and nationally, working closely with the rank and file; and another, a general penetration in the Stalinist ranks. Comrade Cornell says that the comrades become demoralized if they are left to work in the CP. It is because they are isolated. It is very difficult to work in an atmosphere of falsehood and lies. If their work is systematized and they have regular meetings with the committee, are given the necessary help and understanding in meeting their problems and even meet with some success, then there will not be the demoralization. We must reject the sociological fatalism, begin the political work and organize it on a local and national scale.

Lankin: I would like to add another word on what I said. When I said that we must send qualified comrades into the CP, I did not mean that we should send in the leadership. I believe that it is sufficient for this work to send in some wide-awake rank and filers. I believe it is good to send in certain rank-and-file comrades who understand and can explain our program, to work under a committee. Also, there are many ways of joining the CP: through the fraternal organizations, because here they are not given a third degree, through the clubs, or through a union. Some, who are not known, can even join the party directly. Many who join the CP fraternal organizations are approached to join the CP.

Another question you raised. You asked the question whether the Stalinists really have influence through the rank and file or through the top. I believe that the bulk of the influence is only through the top, because they are in a position to buy influence in many cases. When the CP controls a union, it does so because it gives its whole support to a bureaucrat who does not carry a book in the CP.

Gray: When I was in the Young Communist League and in a Trotskyite nucleus within it, we issued a mimeographed paper for a few weeks. The effect of this paper was remarkable even for such a short duration and had it been continued there would have been far better results than there were. The reason — one of the chief reasons — that the paper ceased was because of the lack of guidance and direction from the CLA. [232] The CPers really did read the paper and derived some benefit from it. It caused a great deal of discussion. If it could be done then, it can be done now, because the issues now are much clearer than they were five years ago.

O'Brien: At the time we discussed the project of a bulletin, I felt that we did not have enough people in the CP to carry it out. Through the discussion I realized that it would be done from the outside. But nothing has been done.

Trotsky: Nothing has been done. During the crisis with the

Norman Thomas people such work was a commonplace. After this, the new step is the work within the CP. We also discussed it with the comrades who were here and it was a commonplace that it must be done and it will be done. It has not been done. However that is not a reproach. It is possible that after leaving the Socialist Party a closed organization was created which was satisfied or dissatisfied with itself. As a transitory step it is comprehensible, but it is dangerous. It might degenerate into a sect. Such a danger was vanquished by the entry into the Socialist Party. Now it is necessary to develop our work against the real obstacle.

The voice of the comrades is interesting — please do not polemicize openly against the Stalinists. It is necessary to awaken the opinion of our own comrades. We often say that the real field of activity is the trade union, but there we find the same task, the Stalinists.

TWO STATEMENTS
ON FAMILY MATTERS[233]

Deposition to the Court
January 15, 1939

. . . To His Honor, the president of the Civil Court of the Seine.

Mr. Leon Sedov, known as Trotsky, who is a writer by profession and who resides in the country of Mexico . . .

Having Mr. Malinvaud as counsel,

Has the honor to inform you:

— That his daughter Zinaida married Mr. Platon Volkov, and that from their marriage issued a child, Vsievolod Volkov, born in Leningrad (Russia) in March 1926;

— That his daughter Zinaida died in Berlin in January 1933, and that his son-in-law Platon Volkov disappeared in Russia;

— That the petitioner is the maternal grandfather and sole surviving relative of the minor Vsievolod Volkov;

— That the custody of the child was assumed by another son of the petitioner, Mr. Leon Sedov, who resided in Paris at 26 rue Lacretelle until his death on 16 February 1938;

— That the petitioner desires, as maternal grandfather and sole surviving relative, to assume custody of the child Vsievolod Volkov, and that while waiting for a determination of the personal status of the child and the rulings applicable for the organization of his guardianship, he may have recourse to temporary emergency measures by which the person and property of the child may be immediately placed in his care.

— For these reasons, the petitioner requests, if it may please the Court, to appoint any administrator it may deem proper over the person and property of the child Vsievolod Volkov, grandson of the petitioner. . . .

The "Kidnaping" of Trotsky's Grandson[234]
March 26, 1939

Although Mme. Jeanne Martin des Pallieres didn't have the slightest legal hold over my grandson, I urged her to come to Mexico to live with the child in our house, or at least to discuss and decide the future with us. She refused, and at the same time she tried to gain possession of my archives, for reasons that are not clear.

Since the reports of my friends in Paris had shown me that it was impossible to leave my grandson with this person even for a short time, I referred the matter to the French authorities, through the intermediaries of the French legation in Mexico and my lawyer in Paris, Mr. Gerard Rosenthal.

The qualified authorities have recognized the complete justice of my claim to this child, who now has no relative anywhere in the world besides me. For a transitional period I have entrusted him to my friends in Paris, a move that was endorsed by the judicial administrator. The child is in the best possible hands while he is waiting to rejoin me.

This story of a kidnaping was made up from start to finish by Mme. Martin des Pallieres's unhealthy imagination.

FIGHTING AGAINST THE STREAM[235]

April 1939

James: (1) I should very much like to hear what Comrade Trotsky thinks about the tremendous rise in the fighting temper of the French workers and the actual decline of our movement in that period. At the founding conference there were six sessions devoted to the French question and at the very end there was a dispute about the nature of the resolution to be drawn up. This gives some idea of the difficulty. C. and S. thought that it was almost entirely a question of leadership and organization.[236] Blasco thought that the comrades could analyze the political situation but lacked the capacity to intervene actively in the struggle of the masses. My personal view is that it is due to the social composition of the group, its concentration in Paris and its predominant interest in politics rather than in industry, although I noticed in the middle of 1937 a great change in that direction. I still believe, however, that this is a question that demands careful thought and analysis.

(2) *The Spanish question.* I believe that it is not too late to initiate, from all possible sources, an investigation into the organizational activity of our comrades in Spain, beginning in 1936. From all that I have heard, five hundred well-organized comrades inside the POUM would have been able at least to make an attempt at the seizure of power in May 1937. I believe that we have a great deal to learn from the methods of work pursued by our comrades inside the POUM and outside. And inasmuch as in France, and perhaps in Holland and in Britain, where there are centrist parties between us and the Social Democracy and where it is likely that we may have to work as our comrades had to work in the POUM in Spain, for all those reasons I believe it is important that some work should be done on the actual experiences of our comrades in Spain.

(3) *The British section.* You are familiar with the history of

249

the section: the split in 1936 and the formation of two groups, one consolidated in the Labour Party and one outside. When C. arrived in the summer of 1938, both groups were about seventy strong. The Labour Party group was more stable. The RSL [Revolutionary Socialist League] consisted of a fusion between the old Marxist League, which split with Groves, and the Marxist Group, 237 and was in contact with about twenty admirable comrades from Edinburgh. The pact for unity and peace stipulated that each group was to continue its own activity and after six months a balance was to be drawn. The last news is the friction has continued and that the Labour Party group is now dominant.

There is also another group — Lee's group in the Labour Party 238 — which refused to have anything to do with fusion, saying that it was bound to fail. The Lee group is very active.

I told Comrade C. that I had ultimately arrived at the conclusion (a) that I had no objection to even the larger part of the comrades of the fusion group being in the Labour Party; (b) but that the independent group with its paper should continue. In the last analysis, the fraction in the Labour Party would not gain any large numbers under the present circumstances, and our independence as a group with a paper was absolutely necessary. Wicks, Sumner, Sara, 239 and others of the old Marxist League, who had worked in the Labour Party for four years and were still in it, thoroughly agreed with us that an independent voice was needed. The Labour Party comrades wanted a theoretical paper like the *New International.* We said no; we wanted a paper like the old *Militant,* 240 part theoretical and part agitational. There is not much further to discuss about the English question as one has had time to consider it at a distance. It is clear that no advice or policy can perform miracles.

The position of the ILP, however, is important for us. 241 Organizationally it is weak, but it has four MPs, its paper sells between twenty-five and thirty thousand copies per week, its conferences and statements are published in the bourgeois newspapers, it gets enough financial support to run fifteen candidates in an election (most of them lose their deposit of $750 per candidate). In general, it says much the same sort of thing that we say and it takes away all that moral and financial support which, for instance, is ours in the United States where there is nothing between us and the Social Democracy, such as it is. Furthermore, the ILP is always opening and then closing, but we are unable to take advantage of the consistent splits and general dissatisfaction of the left wing. If we could split the ILP and, as Maxton has threatened to do of his own accord,[242] drive the Scottish members into Scotland and leave the field in England open, we would be able not to create a great party leading the masses immediately, but we would make extraordinary progress.

I believe that the 1936 resolution on the centrist parties,[243] which stated that the ILP would soon descend into Stalinism, was an error and disoriented the English section. At the present time it would seem that our future progress in Britain in regard to the ILP would depend largely on whether our French section is successful in attracting to itself the best elements in the PSOP. Nevertheless, I propose that our British section should not neglect the ILP in any way and by means of pamphlets, in our press and articles, should make a concentrated drive at its weaknesses and divergences and do its best to accentuate the splits which are constantly opening up in it so as to facilitate its destruction.

Finally there is the question of the comrades going into industry as has been done in one or two districts in America where intellectuals, in their determination to get into contact with the masses, have entered the food industry and other industries wherever that was possible; in certain places with great success. It seems to me in France and most certainly in Britain, this is a means which could very well be attempted in order to strengthen that contact with the masses which is one of the great weaknesses of our party in great cities like London, Paris, and to some extent New York; whereas the Belgian party, based on a working class area in the provinces, is extremely well organized, and despite certain political weakness during the past period shows that in any upheaval such as had taken place in France, it is likely to play a far more powerful part and at least to show infinitely greater progress than our French section has shown.

Trotsky: Yes, the question is why we are not progressing in correspondence with the value of our conceptions, which are not so meaningless as some friends believe. We are not progressing politically. Yes, it is a fact, which is an expression of a general decay of the workers' movements in the last fifteen years. It is the more general cause. When the revolutionary movement in general is declining, when one defeat follows another, when fascism is spreading over the world, when the official "Marxism" is the most powerful organization of deception of the workers, and so on, it is an inevitable situation that the revolutionary elements must work against the general historic current, even if our ideas, our explanations, are as exact and wise as one can demand.

But the masses are not educated by prognostic theoretical conception, but by general experiences of their lives. It is the most general explanation — the whole situation is against us. There must be a turn in the class realization, in the sentiments, in the feelings of the masses; a turn which will give us the opportunity for a large political success.

I remember some discussions in 1927 in Moscow after Chiang Kai-shek stilled the Chinese workers. We predicted this ten days before and Stalin opposed us with the argument that Borodin was vigilant,[244] that Chiang Kai-shek would not have the chance to betray us, etc. I believe that it was eight or ten days later that the tragedy occurred,[245] and our comrades expressed optimism because our analysis was so clear that everyone would see it and we would be sure to win the party. I answered that the strangulation of the Chinese revolution is a thousand times more important for the masses than our predictions. Our predictions can win some few intellectuals who take an interest in such things, but not the masses. The military victory of Chiang Kai-shek will inevitably provoke a depression and this is not conducive to the growth of a revolutionary faction.

Since 1927 we have had a long series of defeats. We are similar to a group who attempt to climb a mountain and who must suffer again and again a downfall of stone, snow, etc. In Asia and Europe is created a new desperate mood of the masses. They heard something analogous to what we say ten or fifteen years ago from the Communist Party and they are pessimistic. That is the general mood of the workers. It is the most general reason. We cannot withdraw from the general historic current — from the general constellation of the forces. The current is against us, that is clear. I remember the period between 1908 and 1913 in Russia. There was also a réaction. In 1905 we had the workers with us — in 1908 and even in 1907 began the great reaction.

Everybody invented slogans and methods to win the masses and nobody won them — they were desperate. In this time the only thing we could do was to educate the cadres and they were melting away. There was a series of splits to the right

or to the left or to syndicalism and so on. Lenin remained
with a small group, a sect, in Paris, but with confidence that
there would be new possibilities of a rise. It came in 1913.
We had a new tide, but then came the war to interrupt this
development. During the war there was a silence as of death
among the workers. The Zimmerwald conference was a conference of very confused elements in its majority.[246] In the
deep recesses of the masses, in the trenches and so on, there
was a new mood, but it was so deep and terrorized that we
could not reach it and give it an expression. That is why the
movement seemed to itself to be very poor and even this element that met in Zimmerwald, in its majority, moved to the
right in the next year, in the next month. I will not liberate
them from their personal responsibility, but still the general
explanation is that the movement had to swim against the
current.

Our situation now is incomparably more difficult than that
of any other organization in any other time, because we have
the terrible betrayal of the Communist International, which
arose from the betrayal of the Second International. The degeneration of the Third International developed so quickly
and so unexpectedly that the same generation which heard
its formation now hears us, and they say, "But we have already heard this once!"

Then there is the defeat of the Left Opposition in Russia.
The Fourth International is connected genetically to the Left
Opposition; the masses call us Trotskyists. "Trotsky wishes
to conquer power, but why did he lose power?" It is an elementary question. We must begin to explain this by the dialectic of history, by the conflict of classes, that even a revolution
produces a reaction.

Max Eastman wrote that Trotsky places too much value on
doctrine and if he had more common sense he would not have
lost power.[247] Nothing in the world is so convincing as success
and nothing so repelling as defeat for the large masses.

You have also the degeneration of the Third International
on the one side and the terrible defeat of the Left Opposition
with the extermination of the whole group. These facts are a
thousand times more convincing for the working class than
our poor paper with even the tremendous circulation of 5000
like the *Socialist Appeal*.

We are in a small boat in a tremendous current. There are
five or ten boats and one goes down and we say it was due
to bad helmsmanship. But that was not the reason — it was
because the current was too strong. It is the most general

explanation and we would never forget this explanation in order not to become pessimistic — we, the vanguard of the vanguard. Then this environment creates special groups of elements around our banner. There are courageous elements who do not like to swim with the current — it is their character. Then there are intelligent elements of bad character who were never disciplined, who always looked for a more radical or more independent tendency and found our tendency, but all of them are more or less outsiders from the general current of the workers' movement. Their value inevitably has its negative side. He who swims against the current is not connected with the masses. Also, the social composition of every revolutionary movement in the beginning is not of workers. It is the intellectuals, semi-intellectuals, or workers connected with the intellectuals who are dissatisfied with the existing organizations. You find in every country a lot of foreigners who are not so easily involved in the labor movement of the country. A Czech in America or in Mexico would more easily become a member of the Fourth International than in Czechoslovakia. The same for a Frenchman in the U.S. The national atmosphere has a tremendous power over individuals.

The Jews in many countries represent the semiforeigners, not totally assimilated, and they adhere to any new critical, revolutionary, or semirevolutionary tendency in politics, in art, literature, and so on. A new radical tendency directed against the general current of history in this period crystallizes around the elements more or less separated from the national life of any country and for them it is more difficult to penetrate into the masses. We are all very critical toward the social composition of our organization and we must change; but we must understand that this social composition did not fall from heaven, but was determined by the objective situation and by our historic mission in this period.

It does not signify that we must be satisfied with the situation. Insofar as it concerns France, it is a long tradition of the French movement connected with the social composition of the country. Especially in the past the petty-bourgeois mentality — individualism on the one side, and on the other an *elan*, a tremendous capacity for improvising.

If you compare in the classic time of the Second International you will find that the French Socialist Party and the German Social Democratic Party had the same number of representatives in parliament. But if you compare the organizations, you will find they are incomparable. The French could only collect 25,000 francs with the greatest difficulty but in Germany to send half a million was nothing. The Germans had in the trade unions some millions of workers and the French had some millions who did not pay their dues. Engels once wrote a letter in which he characterized the French organization and finished with, "and as always, the dues do not arrive."

Our organization suffers from the same illness, the traditional French sickness: this incapacity to organize and at the same time lack of conditions for improvisation. Even so far as we now had a tide in France, it was connected with the People's Front. In this situation the defeat of the People's Front was the proof of the correctness of our conceptions just as was the extermination of the Chinese workers. But the defeat was a defeat and it is directed against revolutionary tendencies until a new tide on a higher level will appear in the new time. We must wait and prepare — a new element, a new factor, in this constellation.

We have comrades who came to us, like Naville and others, fifteen or sixteen or more years ago when they were young boys. Now they are mature people and their whole conscious life they have had only blows, defeats, and terrible defeats on an international scale and they are more or less acquainted with this situation. They appreciate very highly the correctness of their conceptions and they can analyze, but they never had the capacity to penetrate, to work with the masses and they have not acquired it. There is a tremendous necessity to look at what the masses are doing. We have such people in France. I know much less about the British situation, but I believe that we have such people there also.

Why have we lost people? After terrible international defeats we had in France a movement on a very primitive and a very low political level under the leadership of the People's Front. The People's Front — I think this whole period — is a kind of caricature of our February revolution. It is shameful in a country like France, which 150 years ago passed through the greatest bourgeois revolution in the world, that the workers' movement should pass through a caricature of the Russian Revolution.

James: You would not throw the whole responsibility on the Communist Party?

Trotsky: It is a tremendous factor in producing the mentality of the masses. The active factor was the degeneration of the Communist Party.

In 1914 the Bolsheviks were absolutely dominating the workers' movement. It was on the threshold of the war. The most exact statistics show that the Bolsheviks represented not less than three-fourths of the proletarian vanguard. But beginning with the February revolution, the most backward people — peasants, soldiers, even former Bolshevik workers — were attracted toward this People's Front current and the Bolshevik Party became isolated and very weak. The general current was on a very low level, but powerful, and moved toward the October Revolution. It is a question of tempo. In France, after all the defeats, the People's Front attracted elements that sympathized with us theoretically but were involved with the movement of the masses and we became for some time more isolated than before. You can combine all these elements. I can even affirm that many (but not all) of our leading comrades, especially in old sections, by a new turn of situation would be rejected by the revolutionary mass movement and new leaders, fresh leadership, will arise in the revolutionary current.

In France the regeneration began with the entry into the Socialist Party. The policy of the Socialist Party was not clear, but it won many new members. These new members were accustomed to a large milieu. After the split they became a little discouraged. They were not so steeled. Then they lost their not-so-steeled interest and were regained by the current of the People's Front. It is regrettable, but it is explainable.

In Spain the same reasons played the same role with the supplementary factor of the deplorable conduct of the Nin group. He was in Spain as [a] representative of the Russian Left Opposition, and during the first year he did not try to mobilize, to organize our independent elements. We hoped that we would win Nin for the correct conception, and so on. Publicly the Left Opposition gave him its support. In private correspondence we tried to win him and push him forward, but without success. We lost time. Was it correct? It is difficult to say.

If in Spain we had had an experienced comrade, our situation would be incomparably more favorable, but we did not have one. We put all our hopes on Nin, and his policy consisted of personal maneuvers in order to avoid responsibility.

He played with the revolution. He was sincere, but his whole mentality was that of a Menshevik. It was a tremendous handicap, and to fight against this handicap only with correct formulas falsified by our own representatives in the first period, the Nins, made it very difficult.

Do not forget that we lost the first revolution in 1905. Before our first revolution we had the tradition of high courage, self-sacrifice, etc. Then we were pushed back to a position of a miserable minority of thirty or forty men. Then came the war.

James: How many were there in the Bolshevik Party?

Trotsky: In 1910 in the whole country there were a few dozen people. Some were in Siberia. But they were not organized. The people whom Lenin could reach by correspondence or by an agent numbered about thirty or forty at most. However, the tradition and the ideas among the more advanced workers was a tremendous capital, which was used later during the revolution, but practically, at this time, we were absolutely isolated.

Yes, history has its own laws which are very powerful — more powerful than our theoretical conceptions of history. Now you have in Europe a catastrophe — the decline of Europe, the extermination of countries. It has a tremendous influence on the workers when they observe these movements of diplomacy, of the armies, and so on, and on the other side a small group with a small paper which makes explanations. But it is a question of his being mobilized tomorrow and of his children being killed. There is a terrible disproportion between the task and the means.

If the war begins now, and it seems that it will begin, then in the first month we will lose two-thirds of what we now have in France. They will be dispersed. They are young and will be mobilized. Subjectively many will remain true to our movement. Those who will not be arrested and who will remain — there may be three or five — I do not know how many, but they will be absolutely isolated.

Only after some months will the criticism and the disgust begin to show on a large scale and everywhere our isolated comrades — in a hospital, in a trench, a woman in a village — will find a changed atmosphere and will say a courageous word. And the same comrade who was unknown in some section of Paris will become a leader of a regiment, of a division, and will feel himself to be a powerful revolutionary leader. This change is in the character of our period.

I do not wish to say that we must reconcile ourselves with the impotence of our French organization. I believe that with the help of the American comrades we can win the PSOP and make a great leap forward. The situation is ripening and it says to us, "You must utilize this opportunity." And if our comrades turn their backs the situation will change. It is absolutely necessary that your American comrades go to Europe again and that they do not simply give advice, but together with the International Secretariat decide that our section should enter the PSOP. It has some thousands. From the point of view of a revolution it is not a big difference, but from the point of view of working it is a tremendous difference. With fresh elements we can make a tremendous leap forward.

Now in the United States we have a new character of work and I believe we can be very optimistic without illusions and exaggerations. In the United States we have a larger credit of time. The situation is not so immediate, so acute. That is important.

Then I agree with Comrade Stanley who writes that we can now have very important successes in the colonial and semicolonial countries. We have a very important movement in Indochina. I agree absolutely with Comrade James that we can have a very important Negro movement, because these people have not passed through the history of the last two decades so intimately. As a mass they did not know about the Russian Revolution and the Third International. They can begin history as from the beginning. It is absolutely necessary for us to have fresh blood. That is why we have more success among the youth. Insofar as we have been capable of approaching them, we have had good results. They are very attentive to a clear and honest revolutionary program.

Great Britain and the ILP? It is also a special task. I followed it a bit more closely when I was in Norway. It seems to me that our comrades who entered the ILP had the same experience with the ILP that our American comrades had with the Socialist Party. But not all our comrades entered the ILP, and they developed an opportunistic policy so far as I could observe, and that is why their experience in the ILP was not so good. The ILP remained almost as it was before while the Socialist Party is now empty. I do not know how to approach it now. It is now a Glasgow organization. It is a local machine and they have influence in the municipal machine, and I have heard that it is very corrupt. It is a separate job of Maxton.

Rebellions of the rank and file are a familiar thing in the ILP. In preparing for a new convention Fenner Brockway becomes a patron of the rebellious section and secures a majority. Then Maxton says he will resign. Then Fenner Brockway says, "No, we will abandon our victory. We can give up our principles, but not our Maxton." I believe that the most important thing is to compromise them — to put them in the mud — the Maxtons and the Brockways. We must identify them with class enemies. We must compromise the ILP with tremendous and pitiless attacks on Maxton. He is the sacrificial goat for all the sins of the British movement and especially the ILP. By such concentrated attacks on Maxton, systematic attacks in our press, we can expedite the split in the ILP. At the same time we must point out that if Maxton is the lackey of Chamberlain, then Fenner Brockway is the lackey of Maxton.

James: What do you think of an independent paper for the work of slashing at Maxton, etc.?

Trotsky: It is a practical question. In France, if our section enters the PSOP I believe that the International Secretariat should publish the *Quatrieme Internationale* for all French-speaking countries twice-monthly. It is simply a question of the juridical possibility. I believe that even if we work inside the Labour Party we must have an independent paper, not as opposed to our comrades within it, but rather to be outside the control of the ILP.

ON THE HISTORY
OF THE LEFT OPPOSITION[248]

April 1939

Trotsky: Comrade James has studied this subject with the greatest attention and the numerous annotations I have made are evidence of the care with which I have read his memorandum. It is important for all our comrades to see our past with insistence on revolutionary clarity. In parts the manuscript is very perspicacious, but I have noticed here the same fault that I have noticed in *World Revolution* — a very good book — and that is a lack of dialectical approach, Anglo-Saxon empiricism, and formalism which is only the reverse of empiricism.

C. L. R. James makes his whole approach to the subject depend on one date — the appearance of Stalin's theory of socialism in a single country — April 1924. But the theory appeared in October 1924. This makes the whole structure false.

In April 1924 it was not clear whether the German revolution was going forward or back.[249] In November '23 I asked that all the Russian comrades in Germany should be recalled. New strata *might* lift the revolution to a higher stage. On the other hand, the revolution might decline. It it declined, the first step of the reaction would be to arrest the Russians as foreign agents of disorder. Stalin opposed me: "You are always too hasty. In August you said the revolution was near; now you say that it is over already." I didn't say that it was over, but suggested that this precautionary step should be taken. By the summer of 1924 Stalin had convinced himself that the German revolution was defeated. He then asked the Red professors to find him something from Lenin to tell the people. They searched and found two or three quotations and Stalin changed the passage in his book. The German revolution had more influence on Stalin than Stalin on the German revolution. In 1923 the whole party was in a fever over the coming revolution. Stalin would not have dared to oppose me on this question at the Central Committee. The Left Opposition was very much to the fore on this question.

James: Brandler went to Moscow convinced of the success of the revolution. What changed him?

Trotsky: I had many interviews with Brandler. He told me that what was troubling him was not the seizure of power, but what to do after. I told him "Look here, Brandler, you say the prospects are good, but the bourgeoisie is in power, in control of the state, the army, police, etc. The question is to break that power. . . ." Brandler took many notes during many discussions with me. But this very boldness of his was only a cover for his secret fears. It is not easy to lead a struggle against bourgeois society. He went to Chemnitz and there met the leaders of the Social Democracy, a collection of little Brandlers. He communicated to them in his speech his secret fears by the very way he spoke to them. Naturally they drew back and this mood of defeatism permeated to the workers.

In the 1905 Russian revolution there was a dispute in the soviet as to whether we should challenge the czarist power with a demonstration on the anniversary of Bloody Sunday. To this day I do not know for certain whether it was the correct thing to do at that time or not. The committee could not decide, so we consulted the soviet. I made the speech, putting the two alternatives in an objective manner, and the soviet decided by an overwhelming majority not to demonstrate. But I am certain that if I had said it was necessary to demonstrate and spoken accordingly we would have had a great majority in favor. It was the same with Brandler. What was wanted in Germany in 1923 was a revolutionary party. . . .

You accuse me also of degeneration when you quote Fischer. But why did I give that interview? In revolution it is always wise to throw on the enemy the responsibility. Thus in 1917 they asked me at the soviet: "Are the Bolsheviks preparing an insurrection?" What could I say? I said, "No, we are defending the revolution, but if you provoke us. . . !" It was the same thing here. Poland and France were using the Russian Bolsheviks as a pretext for preparing intervention and reactionary moves. With the full consent of the German comrades I gave this interview, while the German comrades explained the situation to the German workers. Meanwhile I had a cavalry detachment under Dybenko ready on the Polish border.[250]

James: You would not agree with Victor Serge that the bureaucracy sabotaged the Chinese revolution; in other words, that its attitude to the Chinese revolution was the same as its attitude toward the Spanish?

Trotsky: Not at all. Why should they sabotage it? I was on a committee (with Chicherin, Voroshilov, and some others) on the Chinese revolution.[251] They were even opposed to my attitude, which was considered pessimistic. They were anxious for its success.

James: For the success of the bourgeois democratic revolution. Wasn't their opposition to the proletarian revolution the opposition of a bureaucracy which was quite prepared to support a bourgeois democratic revolution, but from the fact of its being a bureaucracy could not support a proletarian revolution?

Trotsky: Formalism. We had the greatest revolutionary party in the world in 1917. In 1936 it strangles the revolution in Spain. How did it develop from 1917 to 1936? That is the question. According to your argument, the degeneration would have started in October 1917. In my view it started in the first years of the New Economic Policy.[252] But even in 1927 the whole party was eagerly awaiting the issue of the Chinese revolution. What happened was that the bureaucracy acquired certain bureaucratic habits of thinking. It proposed to restrain the peasants today so as not to frighten the generals. It thought it would push the bourgeoisie to the left. It saw the Kuomintang as a body of office-holders and thought it could put Communists into the offices and so change the direction of events. . . . And how would you account for the change which demanded a Canton Commune?[253]

James: Victor Serge says that it was only for the sake of the Sixth World Congress that they wanted the Commune "if only for a quarter of an hour."

Trotsky: It was more for the party internally than for the International. The party was excited over the Chinese revolution. Only during 1923 had it reached a higher pitch of intensity.

No, you want to begin with the degeneration complete. Stalin and Company genuinely believed that the Chinese revolution was a bourgeois democratic revolution and sought to establish the dictatorship of the proletariat and peasantry.

James: You mean that Stalin, Bukharin, Tomsky,[254] Rykov, and the rest did not understand the course of the Russian Revolution?

Trotsky: They did not. They took part and events overwhelmed them. Their position on China was the same they had in March 1917 until Lenin came. In different writings of theirs you will see passages that show that they never understood. A different form of existence, their bureaucratic habits affected their thinking and they reverted to their previous position. They even enshrined it in the program of the Comintern: proletarian revolution for Germany, dictatorship of the proletariat and peasantry for semicolonial countries, etc.

(Comrade Trotsky here asks Van to get a copy of the Draft Program and the extract is read.) I condemned it in my critique of the Draft Program [of the Communist International].

James: What about Bukharin's statement in 1925 that if war came revolutionists should support the bourgeois-Soviet bloc?

Trotsky: After Lenin's testament Bukharin wanted to show that he was a real dialectician.[255] He studied Hegel and on every occasion tried to show that he was a realist. Hence, "Enrich yourselves," "Socialism as a snail's pace," etc.[256] And not only Bukharin, but I and all of us at various times wrote absurd things. I will grant you that.

James: And Germany 1930-33?[257]

Trotsky: I cannot agree that the policy of the International was only a materialization of the commands of Moscow. It is necessary to see the policy as a whole, from the internal and the international points of view, from all sides. The foreign policy of Moscow, and the orientation of the Social Democracy to Geneva could play a role. But there was also the necessity of a turn owing to the disastrous effect of the previous policy on the party inside Russia. After all the bureaucracy is dealing with 160 million people who have been through three revolutions. What they are saying and thinking is collected and classified. Stalin wanted to show that he was no Menshevik. Hence this violent turn to the left. We must see it as a whole, in all its aspects.

James: But the British Stalinist, Campbell, writes that when the British delegation in 1928 was presented with the theory of social fascism it opposed the idea, but soon was convinced that it was correct. . . .[258]

(It was agreed to continue the discussion. During the interval Comrade James submitted a document. Discussion continues:)

Trotsky: I have read your document claiming to clarify the position, but it does not clarify it. You state that you accept my view of 1923, but later in the document I see that you do not really accept it. . . . I find it strange that on the Negro question you should be so realistic and on this be so undialectical.[259] (I suspect that you are just a *little* opportunistic on the Negro question, but I am not quite sure.)

In 1924, Stalin's slogan (socialism in a single country) corresponded to the mood of the young intellectuals, without training, without tradition. . . .

But despite that, when Stalin wanted to strangle the Spanish revolution openly, he had to wipe out thousands of Old Bolsheviks.[260] The first struggle started on the permanent revolution, the bureaucracy seeking peace and quiet.[261] Then into this came the German revolution of 1923. Stalin dared not even oppose me openly then. We never knew until afterwards that he had secretly written the letter to Bukharin saying that the revolution should be held back. Then, after the German defeat, came the struggle over equality. It was in defense of the privileges of the bureaucracy that Stalin became its undisputed leader. . . .

Russia was a backward country. These leaders had Marxist conceptions, but after October they soon returned to their old ideas. Voroshilov and others used to ask me: "But how do you think it possible that the Chinese masses, so backward, could establish the dictatorship of the proletariat?"

In Germany they hoped now for a miracle to break the backbone of the Social Democracy; their politics had failed utterly to detach the masses from it. Hence this new attempt to get rid of it. . . . Stalin hoped that the German Communist Party would win a victory and to think that he had a "plan" to allow fascism to come into power is absurd. It is a deification of Stalin.

James: He made them cease their opposition to the Red Referendum; he made Remmele say "After Hitler, our turn"; 262 he made them stop fighting the fascists in the streets.

Trotsky: "After Hitler, our turn," was a boast, a confession of bankruptcy. You pay too much attention to it.

Schuessler: They stopped fighting in the streets because their detachments were small CP detachments. Good comrades were constantly being shot, and inasmuch as workers as a whole were not taking part, they called it off. It was a part of their zig-zags.

Trotsky: There you are! They did all sorts of things. They even offered the united front sometimes.

James: Duranty said in 1931 that they did not want the revolution in Spain. 263

Trotsky: Do not take what Duranty says at face value. Litvinov wanted to say that they were not responsible for what was happening in Spain. He could not say that himself so he said it through Duranty. Perhaps even they did not want to be bothered about Spain, being in difficulties at home. . . . But I would say that Stalin sincerely wished the triumph of the German Communist Party in Germany 1930-33. . . .

Also you cannot think of the Comintern as being merely an instrument of Stalin's foreign policy. In France in 1934 the Communist Party had declined from 80,000 to 30,000. It was necessary to have a new policy. We do not know the archives of the Comintern, what correspondence passed, etc. At the same time Stalin was seeking a new foreign policy. From one side and the other we have these tendencies which go to make the new turn. They are different sides of the same process. . . . The French Communist Party is not only an agency of Moscow, but a national organization with members of parliament, etc.

All that, however, is not very dangerous, although it shows a great lack of proportion to say that our whole propaganda has been meaningless. If that is so, we are bankrupt. What is much more dangerous is the sectarian approach to the Labour Party.

You say that I put forward the slogan of Blum-Cachin without reservations.[264] Then you remember, "All power to the soviet!" and you say that the united front was no soviet. It is the same sectarian approach.

James: We have had difficulty in England with advocating a Labour government with the necessary reservations.

Trotsky: In France in all our press, in our archives and propaganda, we regularly made all the necessary reservations. Your failure in England is due to lack of ability; also lack of flexibility, due to the long domination of bourgeois thought in England. I would say to the English workers, "You refuse to accept my point of view. Well, perhaps I did not explain well enough. Perhaps you are stupid. Anyway I have failed. But now, you believe in your party. Why allow Chamberlain to hold the power? Put your party in power. I will help you all I can. I know that they will not do what you think, but as you don't agree with me and we are small, I will help you to put them in." But it is very important to bring up these questions periodically. I would suggest that you write an article discussing these points and publish it in our press. *(Comrade James agreed that he would.)*

THE DIEGO RIVERA AFFAIR[265]

Letter to James P. Cannon
October 30, 1938

Dear Friend,

I must occupy you with the question of Diego Rivera. He is extremely dissatisfied with the resolution of the congress.[266]

1) Diego Rivera protested most emphatically against the last paragraph of the resolution, which recommends that Rivera not belong to the Mexican section and that he work directly under the supervision of the Latin American subcommittee.

How did this decision arise? For a year I observed the work of Diego Rivera in the League. It represented for himself a series of useless personal sacrifices and personal offenses. Repeatedly I expressed my opinion in this sense that Diego should not occupy any administrative posts in the League. But as a member of the League he was continually nominated to posts and he couldn't find the possibility to refuse. And then the conflicts, the source of which you know, began again. In this way arose the idea that Diego should not be considered as a member of the Mexican League but as a member of our Pan-American staff. This was my personal idea. I discussed it with Diego himself. He didn't oppose it. At that time he found himself that the best for him as a painter and as a revolutionary would be not to be intricated in the routine work of the Mexican League. In this sense I discussed the question with you. My formulation was, as you surely remember yourself: "Diego is too precious an acquisition of the Fourth International for us to allow the political fate of this acquisition to rest in dependence upon the attitude of Galicia and company." You, Shachtman, and Dunne were completely of the same opinion[267]

I am absolutely sure that *this* is the origin of the last paragraph of the resolution.

But I must recognize that the formulation is not happy and can give pretext to misinterpretations and insinuations. I personally don't believe that it was necessary to *publish* this part of the resolution. 268 But it is done and now it is necessary to explain the real meaning of this decision, namely: (a) The conference didn't of course forbid Diego to belong to the Mexican League. Such a decision would be really incompatible with his revolutionary dignity. As a matter of fact every member of the Fourth International is obliged to belong to the national section. The conference made an *exception* for Diego, giving him the right and the advice not to belong to the Mexican section but to develop his activity on a larger arena: Pan-American and international. The reason for that decision was that some Mexican leaders didn't understand enough the importance for the Fourth International as a whole of such a world figure as Diego Rivera. I believe that in one form or another this idea, which is the genuine sense of the decision of the conference, should. be expressed in our international press. It could be for example done in the form of a statement of the Pan-American Committee in answering questions upon the real meaning of the decision concerning Diego Rivera. In my opinion it should be done as early and as categorically as possible. 269

2) The other objections of Diego Rivera made in personal discussions with me before the publishing of the resolution seem to be blown away by the text of the resolution: (a) Galicia's league is not recognized as our section; (b) The new section should be reconstructed on the base of real work of everyone in accordance with the decisions of the conference, especially in the trade union work. Galicia and Fernandez 270 are deprived of the right to occupy during a year any responsible post in the Mexican section. (c) C. is appointed as the representative of the International Bureau in Mexico. 271

All these decisions correspond in my eyes to the propositions we elaborated here in agreement with Diego himself. (I would for my part oppose putting Fernandez on the same level as Galicia: I would for example prefer that he be demoted for six months only. But this is not important.)

Comrade C. says that all former members of the League are trying to reestablish their reputation. We should not be too confident. The experience of the past here is very bad. For my part I am almost convinced that Galicia will rebegin his maneuvers. The resolution of the conference arms us enough in order to prevent such maneuvers and not to permit him again to win the support of the overwhelming majority of the organization. The future will show how the selection can go on. Carefulness, caution are now obligatory. But it is clear that the whole Mexican experience begins now on a *new, higher* level and under the supervision of our international organization. This new experience will have a great educational value for the members of the future Mexican section.

Concerning the theoretical magazine it should in my opinion remain absolutely independent from the future Mexican section. *Clave* is destined for all Spanish-speaking partisans and sympathizers of the Fourth International. The editorial board is composed of three members of the Fourth International (Diego Rivera, C., and myself) and three sympathizers (the Zamora brothers and Ferrel). For the next period I believe the magazine should continue as it is. This is also the opinion of Diego and C. It would be good that the Pan-American Committee confirms us in the composition of the editorial board and the direct dependence of us three on the Pan-American Committee.

Comradely,

Letter to Charles Curtiss
December 24, 1938

Dear Comrade Curtiss,

In a letter to Comrade Diego I repeat my proposition to separate the two absolutely different questions and arguments, but I ask myself what to do if Diego will not accept this proposition.

I don't believe that we should simply reject the article of Diego as it is.[272] We should propose to the editorial board to publish the article under the personal responsibility of Diego in the Open Forum. At the same time I propose to publish in the name of the editorial board the enclosed short article on the first page of *Clave.*

Best greetings,
Hansen [Trotsky]

A Necessary Statement[273]
January 4, 1939

Over the last few months I've done everything I possibly could to forestall a clash between Comrade Rivera and our international organization. I can present at any moment the entire collection of documents characterizing my efforts. It is hardly necessary to point out that at the same time I tried to preserve relations of sincerity and friendship with Comrade Rivera, despite his more and more ambiguous, or even frankly hostile, attitude toward the Fourth International as well as toward me.

Unfortunately, my efforts have not met with success. Each time I succeeded in smoothing over some conflict or clearing up some misunderstanding, Comrade Rivera undertook a new attack without the slightest concern for the decisions of the international congress, the Pan-American Committee, or even the decisions reached collectively here. There are, I fear, profound political reasons for this attitude. At present, it has led to acts that signify Comrade Rivera's moral break with the Fourth International, and, I have every reason to fear, his preparation for breaking personal relations with me.

By chance I came across a copy of a letter Comrade Rivera sent to Andre Breton, a French writer who is fully worthy of esteem and confidence, but who is not even a member of our organization. This letter represents a venomous attack against the principles I support and even against me, morally. It contains statements that are absolutely false and that can only be intended to compromise me in the eyes of Breton and his friends, and by means that are far from straightforward.

Comrade Rivera states that I ordered his article to be published in the form of a letter (because, you see, I cannot tolerate the free expression of Rivera's ideas on art). However, it was in the presence of Rivera and other comrades that I first became aware of the fact that the article had been published in the form of a letter. I was astonished. In Rivera's presence I expressed my astonishment to the technical editor, going so far as to tell him he had acted contrary to a decision made collectively. Rivera has not forgotten any of that. This leaves just one explanation: he suspects that behind the scenes I acted contrary to the decision openly proposed by me and accepted in good faith by Rivera, and that I feigned astonishment when the technical editor made the change. Well, I reject such a suspicion with the greatest indignation.

After the meeting mentioned above, I spoke with Comrade C. about the change he had made. Here is what I understood from what he told me: It seemed to him that the article was not Marxist or, at least, that it contained anti-Marxist theses. He knew that neither I nor other friends had read the article. Because he took his responsibility as a representative of the IS [International Secretariat][274] seriously, he believed it necessary to disclaim any responsibility in publishing the article. He should have notified his colleagues and the author, but time was short, it seems. In any event, the crime is not overwhelming. But Comrade Diego not only found it necessary to denounce it in . . . Paris, but even to attribute it to me (without giving me the slightest warning) when in reality I knew *absolutely nothing* about it. Moreover, in order to be able to publish Rivera's article, which he expanded at the last moment, Comrade C. cut two of my articles from the issue, articles that the editors had asked me for. For the same reason (lack of time) he did not notify me about the fate of my articles, one of which has lost all news value since then. I learned about the elimination of my two articles at the same meeting at which Diego protested about the change in subtitles. There you have the pure truth.

In the same letter, Comrade Rivera accuses me of having had recourse to Stalinist (but "tender") methods, of having made a coup d'etat in the matter of FIARI, etc. All that is untrue, and Comrade Rivera knows the facts at least as well as I do. To carry out a coup d'etat you have to have a government, or in this case, an organization. Well, here there was not the slightest trace of either. Nothing was done in this area, for reasons we can leave aside for the moment. In the same meeting of five friends I referred to above, I proposed, in Rivera's presence, to form a provisional committee of FIARI to get things moving. Rivera not only did not protest, but willingly accepted the proposal. He said, "Yes, now, after the affair of the O'Gorman frescoes,[275] perhaps we can get something done." I then continued, "But in that case we need a provisional secretary. Who should it be?" It seems to me that it was Comrade A. Z. who proposed the candidacy of Ferrel.[276] I asked Ferrel, "Would that be all right with you?" He replied, "Why not?" or something similar. All this took place without the slightest objection from anyone and in an atmosphere of the greatest cordiality. Where the coup d'etat comes in, I just don't understand. Rivera speaks of Ferrel with a note of disdain. Why? And in particular, why in a letter destined for France? As for myself, I have only known Ferrel for two or three months. When his candidacy for the editorial post came up, Diego's opinion was requested in my presence. He didn't make the slightest objection, and the post of editor is, in spite of everything, a little more important than the post of provisional secretary of an as-yet-nonexistent group of FIARI. Where, therefore, is the evidence of a coup d'etat and my Stalinist methods? I do not understand at all. These two examples are sufficient to characterize Diego's ill will toward me.

As far as I can make out, this ill will is the result of my attempt to have a frank discussion with him about his political activity. I told him that he was organically incapable of carrying out the day-to-day work of a functionary of a workers' organization. On the other hand, however, thanks to his imagination and his powerful creative spirit, he could be extremely useful in the leadership, on condition, naturally, that he recognize the function of the leadership and submit to its discipline, like anyone else. It seemed to me that he decided on the spot to show me that he was capable of performing miracles in politics as well as in art (but politics is much less of an individual affair than art; in fact, you could even say that it is a collective effort by definition). He undertook a series of purely personal adventures — yes, unfortunately, adventures — in the union movement, which produced results that were negative and prejudicial to our movement. Instead of blaming himself, he began to direct his discontent against our International and against me personally.

At the same time, Rivera went through an ideological crisis that was, in its general features, identical to the crises many contemporary intellectuals have gone through: under the pressure of extreme reaction they have abandoned Marxism for some eclectic hodgepodge. In private and semiprivate discussions, Comrade Rivera has begun to defend absolutely anti-Marxist conceptions on the question of the state, the trade unions, the party, the October Revolution, and Bolshevik methods, the social function of art, the role of war in society, and so forth. If it were only a matter of private discussions, we could certainly live with it, as I have tried to do for a whole period. But his concepts, which are never fully formulated, lead him to engage in trade union activity and personal propaganda that are directed against all the fundamental principles of the Fourth International.

The situation has become absolutely intolerable. It is necessary therefore to dispense with all equivocation.

As one can see from the above, there are two aspects to the affair: the personal side and the general side. It is necessary to separate them and to liquidate the first as soon as possible. If Comrade Rivera is ready to recognize that his temperament has led him to take the path of accusations devoid of all foundation, to say the least; if he withdraws his statements in a letter addressed to Breton and sends me a copy, as well as a copy of his previous letter; then I will say no more on this question. It is unnecessary to point out that in this case I will make no use of the present statement. Rivera's setting the record straight can have the character of a personal initiative, but it must be absolutely categorical; that is, it must correspond to reality. After a formal liquidation of the personal incident, the general question remains to be dealt with. Comrade Rivera is a member of the Pan-American Committee, not to mention the Fourth International. We have our congresses, our statutes, our decisions, and our discipline. The congress tried, given Rivera's personality, to create somewhat special conditions for him, freeing him, at least for the difficult period, from the obligation to participate in the work of the Mexican section of the Fourth International. But this decision naturally cannot signify that Comrade Rivera has full freedom to act, under the banner of the Fourth International but against its principles, against its decisions, and against its institutions.

To give most recent examples, let us cite the following. On the editorial board of *Clave*, the Fourth International is represented by Comrades Rivera, C., and Cr.[277] These three comrades are responsible before the Pan-American Bureau for the line of the magazine. But Rivera systematically refuses to consult this three-member Bureau and to submit to its decisions. In the last article on the Ramirez case,[278] Rivera found it necessary, contrary to our previous proposals, to attack everything in Bolshevik politics on the question of trade unions, without clarification, without details, without citations, and without proof. When Cr. and C. proposed that he at least divide the article and hold the second part for the "Open Forum" column in the following issue, he refused to accept the proposal.

It is also necessary to mention that Comrade Rivera's attitude toward Comrade C. is not normal. C. was invited here on the direct initiative of Rivera, who offered C., in conversations with Cannon and others, his full collaboration and all the necessary facilities. C. is a very reserved comrade. He never complains. On the contrary, he does everything to adjust to the situation. But this situation, as far as I can judge, is absolutely intolerable. Far from upholding C.'s authority as the official representative of the IS, Rivera goes ahead with his own work, absolutely independently of C. This creates extremely serious organizational difficulties for C., not to mention the personal difficulties.

How can this political ambiguity be eliminated?

If the differences are really so profound as to require Rivera to carry out his own political line against the line of the Fourth International, a political break is inevitable. It can and must be carried out in a frank, open, and decisive manner. It must be clear to all that from now on the Fourth International has no responsibility for Rivera's political activities. This would be a painful and serious loss, but the present situation is even worse.

If the differences are not (or are not yet) that profound, and if Diego Rivera simply finds that his temperament has carried him beyond the bounds of what our common interests permit, it is up to Rivera himself to draw all the consequences. Time and again I have taken upon myself the initiative for a frank discussion. Now it is Rivera's turn to take this initiative, once he liquidates the personal aspect of the difficulties. I will bring to the new discussion all the goodwill I can muster. If Rivera decides to renew his activity within the normal framework of the Fourth International, all the misunderstandings of the past will be liquidated and close collaboration will once again take their place.

The Source of the Problem[279]
January 11, 1939

If Comrade Van[280] has understood Diego Rivera correctly, he refuses to give public explanations for his resignation from the Fourth International so that . . . he would not hinder my living in his house. Truly, one can hardly believe one's ears. When there are differences within an organization, and when both sides remain loyal to the fundamental principles, an open discussion can have a completely friendly character, without in any way poisoning personal relationships (for example, my discussion with Burnham and Carter, in the United States, or with Craipeau, in France, on the character of the Soviet state, etc.).[281]

What infects the atmosphere and poisons the personal relationships are the unprincipled intrigues and the behind-the-scenes insinuations, which are completely unfounded. In his letter to Breton, Diego Rivera accused me of such acts. To illustrate his accusation, which he has never openly presented to me, he gave only two examples, *which he himself*

invented from start to finish. When I pointed this out to him
in writing, he promised to rectify his false statements. The
next day he refused to do that. Moreover, his statements were
not only false, but even absurd, absolutely contrary to the
actual facts and to my general methods. It is not open and
serious discussion but actions of this type that make moral
solidarity impossible, and preclude benefiting from hospitality.

I will make every effort to overcome the material difficulties
of my somewhat special situation in order to move my dwelling
as soon as possible.

At the same time, I am ready immediately to present to
any commission at all, or to Comrade Rivera himself, copies
of all my correspondence dealing with him. This correspondence
demonstrates that I have always been concerned with empha-
sizing to comrades how important it is that Rivera is in our
ranks and I have always tried to raise his authority in the
eyes of our young friends.

I distinguish between the personal conflict, unilaterally provoked by Diego Rivera, and the political question. If Comrade
Rivera remains in the Fourth International, as I sincerely
hope, I will extend to him the same collaboration as in the
past.

Letter to Frida Rivera
January 12, 1939

Dear Frida,

We here were all very happy, and even proud, of your success in New York, [282] because we consider you as an artistic
ambassador not only from San Angel, but also from
Coyoacan. Even Bill Lander, objective representative of the
American press, informed us that, according to press notices,
you had a genuine success in the States. Our heartiest con-
gratulations.

Then we heard that you were ill, even seriously so. Yesterday Van told us that you were now convalescent and possibly
would go to France within a short time. We all hope that
in France you will find the same success as was yours in the
States.

However, before you leave the New Continent I wish to
communicate to you some complications with Diego, which

are very painful to me and to Natalia and to the whole household.

It is very difficult for me to find out the real source of Diego's discontent. Twice I tried to provoke a frank discussion on the matter, but he was very general in his answers. The only thing I could extract from him was his indignation at my reluctance to recognize those characteristics in him which would make for a good revolutionary functionary. I insisted that he should never accept a bureaucratic position in the organization, because a "secretary" who never writes, never answers letters, never comes to meetings on time and always makes the opposite of the common decision is not a good secretary. And I ask you, why should Diego be a "secretary"? That he is an authentic revolutionary needs no proof; but he is a revolutionary multiplied by a great artist and it is even this "multiplication" which makes him absolutely unfit for routine work in the party. I am certain that in the time of a revolutionary tide he would be invaluable, thanks to his passion, courage, and imagination. In peacetime he is precious on a revolutionary staff which he can inspire by his initiative and ardor. But for routine organizational work, our friend Diego is absolutely unfit.

It seemed as though he had the ambition of proving to me that he was the best bureaucrat in the world and that he had become a great painter only by chance. He began a purely personal activity in the Casa del Pueblo and the CGT and concealed this activity from me and from the other comrades. I was very much alarmed, because I was sure that this personal venture could not end without disagreeable results for the Fourth International and for Diego personally. I believe that it was precisely the fact that Diego "conspired" a bit against me which at the same time irritated him against me and the other comrades. It is the only sound explanation I can find.

In my eyes, the experiments with the Casa del Pueblo and the CGT were not catastrophic, but were very unhappy. The leadership of the CGT turned not to the left, but to the right, and did so in a very cynical manner; I presume that it was the cause of Diego's last explosion against me.

He wrote an absolutely inconceivable letter to Breton. The factual basis of his outburst against me is absolutely false, a pure product of Diego's imagination (I shall ask Van to send you a copy of his refutation of Diego's "grievances"). [283] Diego now says that it is not important. Of course it is not important in itself, but it is an infallible symptom of his genuine

Diego Rivera and Frida Kahlo Rivera.

mood. He told Van that even if the smaller facts were not correct, the larger fact remains true, namely that I wish to *rid myself of Diego*. As "proof" Diego says that I refused to hear a reading of his article on art. Dear Frida, it is absolutely incredible that one finds it necessary to defend himself against such accusations.

Unexpectedly, Diego brought his article on art to a meeting of friends at my house and proposed to read it immediately so that we could give our opinions on it. I remarked that I understood Spanish only when I could have the manuscript before me and that if I only heard it, at least half was lost. That is entirely true. In order to voice an opinion on such an important matter I should have to *study* the article with a pencil in hand. Then I could propose criticism, changes, or amendments without provoking a general discussion about heaven and hell. It was that kind of collaboration we had when Diego wrote for *Las Novedades*. It was even decided, upon my suggestion, that copies of every article should be sent to all interested friends, but Diego forgets the common decisions immediately and then he looks for the most fantastic explanations of the most simple things.

The idea of my wanting to be rid of Diego is so incredible, so absurd, permit me to say, so mad, that I can only shrug my shoulders helplessly. During these months we passed many hours with Natalia in discussing what we could do to clear the atmosphere and to reestablish the old, friendly relationship. Once we visited Diego together with Natalia and passed a very, very good hour with him. Then I visited him alone (in spite of his resistance) and provoked a discussion. After each visit I had the impression that the matter was definitely settled, but the next day it began again and seemed worse than ever.

A few days ago Diego resigned from the Fourth International. I hope that the resignation will not be accepted. For my part, I will do everything possible to settle at least the political matter, even if I am not successful in settling the personal question. However, I believe your help is essential in this crisis. Diego's break with us would signify not only a heavy blow to the Fourth International, but — I am afraid to say it — would mean the moral death of Diego himself. Apart from the Fourth International and its sympathizers I doubt whether he would be able to find a milieu of understanding and sympathy, not only as an artist but as a revolutionist and as a person.

Now, dear Frida, you know the situation here. I cannot believe that it is hopeless. In any case, I would be the last to abandon the effort to reestablish the political and personal friendship and I sincerely hope that you will collaborate with me in that direction.

Natalia and I wish you the best of health and artistic success and we embrace you as our good and true friend.

Clave's Statement on Rivera's Resignation[284]
January 17, 1939

The editorial board of *Clave* does not know and thus cannot enter into an analysis of the circumstances which provoked the resignation of Comrade Diego Rivera, but in view of our complete theoretical and political solidarity we are sure that these circumstances cannot be other than of a secondary and transitory nature. However, the resignation in itself can provoke a very disadvantageous impression and thus prejudice our common cause. That is why we cannot accept Comrade Diego Rivera's resignation.

We propose that if it is absolutely necessary, a leave of absence can be granted him for one or two months, on the firm conviction that Comrade Rivera will continue an uninterrupted collaboration, which is highly appreciated by the editorial board as well as by all serious readers.

Suggestions for a Reply
from the Pan-American Committee and the IS
January 1939

Dear Comrade:

Your letter of January 7, announcing your desire to resign from the Fourth International, is an absolutely unexpected and unmotivated blow to us.

You indicate that the Pan-American Committee did not define the character of your work and that this contributed to your "complete inactivity," which in its turn created misunderstandings which could be exploited by our enemies.

Permit us to say, dear comrade, that all this is far from corresponding to reality. The only misunderstanding which could have been produced by the overly general formulation of the decision concerning you was eliminated by the official interpretation of the Pan-American Committee, which was published in our press. This interpretation indicated that our congress was far from the idea of depriving you of your *right* to participate in the Mexican movement. It depended entirely on you whether or not this right would be used in the given transitional stage.

You also agreed with the delegation of the SWP that Comrade C., delegated on your personal initiative, would collaborate with you as closely as possible. We considered this collaboration as the most important lever for the restoration of our Mexican section.

Finally, with your full agreement, you, together with other comrades, were delegated as our representative on the editorial board of *Clave*. It is not necessary to indicate here the importance of this review for all Spanish-speaking countries and for the entire Fourth International. We can see, with full satisfaction, that far from "complete inactivity," you contributed very important theses, articles, and notes to *Clave*.

If the character of your practical participation in the daily work appears unsatisfactory to you, you can propose any change you find reasonable. Needless to say, we will give any such proposals the greatest attention.

In view of these facts and circumstances, we cannot see how our enemies can exploit your further participation in the Fourth International, the only revolutionary organization, existing now under the blows and persecutions of innumerable enemies. On the other hand, it is absolutely clear that a resignation will give these enemies ammunition for their slanders and intrigues.

A resignation from a revolutionary organization can be justified in only one case, namely that of irreconcilable, principled divergences. However, even in this case, the separation should nominally be preceded by a friendly discussion of the points of difference, with a sincere desire on both sides to assure collaboration as far as is humanly possible. From your letter we see with great satisfaction and pleasure that you remain "in complete sympathy with the Fourth International." Under these conditions we cannot but consider your resignation as a complete misunderstanding, provoked by secondary episodes.

Dear Comrade Rivera, we do not accept your resignation. We continue to be in complete sympathy with you, not only as a great painter, but as a fighter for the Fourth International.

Letter to Charles Curtiss
January 18, 1939

Dear Comrade Curtiss:

So far as I understood Comrade Rivera's new arguments which you transmitted to me orally yesterday, Rivera refused to participate in collective work because of . . . my presence. At the same time he denied any principled divergence.

This time his accusations concern my bad "methods," more concretely, he accuses me of intrigues against him behind the scenes. I do not wish to insist here that this accusation is more false and fantastic than all the others; but I believe that a *party* man who accuses another of such "terrible" intrigues which hinder him from participating in the work is obliged to prove it through the regular party channels.

Please ask Comrade Rivera if he is ready to prove his accusations before a commission appointed by the Pan-American Committee or by the International Secretariat.

With best comradely greetings.

L. Trotsky

Letter to Charles Curtiss
February 14, 1939

Dear Comrade Curtiss,

I must ask for your intervention in a matter which may seem to be of a personal character, but which has a general political importance.

You know, as do all the other comrades, of the generosity with which Diego Rivera and his family helped us during our installation and ultimate sojourn in Mexico. 285 I accepted this help, especially the housing, because it came from a person whom I considered not only as a devoted militant of the Fourth International, but also as a personal friend. Now, as you know, the situation has undergone a radical change. I did everything I could to settle the crisis provoked by Diego Rivera's attempts to perform political miracles beside the Fourth International and against it. I did not succeed. The intervention of the Pan-American Bureau also seems to be without results. Diego Rivera even refused to correct absolutely false affirmations against me which he made behind my back. It is not necessary to go into detail again here, but it is morally and politically impossible for me to accept the hospitality of a person who conducts himself not as a friend but as a venomous adversary.

We are now looking for another house. Unfortunately, the experiences of the past two years have showed us that it is very difficult, if not impossible, to find a house which is more or less convenient from the point of view of security. In any case, we are compelled to live in this house until we find another. Through Comrade Van I proposed to pay a monthly rental to Diego Rivera, but he refused categorically. He refused a common collaboration. He refused to correct his false and hostile assertions. Yet he wishes to impose his "generosity" upon me, using the special conditions which hinder me from moving freely from one house to another. I refuse to qualify this attitude.

I am enclosing two hundred pesos (a modest monthly rental) and I ask you to visit Diego Rivera and to explain to him again that he puts himself in a more and more false position; and that under the given conditions he cannot refuse to accept the payment. If in spite of all this he refuses, please transmit this payment to the treasury of *Clave,* noting it as the rent which Diego Rivera has not accepted. In this case, I shall consider Rivera's attitude as moral pressure to force me to move from the house immediately, regardless of whether we have or have not found another.

Comradely yours,
Leon Trotsky

P. S. — The allegation that the house belongs to Frida Rivera and not to Diego Rivera has neither sense nor value. Diego Rivera disposed of the house freely, made new acquisitions, reconstructions, and so on. The allegation is only a subterfuge in order to complicate a very simple question.

L. T.

Letter to Charles Curtiss
February 15, 1939

Dear Comrade:

I am again astonished by the attitude of Diego Rivera. He proclaimed many times, and also in conversations with you, that he wished to resign from political activity and thus from the Fourth International—that he wished to devote his time exclusively to painting, and so on. Now it seems that he has transformed the Casa del Pueblo into the Partido Revolucionario Obrero y Campesino [Revolutionary Workers and Peasants Party] for the purpose of participating actively in the presidential campaign in favor of one of the candidates.[286] Of course, it is his own affair and he has the full right to make one more political mistake instead of one good painting. However, I must confess that Rivera's new political activity creates a very delicate situation for me personally. Many people will believe that Rivera acts in solidarity with me and that through him, I am interfering in the presidential campaign. At least the stupid people can believe it and they are numerous.

What can be done? I believe it becomes absolutely necessary to publicly separate me politically from Diego Rivera. The matter is very disagreeable in every respect, but on the other hand it becomes more and more impossible for the Fourth International in general and for me personally — for double reasons — to carry any responsibility for Rivera's political improvisations, which become increasingly dangerous. I hope to see you within the next few days and discuss the matter with you.

Please send a copy of this letter, with discretion, to the Pan-American Committee and to the International Secretariat.

Comradely yours,
Leon Trotsky

Letter to the Pan-American Committee
March 22, 1939

Dear Comrades,

I am very embarrassed at being obliged to take your time for a matter which has a semi-personal character. I did everything that I could in order to settle the matter personally with the help of Comrade Curtiss; but I did not succeed. After a series of written and oral declarations about his resignation from the Fourth International, Comrade D. Rivera now makes a definite declaration, in essence, that the reason for his withdrawal from our international organization is my attitude toward him. When he first hinted this I visited him immediately and asked him what it was all about. I gave him all the explanations I could and we separated in the friendliest mood, at least on my part. After the incident of Comrade Rivera's letter to Breton, he repeated, in a very vague form, his complaints against my attitude toward him. I proposed that we

(Top) Rose Karsner (left) and J.P. Cannon; (bottom) V.R. Dunne (left) and Max Shachtman.

immediately invite the Pan-American Committee to create a special, discreet, and authoritative commission to which I would present all my correspondence concerning D. Rivera and all the necessary explanations. I was certain that I could prove that in my words and actions concerning Comrade Rivera there was nothing but friendship and care for his work and his personal reputation in our ranks. I believe that Comrades Cannon, Shachtman, and Vincent Dunne could give important testimony on this question. But Comrade Rivera refused to agree to such an investigation and declared to Comrade Curtiss "that there was no need for a commission as there were no accusations" . . . that he "simply did not feel comfortable" in my presence. Of course, there was nothing I could do to remedy a situation created by imponderable elements. In any case, after his formal declaration that he had nothing with which to reproach me personally, I felt that I could consider the personal side of the matter settled. I saw no reason to disquiet you.

But then, at his next meeting with Comrade Curtiss, Comrade Rivera not only repeated the personal accusations, but gave them the sharpest expression: that I, "while fighting against the methods of Stalinism, was using them" myself; . . . that [I was] reading his mail, "which was a typical act of the GPU, an act [that], if revealed publicly, would result in the condemnation of LDT by all the workers." Of course, I could not let such accusations pass without rectification. I immediately informed Comrade Curtiss, as your representative, that I would send all the documents to the Pan-American Committee, and if necessary to the International Secretariat.

In the meantime, D. Rivera found it necessary himself to give a written explanation of his resignation. This explanation does not repeat the sharp accusations made in his discussions with Comrade Curtiss, but gives as his reason for so important a step as the abandonment of a revolutionary organization, my allegedly hostile and unjustified accusations against him personally.

D. Rivera takes a passage from a letter which I wrote to Frida Rivera with the purpose of winning her help in making Diego Rivera change his decision. I did not succeed; but how could this letter, which was written *after* the resignation, explain the resignation itself? You can see from the letter itself that it was far from being hostile or unappreciative of Comrade Rivera. I simply insisted on my opinion that by his character, his occupation, and his life, he was not suited to be a party *functionary*. But that does not indicate a lack of appreciation. Not every member of the organization, nor even of the staff, is obliged to be a secretary. This post demands very concrete qualities, and in every instance in which Rivera functioned as a secretary it was disadvantageous to the organization and to himself. My opinion may be wrong (I am sure that it is correct); but how can my personal *opinion* on this specific question be considered a cause for resignation, even if we ignore the chronological fact that the letter was written after the resignation?

The other accusation reads, "I am, therefore, in the opinion of Comrade Trotsky, a liar and an anti-Marxist traitor" (in Rivera's letter of March 19 to the PAC). Here Comrade Rivera quotes not my words, but my "opinions." This deals with the incident in connection with Rivera's letter to Breton. The entire incident is exhaustively presented in the enclosed documents. Rivera is aware of all these documents, yet in spite of this he permits himself to put in ironical quotation marks the words "by chance."

It is a repetition, in a vaguer form, of his assertion that I used the methods of the GPU. One might imagine that I found the letters on Diego Rivera's desk or that I searched for them. However, it is sufficient to consider the matter calmly for a moment to realize that I could not suspect, after our very friendly meeting mentioned above, that Rivera would write an extremely hostile letter against me with a series of absolutely unjustified accusations and that a copy of this letter is to be found in my home on the desk of my [closest] collaborator, where he ordinarily leaves the copies of my French letters for my wife. Or will Rivera say that I am suspicious of Van himself and that it was with this view that I looked at the documents in his room? It is so absurd that it does not warrant further analysis. I repeat, the documents are self-explanatory.

But can the way in which the letter came into my hands justify the *content* of the letter? I doubt it very much. Andre Breton is our mutual friend and he is well aware of my genuine attitude toward Diego Rivera. During his stay here I wrote my article for the *Partisan Review* and the part concerning Rivera met with a warm appreciation from both of them. 287 In his letter, Rivera found it necessary to show Breton that his attitude toward me had changed radically. That was his right; but in order to explain this change he quoted two "facts" which are the product of his suspicious imagination.

During the writing of Rivera's letter, Van called his attention to the fact that his assertions were not correct. Rivera *promised to show the letter to me* and to make the necessary explanations. It would have been more correct to have shown me the letter *before* sending it, but he did not show it to me even after he sent it. Such are the facts.

In writing, I proposed to Rivera to retract his absolutely false assertions in a letter to Breton and I declared that in this case I would consider the matter settled. In the conversation with Van, Rivera immediately agreed and convoked Van for the common work. The following day he refused. After a further insistence, he agreed, convoked Van again, and again refused. Such are the facts. I did not call Rivera a "liar." I proposed only that he either accept my proposal of an authoritative commission which would study all my acts and documents concerning Rivera, or that he retract his false assertions. He refused to accept the commission and he repeated his false assertions.

In order to make these incredible facts a bit more comprehensible, I must quote some examples of what might be considered our "conflicts" with Rivera and explain, at least partially, the accumulation of hostility in his attitude toward me.

After my statement in favor of China against Japan, Eiffel declared that I was directed by my wish to be agreeable to the Mexican government — to prove that in case of a conflict I would be in favor of Mexico. Rivera was very indignant at this miserable man's assertion that my opinions or actions on fundamental questions could be directed by personal considerations. He was even more indignant at the fact that a political adversary tried to compromise my asylum by such false assertions and "revelations." In this article, Rivera hinted that Eiffel was an agent of the GPU or the Gestapo. Rivera's indignation was correct, but his hint was not. He did not have the slightest proof. In a mild and friendly way, I gave him to understand it. He became indignant; he repeated he was "sure," that he was "convinced," and so on.

In a campaign against the high cost of living, Galicia called the people to a "general strike," "direct action," and "sabotage." It coincided with the accusations of sabotage in the Moscow trials and so was doubly stupid and criminal. This time, in conversations, Rivera declared that Galicia was an agent of the GPU. In a very friendly form I repeated my warning. On his part, Galicia expressed the opinion that I was against sabotage because I was concerned with the question of asylum. In this stupid and miserable assertion Rivera found new proof that Galicia was an agent of the GPU. I opposed this view.

Meanwhile the published accusation against Eiffel had circulated around the world through Oehler, Vereecken, Sneevliet, and others. Some of the ultraleftists addressed Rudolf Klement, as our international secretary, with a demand for proof or refutation. Vereecken was especially active and tried to mobilize our Belgian section. Comrade Klement addressed a letter to the Mexican section asking for an explanation. He was sure that the assertion had been made by some young, inexperienced, and hot-headed comrade, and proposed to rectify the matter in order to deprive the ultraleftist "roosters" of a supplementary weapon. After reading the letter in my presence, Rivera declared that Klement was an agent of the GPU. It sounds incredible, but it was so. I protested a bit more vigorously this time. However, Rivera energetically repeated his assertion to me, to Van, and, I believe, to other comrades. Klement disappeared. Rivera said, "You see, I was right." When the French comrades recognized the mutilated body, he said that it was all a machination of the GPU, that it was not really Klement's body, etc.

Rivera had never met Rudolf Klement. He knew nothing about him. He had received from him a very warm personal letter of invitation to our International Congress. But it was sufficient for him that Klement asked for an explanation of a false assertion of which he did not even know the author, to proclaim him an agent of the GPU.

I could quote a series of analogous facts concerning Mexicans (O'Gorman, Hidalgo, General Mujica, and others)[288] against whom Rivera launched the severest accusations of a personal kind, but which did not hinder him from completely reversing his attitude toward these persons within the next two weeks.

A tremendous impulsiveness, a lack of self-control, an inflammable imagination, and an extreme capriciousness — such are the features of Rivera's character. I suppose these features are intimately connected with his artistic temperament and possibly form the negative side of his temperament. It is sufficient to discuss with him for an hour in order to observe this shadowy side of his great personality. I have not been and I will not be in the slightest inclined to exaggerate these features or be intolerant of them. Our friends, especially Cannon, Shachtman, and Vincent Dunne, know this very well. On the contrary, in conversations and correspondence with comrades about Rivera, it has always been my purpose to reconcile them to his extreme impulsiveness, his exaggerations, etc., and not to permit them to forget his great qualities because of the negative sides of his temperament. I was always preoccupied by this aim, not only in the personal interest of Rivera, whom I considered as my friend, but in the interests of our party, which was honored by the participation in its ranks of so eminent a personality. At the same time, of course, I could not admit all his fantastic hypotheses, exaggerations, and often venomous assertions against friends, comrades, and third neutral persons. I never considered my disagreements, my criticisms, or my friendly warnings as reasons for hostility, not to speak of a resignation from the Fourth International. Rivera was not obliged to follow my advice or to heed my warnings. But he could not tolerate any disagreements with his opinions and appreciations, which were often very contradictory. He felt even the friendliest criticism (as we see in the case of Rudolf Klement) to be a terrible intrigue, a machination directed against him personally.

So, in this long series of personal disqualifications and ruptures, my turn came. All my efforts to calm Rivera and to win him to a more realistic appreciation of our actual relationship remained unsuccessful. Now, with the same insistence with which he accused Klement of being an agent of the GPU, he repeats that I used the methods of the GPU against him. And so on.

This, I hope, gives you an explanation of the "conflict." And I hope that this gives you an explanation of why I believe that a comrade with such an exceptional mentality cannot be a good "secretary" of a workers' organization.

What is to be done now?

In view of the fact that Diego Rivera rejected the creation of a commission and that he continues to repeat his accusations after he had retracted them, I must insist, dear comrades, that *the Pan-American Committee itself or through a special commission investigate the matter in order to establish whether or not Rivera's assertions are true that I committed acts against him which could be considered disloyal and would meet with the disapproval of the workers, as he affirms.* Certainly the importance of the matter is clear enough to everyone so that I do not have to insist upon this point.

Fraternally yours,

P. S.—I have not entered at all into the theoretical and political disagreements. Thanks to Comrade Curtiss, I read a
program which Rivera elaborated for the CGT, an article
written by Rivera for *Clave* and not published, and finally the
program of the Partido Revolucionario Obrero y Campesino.
This series of incredible zigzags clearly shows that, pushed by
purely personal impulsions in the search for some political
magic, Rivera heaps error upon error prejudicial to the workers' movement and to himself. I am sure that your representative has sent you all these documents and thus you can appreciate the recent political activities with facts and documents
in hand.

Letter to James P. Cannon
March 27, 1939

Dear Friend,

You remain silent as before. A bad sign!

You know the trouble we are having here with the painter
and you are not astonished, because you warned us many
times about his fantastic political ideas. For quite a long time,
I believe for about a year and a half, he tried to impose some
discipline upon himself; but around the time of the International
Congress he became dissatisfied and disquieted. I shall give
you some examples of his preoccupations so that you can communicate them to other friends.

All decisions made here concerning the Mexican section were
made with the full agreement of the painter and with a view
to not exposing him to constant attacks (you know that the organization condemned him unanimously—no one undertaking
his defense); but after the decisions were made and ratified by
the conference, he found that he had not been sufficiently defended. He was extremely dissatisfied with the decision, terribly ex-
aggerating some unhappy formulations. But this was not
enough; he declared that the *Socialist Appeal* had deliberately
published the decision about Molinier and the decision about
him symmetrically in order to identify them.[289]

He demanded the immediate exclusion of all members of the
organization who had made accusations against him. He demanded my intervention in that direction and I had an unfor-
gettable discussion with him about the matter. He asked me
to expel Galicia immediately. "How can I do it?" I asked in
full astonishment. "But you are the leader." "You have an ex-

traordinary conception of the so-called leadership, my dear friend," I answered, "it is a bit like Stalinism." "Yes," he answered, with the childishness which characterizes him, "they say that I am worse than the Stalinists." But he returned to the matter many times, especially after the arrival of Comrade C.

You probably know that the painter himself proposed this candidate and gave me a very eulogistic characterization of the comrade. I asked G. about him and he confirmed the characterization. It was thus agreed that Comrade C. would work here as a representative. But C. could not work other than on the basis of the conference decision and so provoked a sharp dissatisfaction on the part of the painter, who practically boycotted him. I attracted the painter's attention to the fact that C. was appointed on his initiative and that C. was working as a loyal representative of the International Secretariat, whose duty it was not to overthrow, but to realize the decisions of the conference. That was practically enough for the painter to begin his independent political activity.

After his condemnation by the organization, he told me many times that the entire organization was a mistake, that he had never wished to work within it, but that this was imposed upon him by Shachtman and the others during their first trip to Mexico; that it would be very easy for him to create a genuine section of hundreds of workers, and so on. I was skeptical, but silent. He then began opposing the Casa del Pueblo to the section and personally to C. Unfortunately, it seems that the question of money played an important part here. (The American comrades Cannon, Shachtman, and Dunne found out very easily that a very important cause of the sharp explosion between the organization and the painter, apart from his temperament, lay in the fact that the organization was directly dependent upon him financially. By common agreement it was decided that in the future he would give his money to the Pan-American Committee, which would distribute it.) In creating his own party, the painter began to subsidize the Casa del Pueblo directly and created a most degrading state of dependence of a workers' organization on an individual.

In the course of the last four or five months, the painter made an attempt to fraternize with the anarchist CGT, and the Casa del Pueblo followed him in this direction. He invented a special historic philosophy and a special program for this fraternization. You have the program — a mixture of Marxist remnants with anarchist and vulgar democratic prejudices. It seems that the leaders of the CGT agreed with the document in a friendly way, but only in order to abandon their anarchism and to pass into the camp of the most reactionary bourgeois politicians.

I forgot to mention that a month or so before this experience, he won the Casa del Pueblo for a proclamation of adherence to the Fourth International. In a manifestation [demonstration], they held aloft the banner of the Fourth International. But it was only a measure of protection against the Fourth International. When I asked the leaders why they did not wish to work with our section or with Comrade C. personally, they answered verbally that there was no necessity to do so, because they already belonged to the Fourth International and it was better for them to work in other trade union organizations.

Several weeks later the painter decided to carry on presidential politics and the Casa del Pueblo followed him again. Now they formed a special party with its own program, written by the painter in five or ten minutes on his knee.

The painter declared that the Mexican section of the Fourth International had decided not to participate in the elections for fear of endangering my asylum. Here he repeats the most vicious accusations of Eiffel and Galicia, who, for this very reason, he called agents of the GPU.

Here I must introduce the incident in connection with the O'Gorman frescos. The painter and his friend organized a very sharp protest action, as usual without any participation on my part. During this campaign I had only one accidental discussion on the matter with the painter. I told him that this story had nothing in common with the story of the frescos in the Rockefeller Building. The Mexican government expropriated the oil enterprises and had to sell the oil. The democracies boycotted the oil and the fascists purchased it; but they would also begin to boycott it if the Mexican government placed caricatures of them in government buildings. Mexico is an oppressed country and she cannot impose her oil on others by battleships and guns. If the boss forces the workers to remove a portrait of Marx from the workers' room, the workers must obey in order to avoid being thrown into the street. Mexico's position toward the big, imperialist countries is similar to that of the worker toward the boss. For example, during the Brest-Litovsk regime we could not place caricatures of Wilhelm II in our public buildings, nor even publish them in the official government paper. It is a question of the relationship of forces, not of principles. I tried to explain all this to the painter. But he af-

firmed that the government, and especially Mujica (it was in his
department), were reactionary bootlickers of Hitler and Mussolini and that they would do anything in order to prove themselves anti-Semites and so on. And he mentioned that he had
broken off all relations with Hidalgo, who had tried to defend
his "reactionary master, Mujica." I understood the hint and
abandoned the discussion.

You can imagine how astonished I was when Van accidentally
met the painter, in company with Hidalgo, leaving the building
of the Pro-Mujica Committee carrying bundles of pro-Mujica
leaflets which they were loading into the painter's stationwagon.
I believe that this was the first we learned of the new turn, or
the passing of the painter from "third period anarchism" to
"people's front politics." The poor Casa del Pueblo followed
him on all these steps.

We were very patient, my dear friend. We hoped that in spite
of everything we would be able to retain the fantastic man for
our movement. I remained aside and Comrade C. did everything that could possibly be done. All in vain.

Now you know his personal accusations against me. They
arose unexpectedly, even for himself. He was discontented with
our slowness, our concilatory attitude toward Galicia and company, etc. He wished to perform a miracle, at any price. In
his fantastic mind, he came somehow to hope that after achieving success in dominating the Casa del Pueblo and the CGT
he could come to us triumphant and we would recognize his
mastery. But his fiascos made him nervous and hostile toward
us. As he accused Shachtman of responsibility for his own misfortune with the Mexican League, he now began to accuse me
of responsibility for his own mistakes and fantastic jumps. It
was in this mood that he dictated his fantastic letter to Andre
Breton. He could not find even a little fact with which to reproach me, so he simply invented two stories, which all friends,
particularly C. and Van, know to be absolutely false. A copy
of this fantastic letter, unsigned, fell into Natalia's hands by
pure chance. You can imagine my astonishment and my personal disgust. I asked Van for an explanation. He told me that
the painter had promised to show me the letter personally. In
spite of everything I tried to settle this question as discreetly
as possible through the intervention of Van and then of C. I
asked only that he recognize that both examples of my "lack
of loyalty" happened to be misunderstandings (I did not even
ask him to recognize that he had actually invented them). He
agreed, he refused, he agreed again and refused again. I sent

him a copy of all the documents destined for the Pan-American Committee. Comrade C. made an ultimate effort to make him retract his false assertions. He refused and even showed C. a letter to Bertram Wolfe[290] announcing his break with us for our opportunism and so on.

Now we must show this fantastic personality a firm hand. There are two questions: one personal and the other political. I begin with the smaller of the two, the personal question.

The Pan-American Committee cannot help but pronounce its opinion about the painter's three accusations: (a) That I prevailed upon Comrade C. to publish the painter's article on art not as an article, but as a letter. (All the elements of this "accusation" are well known to Comrades Van, C., and two or three others.) (b) That I engineered a coup d'etat in the FIARI by appointing Ferrel as secretary. The whole "drama" happened with the participation of the painter and with his agreement. Ferrel's candidacy was proposed by Zamora and accepted by everyone, including the painter. (The witnesses were Comrades C., Van, Ferrel himself, and Zamora.) (c) That I used GPU methods in connection with the painter's correspondence with Breton. This matter is exhaustively explained in my letter to the Pan-American Committee and in the documents. I can only mention here that quotations from this letter are printed in the French *Cle* (these parts are also directed against me, but anonymously and on an alleged principled plane). Here I must ask of the Pan-American Committee a very clear and categoric statement, even if a special investigation should be considered necessary, for the question can provoke international repercussions. Provoked by his apparent impunity, the painter adds some new detail every day and perfects the picture of his accusations. You know him well enough personally to understand me. We must be armed against his fantastic slanders. I do not propose the publication of the Pan-American Committee's verdict, but it must be communicated to the interested people, including the painter himself, with the warning that if the false assertions continue to be spread in the future, the verdict will be published.

So far as the political side of the question is concerned, in my opinion, we must immediately publish a categoric statement about the painter's political activities in the past period, declaring that the documents he has elaborated are in complete contradiction to Marxism and to the decisions of the Fourth International, and that even without his resignation, he has, by his activities, put himself outside the Fourth International.

The workers' movement is not a free field for individual experiments. I believe that such a resolution should be accepted and published as quickly as possible, and even released through the bourgeois agencies.

I think that in the Pan-American Committee's statement it would be necessary to explain that in spite of its individual peculiarities, the painter's case is a part of the retreat of the intellectuals. Some of them were very "sympathetic" to us insofar as they considered us as persecuted people who needed their protection. But now, when we are becoming a political factor, with our own aims and discipline, they have become more and more "disenchanted" with us, and after some jumps to the ultraleft, they look for a haven in the bourgeois public opinion of their fatherland. Our painter is only more gifted, more generous, and more fantastic than the others, but he is, nevertheless, one of them.

An article on the matter should be published in the *New International,* and the political decision should be printed in the *Socialist Appeal.* [291]

I hope that I have given you the most important information, which you can place at the disposal of the Pan-American Committee.

Comradely,
V. T. O'Brien [Trotsky]

Statement of the Pan-American Committee
April 5, 1939

Comrade Diego Rivera's rectification of March 20 concerning the creation of the Partido Revolucionario Obrero y Campesino [Revolutionary Workers and Peasants Party] only serves to make even clearer the fundamental differences between us, concerning not only the question of the elections, but the fundamental principles of the proletarian class struggle.

It is not necessary to enter into a discussion of who took the initiative in the creation of the new party: the workers of the Casa del Pueblo or Diego Rivera himself. It is sufficient for us that he is the political secretary of the party and thus carries the whole responsibility for this body and its politics.

We consider a proletarian party as the main instrument in the liberation of the working class. The base of such a party must include not empirical and conjunctural demands but a program of transitional slogans, [292] and what is more important, the program of social revolution. The idea that one can create a party "ad hoc" for a concrete conjuncture is absolutely incredible and opportunistic in its essence. A workers' party with a so-called minimum program is *eo ipso* a bourgeois party. It is a party which makes the workers support bourgeois politics or bourgeois politicians.

A revolutionary Marxist workers' party could discuss the question of whether or not it was advisable in this concrete situation to support one of the bourgeois candidates. We are of the opinion that under the given conditions it would be false. But the question placed before us by Diego Rivera's activity is incomparably more important. In reality, Comrade Rivera organized and is leading a new party on a petty-bourgeois, reformist program, without any international connections, with an anti-Marxist name (a party of workers and peasants), and opposes this party to the Fourth International as opportunist in its policy in the elections.

Imagine for a moment that our policy toward the elections is false; but it is an episodic question. Can one imagine that a Marxist puts the difference about this secondary or tertiary question above the program of the world revolution, breaks his international connections, and participates in a new party as a political secretary?

This fact alone shows that the divergences are incomparably deeper than Comrade Rivera, in his fantastic impulsiveness, believes.

We must add that before the absolutely unexpected creation of the new party, he elaborated another program for an alliance with the CGT, which called itself anarchistic. This program of Comrade Rivera's contained absolutely impermissible concessions to the anarchist doctrines. As we know, the alliance was not realized because the supposed allies, the heads of the CGT, abandoned their alleged anarchism for an open reactionary, bourgeois policy.

After this Comrade Rivera elaborated a document in which he accused the Third International of Lenin and the Fourth International of transforming the "anarchists" into bourgeois reactionaries. Of course we could not accept this apology for the anarchist bourgeois fakers and these accusations against the Marxist Internationals.

Now Comrade Rivera invokes letters of Comrade Trotsky. We cannot enter into this matter, which has nothing to do with our fundamental divergences. We simply mention that Comrade Trotsky's letters were written after Diego Rivera's resignation and thus could not have caused the resignation.

After his resignation Comrade Rivera declared that he would remain an active sympathizer. If there is any sense in human words, then an active sympathizer would mean a person who helps the party from the outside. But can we call anyone a sympathizer who creates a new party, opposing it to the Fourth International and its Mexican section? Is it possible to believe that the political secretary of a workers' and peasants' party with a petty-bourgeois, reformist program has no divergences with the Fourth International?

We all did everything in our power to restrain Diego Rivera from taking irreparable steps. We did not succeed. Driven by his own temperament and his fantastic mind, he committed a series of errors; and every error was a further reason for him to look for some sort of miracle which could show people that he was that he was right. In this way he tried to oppose the Casa del Pueblo to the Fourth International, to win the CGT, and now he is leading the Revolutionary Workers and Peasants Party. It is absolutely clear to every Marxist that the new enterprise will be an inevitable fiasco for which we cannot carry the slightest responsibility before the workers of Mexico and of the world. We must state openly that not only has Rivera resigned from the Fourth International, but that by his political activity he puts himself fundamentally outside the Fourth International. Where principles are involved we cannot permit any concessions, even toward such an important figure as Diego Rivera.

We cannot guess whether the new inevitable debacle will teach Comrade Rivera the road back to the Fourth International or whether he will be definitely absorbed by the current of intellectuals who are now breaking with Marxism in favor of a mixture of anarchism, liberalism, individualism, and so on. Needless to say, we hope that the first alternative will be realized.

MORE ON OUR WORK
IN THE COMMUNIST PARTY[293]

April 10, 1939

Dear Comrade Cannon:

You have surely received the minutes of the discussion concerning the work of our party within the Communist Party [see p. 237]. I was astonished to hear that some comrades deny the utility of such a work. The recent happenings show that we do not have the slightest connection with the Communist Party and that we know practically nothing about its internal life. I continue to be of the opinion that it is necessary to create a special, secret commission for this purpose, to be headed by a member of the Political Committee. The difficulties are not insurmountable at all — only a very systematic and persistent work is necessary. I doubt that we can make an important step forward if we neglect this kind of work. It is not possible to conduct a war if one remains blind, that is, without serious and systematic reconnaissance. I believe that the neglect of this question is in the same category as, let us say, the denying of the defense guard.[294] That is to say, it is a result of a misunderstanding of the whole epoch: the terrible tension of its social and political relations and the permanent danger of explosions. We cannot proceed blindly; we must have open eyes. In the service of reconnaissance are the eyes of the army. The army is small — its service will be modest; but it must grow parallel with the party.

We have already had some discussions with Comrade James. The two most important were on the Negro question. He presented an important and very good statement. I do not accept his categorical rejection of self-determination (an independent state) for the American Negro. As a party, we do not enter into the making of the decision, either one way or the other. We say to the Negroes, "You must decide whether or not you

298

wish the separation. If you decide in the affirmative, we as a party will help you with all our power to realize your decision; and in this way the separation of states will assure the brotherhood of workers of both colors. This is what we want above all."

The rest of his statement is very good. The party cannot postpone this extremely important question any longer. James's sojourn in the States is very important for the serious and energetic beginning of this work.

I await with impatience the information from you concerning France.

With best regards to Rose and to you.

Yours fraternally,
V. T. O'Brien [Trotsky]

GREETINGS TO CARLO TRESCA[295]

April 10, 1939

Dear Comrade Tresca:

In spite of all the profound divergences, which neither you nor I have the habitude to deny or attenuate, I hope that you will permit me to express the deepest esteem for you, as for a man who is every inch a fighter. Your sixtieth birthday is being celebrated by your friends and I take the liberty of including myself among them. I hope that your moral vigor and revolutionary ardor will be conserved for a long time to come. I embrace you wholeheartedly.

Yours,
Leon Trotsky

THE UKRAINIAN QUESTION[296]

April 22, 1939

The Ukrainian question, which many governments and many "socialists" and even "Communists" have tried to forget or to relegate to the deep strongbox of history, has once again been placed on the order of the day and this time with redoubled force. The latest aggravation of the Ukrainian question is most intimately bound up with the degeneration of the Soviet Union and of the Comintern, the successes of fascism, and the approach of the next imperialist war. Crucified by four states, the Ukraine now occupies in the fate of Europe the same position that was once occupied by Poland, with this difference — that world relations are now infinitely more tense and the tempos of development accelerated. The Ukrainian question is destined in the immediate future to play an enormous role in the life of Europe. It was not for nothing that Hitler so noisily raised the question of creating a "Greater Ukraine," and likewise it was not for nothing that he dropped this question with such stealthy haste.

The Second International, expressing the interests of the labor bureaucracy and aristocracy of the imperialist states, completely ignored the Ukrainian question. Even its left wing did not pay the necessary attention to it. Suffice it to recall that Rosa Luxemburg, for all her brilliant intellect and genuinely revolutionary spirit, found it possible to declare that the Ukrainian question was the invention of a handful of intellectuals. This position left a deep imprint even upon the Polish Communist Party. The Ukrainian question was looked upon by the official leaders of the Polish section of the Comintern as an obstacle rather than a revolutionary problem. Hence the constant opportunist attempts to shy away from this question, to suppress it, to pass it over in silence, or to postpone it to an indefinite future.

The Bolshevik Party, not without difficulty and only gradually under the constant pressure of Lenin, was able to acquire a correct approach to the Ukrainian question. The right to self-determination, that is, to separation, was extended by Lenin equally to the Poles and to the Ukrainians. He did not recognize aristocratic nations. Every inclination to evade or postpone the problem of an oppressed nationality he regarded as a manifestation of Great Russian chauvinism.

After the conquest of power, a serious struggle took place in the party over the solving of the numerous national problems inherited from old czarist Russia. In his capacity as people's commissar of nationalities, Stalin invariably represented the most centralist and bureaucratic tendency. This evinced itself especially on the question of Georgia and on the question of the Ukraine. 297 The correspondence dealing with these matters has remained unpublished to this day. We hope to publish a section of it — the very small section which is at our disposal. Every line of Lenin's letters and proposals vibrates with an urge to accede as far as possible to those nationalities that have been oppressed in the past. In the proposals and declarations of Stalin, on the contrary, the tendency toward bureaucratic centralism was invariably pronounced. In order to guarantee "administrative needs," i.e., the interests of the bureaucracy, the most legitimate claims of the oppressed nationalities were declared a manifestation of petty-bourgeois nationalism. All these symptoms could be observed as early as 1922-23. Since that time they have developed monstrously and have led to outright strangulation of any kind of independent national development of the peoples of the USSR.

In the conception of the old Bolshevik Party, Soviet Ukraine was destined to become a powerful axis around which the other sections of the Ukrainian people would unite. It is indisputable that in the first period of its existence Soviet Ukraine exerted a mighty attractive force, in national respects as well, and aroused to struggle the workers, peasants, and revolutionary intelligentsia of Western Ukraine enslaved by Poland. But during the years of Thermidorean reaction, the position of Soviet Ukraine and together with it the posing of the Ukrainian question as a whole changed sharply. The more profound the hopes aroused, the keener was the disillusionment.

The bureaucracy strangled and plundered the people within Great Russia, too. But in the Ukraine matters were further complicated by the massacre of national hopes. Nowhere did restrictions, purges, repressions, and in general all forms of bureaucratic hooliganism assume such murderous sweep as they did in the Ukraine in the struggle against the powerful, deeply rooted longings of the Ukrainian masses for greater freedom and independence. To the totalitarian bureaucracy, Soviet Ukraine became an administrative division of an economic unit and a military base of the USSR. To be sure, the Stalin bureaucracy erects statues to Shevchenko but only in order more thoroughly to crush the Ukrainian people under their weight and to force it to chant paeans in the language of the Kobzar to the rapist clique in the Kremlin.[298]

Toward the sections of the Ukraine now outside its frontiers, the Kremlin's attitude today is the same as it is toward all oppressed nationalities, all colonies, and semicolonies, i.e., small change in its international combinations with imperialist governments. At the recent eighteenth congress of the " Communist Party," Manuilsky, one of the most revolting renegades of Ukrainian communism, quite openly explained that not only the USSR but also the Comintern (the "gyp-joint," according to Stalin's formulation) refused to demand the emancipation of oppressed peoples whenever their oppressors are not the enemies of the ruling Moscow clique. India is nowadays being defended by Stalin, Dimitrov, and Manuilsky against—Japan, but not against England. Western Ukraine they are ready to cede forever to Poland in exchange for a diplomatic agreement which appears profitable at the present time to the bureaucrats of the Kremlin. It is a far cry from the days when they went no further than episodic combinations in their politics.

Not a trace remains of the former confidence and sympathy of the Western Ukrainian masses for the Kremlin. Since the latest murderous "purge" in the Ukraine no one in the West wants to become part of the Kremlin satrapy which continues to bear the name of Soviet Ukraine. The worker and peasant masses in the Western Ukraine, in Bukovina, in the Carpatho-Ukraine are in a state of confusion: Where to turn? What to demand? This situation naturally shifts the leadership to the most reactionary Ukrainian cliques who express their "nationalism" by seeking to sell the Ukrainian people to one imperialism or another in return for a promise of fictitious independence. Upon this tragic confusion Hitler bases his policy in the Ukrainian question. At one time we said: but for Stalin (i.e., but for the fatal policy of the Comintern in Germany) there would have been no Hitler. To this can now be added: but for the rape of Soviet Ukraine by the Stalinist bureaucracy there would be no Hitlerite Ukrainian policy.

We shall not pause here to analyze the motives that impelled

Hitler to discard, for the time being at least, the slogan of a Greater Ukraine. These motives must be sought in the fraudulent combinations of German imperialism on the one hand, and on the other in the fear of conjuring up an evil spirit whom it might be difficult to exorcize. Hitler gave Carpatho-Ukraine as a gift to the Hungarian butchers. This was done, if not with Moscow's open approval then in any case with confidence that approval would be forthcoming. It is as if Hitler had said to Stalin: "If I were preparing to attack Soviet Ukraine tomorrow I should have kept Carpatho-Ukraine in my own hands." In reply, Stalin at the eighteenth party congress openly came to Hitler's defense against the slanders of the "Western democracies." Hitler intends to attack the Ukraine? Nothing of the sort! Fight with Hitler? Not the slightest reason for it. Stalin is obviously interpreting the handing over of Carpatho-Ukraine to Hungary as an act of peace.

This means that sections of the Ukrainian people have become so much small change for the Kremlin in its international calculations. The Fourth International must clearly understand the enormous importance of the Ukrainian question in the fate not only of Southeastern and Eastern Europe but also of Europe as a whole. We are dealing with a people that has proved its viability, that is numerically equal to the population of France and occupies an exceptionally rich territory, which, moreover, is of the highest strategical importance. The question of the fate of the Ukraine has been posed in its full scope. A clear and definite slogan is necessary that corresponds to the new situation. In my opinion there can be at the present time only one such slogan: *A united, free, and independent workers' and peasants' Soviet Ukraine.*

This program is in irreconcilable contradiction first of all with the interests of the three imperialist powers, Poland, Rumania, and Hungary. Only hopeless pacifist blockheads are capable of thinking that the emancipation and unification of the Ukraine can be achieved by peaceful diplomatic means, by referendums, by decisions of the League of Nations, etc. In no way superior to them of course are those "nationalists" who propose to solve the Ukrainian question by entering the service of one imperialism against another. Hitler gave an invaluable lesson to those adventurers by tossing (for how long?) Carpatho-Ukraine to the Hungarians who immediately slaughtered not a few trusting Ukrainians. Insofar as the issue depends upon the military strength of the imperialist states, the victory of one grouping or another can signify only a new dismemberment and a still more brutal subjugation of the Ukrainian people. The program of independence for the Ukraine in the epoch of imperialism is directly and indissolubly bound up with the program of the proletarian revolution. It would be criminal to entertain any illusions on this score.

But the independence of a United Ukraine would mean the separation of Soviet Ukraine from the USSR, the "friends" of the Kremlin will exclaim in chorus. What is so terrible about that?—we reply. The fervid worship of state boundaries is alien to us. We do not hold the position of a "united and indivisible" whole. After all, even the constitution of the USSR acknowledges the right of its component federated peoples to self-determination, that is, to separation. Thus, not even the incumbent Kremlin oligarchy dares to deny this principle. To be sure it remains only on paper. The slightest attempt to raise the question of an independent Ukraine openly would mean immediate execution on the charge of treason. But it is precisely this despicable equivocation, it is precisely this ruthless hounding of all free national thought, that has led the toiling masses of the Ukraine, to an even greater degree than the masses of Great Russia, to look upon the rule of the Kremlin as monstrously oppressive. In the face of such an internal situation it is naturally impossible even to talk of Western Ukraine voluntarily joining the USSR as it is at present constituted. Consequently, the unification of the Ukraine presupposes freeing the so-called Soviet Ukraine from the Stalinist boot. In this matter, too, the Bonapartist clique will reap what it has sown.

But wouldn't this mean the military weakening of the USSR?—the "friends" of the Kremlin will howl in horror. We reply that the weakening of the USSR is caused by those ever-growing centrifugal tendencies generated by the Bonapartist dictatorship. In the event of war the hatred of the masses for the ruling clique can lead to the collapse of all the social conquests of October. The source of defeatist moods is in the Kremlin. An independent Soviet Ukraine, on the other hand, would become, if only by virtue of its own interests, a mighty southwestern bulwark of the USSR. The sooner the present Bonapartist caste is undermined, upset, crushed, and swept away, the firmer the defense of the Soviet Republic will become and the more certain its socialist future.

Naturally an independent workers' and peasants' Ukraine

might subsequently join the Soviet Federation; but voluntarily, on conditions that it itself considers acceptable, which in turn presupposes a revolutionary regeneration of the USSR. The genuine emancipation of the Ukrainian people is inconceivable without a revolution or a series of revolutions in the West which must lead in the end to the creation of the Soviet United States of Europe. An independent Ukraine could and undoubtedly will join this federation as an equal member. The proletarian revolution in Europe, in turn, would not leave one stone standing of the revolting structure of Stalinist Bonapartism. In that case the closest union of the Soviet United States of Europe and the regenerated USSR would be inevitable and would present infinite advantages for the European and Asiatic continents, including of course the Ukraine too. But here we are shifting to questions of second and third order. The question of first order is the revolutionary guarantee of the unity and independence of a workers' and peasants' Ukraine in the struggle against imperialism on the one hand, and against Moscow Bonapartism on the other.

The Ukraine is especially rich and experienced in false paths of struggle for national emancipation. Here everything has been tried: the petty-bourgeois Rada [government] and Skoropadsky, and Petlura, and "alliance" with the Hohenzollerns, and combinations with the Entente.[299] After all these experiments, only political cadavers can continue to place hope in any one of the factions of the Ukrainian bourgeoisie as the leader of the national struggle for emancipation. The Ukrainian proletariat alone is capable not only of solving the task — which is revolutionary in its very essence — but also of taking the initiative for its solution. The proletariat and only the proletariat can rally around itself the peasant masses and the genuinely revolutionary national intelligentsia.

At the beginning of the last imperialist war the Ukrainians Melenevski ("Basok") and Skoropis-Yeltukhovski attempted to place the Ukrainian liberation movement under the wing of the Hohenzollern general Ludendorff. They covered themselves in so doing with left phrases. With one kick the revolutionary Marxists booted these people out. That is how revolutionists must continue to behave in the future. The impending war will create a favorable atmosphere for all sorts of adventurers, miracle-hunters, and seekers of the golden fleece. These gentlemen, who especially love to warm their hands in the vicinity of the national question, must not be allowed within artillery range of the labor movement. Not the slightest compromise with imperialism, either fascist or democratic! Not the slightest concession to the Ukrainian nationalists, either clerical-reactionary or liberal-pacifist! No "People's Fronts"! The complete independence of the proletarian party as the vanguard of the toilers!

This appears to me the correct policy on the Ukrainian question. I speak here personally and in my own name. The question must be opened up to international discussion. The foremost place in this discussion must belong to the Ukrainian revolutionary Marxists. We shall listen with the greatest attention to their voices. But they had better make haste. There is little time left for preparation!

LETTER TO EMRYS HUGHES[300]

April 22, 1939

Dear Comrade Hughes,

Thank you sincerely for your letter of April 3. Undoubtedly there are thousands upon thousands of British workers and honest and revolutionary intellectuals who think as you do. They are simply stifled, but not so much by the state machine as by the machine of the official workers' organizations. The war they are preparing will break both these machines.

In the catastrophe of war, the most disoriented, confused, and cowardly will be the present magnificent leaders of the workers' organizations, of the Second and Third Internationals. The masses will look for a new orientation, a new direction, and will find them.

You are right that the first chapter of the war will be a chapter of nationalistic madness. But the more terrible the war and the war hysteria, the more crushing will be the mass reaction. Not to lose one's head and to look toward the future—the near future—with open eyes, is the highest revolutionary duty.

With fraternal greetings,
Leon Trotsky

THE CRISIS IN THE FRENCH SECTION[301]

Letter to James P. Cannon
December 5, 1938

Dear Friend:

I am really embarrassed about formulating my opinion upon this very complicated and important question without possessing the necessary material. For a long time I have abandoned the reading of French papers. I read the publications of our own party insufficiently. That is why my appreciation can have only a very general and abstract character absolutely insufficient for practical decisions.

I heard about the tendency to enter the PSOP [Workers and Peasants Socialist Party] for the first time on the eve of the Sudeten crisis. My position was: if war comes, events can find our party dissolved at the most critical moment in the nebulous spot of the PSOP. In such situations it is absolutely necessary to have pure independence of decision and action. Ten internationalists can do good work whereas thousands of centrists can only aggravate the confusion. In this sense I expressed my opinion through Van.

The world crisis passed over—for a certain time—but now the internal French crisis is in full upsurge.[302] What is the influence of this crisis upon our organization and upon the PSOP? That is the question.

In 1936 we observed in France a genuine prerevolutionary situation and even more than that, a mass uprising which could have and should have transformed itself with a minimum of revolutionary leadership into the battle for power. But every revolution, even with people who accomplish a dozen, begins with a kind of "February" stage. It is with illusions, stupid confidence, and so on. The Peoples' Front coalition, absolutely impotent against fascism, war, reaction, etc., showed itself to be a tremendous counterrevolutionary brake upon the mass movement, incomparably more powerful than the February coalition in Russia, because: (a) We didn't have

309

such an omnipotent workers' bureaucracy, including the trade union bureaucracy; (b) We had a Bolshevik party. During almost three years the machine of the Peoples' Front prevented the transformation of the prerevolutionary situation into a revolutionary one. What are now the consequences of this vile work upon the mentality of the masses is absolutely impossible to say from afar. One part of the masses should have become more impatient and aggressive, another part demoralized, a large in-between stratum disoriented. What is the relation of forces among these three parts? It is a decisive question, which even in France can be resolved only by action or by an attempt at action.

What is the influence of this sharp turn (the breakdown of the Peoples' Front) upon the PSOP? I don't know even the social composition of the PSOP. I doubt very much that it is a good one. Are they connected with the trade unions? Is there not a danger that our entrance into the PSOP can in a critical moment separate us from the trade unions, involving us in endless discussion with petty-bourgeois socialists? I don't know this.

The purely formal question — through a congress or through summit agreement — has a secondary, tertiary importance. The social composition of the PSOP and the possibilities for us are decisive.

Rous threatens a split. I agree fully with you that we must have an immediate, active, and aggressive policy; I agree with this so completely that I would prefer a split to the present stagnation. The split on such a practical question (how to conquer the PSOP) can have a very brief character. The fraction guided by Rous could show what they are capable of doing inside the PSOP and in case of their success they will inevitably win the others. You proposed in Paris that our party send an important fraction inside the PSOP. The split would signify such a penetration into the PSOP of a part of our comrades. I don't neglect the danger connected with every split, but I am trying to analyze this variant as a lesser evil in comparison with doing nothing.

It is not necessary to say that your presence now in France would be of the greatest importance. France is today the immediate battlefield, and not the United States. This should be considered also from a financial point of view. If you go to France (and I am absolutely in favor of such a decision) you should have a modest treasury for the needs of the French party in the next period.[303]

I believe Rosmer could be very helpful to you,[304] especially for the conversations with the PSOP, information, advice, and so on, but I doubt that he would be ready to enter the movement actively. He is not young . . . sick and tired. Pivert is a very, very deteriorated edition of Karl Liebknecht. The fact that after long oscillations he committed a split speaks for him, at least for his honesty, but it is a centrist honesty. How far is he capable of going under the pressure of events?

That is all, dear friend, that I can say about the matter in a hurry; I wish to send this letter tomorrow morning by airmail. Possibly I will write in one or two days again.

Hansen [Trotsky]

Letter to James P. Cannon
April 8, 1939

Dear Comrade:

I am very, very disquieted at not receiving any information from you about the happenings in France and especially about your plans for the future.[305] I can understand that you found it necessary to interrupt your sojourn in France and to abandon the leaders of the POI to their own helplessness. But such a situation cannot last for a long time. We must elaborate a solution in one direction or the other. It is necessary not only for the French party, but also for the American section; after the great effort of the American comrades, a disappointment can have very negative consequences.

I have some hypothetical propositions, but they are too vague and I prefer to have your information and suggestions before formulating some concrete propositions.

I should also be very glad to hear from you as to how you found the American party after your absence.

Warmest greetings from Natalia and myself to you both.

Comradely yours,
L. Trotsky

Letter to the Political Committee of the SWP
April 18, 1939

Dear Friends:

I continue to be very disquieted about your complete silence in general and on the French question in particular. The decisions about the matter in the National Committee minutes seem to be correct, but they are not concrete concerning the dates, the practical means, the persons, and so on.

I had some propositions to make, but I waited for word from Comrade Cannon in order to check them in the light of his experience before presenting them to you. However, I see now that Comrade Cannon is on a leave of absence and I am afraid to lose much time, which is very precious in this affair.

My preliminary propositions are:

1. To send immediately one or two comrades to France with credentials giving them full power from the SWP, the Pan-American Committee, the Mexican section, a letter from Crux [Trotsky], and so on (I believe even with special resolutions from party meetings in New York and other important branches).

2. During two or three days, these two comrades together with the IS [should] examine the work of the POI during the last critical period in order to establish: whether they have changed their methods; whether they have had some success; whether there is a chance of their having success in the near future.

3. In the same manner check the activity of the Fourth Internationalists inside the PSOP—since their entrance.

4. If it happens that the POI has not advanced at all, the IS, with the American comrades, should make, not a proposal, but a definite decision approximately as follows:

a. All members of the POI and the youth are obliged to enter the PSOP within the next week.

b. Naville (and two or three others) are not to enter the PSOP but should devote all their work to the IS.

c. *La Lutte Ouvriere* will be discontinued.

d. The magazine, *Quatrieme Internationale,* becomes a publication of the IS for all French-speaking countries. The editorial board is composed of Naville, some other French comrade, one Belgian comrade, one American comrade, and one from the youth. The magazine becomes a semimonthly.

e. Those who refuse to follow this decision will be abandoned to their own fate without any subsidy from the International. They will not be expelled, under the condition that in their independent activity they do not try to sabotage the work inside the PSOP. After three months or so, the IS will check the activity of these "outsiders" and make a definite decision.

The propositions are more or less self-explanatory. It would be very difficult for Naville and some of the others to work in the PSOP and it is not at all sure that they would be accepted. The proposed decision would settle the matter with a minimum amount of friction.

Our theoretical and political superiority over the leadership of the PSOP can very well be demonstrated in the semimonthly magazine (under the condition that the composition of the editorial board excludes a specific anti-entrist policy).

A small part of the French fund can be utilized for the support of the semimonthly magazine. The bulk of the fund should be preserved until such time as the organizational matters are settled and a large activity can be developed.

Every means should be applied in order to make the decision of the IS as authoritative and imperative as possible. For example, the whole National Committee of the Belgian section should be involved in the action. The decision should be signed by all the members of the International Secretariat, the American representatives, all the members of the American National Committee, all the members of the Pan-American Committee, and so on.

We must act immediately and with extreme vigor, otherwise the disintegration of the French section will have a most dispiriting effect on all the other sections and would terribly handicap the development of our party in the States.

This letter is not at all destined for any kind of publication. It can be communicated only to the National Committee and to the Pan-American Committee. For France and other sections, I shall write another letter when I know your decision. I hope to receive your reply as quickly as possible.

Comradely,

Letter to the Political Committee of the SWP
April 22, 1939

cc: Cannon, Shachtman, Abern, Burnham

Dear Comrades:

Rous's last letters to you and to me indicate an extremely acute situation between the POI, the fraction in the PSOP, and the IS. An explosion is possible any day, as is also an explosion inside the POI. One almost has the impression that somebody is consciously provoking the dissensions in order to break the movement in France.

The American comrades made an excellent effort to aid the French. But if they stop now and abandon the French organization to itself, the result will be catastrophic. A postponement for several weeks, even for one week, is equivalent to abandonment. We have no time for new discussions about the matter. We must intervene *immediately*.

In my opinion, two comrades should go to France. One of them should be Cannon, not only because of his intimate acquaintance with the matter, but also to demonstrate that we all agree with the fundamental line of his attitude. Cannon's sojourn in France could be short — one or two weeks.

Shachtman should also go *immediately*, simultaneously with Cannon, without the slightest postponement, and should remain there for a longer time. We cannot repeat the omission made after the congress and for which we are now paying very dearly.

Since Klement's death we do not have an IS. Naville is now the secretary, but he is in a minority in the IS on the most acute and important matter — the French question. He simply seems not to convoke the IS. His attitude, as in every critical situation, is passive resistance toward the French section as well as toward the IS.

At the same time, I propose the reinforcement of the Pan-American Committee, not only as the Pan-American Committee, but as an unofficial substitute for the IS during the transitory period. It is necessary to introduce very authoritative comrades into the PAC, to publish a semimonthly bulletin in the name of the PAC, not only in Spanish, but in English, and if possible in French. This activity would be a rehearsal for the time of war in Europe.

Regarding my concrete proposals concerning France, which were formulated in my last letter (these proposals are along the line of your own decisions and the activity of Cannon in France) — after receiving Rous's letters I am more sure of their correctness than before. Naville's attitude shows that he is only waiting for a forceful order and his attitude is simply the reflection of the mood of his followers.

The personal question of two comrades who ask to reenter can be resolved only with the help of the American comrades. 306 Rous asks me to intervene through correspondence. It is impossible; I do not know the concrete situation and I have heard only one side.

Everything depends upon the immediate trip to Europe. We have no more time for discussion. We have a military situation in our own ranks as in Europe in general. After tomorrow the war can block the trip. It is necessary to go tomorrow at any price. Please excuse my insistence. It is not an American question. It is not even a French question. It is an international question of vital importance.

I will await your answer with the greatest impatience.

Comradely,

P. S. — To make them wait for some time with their decisions, it is necessary to cable them as to the date on which the comrades will arrive in Paris.[307]

Letter to the International Secretariat [308]
July 27, 1939

Dear Comrades:

A few days ago I sent you a copy of my reply to the French group that has broken with the Fourth International and continues to call itself the POI.[309] When — not without a certain satisfaction — I became aware of their statement that they don't want to fight against the Fourth International, I did not yet have my hands on the so-called internal bulletin of this group. I now see that their statement had a character that was purely diplomatic, not to say hypocritical. Boitel's report is a venomous and malicious document.[310] He attacks Comrade Cannon personally, as if Comrade Cannon had acted arbitrarily and on his own initiative, and not in full accord with his party, the International Secretariat, the Belgian party, and all the other key bodies of our International.

Moreover, this development is classical. When you end up a failure, the first thing you do is set about denouncing the vicious methods of the Fourth International. Boitel only imitates Molinier, Vereecken, and the others.

My best regards,

ON LABORDE
AND TROTSKYISTS IN GENERAL [311]

April 28, 1939

La Voz de Mexico[312] has expressed its conviction that the recent tragic train wreck was the handiwork of the forces of reaction and of Trotsky in particular. Despite the reliability of such a source, at first glance this report hardly seemed likely. However, recalling the Moscow trials, in which Trotskyists accused themselves of even more monstrous crimes, we decided with our modest forces to conduct a meticulous investigation of this case. And this investigation has yielded far better results than we had hoped for at the outset.

Trotsky is dear to us, but the truth is dearer still. The documents that have fallen into our hands prove beyond a shadow of a doubt that the principal organizer of the train wreck is a conspirator known to be living in Coyoacan. In the process, we also succeeded in discovering the identity of his principal accomplices. It is clear that Trotsky transmitted the most criminal of his commands through — would you have believed it? — Hernan Laborde. Many people may find this inconceivable since Laborde is known as the leading enemy of Trotskyism in Mexico. However, the only people who can argue this way are either extremely naive or miserable hypocrites who are not aware of the diabolical duplicity of the Trotskyists.

Like Radek, Pyatakov, and dozens of others, who seemed to be whipping up a rabid campaign against Trotsky but who were actually his secret agents, Hernan Laborde only masquerades as a Stalinist in order to carry out his Trotskyist intrigues more effectively. The proof? There is more than enough. Let us take the simplest, clearest example. Many people have more than once expressed their amazement at seeing at the head of the Mexican Communist Party a person whose speeches, declarations, and even denunciations are characterized by extraordinary imbecility. In truth, only innocent naivete

could take this imbecility for good coin. Carrying out the diabolical designs of the Fourth International, Hernan Laborde
delights in passing himself off as an idiot in order the better
thus to discredit the Comintern. So that everywhere everyone
will say that there is a man without wits or conscience at the
head of the Mexican section of the Comintern!

The mask of imbecility is necessary for this cunning Trotskyist to better carry out his intrigues.

As for Laborde's direct participation in the train wreck—
this has been clearly established. In the drawer of our desk
we have two nuts unscrewed by Laborde the night before the
train wreck. An investigation will certainly establish the fact
that the finger prints on them are those of the Mexican Trotskyist. Moreover, we don't really need much physical evidence.
Just like the other double-dealers, Laborde has been persuaded
to publicly confess his crimes. We are informed by reliable
sources that Vyshinsky has already sent him a first-class ticket
for a trip to Moscow. We hope that this time Laborde will not
remain incognito in the United States, but will, in fact, deliver himself up to the GPU. It is the best thing he could do
for the workers' movement. After Comrade Beria has performed the ritual surgical operation on him, the editors of
La Voz de Mexico will dedicate a heartfelt obituary to their
leader and friend—which will end with the words: "Another
Trotskyite mad dog has just been liquidated. Long live Stalin,
the father of the peoples!" And the whole Mexican "Communist"
Party will reply in unison: "Amen!"

THE BONAPARTIST PHILOSOPHY
OF THE STATE [313]

May 1, 1939

One of the central points in Stalin's report at the eighteenth party congress in Moscow was undoubtedly a new theory of the state promulgated by him. Stalin ventured into this dangerous field not from any innate inclination but out of necessity. Only a short time ago, the jurists Krylenko and Pashukanis, both orthodox Stalinists, were removed and crushed for having repeated the ideas of Marx, Engels, and Lenin to the effect that socialism implies a gradual withering away of the state. [314] This theory cannot possibly be accepted by the reigning Kremlin. What, wither away so soon? The bureaucracy is only beginning to live. Krylenko and Pashukanis are obviously — "wreckers."

The realities of Soviet life today can indeed be hardly reconciled even with the shreds of old theory. Workers are bound to the factories; peasants are bound to the collective farms. Passports have been introduced. Freedom of movement has been completely restricted. It is a capital crime to come late to work. Punishable as treason is not only any criticism of Stalin but even the mere failure to fulfill the natural duty to get down on all fours before the "Leader." The frontiers are guarded by an impenetrable wall of border-patrols and police dogs on a scale heretofore unknown anywhere. To all intents and purposes, no one can leave and no one may enter. Foreigners who had previously managed to get into the country are being systematically exterminated. The gist of the Soviet constitution, "the most democratic in the world," amounts to this, that every citizen is required at an appointed time to cast his ballot for the one and only candidate handpicked by Stalin or his agents. The press, the radio, all the organs of propaganda, agitation, and national education are completely in the hands of the ruling clique. During the last five years no less than half a million members, according to official figures, have been expelled from the party. How many have been shot, thrown into jails and concentration camps, or exiled to Siberia, we do not definitely know. But undoubtedly hundreds of thousands of party members have shared the fate of millions of nonparty people. It would be extremely difficult to instill in the minds of these millions, their families, relatives, and friends, the idea that the Stalinist state is withering away. It is strangling others, but gives no sign of withering. It has instead brought the state to a pitch of wild intensity unprecedented in the history of mankind.

Yet the official edict is that socialism has been realized. According to the official text, the country is on the road to complete communism. Beria will disabuse the doubters. But here the main difficulty presents itself. To believe Marx, Engels, and Lenin, the state is the organ of class rule. Marxism has long ago exposed all other definitions of the state as theoretical falsifications which serve to cover up the interests of the exploiters. In that case, what does the state mean in a country where "classes have been destroyed"? The sages in the Kremlin have more than once racked their brains over this question. But, of course, they first proceeded to arrest all those who reminded them of the Marxian theory of the state. Since this alone cannot suffice, it was necessary to provide some semblance of theoretical explanation for Stalinist absolutism. Such an explanation was forthcoming in two installments. At the seventeenth party congress, five years ago, Stalin and Molotov explained that the police state was needed for the struggle against the "remnants" of old ruling classes and especially against the "splinters" of Trotskyism. These remnants and splinters, they said, were, to be sure, insignificant. But because they were extremely "rabid" the struggle against them demanded utmost vigilance and ruthlessness. This theory was exceptionally idiotic. Why should a totalitarian state be required for a struggle against "impotent remnants" when Soviet democracy proved wholly adequate for the overthrow of the ruling classes themselves? No answer was ever given to this question.

But even so, this theory of the era of the seventeenth congress had to be discarded. The last five years have in a large measure been devoted to destroying the "splinters of Trotskyism." The party, the government, the army, and the diplomatic corps have been bled white and beheaded. Things had gone so far that Stalin at the last congress was forced, in order to calm his own apparatus, to promise that he would not in the future resort to wholesale purges. This, of course, is a lie. The Bonapartist state will find itself compelled likewise in the future to devour society physically as well as spiritually. This cannot be admitted by Stalin. He swears that purges will not be renewed. If that is so, and if the "splinters" of Trotskyism together with the "remnants" of old ruling classes have been completely destroyed, then the question arises: "Against whom is the state necessary?"

This time, Stalin replies: "The need of the state arises from the capitalist encirclement and the dangers flowing therefrom to the land of socialism." With the monotony of a theology student that is so habitual with him, he repeats and rehashes this idea over and over again: "The function of military suppression within the country has fallen away, has withered away . . . the function of military defense of the country from outside attacks has remained completely preserved." And further on: "As regards our army, our punitive organs, and our intelligence service, their barb is aimed no longer inwardly within the country, but outwardly against the external enemy."

Let us for the sake of argument allow that all this is actually the case. Let us allow that the need of preserving and strengthening the centralized bureaucratic apparatus arises solely from the pressure of imperialism. But the state by its very nature is the rule of man over man. Socialism on the other hand aims to liquidate the rule of man over man in all its forms. If the state is not only preserved but strengthened, becoming more and more savage, then it means that socialism has not yet been achieved. If the privileged state apparatus is the product of capitalist encirclement then it means that in a capitalist encirclement, in an isolated country, socialism is not possible. Trying to extricate his tail, Stalin is thus caught by the snout. Justifying his Bonapartist rule, he refutes in passing his principal theory of building socialism in one country.

Stalin's new theory is correct, however, only in that section which refutes his old theory; in everything else it is entirely worthless. For the struggle against imperialist danger, the workers' state naturally requires an army, a commanding staff, an intelligence service, etc. But does this mean that the workers' state requires colonels, generals, and marshals, with their corresponding emoluments and privileges? On October 31, 1920, at a time when the spartan Red Army was still without a special officer corps, a special decree relating to the army was

issued and in it was stated: "Within the military organization . . . there exists inequality which is in some cases quite
understandable and even unavoidable but which is in other
cases absolutely uncalled for, excessive, and sometimes
criminal." The concluding section of this decree reads as follows: "Without posing the unattainable task of immediately
eliminating any and all prerogatives in the army, we must
systematically strive really to reduce these privileges to the
bare minimum; and to eliminate as quickly as possible all
those privileges which do not at all flow from the requirements
of the military art and which cannot but offend the feeling of
equality and comradeship of the Red Army men." This was the
fundamental line of the Soviet government during that period.
The policy nowadays is taking a diametrically opposite direction. The growth and strengthening of the military and civil
caste signifies that society is moving not toward but away from
the socialist ideal — regardless of who is guilty, whether foreign
imperialists or domestic Bonapartists.

The same thing holds for the intelligence service, in which
Stalin sees the quintessence of the state. At the congress, where
GPU agents well-nigh composed the majority, he lectured as
follows: "The intelligence service is indispensable for appre-
hending and punishing spies, assassins, and wreckers whom
foreign intelligence services send into our country." Of course,
no one will deny the need of an intelligence service against the
intrigues of imperialism. But the crux of the question is in the
position occupied by the organs of this intelligence service in
relation to the Soviet citizens themselves. A classless society
cannot fail to be bound with ties of internal solidarity. Stalin
in his report referred many times to this solidarity, celebrated
as "monolithic." Yet spies, wreckers, and saboteurs need a
cover, a sympathetic milieu. The greater the solidarity in
a given society and the more loyal it is to an existing regime
the less room remains for antisocial elements. How then explain
that in the USSR, if we are to believe Stalin, everywhere such
crimes are being committed as are not to be met with in decaying bourgeois society. After all, the malice of imperialist states
is not sufficient in itself. The activity of microbes is determined
not so much by how virulent they are as by the resistance they
encounter in the living organism. How are the imperialists able
to find in a "monolithic" socialist society a countless number of
agents who occupy, moreover, the most prominent posts? Or,
to put it differently, how does it happen that spies and diver-

sionists are able to occupy in a socialist society positions as members and even heads of the government, members of the Political Bureau,[315] and the most prominent posts in the army? Finally, if the socialist society is so lacking in internal elasticity that to save it one must resort to an all-powerful, universal, and totalitarian intelligence service, then things must be very bad indeed when at the head of the service itself appear scoundrels like Yagoda, who has to be shot, or Yezhov, who has to be driven away in disgrace. Who is there to depend on? Beria? The knell will soon sound for him, too!

As a matter of fact, it is well known that the GPU destroys not spies and imperialist agents but the political opponents of the ruling clique. All that Stalin is trying to do is raise his own frame-ups to a "theoretical" level. But what are the reasons compelling the bureaucracy to cloak its real goals and to label its revolutionary opponents as foreign spies? Imperialist encirclement does not explain these frame-ups. The reason must be of an *internal* nature, i.e., they must flow from the very structure of Soviet society.

Let us try to find some supplementary evidence from the lips of Stalin himself. Without any connection with the rest of his report, he states the following: "Instead of the function of coercion there has manifested itself in the state the function of safeguarding socialist property against thieves and embezzlers of national wealth." Thus it turns out that the state exists not only against foreign spies but also against domestic thieves. And moreover the rule of these thieves is so great that it justifies the existence of a totalitarian dictatorship and even provides the foundation for a new philosophy of the state. It is quite obvious that if people steal from one another then cruel misery and glaring inequality inciting to theft still rule in society. Here we probe closer to the root of things. Social inequality and poverty are very important historical factors which by themselves explain the existence of the state. Inequality always requires a safeguard; privileges always demand protection; and the encroachments of the disinherited require punishment. This is precisely the function of the historical state!

As regards the structure of "socialist" society, what is important in Stalin's report is not what he said but what he passed over in silence. According to him, the number of workers and civil employees increased from twenty-two million in 1933 to twenty-eight million in 1938. The above category of "employees" embraces not only clerks in a cooperative store, but also members of the Council of People's Commissars. Workers and employees are here lumped together, as always in Soviet statistics, so as not to reveal how large the bureaucracy is numerically and how swiftly it is growing, and above all how rapidly its income is increasing.

In the five years that have elapsed between the last two party congresses, the annual wage fund of workers and employees has increased, according to Stalin, from thirty-five billions to ninety-six billions, i.e., almost threefold (if we leave aside the change in the purchasing power of the ruble). But just how are these ninety-six billions divided among the workers and employees of various categories? On this score, not a word. Stalin only tells us that "the average annual wage of industrial workers, which in 1933 amounted to 1,513 rubles, rose in 1938 to 3,447 rubles." The reference here is surprisingly only to *workers;* but it is not difficult to show that it is a question as before of both workers and employees. It is only necessary to multiply the annual wage (3,447 rubles) by the total number of workers and employees (twenty-eight million) for us to obtain the total annual wage fund of workers and employees mentioned by Stalin, namely ninety-six billion rubles. To embellish the position of workers, the "Leader" thus permits himself the cheapest kind of trickery of which the least conscientious bourgeois journalist would have been ashamed. Consequently, if we leave aside the change in the purchasing power of the currency, the average annual wage of 3,447 rubles signifies only this, that if the wages of the unskilled and skilled workers, Stakhanovists,[316] engineers, directors of trusts, and People's Commissars of Industry are lumped together, then we obtain an average of less than 3,500 rules a year per person. What has been the increase in the pay of workers, engineers, and the highest personnel in the last five years? How much does an unskilled worker receive annually at present? Of this not a word. Average statistics for wages, income, etc., have always been resorted to by the lowest type of bourgeois apologists. In cultured countries this method has virtually been discarded since it no longer deceives anybody; but it has become the favorite method in the land where socialism has been achieved and where all social relations ought to be marked by their crystal clarity. Lenin said: "Socialism is bookkeeping." Stalin teaches: "Socialism is bluffing."

Over and above everything else, it would be the crudest kind of blunder to think that the above-mentioned average sum cited by Stalin includes *all* of the income of the highest "employees," i.e., the ruling caste. In point of fact, in addition to their official and comparatively modest salaries, the so-called responsible "workers" receive secret salaries from the treasuries of the Central Committee or local committees; they have at their disposal automobiles (there even exist special plants for the production of finest automobiles for the use of "responsible workers"), excellent apartments, summer homes, sanatoria, and hospitals. To suit their needs or their vanity all sorts of "Soviet palaces" are erected. They almost monopolize the highest institutions of learning, the theatres, etc. All these enormous sources of income (they are expenses for the state) are of course not included in the ninety-six billions referred to by Stalin. And yet Stalin does not even dare to broach the question of just how the legal wage fund (ninety-six billions) is apportioned between workers and employees, between unskilled workers and Stakhanovists, between the upper and lower tiers of employees. There is no doubt that the lion's share of the increase of the official wage fund went to the Stakhanovists, for premiums to engineers, and so on. By operating with averages whose accuracy does not inspire confidence, by lumping workers and employees into a single category, by merging the summits of the bureaucracy with the employees, by passing in silence over secret funds of many billions, by "forgetting" to refer to the employees and mentioning only workers in determining "the average wage," Stalin pursues a simple goal: to deceive the workers, to deceive the entire world, and to hide the vast and ever-growing income of the privileged caste.

"The defense of socialist property against thieves and embezzlers" thus signifies, nine times out of ten, the defense of the income of the bureaucracy against any encroachments by the unprivileged sections of the population. Nor would it be amiss to add that the secret income of the bureaucracy, without a basis either in the principles of socialism or in the laws of the country, is nothing else but theft. In addition to this legalized thievery there is illegal supertheft to which Stalin is compelled to shut his eyes because thieves are his strongest support. *The Bonapartist apparatus of the state is thus an organ for defending the bureaucratic thieves and plunderers of national wealth.* This theoretical formula comes much closer to the truth.

Stalin is compelled to lie about the social nature of his state for the same reason that he must lie about the workers' wages. In both instances he comes forward as the spokesman of privileged parasites. In the land that has gone through the proletarian revolution, it is impossible to foster inequality, create an aristocracy, and accumulate privileges save by bringing down upon the masses floods of lies and ever more monstrous repressions.

Embezzlement and theft, the bureaucracy's main sources of income, do not constitute a system of exploitation in the scientific sense of the term. But from the standpoint of the interests and position of the popular masses it is infinitely worse than any "organic" exploitation. The bureaucracy is not a possessing class, in the scientific sense of the term. But it contains within itself to a tenfold degree all the vices of a possessing class. It is precisely the absence of crystallized class relations and their very impossibility on the social foundation of the October Revolution that invest the workings of the state machine with such a convulsive character. To perpetuate the systematic theft of the bureaucracy, its apparatus is compelled to resort to systematic acts of banditry. The sum total of all these things constitutes the system of Bonapartist gangsterism.

To believe that *this* state is capable of peacefully "withering away" is to live in a world of theoretical delirium. The Bonapartist caste must be smashed, the Soviet state must be regenerated. Only then will the prospects of the withering away of the state open up.

NATIONALIZED INDUSTRY
AND WORKERS' MANAGEMENT[317]

May 12, 1939

In the industrially backward countries foreign capital plays a decisive role. Hence the relative weakness of the *national* bourgeoisie in relation to the *national* proletariat. This creates special conditions of state power. The government veers between foreign and domestic capital, between the weak national bourgeoisie and the relatively powerful proletariat. This gives the government a Bonapartist character of a distinctive character. It raises itself, so to speak, above classes. Actually, it can govern either by making itself the instrument of foreign capitalism and holding the proletariat in the chains of a police dictatorship, or by maneuvering with the proletariat and even going so far as to make concessions to it, thus gaining the possibility of a certain freedom toward the foreign capitalists. The present policy [of the Mexican government] is in the second stage; its greatest conquests are the expropriations of the railroads and the oil industries.

These measures are· entirely within the domain of state capitalism. However, in a semicolonial country state capitalism finds itself under the heavy pressure of private foreign capital and of its governments, and cannot maintain itself without the active support of the workers. That is why it tries, without letting the real power escape from its hands, to place on the workers' organizations a considerable part of the responsibility for the march of production in the nationalized branches of industry.

What should be the policy of the workers' party in this case? It would of course be a disastrous error, an outright deception, to assert that the road to socialism passes, not through the proletarian revolution, but through nationalization by the bourgeois state of various branches of industry and their transfer into the hands of the workers' organizations. But it is not a question of that. The bourgeois government has itself carried through the nationalization and has been compelled to ask

participation of the workers in the management of the nationalized industry. One can of course evade the question by citing
the fact that unless the proletariat takes possession of the power, participation by the trade unions in the management of the
enterprises of state capitalism cannot give socialist results.
However, such a negative policy from the revolutionary wing
would not be understood by the masses and would strengthen
the opportunist positions. For Marxists it is not a question of
building socialism with the hands of the bourgeoisie, but of
utilizing the situations that present themselves within state capitalism and advancing the revolutionary movement of the
workers.

Participation in bourgeois parliaments can no longer give
important positive results; under certain conditions it even
leads to the demoralization of the worker-deputies. But this
is not an argument for revolutionists in favor of antiparlia-
mentarism.

It would be inexact to identify the policy of workers' participation in the management of nationalized industry with the
participation of socialists in a bourgeois government (which
we called *ministerialism*). All the members of the government
are bound together by ties of solidarity. A party represented
in the government is answerable for the entire policy of the
government as a whole. Participation in the management of
a certain branch of industry allows full opportunity for political opposition. In case the workers' representatives are in a
minority in the management, they have every opportunity
to declare and publish their proposals, which were rejected by
the majority, to bring them to the knowledge of the workers, etc.

The participation of the trade unions in the management of
nationalized industry may be compared to the participation
of socialists in the *municipal governments,* where the socialists sometimes win a majority and are compelled to direct an
important municipal economy, while the bourgeoisie still has
domination in the state and bourgeois property laws continue.
Reformists in the municipality adapt themselves passively to
the bourgeois regime. Revolutionists in this field do all they
can in the interests of the workers and at the same time teach
the workers at every step that municipality policy is powerless without conquest of state power.

The difference, to be sure, is that in the field of municipal
government the workers win certain positions by means of
democratic elections, whereas in the domain of nationalized

industry the government itself invites them to take certain posts. But this difference has a purely formal character. In both cases the bourgeoisie is compelled to yield to the workers certain spheres of activity. The workers utilize these in *their own* interests.

It would be light-minded to close one's eye to the dangers that flow from a situation where the trade unions play a leading role in nationalized industry. The basis of the danger is the connection of the top trade union leaders with the apparatus of state capitalism, the transformation of mandated representatives of the proletariat into hostages of the bourgeois state. But however great this danger may be, it constitutes only a part of a general danger, more exactly, of a general sickness: that is to say, the bourgeois degeneration of the trade union apparatuses in the imperialist epoch not only in the old metropolitan centers but also in the colonial countries. The trade union leaders are, in an overwhelming majority of cases, *political* agents of the bourgeoisie and of its state. In nationalized industry they can become and already are becoming direct *administrative* agents. Against this there is no other course than the struggle for the independence of the workers' movement in general, and in particular through the formation within the trade unions of firm revolutionary nuclei, which, while at the same time maintaining the unity of the trade union movement, are capable of struggling for a class policy and for a revolutionary composition of the leading bodies.

A danger of another sort lies in the fact that the banks and other capitalist enterprises, upon which a given branch of nationalized industry depends in the economic sense, may and will use special methods of sabotage to put obstacles in the way of the workers' management, to discredit it and push it to disaster. The reformist leaders will try to ward off this danger by servile adaptation to the demands of their capitalist providers, in particular the banks. The revolutionary leaders, on the contrary, will draw the conclusion, from the sabotage by the banks, that it is necessary to expropriate the banks and to establish a *single national bank,* which would be the accounting house of the whole economy. Of course this question must be indissolubly linked to the question of the *conquest of power by the working class.*

The various capitalist enterprises, national and foreign, will inevitably enter into a conspiracy with the state institutions to put obstacles in the way of the workers' management of nationalized industry. On the other hand, the workers' organizations that are in the management of the various branches of nationalized industry must join together to exchange their experiences, must give each other economic support, must act with their joint forces on the government, on the conditions of credit, etc. Of course such a central bureau of the workers' management of nationalized branches of industry must be in closest contact with the trade unions.

To sum up, one can say that this new field of work includes within it both the greatest opportunities and the greatest dangers. The dangers consist in the fact that through the intermediary of controlled trade unions state capitalism can hold the workers in check, exploit them cruelly, and paralyze their resistance. The revolutionary possibilities consist in the fact that basing themselves upon their positions in the exceptionally important branches of industry, the workers can lead the attack against all the forces of capital and against the bourgeois state. Which of these possibilities will win out? And in what period of time? It is naturally impossible to predict. That depends entirely on the struggle of the different tendencies within the working class, on the experience of the workers themselves, on the world situation. In any case, to use this new form of activity in the interests of the working class, and not of the labor aristocracy and bureaucracy, only one condition is needed: the existence of a revolutionary Marxist party that carefully studies every form of working class activity, criticizes every deviation, educates and organizes the workers, wins influence in the trade unions, and assures a revolutionary workers' representation in nationalized industry.

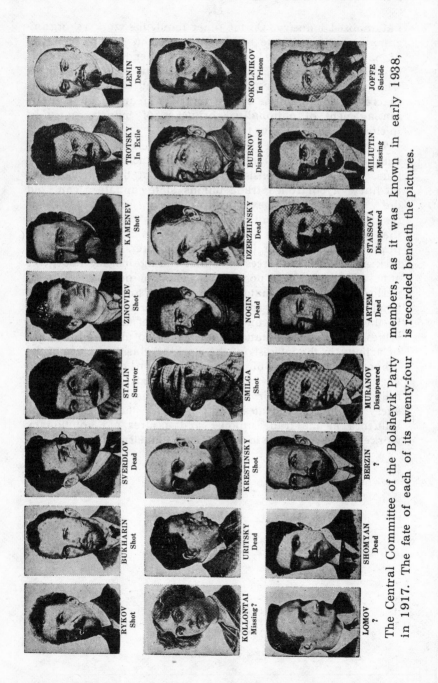

RYKOV
Shot

BUKHARIN
Shot

SVERDLOV
Dead

STALIN
Survivor

ZINOVIEV
Shot

KAMENEV
Shot

TROTSKY
In Exile

LENIN
Dead

KOLLONTAI
Missing ?

URITSKY
Dead

KRESTINSKY
Shot

SMILGA
Shot

NOGIN
Dead

DZERZHINSKY
Dead

BUBNOV
Disappeared

SOKOLNIKOV
In Prison

LOMOV
?

SHOMYAN
Dead

BERZIN
?

MURANOV
Disappeared

ARTEM
Dead

STASSOVA
Disappeared

MILIUTIN
Missing

JOFFE
Suicide

The Central Committee of the Bolshevik Party
in 1917. The fate of each of its twenty-four
members, as it was known in early 1938,
is recorded beneath the pictures.

A GRAPHIC HISTORY OF BOLSHEVISM [318]

June 7, 1939

Printed below is the history of the Central Committee of the
Bolshevik Party in statistical form. These tables, carefully compiled from data in the Soviet press, are eloquent enough in
themselves. But it would not be superfluous to append a brief
commentary as an introduction to them.

Beginning with the sixth party congress (July 1917) there
were thirteen party congresses held in a period of twenty-two
years. Between the sixth and the seventh congresses eight
months elapsed. The next six congresses were held at intervals of one year; furthermore, under Lenin this interval fixed
in the party statutes was very rigidly observed. Thereafter,
the schedule was violated. The twelfth congress was convened
in April 1923 and the thirteenth was held in May 1924, after
a month's delay. The next congress, the fourteenth, was held
only in December 1925, that is, one year and a half later.
The fifteenth party congress, at which the Left Opposition was
expelled from the party, was convened in December 1927, that
is, two years after the fourteenth. Violations of the party statutes
had already become the rule. The sixteenth congress was called
only after a lapse of two and a half years, in June 1930.
But even this interval was found to be too brief. The seventeenth party congress was called after three years and eight
months had elapsed. Finally, the last congress — the eighteenth —
was held in March of this year, more than five years after
the preceding one.

This prolongation of time intervals was of course no accident.
In the years of the revolution and the civil war the party found
it possible to adhere to its own statutes; the Central Committee
remained an organ subject to the control of the party. The
Central Committee began to rise above the party simultaneously
with the rise of the Soviet bureaucracy over the workers' state.
The control of the party, however terrorized, became an irk-
some fetter for the Central Committee. The intervals between the

congresses were henceforth determined to an ever larger measure by the administrative exigencies of the ruling nucleus
in the Central Committee, that is, Stalin's clique. Thus, the
fourteenth congress was convened after a half year's delay in
connection with the internal struggle in the "triumvirate" (Stalin, Zinoviev, Kamenev). 319 Before presenting himself at the
congress, Stalin had to make sure of his majority in the provinces. It was no longer a question of solving controversial
issues, nor of exercising control over the CC, but of setting
the seal of approval on accomplished facts. The fifteenth congress was convened for the sole purpose of drawing the balance
sheet of the strangulation of the Left Opposition. The time
for its convocation was determined by this very task. An identical task was fulfilled by the sixteenth congress, this time in
relation to the Right Opposition. 320 The seventeenth congress
was called only after the crisis in collectivization had passed
its acutest phases and the CC was already in position to report certain "consoling" items. Finally, the eighteenth congress
was convened after the purges of Yagoda, Yezhov, and Beria
had succeeded in rooting out opposition, terrorizing the party,
and reconstituting the ruling apparatus in the state and the
army. The interrelationship between the party and the apparatus
has been stood completely on its head.

The choice of the personnel of the CC was not left to chance
but came as the result of years of work, testing, and selection. It was only in the nature of things that a stable nucleus
should be formed in the personnel of the CC which was reelected from one year to the next. The CC was renewed on
the one hand by the dying out of the older members and on
the other by the coming to the fore of younger forces. Generally speaking, as appears from Table 1, from 60 percent to
86 percent of the outgoing CC composed the members of the
incoming committees up to the seventeenth congress. The foregoing statement must be qualified to this effect, that these bare
percentages do not of themselves provide a sufficiently correct picture of the actual process whereby the CC had been
renewed. During the first seven congresses — from the sixth to
the twelfth — one and the same nucleus was in reality reelected,
and the changes in the composition of the CC amounted to
the inclusion of new elements, who were then subjected to test
and selection. The thirteenth congress marked a breaking point.
In the initial period of Thermidor, changes in the political
character of the Bolshevik staff were attained through an arti-
ficial expansion of the CC, i.e., by a dilution of the old revo-

lutionists with new officeholders grateful for a rapid career and firmly clinging to the coattails of the general secretary. Up to 1923 the number of members of the CC varied between fifteen and twenty-seven. From 1923 on, it was increased first to forty and later to seventy-one. Stalin's clique found it easier at the outset to introduce docile or semidocile novices into the CC than to remove immediately the basic nucleus of Lenin's party. Toward the latter part of 1927 a stabilization was achieved with respect to the number of members but there began a shunting of the old Leninist nucleus. However, even as pariahs, the Old Bolsheviks represented a political danger. A far greater danger was the growth of the Fourth International. Stalin in his own fashion "combined" these two dangers to as to cope with them through the medium of Yagoda and Yezhov. The shunting aside of Old Bolsheviks, as well as the revolutionists of the new generation, was supplanted by a drive to exterminate them physically.

Of necessity, these complex processes are abstracted from Table I. It only registers in figures the proportions to which each new Central Committee was renewed. As we have already observed, up to a certain time each CC passed on to its successor from 60 percent to 86 percent of its personnel. In the last five years we find this continuity violently disrupted. The eighteenth congress held in March of this year took over from the outgoing CC only 22.5 percent of its members! The personnel of the CC which in the preceding eleven years had smashed the Left Opposition and then the Joint Opposition and then the Right Opposition, and had secured the complete "monolithism" of Stalin's party thus proved to have consisted of more than three-quarters traitors, betrayers, or just plain "enemies of the people."

Table II shows how many members from the staff of each of the preceding twelve Central Committees have been preserved in the composition of the present Central Committee; and it also registers the fate suffered by the members who were removed. As an example we take the Central Committee that was elected in August 1917 and led the October Revolution. This historical staff consisted of twenty-one members. Of them only one remains at the present time in the party leadership — Stalin. Seven have died of disease or have fallen at the hands of the enemy (we shall not engage in a dispute over the causes). Shot or condemned to the firing squad — seven; three have disappeared during the purges; three others have been liquidated politically — and perhaps also physically: a total of thirteen, that is, almost 62 percent of the participants in the October staff turned out to be "enemies of the people." Stalin here provides a statistical confirmation *sui generis* of the hoary theory of Miliukov-Kerensky that the October Revolution was the handiwork of the agents of the German general staff.

The tenth congress, held in March 1921, which launched the "New Economic Policy," elected a Central Committee of twenty-four members. At the present time, participating in the leadership are five of them, that is, about 20 percent. Fifteen members, that is 62.5 percent have been liquidated physically and politically. The fifteenth congress which expelled the "Trotskyists" in December 1927 established a Central Committee of seventy-one members. Of them, ten have remained at the present time in the party leadership, i.e., 14 percent; fifty men have been liquidated, i.e., over 70 percent. Of the personnel of the CC established by the sixteenth congress (1930), 76 percent have been exterminated physically and politically. Lastly, of the seventy-one members of the CC elected by the seventeenth congress (1934), only sixteen souls now remain in the leadership; forty-eight have been liquidated, i.e., 67.6 percent. We cannot tell as yet just how or to what extent the incumbent CC will be extirpated, but its horoscope is a dark one.

In the sphere of candidates the purges have taken even a more devastating toll. At the last congress less than 12 percent of the candidates to the previous CC were reelected; 86.7 percent of the candidates have been liquidated physically and politically. In almost all the congresses we observe the workings of one and the same law: the proportion of reelected candidates is smaller while the proportion of those liquidated is much larger than the corresponding proportions among the actual members. This fact is of exceptional interest: the fate of the candidates, recruited from among new party cadres, indicates the direction in which the new party bureaucracy is developing. Contrary to the constantly reiterated assertions that the youth is unconditionally "loyal" to Stalin it turns out that the proportion of "traitors," "betrayers," and generally unreliable elements among the young cadres is even larger than among the personnel of the Old Guard. This is the irrefutable testimony of figures! However, the difference lies in this, that the "criminals" from among the Old Guard were in most instances guilty of devotion to the revolutionary tradition, whereas the "criminals" from among the young bureaucracy are apparently pulling more resolutely than Stalin himself in the direction of class society. But both the former and the latter are dangerous!

The changes in the composition of the CC were accompanied by even more drastic changes in its role. The old Bolshevik CC was the undisputed leader of the party and was most conscientious in its attitude toward questions of theory and the voice of the workers. The incumbent CC has no independent meaning whatever. It is handpicked as an auxiliary to the ruling nucleus, and it is altered by the nucleus in the interval between the congresses. Changes in the personnel of the CC are effected through the state apparatus, or to put it more correctly, through certain "secret" departments of this apparatus, above all the GPU. Among the staff of seventy-one members of the incumbent CC there is Beria, the head of the GPU, and Vyshinsky, former chief prosecutor, now Molotov's deputy. Beria's past in the party is at best an obscure one. Vyshinsky's past in the party is quite clear: he adhered to Menshevism in the "heroic" periods of his career, at a time when it was impossible not to belong to a "leftist" party; but for the most part he was an attorney for the oil trust. He appeared on the Soviet arena during the period of the crushing of the Trotskyist opposition. This individual did not become a Bonapartist lackey; he was born such. Stalin leans not upon the CC but on Beria, Vyshinsky, and their assistants in whose presence the ordinary members of the CC quake.

From among the diplomats, the personnel of the latest CC includes Litvinov and Potemkin. Litvinov is an Old Bolshevik who participated in the party from its day of foundation. Potemkin is a former bourgeois professor who joined the Bolsheviks after they were victorious; and who enjoyed, as an avowed and importunate courtier, the merited contempt of all those who knew him. Today Potemkin has not only replaced Litvinov as head of the diplomatic corps but he also plays a far more important part in the party line than does Litvinov. From among the old military men in the CC there is Budenny[321] who has no essential ties with the party; and among the candidates there is the former General Shaposhnikov.[322] Shaposhnikov's political physiognomy may be characterized by the fact that during the Soviet-Polish war, the then head of the War Department suspended the publication of the periodical *Voennoe Delo* ["Military Affairs"] in which Shaposhnikov had printed an exceptionally coarse chauvinist article in the style of the good old czarist days ("the scheming

Poles," and so on). Even as a military man, Shaposhnikov is lacking in any stature. He is a docile functionary of the czarist general staff, and nothing more; his political stature calls for absolutely no comments. Surviving the purge that has destroyed the flower of the commanding staff, Shaposhnikov is today along with Potemkin a figure symbolic of the Stalinist CC.

The Central Committee as a committee is a many-headed myth. It goes without saying that the most important questions, such as purging the CC itself, cannot even be discussed in the Committee, inasmuch as 32.4 percent of its members cannot possibly pass a decision to destroy 67.6 percent. Such questions are decided by the super-Central Committee of Stalin-Yagoda-Yezhov-Vyshinsky. The fate of the party depends as little on the CC as the fate of the latter does on the party.

The Political Bureau, in its turn, does not at all depend on the CC. This is most glaringly demonstrated in the fact that the Political Bureau has undergone relatively little change in the Stalinist era, while the CC "electing" it has been periodically subjected to extermination. But this immutable Political Bureau serves itself only as a more or less stable piece of decoration. It wields no power. In contrast to the CC, the Political Bureau is composed predominantly of Old Bolsheviks. Of them, Stalin alone served as a member of the Political Bureau under Lenin; Kalinin was for a while a candidate. [323] The majority of the remaining members, men like Molotov, Andreyev, Voroshilov, Kaganovich, Mikoyan[324] are by no means youngsters whose talents bloomed in the recent period. They were sufficiently well known fifteen and even twenty years ago; but it was precisely for this reason that the idea never entered anyone's mind that these people were capable of leading the party. They are kept in the Political Bureau primarily because in the guise of "Old Bolsheviks" they provide a species of cover for shysters of the Vyshinsky-Beria-Potemkin-et al. type. On every important question Stalin confronts his "Political Bureau" with an accomplished fact.

To sum up, on the basis of the tables printed below, we can draw two extremely important conclusions:

1. What is now being designated as party "monolithism" has acquired a social and political content which is the diametrical opposite of Bolshevism. A genuine Bolshevik party prides itself on its unanimity but only in the sense that it groups the vanguard of the workers on the basis of an irreconcilable revolutionary program. The party demarcates itself

from all other tendencies along the line of the proletarian class struggle. The Stalinist party has the following characteristic trait: there is a systematic shift away from proletarian politics toward the policy of defending the privileged layers (the kulak [rich peasant], the Nepman, the bureaucrat, in the first period; the bureaucrat, the labor and *kolkhoz* [collective farm] aristocracy, in the second period). This social shift is intimately bound up with the recasting of the entire program in both domestic as well as world politics (the theory of socialism in one country, the struggle against equality, the defense of imperialist democracy, People's Fronts, etc.) The ruling apparatus systematically adapts the party and its institutions to this changing program, that is, in the service of new and ever more privileged social layers. The principal methods of this adaptation are the dictatorial purges. The monolithism of the party signifies today not its unity on the basis of the proletarian program but its docility to the apparatus that betrays this program. Renewals in the personnel of the CC have reflected and continue to reflect the social shift of the party from the oppressed to the oppressors.

2. The second conclusion is indissolubly linked with the first. The unimpeachable language of figures mercilessly refutes the assertion so current among the democratic intellectuals that Stalinism and Bolshevism are "one and the same." Stalinism originated not as an organic outgrowth of Bolshevism but as a negation of Bolshevism consummated in blood. The process of this negation is mirrored very graphically in the history of the Central Committee. Stalinism had to exterminate first politically and then physically the leading cadres of Bolshevism in order to become what it now is: an apparatus of the privileged, a brake upon historical progress, an agency of world imperialism. Stalinism and Bolshevism are mortal enemies.

TABLE I				
Congress	Date of Congress	(1) CC members (2) Candidates	Former CC members and candidates reelected	
			No.	%
VI	July 1917	21 4	– –	– –
VII	March 1918	15 8	13 2	86.6 25.0
VIII	March 1919	19 8	12 1	63.0 12.5
IX	Mar-Apr. 1920	19 12	13 3	68.4 25.0
X	March 1921	24 15	15 4	62.5 25.6
XI	Mar-Apr. 1922	27 19	20 7	74.0 36.8
XII	April 1923	40 17	24 10	60.0 58.8
XIII	May 1924	53 34	37 10	69.8 29.4
XIV	December 1925	63 43	49 22	77.7 51.1
XV	December 1927	71 50	52 39	73.2 78.0
XVI	June-July 1930	71 67	57 39	80.3 58.2
XVII	February 1934	71 68	56 36	78.9 52.9
XVIII	March 1939	71 68	16 8	22.5 11.7

			TABLE II									
							Victims of Thermidor					
Congress	Date of Congress	(1) CC members (2) Candidates	In party leadership at present		Deceased		By court decision	Suicide	Disappeared	Politically Liquidated	Total	
			No.	%	No.	%					No.	%
VI	July 1917	21	1	4.8	7	33.3	7	—	3	3	13	61.9
		4	—	—	—	—	—	2	2	—	4	100.0
VII	March 1918	15	2	13.3	5	33.3	5	—	3	—	8	53.3
		8	—	—	2	25.0	—	1	4	1	6	75.0
VIII	March 1919	19	2	10.5	3	15.8	9	1	3	1	14	73.7
		8	2	25.0	2	25.0	1	—	2	1	4	50.0
IX	Mar-Apr. 1920	19	3	15.8	3	15.8	10	1	2	—	13	68.4
		12	2	16.6	3	25.0	—	—	4	3	7	58.3
X	March 1921	24	5	20.8	4	16.6	7	1	2	5	15	62.5
		15	—	—	3	20.0	3	—	7	2	12	80.0
XI	Mar-Apr. 1922	27	6	22.2	5	18.5	9	1	4	2	16	59.2
		19	3	15.8	3	15.8	2	—	6	5	13	68.4
XII	April 1923	40	7	17.5	7	17.5	11	1	9	5	26	65.0
		17	2	11.8	1	5.9	1	1	3	9	14	82.3
XIII	May 1924	53	9	17.0	8	15.0	10	1	16	9	36	67.9
		34	2	5.8	—	—	3	1	9	19	32	94.1
XIV	December 1925	63	10	15.8	9	14.3	10	1	17	16	44	69.8
		43	3	6.9	2	4.6	4	3	10	21	38	88.4
XV	December 1927	71	10	14.0	11	15.5	5	3	25	17	50	70.4
		50	5	10.0	1	2.0	3	1	12	28	44	88.0
XVI	June-July 1930	71	11	15.5	6	8.4	6	4	25	19	54	76.0
		67	4	6.0	1	1.5	7	—	21	34	62	92.0
XVII	February 1934	71	17	24.0	6	8.4	11	1	24	12	48	67.6
		68	8	11.8	1	1.5	8	2	20	29	59	86.7

TEN YEARS[325]

June 10, 1939

The *Biulleten Oppozitsii* has been in existence for ten years. At the time it was founded, it was already clear that the Thermidorean reaction in the USSR would endure until it met with decisive resistance. Domestic resistance could hardly be counted upon inasmuch as the revolution had already in a large measure spent its fighting resources. The international situation, however, was or appeared to be far more favorable than it is today. Mighty labor organizations flourished in Germany. It was possible to hope that under the influence of the terrible lessons of the past, the German Communist Party would take the road of the class struggle and pull along the French proletariat. Two years after our publication was launched, the Spanish revolution, which might have become the starting point for a whole series of revolutions in Europe, erupted. In the minds of the editorial board of the *Biulleten* the fate of the USSR was always indissolubly linked with the fate of the world proletariat. Every revolutionary conflict opened at least a theoretical possibility of regenerating that which once had been the Communist International. But at each new stage of development a tombstone had to be placed over these expectations.

We have often been accused of having been too belated in declaring the Moscow International a corpse. We are not ready to recant on this score. It is better to delay a burial than to bury the not-dead. Whenever it is a question of contending living forces, one can foresee a priori the general trend of the movement; but it is extremely difficult, if not impossible, to forecast its stages and time intervals. Only when it became revealed that no open indignation was aroused in the ranks of the Communist International after the latter had surrendered without a struggle the most important position in Germany did it become clear that no hopes remained for the regeneration of this organization. By virtue of this very fact, the hour struck — not for vacillation or hesitation, as was the opinion of the participants in the defunct London Bureau, but for systematic work under the banner of the Fourth International.

So, too, in relation to the Soviet state our hopes and expectations have undergone in ten years an evolution determined not by our subjective likes or dislikes but by the general course of development. Political prognosis is only a working hypothesis. It must be constantly checked, rendered more precise, brought closer to reality. It was utterly impossible to have measured a priori how strong would be the internal resistance of the Bolshevik Party to the onset of Thermidor. Despite the disillusion and the fatigue of the masses, this resistance evidenced itself. Proof of it are the countless "purges," the massacre of entire revolutionary generations. But, in the circumstances of the defeats of the world proletariat, the Thermidorean reaction in the USSR proved stronger than the resistance of Bolshevism. In 1929, when the *Biulleten* was launched, this variant in perspectives was already a probability. But to have chosen beforehand this variant as the sole possibility would have signified the surrender of a position without a battle, that is, treacherous capitulation. Only the complete and manifest strangulation of the Bolshevik Party along with the complete prostitution of the Comintern removed the ground from under the program of "reforming" the Soviet state, placing on the order of the day the antibureaucratic revolution.

We have often been and are still being indicted for not having to this very day declared the USSR not to be a workers' state. Our critics have refrained, however, from giving *their* definition of the Soviet state, if we leave aside the term "state capitalism" which is applied by them equally to the USSR, Germany, and Italy. We have rejected, and still reject, this term, which while it does correctly characterize certain features of the Soviet state, nevertheless ignores its fundamental difference from capitalist states, namely, the absence of a bourgeoisie, as a class of property-owners, the existence of the state form of ownership of the most important means of production, and finally planned economy, made possible by the October Revolution. Neither in Germany nor in Italy does the foregoing exist. The proletariat, in overthrowing the Bonapartist oligarchy, will lean on this social foundation.

*   *   *

The last decade was a decade of defeats and retreats of the proletariat, a decade of victories of reaction and counterrevolution. This era has not terminated; the greatest evils and bestialities are still ahead. But the approaching denouement is presaged precisely by the extraordinary tension. In international relations this denouement means war. Abstractly speaking, it would have been far better had the war been forestalled by the proletarian revolution. But this did not occur and — we must say flatly — the remaining chances for it are few. The war is advancing far more speedily than the rate at which new cadres of the proletarian revolution are being formed. Never before has historical determinism assumed so fatalistic a form as it does nowadays. All the forces of old society — fascism and democracy, and social patriotism and Stalinism — stand equally in fear of war and keep heading towards it. Nothing will help them. They will make the war and will be swept away by the war. They have fully earned it.

The Social Democracy and the Comintern are concluding deals with democratic imperialism "against fascism" and "against war." But their "lesser evil" inescapably retreats before a greater evil. Should capitalism, with the aid of the two Internationals, succeed in maintaining itself for another decade, then the methods of fascism will no longer be adequate. Military conquests can achieve only a shift of poverty from one country to another, while at the same time narrowing the base upon which all countries rest. A superfascism will become necessary, with such legislation as harks back to the time of Herod and the slaughter of innocent babes, so as to preserve the dictatorship of the trusts. In that event, the corroded Internationals will doubtless proclaim as a holy duty an alliance with fascism — a lesser evil in the face of a Herod threatening no longer civilization alone but the very existence of mankind. For Social Democrats and Stalinists there is not and there cannot be — either in China, Germany, Spain, France, or anywhere in the world — such conditions as would give the proletariat the right to play an independent role; the one thing that the workers are good for is to support one form of banditry against another. There are no limits within capitalism itself as to the depths to which it can sink; this is likewise true of its shadows:

the Second and Third Internationals. They will be the first to be crushed by the war they are themselves preparing. The only world party unafraid of war and its consequences is the Fourth International. We should have preferred another way; but we shall take confidently also the path into which the present masters of the situation are shoving mankind.

* * *

The *Biulleten* does not stand alone. Publications of the same spirit appear in dozens of countries. Many articles of the *Biulleten* have been translated during the last decade into dozens of languages. True enough, there remain quite a few left philistines who turn up their noses loftily at our small publications and their small circulation. But we would not swap our *Biulleten* for the Moscow *Pravda,* with all its rotary presses and trucks. Machines may and will pass from one hand to another under the influence of ideas that sway the masses. Neither the Second nor the Third International has a single idea left. They only reflect the mortal fears of the ruling classes. The ideas that comprise the heritage of the Fourth International have a colossal dynamic force lodged in them. The impending events will annihilate all that is decrepit, putrescent, and out-lived, clearing the arena for a new program and a new organization.

But even today, at the peak of reaction, we derive priceless satisfaction from the knowledge that we have observed the historical process with our eyes open; that we have analyzed realistically each new situation, foreseen its possible consequences, warned of its dangers, indicated the correct road. In everything essential our analysis and our prognosis have been confirmed by events. We did not achieve miracles. Generally speaking, miracles do not enter into our field of specialty. But together with our reader-friends we have learned how to think as Marxists in order when the hour strikes to act as revolutionists. The *Biulleten* enters into its second decade with an immutable faith in the triumph of its idea.

* * *

For almost nine years, the publication of the *Biulleten* was

in the hands of L. L. Sedov. To this cause he gave the better
part of his youth. Unwaveringly devoted to the cause of revolutionary socialism, Sedov did not flinch once throughout the
hard years of reaction. He always lived in the expectation
of a new revolutionary dawn. It did not fall to his lot to meet
it himself. But like all genuine revolutionists he worked for
the future. And the future will disappoint neither him nor us.

*   *   *

The publication of the *Biulleten* would have been impossible
without the aid of loyal friends. To all of them we send our
fraternal gratitude. We are banking firmly in the future on
their help, which we need today more than ever before.

SOVIET PLUTARCHS [326]

June 10, 1939

In the time of King David the chronicler was a certain man by the name of Gad. [327] Whether he was an academic is unknown. But the historian Yaroslavsky certainly is descended in direct line from this Gad. And all the other Stalin historians — the authors of the school "history" of Russia, and the authors of the "history" of the party — certainly belong to the tribe of Gad.

There are rumors going around that in view of the special services rendered by this corporation in the "purging" of history, the Kremlin intends to introduce a special mark of distinction: the Order of Plutarch. However, Yaroslavsky himself is risking confusion being sown among the people by this name. Plutarchs? Some man in the street, who hasn't a classical education, will wonder. Plut-archs? or maybe simply arch-pluts? [328]

TOWARD A BALANCE SHEET
OF THE PURGES [329]

June 10, 1939

Walter Duranty, correspondent of the *New York Times,* whom the Kremlin has always entrusted with its dirtiest journalistic tasks, considers it necessary now to report that the purge far exceeded in size everything known about it abroad. Half of the expelled Communists have returned to the ranks of the party again. But how many innocent nonparty people suffered, etc.!

Walter Duranty's indignation has been ordered from him by the Kremlin this time too. Stalin now has to have his own lackeys as indignant as possible over the outrages and crimes that have been committed. They thus lead public opinion to believe that Stalin himself is full of indignation, and that consequently the forgeries, provocations, arbitrary exiles, and shootings took place without his knowledge and against his will. Only inveterate fools, of course, are capable of believing this. But even people who are not stupid are inclined to go to meet Stalin, on this question, at least halfway; yes, they say, Stalin was doubtless the culprit of the last wave of terror; but he wanted to limit it within the framework of political expediency, i.e., exterminate those it was necessary for his regime to exterminate. Meanwhile, the unreasonable and demoralized executants, guided by interests of a lower order, gave the purge a completely monstrous dimension and thus produced general indignation. Stalin, of course, is not guilty of these exaggerations, this senseless, even from the viewpoint of the Kremlin, extermination of hundreds of thousands of "neutral" people.

However much this reasoning may win over the thinking of ordinary people, it is false from start to finish. It supposes, above all, that Stalin himself is more limited than he actually is. But he has available, especially in this field, sufficient experience to be able to say what size a purge has to be in the apparatus that he took the major part in creating and forming. The preparation, as is well known, took a long time. It started with the expulsion from the party, in 1935, of tens of thousands

346

of long repentant oppositionists. Nobody understood these measures. Least of all, of course, those expelled themselves. Stalin's task was to kill the Fourth International and exterminate in passing the old generation of Bolsheviks, and from the subsequent generations all those who were morally connected with the tradition of the Bolshevik Party. In order to carry out such a monstrous plan, the like of which cannot be found in the pages of human history, the apparatus itself had to be caught in pincers. It was necessary to make every GPU agent, every Soviet official, every member of the party, feel that the slightest deviation from this or that diabolic assignment would mean the death of the recalcitrant and the destruction of his family and friends. Any thought of resistance in the party or in the working masses had to be killed in advance. It was thus a matter not of chance "exaggerations," not of unreasonable zeal on the part of the executants, but of a necessary condition of the success of the basic plan. As executant was required a hysterical villain like Yezhov; Stalin saw his character and the spirit of his work in advance, and prepared to reject him when the basic aim was reached. In this field, the work went according to plan.

Even in the period of struggle with the Left Opposition, Stalin initiated the clique of his nearest co-thinkers into his greatest sociological and historical discovery: all regimes in the past fell as a result of the indecision and vacillation of the ruling class. If the state power has sufficient ruthlessness in struggle with its foes, not stopping at mass extermination, it will always manage to cope with all dangers. Already in autumn 1927 this wisdom was being repeated by Stalin's agents in all keys with the aim of preparing the public opinion of the party for the coming purges and trials. Today, it may seem to the Kremlin bosses — in any case it seemed so to them yesterday — that the great theorem of Stalin has been confirmed by facts. But history will destroy the police illusion, this time too. When a social or political regime reaches irreconcilable contradictions with the demands of the development of the country, repressions can certainly prolong its existence for a certain time, but in the long run the apparatus of repression itself will begin to break, grow dull, crumble. Stalin's police apparatus is entering just this stage. The fates of Yagoda and Yezhov foretell the coming fate not only of Beria, but also of the common boss of all three.

1917-1939 [330]

June 10, 1939

The manifesto with which the sixth congress of the party (July 1917) finished its work proclaimed: "From the very beginning the Russian proletariat understood that for the success of the Russian Revolution an international uprising of the proletarians of Europe . . . was necessary." Let us remember that because of the absence of the party leaders, Stalin, along with Sverdlov[331] and Bukharin, led this congress.

"The entrance of America into the war"—went on the manifesto—"inspired the allied imperialists even more. . . . They knew very well the value of this great democracy, which electrocutes its socialists, stifles small nations with gun in hand . . . and through the mouths of its diplomats, incomparable for naked cynicism, talks about eternal peace. The American millionaires, their cellars filled with gold minted from the blood of those who are dying on the fields of a Europe laid waste, have joined their weapons, their finances, their counterespionage and their diplomats to crush their German colleagues in world plunder, and stretch tighter the noose round the neck of the Russian Revolution."

Although Russia was at that time certainly the freest of all democracies in the world, the manifesto branded the "defense of the fatherland" as betrayal. "The Russian petty-bourgeois democracy, in the person of the SR and Menshevik parties, has been drawn into the current of general imperialist policy. In this respect, there has taken place a complete equalization of the policy of the social patriots of all countries, who have finally in Russia turned into direct agents of imperialism."

It is sufficient to put just one of these extracts from the manifesto alongside not only the actions of Soviet diplomacy but even the documents of the present Comintern, to measure the difference between proletarian revolution and Thermidorean reaction!

FOR A COURAGEOUS REORIENTATION [332]

June 16, 1939

Dear Friend:

I have just received Goldman's letter. Concerning the Marxist center, it is a purely tactical question and I believe we can give the IS full freedom in maneuvering on this question. [333] I see no principled objection to a repetition of the experiment of direct contact with the centrists busy with the creation of the new international. Our representatives can lose nothing and gain something if they are firm in the essence and elastic in the form.

The prewar situation, the aggravation of nationalism, and so on, is a natural hindrance to our development and the profound cause of the depression in our ranks. But it must now be underlined that the more the party is petty bourgeois in its composition, the more it is dependent upon the changes in the official public opinion. It is a supplementary argument for the necessity for a courageous and active reorientation toward the masses. (The Negro question takes on a new importance. The Negroes will hardly be patriotic in the coming war.)

The pessimistic reasonings you mention in your article are, of course, a reflection of the patriotic, nationalistic pressure of the official public opinion. "If fascism is victorious in France, . ." "if fascism is victorious in England, . ." and so on. The victories of fascism are important, but the death agony of capitalism is more important. Fascism accelerates the new war and the new war will tremendously accelerate the revolutionary movement. In case of war every small revolutionary nucleus can and will become a decisive, historic factor in a very short time. It is shameful that revolutionaries see only one side of the present historic development — its dark, reactionary side — and ignore the approach of a general denouement in which the Fourth International will have the same role to play as did the Bolsheviks in 1917.

Comradely,
Trotsky

THE RIDDLE OF THE USSR [334]

June 21, 1939

Two features are characteristic of the present international policies of the great powers. First, the absence of any system or consistency in their actions. Particularly fantastic oscillations have been exhibited recently by that country which has historically been the model of ponderous stability, namely Great Britain. At the time of the Munich agreement, in September of last year, Chamberlain proclaimed "a new era of peace" based on the cooperation of four European powers. The unofficial slogan of the Conservatives [335] in those days was: "give Germany a free hand in the East." Today all the efforts of the British government are concentrated on concluding an agreement with Moscow — against Germany.

The London stock exchange, which at the time welcomed the Munich agreement with an upward movement in stock prices, is now adapting the state of its nerves to the course of the Anglo-Soviet negotiations. France obediently follows England in these zigzags: there is nothing else it can do. The constant element in Hitler's policy is its aggressive dynamism, but that is all. No one knows where Germany will strike next. It is possible that at this moment Hitler himself does not know. The ups and downs of the "Neutrality" Act in the United States illustrate the same theme.

The second feature of international politics, closely connected with the first, is that no one believes what anyone else says or even what he himself says. Any treaty presupposes a minimum of mutual trust, and a military alliance even more so. But the conditions of the Anglo-Soviet talks show only too clearly no such confidence exists there. This is not at all a question of abstract morality; it is simply that the present objective situation of the world powers, for all of whom the globe has become too small, excludes any possibility of a consistent policy that can predict the future and be relied upon.

Each government is trying to insure itself against at least two eventualities. Hence the appalling duplicity of world politics, its insincerity and its convulsiveness. The more inexorably and tragically emerges the general forecast that mankind is advancing toward a new catastrophe, with its eyes closed, the more difficult does it become to make detailed forecasts as to what England or Germany will do tomorrow, which side Poland will take, or what position Moscow will adopt.

There is especially little data for an answer to the last question. The Soviet press scarcely bothers with international politics. Precisely why Mr. Strang came to Moscow and what he is doing there are no business of the Soviet citizens. [336] Dispatches from abroad are usually printed on the back page and usually are given a "neutral" presentation. The conclusion of the Italo-German alliance or the fortification of the Aland Islands is reported as if these events happened on Mars. [337]

This sham objectivity serves to leave the Kremlin's hands free. The world press more than once in the past has written about the "impenetrability" of Soviet aims and the "unpredictability" of the Kremlin's methods. We shall get nearer to solving the "impenetrable" enigma the more decisively we replace speculations about Stalin's subjective sympathies and antipathies by an objective evaluation of the interests of the Soviet oligarchy which Stalin merely personifies.

Mainsprings of the Kremlin's Policy

Nobody "wants" war and many, above that, "hate" it. This only means that everyone would prefer to gain his ends by peaceful means. But that does not at all mean that there will be no war. The ends, alas, are contradictory, and do not permit reconciliation. Stalin wants war less than anyone since he is more afraid of it than anyone. There are sufficient reasons why. The "purges," monstrous both in scale and methods, reflect the unbearable tension in relations between the Soviet bureaucracy and the people. The flower of the Bolshevik Party, the leaders of the economy and the diplomatic service, have been exterminated. The flower of the general staff, the heroes and idols of the army and navy, have been exterminated. Stalin carried out this purge not as the vain caprice of an oriental despot; he was compelled to do it by his struggle to preserve power. This must be thoroughly understood.

If we follow the life of the USSR from day to day in the Soviet press, reading attentively between the lines, it becomes perfectly clear that the ruling stratum feels it is the object of universal hatred. Among the popular masses the threat runs: "When war comes, we'll show them." The bureaucracy trembles for its recently won positions. Caution is the predominant characteristic of their leader, especially in the field of world affairs. The spirit of daring is utterly alien to him. He does not stop, it is true, at the use of force on an unprecedented scale, but only on condition that he is assured in advance of impunity.

On the other hand, he easily resorts to concessions and retreats when he is uncertain of the outcome of a struggle. Japan would never have got involved in a war with China if it had not known beforehand that Moscow would not take advantage of a favorable pretext to intervene. At the party congress in March of this year Stalin openly declared for the first time that economically the Soviet Union is still very far behind the capitalist countries. He had to make this admission not only in order to explain the low standard of living of the masses but also to justify his retreats in the field of foreign policy. Stalin is prepared to pay very dearly, not to say any price, for peace. Not because he "hates" war but because he is mortally afraid of its consequences.

From this standpoint it is not difficult to evaluate the comparative benefits for the Kremlin of the two alternatives: agreement with Germany or alliance with the "democracies." Friendship with Hitler would mean immediate removal of the danger of war on the Western front, and thereby a great reduction of the danger of war on the Far Eastern front. An alliance with the democracies would mean only the possibility of receiving aid in the event of war. Of course, if nothing is left but to fight, then it is more advantageous to have allies than to remain isolated. But the basic task of Stalin's policy is not to create the most favorable conditions in the event of war, but to avoid war. This is the hidden meaning of the frequent statements by Stalin, Molotov, and Voroshilov that the USSR "needs no allies."

True, it is now being declared that a reconstitution of the Triple Entente is a sure means of preventing war. No one, however, explains why the Entente failed to secure this result twenty-five years ago. The establishment of the League of Nations was motivated precisely by the argument that otherwise the division of Europe into two irreconcilable camps would inevitably lead to a new war.

Now, as a result of the experience of "collective security," [338] the diplomats have come to the conclusion that the splitting of Europe into two irreconcilable camps is capable of . . . preventing war. Believe this who can! The Kremlin, anyway, does not believe it. Agreement with Hitler would mean insuring the border of the USSR on condition that Moscow cut itself off from European politics. Stalin would like nothing better. Alliance with the democracies would insure the borders of the USSR only to the same extent that it insured all other borders in Europe, making the USSR their guarantor and thereby eliminating the possibility of Soviet neutrality. To hope that a reconstitution of the Triple Entente would be capable of perpetuating the status quo, eliminating the possibility of any border being violated, would be to live in the realm of illusion. Perhaps the danger of war would, for a time, be less urgent for the USSR; but, in return, it would become immeasurably more extensive. An alliance of Moscow with London and Paris would mean for Hitler that henceforth he would have against him all three states at once, whichever border he violated. Faced with such a risk, he would most probably choose the most gigantic throw of all, that is, a campaign against the USSR. In that event, the "insurance" provided by the Entente could easily be transformed into its opposite.

In all other respects too, agreement with Germany would be the best solution for the Moscow oligarchy to take. The Soviet Union could systematically supply Germany with almost all the kinds of raw materials and foodstuffs it lacks. Germany could supply the Soviet Union with machinery, industrial products, and also necessary technical advice for both general and war industry. Gripped in the vise of an agreement between these two giants, Poland, Rumania, and the Baltic states would have no choice but to renounce all thought of independent policies and to restrict themselves to the modest benefits to be derived from collaboration and transit facilities. Moscow would willingly grant Berlin full freedom in its foreign policy in all directions but one. Whoever, in these conditions, so much as mentions the "defense of the democracies" would immediately be declared by the Kremlin to be a Trotskyist, an agent of Chamberlain, a hireling of Wall Street, and—be immediately shot.

From the first day of the National Socialist regime Stalin has systematically and steadily shown his readiness for friendship with Hitler. Often this has taken the form of open declarations, more often of hints, meaningful silences, or alternating emphases, which might be unnoticed by Soviet citizens but nevertheless unfailingly got through to where they were meant to go. W. Krivitsky, former chief of Soviet intelligence in Europe, [339] recently described the work carried on behind the scenes in this direction. Only after a series of extremely hostile rejoinders by Hitler to this Soviet policy did the turn begin toward the League of Nations, collective security, and Popular Fronts. This new diplomatic tune, supported by the big drums, kettledrums, and saxophones of the Comintern, has become over the last few years more and more a menace to the eardrums. But every time there was a moment of quiet one could hear underneath it, softer, somewhat melancholy, but more intimate notes intended for the ears of Berchtesgaden. [340] In this apparent duality there is an undoubted inner unity.

The entire world press drew attention to the frankness with which Stalin, in his report to the last party congress in March of this year, made advances to Germany while simultaneously hitting out at England and France as "provokers of war, used to lighting the fires with other people's hands." [341] But the supplementary speech by Manuilsky on Comintern policy passed completely unnoticed, although Stalin had edited this speech too. For the first time, Manuilsky replaced the traditional demand for the freeing of all colonies by a new slogan: "the realization of the right of self-determination of peoples *enslaved by the fascist states. . . .* The Comintern thereby demands free self-determination for Austria, . . the Sudetenland, . . Korea, Formosa, Abyssinia [Ethiopia]. . . ." As regards India, Indochina, Algeria, and the other colonies of Great Britain and France, Stalin's agent confined himself to an inoffensive desire for "improvement in the position of the working masses." At the same time he demanded that the colonial peoples henceforth "subordinate" their struggle for freedom "to the interests of the defeat of fascism, the worst foe of the working people." In other words, the British and French colonies are obliged, according to the Comintern's new theory, to support the countries that rule them against Germany, Italy, and Japan.

The glaring contradiction between the two speeches is in fact a sham. Stalin took upon himself the most important part of the task: a direct offer to Hitler of an agreement against the democratic "provokers of war." To Manuilsky he entrusted the frightening of Hitler with the prospect of a rapprochement between the USSR and the democratic "provokers," incidentally explaining to the latter the enormous advantages for them of an alliance with the USSR: no one but the Kremlin, the old friend of oppressed peoples, could inspire the colonies with the idea that it was necessary for them to remain loyal to their democratic rulers during a war with fascism. These are the mainsprings of Kremlin policy, the unity underlying the outward contradictions in it. From start to finish it is determined by the interests of the ruling caste, which has abandoned all principles except the principle of self-preservation.

Hitler and the USSR

Mechanics teaches us that force is determined by mass and speed. The dynamics of Hitler's foreign policy has assured for Germany a commanding position in Europe, and to some extent in the whole world. For how long is another question. If Hitler were to restrain himself (if he *could* restrain himself), London would once more turn its back on Moscow. On the other hand, the reply which is hourly expected from Moscow to London's proposals depends much more on Hitler than on Stalin. If Hitler at last responds to Moscow's diplomatic advances, Chamberlain will be rebuffed. If Hitler vacillates or seems to, the Kremlin will do all in its power to drag out the negotiations. Stalin will sign a treaty with England only if he is convinced that agreement with Hitler is out of his reach.

Dimitrov, the secretary of the Comintern, carrying out Stalin's commands, announced soon after the Munich agreement a precise calendar of Hitler's next campaigns of conquest. Hungary would be subjected in the spring of 1939; *in the autumn of the same year, Poland would be invaded.* Yugoslavia's turn would come in the following year. In the autumn of 1940 Hitler would invade Rumania and Bulgaria. In the spring of 1941 blows would be struck at France, Belgium, Holland, Denmark, and Switzerland. Finally, in the autumn of 1941, Germany intended to begin its offensive against the Soviet Union.

It is possible that this information — in less precise form, of course — was obtained by Soviet intelligence. But it is also possible that it was a product of pure speculation, having the aim of showing that Germany intended first to crush its Western neighbors, and only afterward to turn its guns against the Soviet Union. To what extent will Hitler be guided by Dimitrov's timetable? Around this question guesses and plans are revolving in the various capitals of Europe.

The first chapter of Hitler's world plan, the creation of a broad national base plus a springboard in Czechoslovakia, has been completed. The next stage of German aggression can have two variants. Either an immediate agreement with the USSR, so as to have his hands free for the Southwest and the West; in that case, plans relating to the Ukraine, the Caucasus, and the Urals would find their place in Hitler's third chapter. Or else — an immediate blow at the East, the dismemberment of the Soviet Union, securing the Eastern rear. In that case, the attack on the West would be the third chapter.

A firm agreement with Moscow, fully in the spirit of the Bismarck tradition, would not only mean enormous economic benefits for Germany but would also allow it to operate an active world policy. However, from the day of his accession to power, Hitler has spurned the outstretched hand of Moscow. Having crushed the German "Marxists," Hitler could not in the first years of his rule weaken his internal position by a rapprochement with "Marxist" Moscow. More important, though, were considerations of foreign policy. To induce England to close its eyes to Germany's illegal rearmament and violations of the Versailles treaty, Hitler had to put on a show as the defender of European culture from Bolshevik barbarism. Both of these factors have now lost a great deal of their importance. Inside Germany, the Social Democratic and Communist parties, having disgraced themselves by their shameful capitulation to the Nazis, are now a negligible quantity. In Moscow, all that remains of Marxism are some poor busts of Marx.

The creation of a new privileged stratum in the USSR and the repudiation of the policy of international revolution, reinforced by the mass extermination of revolutionaries, have enormously reduced the fear that Moscow used to inspire in the capitalist world. The volcano is extinct, the lava has turned cold. The capitalist states would, of course, now as ever, willingly facilitate the restoration of capitalism in the USSR. But they no longer regard that country as a hotbed of revolution. No need is felt any more for a leader for a crusade against the East. Hitler himself understood earlier than others the social significance of the Moscow purges and show trials, for to him, at any rate, it was no secret that neither Zinoviev, nor Kamenev, nor Rykov, nor Bukharin, nor Marshal Tukhachevsky, nor the dozens and hundreds of other revolutionaries, statesmen, diplomats, and generals were *not* his agents.

Hitler's need to hypnotize Downing Street with the notion of a community of interests against the USSR has ceased too, for he has received from England more than he had hoped for—everything he could possibly receive without recourse to arms. If, nevertheless, he is not meeting the Kremlin halfway, this is evidently because he is afraid of the USSR. With its 170 million people, its inexhaustible natural resources, its undoubted achievements in industrialization, the increase in its means of communication, the USSR—so Hitler thinks—would immediately overrun Poland, Rumania, and the Baltic countries, and bring its entire mass up to the borders of Germany as soon as the Third Reich was involved in a struggle for the redivision of the world. In order to be able to grab the English and French colonies, Hitler must first secure his rear, and is meditating a preventive war against the USSR.

True, the German high command knows well, from past experience, the difficulties of occupying Russia or even just the Ukraine. However, Hitler counts on the instability of the Stalin regime. A few serious defeats for the Red Army, he thinks, will suffice to bring down the Kremlin government. And since there are no organized forces in the country, and the White emigres are quite alien to the people, after Stalin's fall chaos will reign for a long time, and this can be utilized, on the one hand, for direct economic plundering—seizure of gold reserves, removal of all kinds of raw materials, etc.— and, on the other, for a blow against the West. Uninterrupted trade relations between Germany and the USSR—today there is once again talk of the arrival in Moscow of a delegation of industrialists from Berlin—do not in themselves mean a

long period of peace ahead. At best they mean that the date
of the war has not yet been decided. Credits for a few hundred
million marks cannot put off the war for a single hour, because in the war what is at stake is not hundreds of millions,
but tens of billions, the conquest of countries and continents,
a new partition of the world. Lost credits will, if necessary,
be put down to petty expenses incurred in a bigger enterprise.
At the same time, the offer of new credits not long before launching a war would be not a bad way of putting one's adversary off the scent. In any case, it is precisely now, at the critical moment of the Anglo-Soviet talks, that Hitler is deciding
which way to direct his aggression — East or West?

Future of Military Alliances

It may seem that to distinguish between the "second" and
"third" chapters in the impending German expansion is a pe-
dantic exercise: a renewal of the Triple Entente would deprive
Hitler of the opportunity to carry out his plans in stages and
alternate his blows, because, regardless of where the conflict
began, it would immediately spread to all Germany's borders.
This idea is true, however, only in part.

Germany occupies a central position in relation to its future
enemies; it can maneuver by throwing its reserves along internal operational lines in the most important directions. To
the extent that the initiative in military operations will be Germany's — and at the beginning of the war it will undoubtedly
be Germany's — that state will at any given moment select
the main enemy to be dealt with, treating the other fronts as
secondary. Unity of action between Britain, France, and the
USSR could, certainly, restrict to a considerable degree the
freedom of action of the German high command; and for that,
of course, a tripartite alliance would be necessary. But this
unity of action must be realized in fact. Meanwhile, the tense
struggle going on over the terms of the pact has already
shown how much each of the participants is striving to preserve its own freedom of action at the expense of its future
ally. If one or another member of the new Triple Entente considered it more expedient to stand aside at the moment of
danger, Hitler is quite ready to provide the juridical basis
for a tearing up of the pact: for that purpose it would suffice to cover the outbreak of the war with such diplomatic

maneuvers as would make it very hard to define the "aggressor" — at least from the standpoint of the member of the Triple Entente interested in clouding the issue. But even apart from this extreme case of open "betrayal" there remains the question of the *extent* to which the pact would be honored. If Germany strikes at the West, Britain will immediately come to the help of France with all its forces because, there and then, the fate of Britain itself will be at stake.

The situation would be regarded quite differently, however, if Germany were to transfer its main forces to the East. Britain and France would not be interested, of course, in seeing a decisive victory by Germany over the Soviet Union, but they would have nothing against a mutual weakening of these two countries. Hitler's tasks in the East, in view of the probable resistance of Poland and Rumania, and in view of the immense distances and masses of population, are so immense that even with the most favorable course of operations for him, they would demand very great forces and considerable time.

During all this first period, which events may make longer or shorter, Britain and France would enjoy comparative comfort for mobilizing, shipping British troops across the Channel, concentrating forces, and choosing the appropriate moment — leaving the Red Army to bear the whole brunt of the German attack. If the USSR should then find itself in a difficult situation, the Allies could lay down new terms for their aid, which the Kremlin could find hard to reject. When Stalin said in March at the party congress that Britain and France were interested in kindling war between Germany and the Soviet Union, so as to appear on the scene at the last moment with fresh forces as arbiter, he was not wrong.

But it is equally true that if Hitler distracts attention by making a fuss about Danzig and then strikes with his main force at the West, Moscow will want to take full advantage of its position.[342] The border states will help it to do this, willy-nilly. A direct attack by Hitler upon Poland would, of course, quickly arouse suspicion in the USSR, and the Warsaw government would itself call on the Red Army for help. On the other hand, if Hitler marched westward or southward, Poland, and Rumania too, would, with the tacit approval of the Kremlin, oppose with all their might the entrance of the Red Army into their territories. The main weight of the German blow would thus be borne by France. Moscow would wait it out. However precisely the new pact might be formulated on paper, the Triple Entente would remain not only a military alliance but also a triangle of antagonistic interests. Moscow's suspicions are all the more natural since it will never succeed in setting France against Britain or Britain against France; but these countries will always find a common language for joint pressure on Moscow. Hitler can make successful use of this antagonism among the allies themselves.

But not for long. In the totalitarian camp the contradictions will break out too, a little later, perhaps, but all the more violently. Even leaving aside distant Tokyo, the Berlin-Rome "axis" seems firm and reliable only because Berlin outweighs Rome so much and Rome is directly subordinated to Berlin. This circumstance doubtlessly produces greater concord and faster action. But only within certain limits. All three members of this camp are distinguished by the extreme range of their pretensions, and their worldwide appetites will come into violent conflict long before they reach satiety. No "axis" will stand up to the burden of the coming war.

What has been said does not, of course, deny any significance at all to international treaties and alliances, which one way or another will determine the initial positions of states in the coming war. But this significance is very limited. Once unleashed, the war will quickly outgrow the framework of diplomatic agreements, economic plans and military calculations. An umbrella is useful as a protection against London rain. But it cannot protect against a cyclone. Before reducing a substantial area of our planet to ruins, the cyclone of war will break not a few diplomatic umbrellas. The "sacredness" of treaty obligations will be revealed as a trifling superstition when people begin to write amid clouds of poison gas. *Sauve qui peut* (every man for himself) will be the slogan of governments, nations, and classes. Treaties will prove no more stable than the governments that made them. The Moscow oligarchy in any case will not survive the war it so deeply fears. The fall of Stalin will not, however, save Hitler, who with the infallibility of a sleepwalker is being drawn toward the greatest catastrophe in history. Whether the other participants in the bloody game will gain from this is a separate question.

THE KREMLIN IN WORLD POLITICS[343]

July 1, 1939

Moscow is being invited, Moscow is being cajoled, Moscow is being implored to join the "peace front" and come to the defense of the status quo. Moscow, in principle, consented long ago, but it now doubts that the capitalist democracies are ready to fight for the existing order with the necessary energy. This paradoxical redistribution of roles shows that something has changed under the sun, not as much on the Thames and the Seine as on the Moscow River. As always in processes of an organic character, the changes have matured gradually. However, under the influence of a great historical impact they appear suddenly and this is precisely why they shock the imagination.

In the last fifteen years Soviet foreign policy has undergone an evolution no less great than the internal regime. Bolshevism declared in August 1914 that the borders of the capitalist states with their customhouses, armies, and wars were obstacles to the development of world economics as great as the provincial customs of the Middle Ages were for the formation of the nations. Bolshevism saw its historic mission in the abolition of national borders in the name of the Soviet United States of Europe and of the world. In November 1917 the Bolshevist government began with an implacable struggle against all bourgeois states, independent of their political form. Not because Lenin did not assign, in general, importance to the difference between military dictatorship and parliamentary democracy, but because in his eyes the foreign policy of a state is determined not by its political form, but by the material interests of the ruling class. At the same time the Kremlin of that period made a radical distinction between imperialist, colonial, or semicolonial nations and was entirely on the side of the colonies against the mother countries, irrespective, here also, of the political form of either.

It is true that from the beginning the Soviet government did not abstain, in the struggle to defend itself, from utilizing the contradictions between bourgeois states and made temporary agreements with some against others. But then the question was of agreements of a limited character and specific type: with defeated and isolated Germany, with semicolonial countries such as Turkey and China, and finally, with Italy, wronged at Versailles. The fundamental rule of the Kremlin's policy was, moreover, that such an agreement of the Soviet government with a bourgeois state did not bind the corresponding national section of the Communist International. Thus, in the years following the Treaty of Rapallo [344] (April 1922), when an economic and partial military collaboration was established between Moscow and Berlin, the German Communist Party openly mobilized the masses for a revolutionary insurrection, and if it did not succeed in accomplishing it, that is not at all because it was hindered by Kremlin diplomacy. The revolutionary tendency of the policy common to the Soviet government and to the Comintern excluded in this period, of course, the possibility of the Soviet Republic's participation in a system of states interested in the preservation of the existing order.

Fear of the Kremlin's revolutionary role remained in force in the diplomatic chancelleries of Europe and America much longer than the revolutionary principles in the Kremlin itself. In 1932, when Moscow's foreign policy was entirely impregnated with a spirit of national conservatism, the French semi-official paper, *Le Temps*, wrote with indignation of "the governments which imagine that they can, without danger to themselves, introduce the Soviets into their game against other powers." A close contiguity to Moscow threatens "a disintegration of the national forces." In Asia, as in Europe, the Soviets "create disorder, exploit misery, provoke hate and the sentiment of vengeance, speculate shamelessly with all international rivalries." France, the country most interested in maintaining the Versailles peace, still remained enemy number one of the Kremlin. The second place was occupied by Great Britain. The United States, because of its remoteness, was in the third rank. Hitler's coming to power did not immediately change this estimate. The Kremlin wanted, at all costs, to maintain with the Third Reich the relations that had been established with the government of Ebert and Hindenburg, [345] and continued a noisy campaign against the Versailles treaty. But Hitler obstinately refused to answer these advances. In 1935 the Franco-Soviet Alliance was concluded, without a military covenant, however — somewhat like a knife without a blade. Eden visited Moscow but was forced to resign. [346] Meanwhile, Europe enriched itself with the experience of the Munich accord. Many diplomatic chancelleries and semi-official publications were hastily obliged to change their positions. On the 12th of June of this year, when Mr. Strang flew from London to Moscow, the same *Temps* wrote on the necessity of "inducing Soviet Russia to accelerate the conclusion of the Anglo-Franco-Russian Pact." The contiguity to Moscow has ceased, apparently, to threaten the "disintegration of the national forces."

The Kremlin's transformation from a revolutionary factor in world politics into a conservative one was brought about, of course, not by the change in the international situation, but by internal processes in the country of Soviets itself, where above the revolution and above the people a new social stratum has arisen, very privileged, very powerful, very greedy — a stratum with something to lose. Since it has only recently subjugated the masses to itself, the Soviet bureaucracy does not trust them any more than any other ruling class in the world fears them. International catastrophes can bring it nothing, but can deprive it of a great deal. A revolutionary uprising in Germany or Japan might, it is true, ameliorate the Soviet Union's international situation; but in return it would threaten to awaken revolutionary traditions inside the country, set in motion the masses and create a mortal danger for the Moscow oligarchy. The passionate struggle which unexpectedly and, as it seemed, without exterior inducement, was unfolding in Moscow around the theory of "permanent revolution," appeared for a long time to the external observer as a scholastic quarrel; but, in reality beneath it is a profound material basis: the new ruling stratum attempted to insure its conquests theoretically against the risk of an international revolution. Precisely at that time the Soviet bureaucracy began to tend toward the conclusion that the social question was resolved, since the bureaucracy had resolved its own question. Such is the sense of the theory of "socialism in one country."

Foreign governments have long suspected that the Kremlin was only screening itself with conservative formulas, and that it was in this way concealing its destructive schemes. Such a "military ruse" is possible, perhaps, on the part of an iso-lated person or a closely welded group for a short time; but it is absolutely inconceivable for a powerful state machine over many years. The preparation of the revolution is not alchemy which can be carried on in a cellar; it is assured by the con-tents of the agitation and propaganda and by the general direction of policies. It is impossible to prepare the proletariat for overthrowing the existing system by defending the status quo.

* * *

The evolution of the Kremlin's foreign policy has directly determined the fate of the Third International, which has been gradually transformed from a party of the international revo-lution into an auxiliary weapon of Soviet diplomacy. The specific weight of the Comintern declined simultaneously, as very clearly appears in the successive changes in its ruling personnel. In the first period (1919-23) the Russian delegation in the leadership of the Comintern consisted of Lenin, Trotsky, Zinoviev, Bukharin, and Radek. After Lenin's death and the elimination of Trotsky, and subsequently of Zinoviev, from the leadership, the direction was concentrated in the hands of Bukharin under the control of Stalin, who until then had stood aside from the international labor movement. After Bukharin's fall, Molotov, who had never troubled himself with the theory of Marxism, who does not know any foreign country or any foreign language, became, unexpectedly for everybody and for himself, the head of the Comintern. But soon it was necessary for Molotov to act as president of the Council of People's Com-missars, replacing Rykov, who had fallen into disgrace. Manuil-sky was appointed to the direction of the "world proletariat" — evidently only because he was not fit for any other task. Manuilsky rapidly exhausted his resources and in 1934 was replaced by Dimitrov, a Bulgarian worker, not lacking in personal audacity, but limited and ignorant. Dimitrov's ap-pointment was utilized for a demonstrative change of policy. The Kremlin decided to throw away the ritual of revolution and to openly attempt a union with the Second International, with the conservative bureaucracy of the trade unions, and through their intermediary with the liberal bourgeoisie. The era of "collective security" in the name of the status quo and of "People's Fronts" in the name of democracy was opened.

For the new policy new persons were necessary. Through a series of internal crises, removals, purges, and outright bribery, the various national parties were gradually adapted to the new demands of the Soviet bureaucracy. All the intelligent, independent, critical elements were expelled. The example was set by Moscow with its arrests, staged trials, and interminable executions. After the assassination of Kirov (December 1, 1934) several hundred foreign Communist emigres, who had become a burden to the Kremlin, were exterminated in the USSR. Through a ramified system of espionage, a systematic selection of careerist functionaries, ready to carry out every commission, was accomplished. At all events the purpose was obtained: the present apparatus of the Comintern consists of individuals who by their character and education represent the direct opposite of the revolutionary type.

In order not to lose influence with certain circles of workers, the Comintern is obliged, to be sure, to have recourse from time to time to demagogy. But this does not go beyond some radical phrases. These individuals are not capable of any real struggle, which demands independent thought, moral integrity, and mutual confidence. Already in 1933 the Communist Party of Germany, the most numerous section of the Comintern next to the USSR, was impotent to offer any resistance to the coup d'etat of Hitler. This shameful capitulation forever marked the end of the Comintern as a revolutionary factor. Since then it sees as its principal task the convincing of bourgeois public opinion of its respectability. In the Kremlin, better than anywhere else, they know the price of the Comintern. They conduct themselves toward the foreign Communist parties as if the latter were poor relatives, who are not exactly welcome and very greedy. Stalin surnamed the Comintern the "gyp-joint." Nevertheless, if he continues to sustain these "gyp-joints," it is for the same reason that other states maintain ministries of propaganda. This has nothing in common with the tasks of the international revolution.

A few examples will best show how the Kremlin makes use of the Comintern, on the one hand, to maintain its prestige in the eyes of the masses; on the other, to prove its moderation to the ruling classes. Moreover, the first of these tasks retreats more and more before the latter.

During the Chinese revolution of 1927 all the conservative papers in the world, particularly the English, represented the Kremlin as an incendiary. In reality the Kremlin feared, even more than anything else, that the Chinese revolutionary masses would go beyond the limits of the national bourgeois revolution. The Chinese section of the Comintern was, on the categorical injunction of Moscow, subordinated to the discipline of the Kuomintang, in order thus to forestall any suspicion of the Kremlin's intentions of shaking the basis of private property in China. Stalin, Molotov, Voroshilov, and Kalinin sent instructions by wire to the leaders of the Chinese Communist Party to restrain the peasants from seizing large estates, in order not to frighten Chiang Kai-shek and his officers. The same policy is carried out now in China, during the war with Japan, in a much more decisive manner: the Chinese Communist Party is completely subordinated to the government of Chiang Kai-shek and by Kremlin command has officially abandoned the teaching of Marx in favor of that of Sun Yat-sen, founder of the Chinese Republic.

The task was more difficult in Poland with its old revolutionary traditions and its strong Communist Party, which has passed through the school of czarist illegality. Since it was seeking the friendship of the Warsaw government, Moscow first prohibited the launching of the demand for the self-determination to the Polish Ukrainians; next it ordered the Polish Communist Party to patriotically sustain their government. Inasmuch as it encountered resistance, Moscow dissolved the Communist Party, declaring that its leaders, old and known revolutionists, were agents of fascism. During his recent visit to Warsaw, Potemkin, assistant people's commissar for foreign affairs, assured Colonel Beck[347] that the Comintern will not resume its work in Poland. The same pledge was given by Potemkin in Bucharest. The Turkish section of the Comintern was liquidated even earlier in order not to dampen the friendship with Kemal Pasha.

The policy of the "People's Fronts" carried out by Moscow signified in France the subordination of the Communist Party to the control of the Radical Socialists, who, in spite of their name, are a conservative bourgeois party. During the tempestuous strike movement in June 1936, with the occupation of the mills and factories, the French section of the Comintern acted as a party of democratic order; it is to them that the Third Republic is indebted in the highest degree for preventing the movement from taking openly revolutionary forms. In England, where if the war does not intervene we can expect a supplanting of the Tories now in power by the Labour Party, the Comintern directs a constant propaganda in favor of a bloc with the Liberals,[348] in spite of the obstinate opposition of the English Labourites. The Kremlin fears that a purely workers' government, in spite of its moderation, would engender extraordinary demands by the masses, provoke a social crisis, weaken England, and untie Hitler's hands. Hence comes the aspiration to place the Labour Party under the control of the liberal bourgeoisie. However paradoxical it may be, the concern of the Moscow government nowadays is the protection of private property in England!

It is difficult to conceive of a sillier invention than the references of Hitler and Mussolini to the Spanish events as proof of the revolutionary intervention of the Soviet Union. The Spanish revolution, which exploded without Moscow and unexpected by it, soon revealed a tendency to take a socialist character. Moscow feared above all that the disturbance of private property in the Iberian peninsula would bring London and Paris nearer to Berlin against the USSR. After some hesitations, the Kremlin intervened in the events in order to restrict the revolution within the limits of the bourgeois regime.

All the actions of the Moscow agents in Spain were directed toward paralyzing any independent movement of the workers and peasants and reconciling the bourgeoisie with a moderate republic. The Spanish Communist Party stood in the right wing of the People's Front. On December 21, 1936, Stalin, Molotov, and Voroshilov, in a confidential letter to Largo Caballero, insistently recommended to the Spanish premier at that time that there be no infringement of private property, that guarantees be given to foreign capital against violation of freedom of commerce and for maintaining the parliamentary system without tolerating the development of soviets. This letter, recently communicated by Largo Caballero to the press through the former Spanish ambassador in Paris, L. Araquistain (*New York Times*, June 4, 1939)[349] summed up in the best manner the Soviet government's conservative position in the face of socialist revolution.

We must, moreover, do justice to the Kremlin — the policy did not remain in the domain of words. The GPU in Spain carried out ruthless repressions against the revolutionary wing ("Trotskyists," POUMists, left socialists, left anarchists). Now, after the defeat, the cruelties and frame-ups of the GPU in

Spain are voluntarily revealed by the moderate politicians, who largely utilized the Moscow police apparatus in order to crush their revolutionary adversaries.

Especially striking is the Kremlin's change of attitude toward the colonial peoples, who have lost for it any particular interests, since they are not the subjects but the objects of world politics. At the last convention of the party in Moscow (March 1939) the refusal of the Comintern to demand freedom for the colonies that belong to democratic countries was officially proclaimed. On the contrary, the Comintern enjoined these colonies to sustain their masters against fascist pretensions. In order to demonstrate to London and Paris the high value of an alliance with the Kremlin, the Comintern is agitating in British India, as in French Indochina, against the Japanese danger and not at all against French and British domination. "The Stalinist leaders have made a new step in the way of treason," wrote the Saigon workers' paper, *La Lutte* [The Struggle] on April 7 of this year. "Taking off their revolutionary masks, they have become champions of imperialism and express themselves openly against the emancipation of oppressed colonial peoples." It merits attention that in the elections for the colonial council, the candidates of the party represented by the quoted newspaper received in Saigon more votes than the bloc of the Communists and the governmental party. In the colonies, Moscow's authority is declining rapidly.

As a revolutionary factor, the Comintern is dead. No force in the world will ever revive it. Should the Kremlin once again turn its policy toward revolution, it would not find the necessary instruments. But the Kremlin does not want that and cannot want it.

*   *   *

The triple military alliance, which must include a covenant of the general staffs, supposes not only a community of interests, but also an important degree of mutual confidence. It is a question of a common elaboration of military plans and the exchange of the most secret information. The purge of the Soviet command is still in the minds of all. How can London and Paris agree to confide their secrets to the general staff of the USSR, at whose head only yesterday were "foreign agents"? If Stalin needed more than twenty years to discover

spies in such national heroes as Tukhachevsky, Yegorov, Gamarnik, Bluecher, Yakir, Uborevitch, Muralov, Mrachkovsky,
Dybenko, and others, what ground is there for hoping that the
new military chiefs, who are absolutely drab and unknown
persons, will be more secure than their predecessors? London
and Paris were not affected, however, by such fears. Not astonishing: the interested governments and their staffs read very
well between the lines of the Moscow indictments. At the trial
in March 1938, the former Soviet ambassador to England,
Rakovsky, declared himself sole agent of the intelligence service.
The backward strata of Russian and English workers can
believe this. But not the intelligence service; it knows its own
agents very well. Only on the basis of this single fact — and
there are hundreds of them — it was not difficult for Chamberlain
to make a decision as to the relative value of the accusations
against Marshal Tukhachevsky and other military chiefs. At
Downing Street as well as on the Quai d'Orsay there are no
romantics, no naive dreamers. They know there with what
materials history is made. Many people, of course, frown at
the mention of the monstrous frame-ups. But in the long run
the Moscow trials, with their fantastic accusations and their
entirely real executions, strengthened the confidence of these
circles in the Kremlin as a factor of law and order. The wholesale extermination of the heroes of the civil war and of all the
representatives of the younger generation connected with them
was the most convincing proof that the Kremlin does not pre-
tend to use cunning, but liquidates the revolutionary past
seriously and definitely.

From the time they prepared themselves to enter a military
alliance with the state spawned by the October Revolution,
England and France answered in reality for the Kremlin's
fidelity before Rumania, Poland, Latvia, Estonia, Finland,
before all the capitalist world. And they are right. There is not
the slightest danger that Moscow, as it was predicted many
times before, will attempt to use its participation in world
politics to provoke war: Moscow fears war more than anything
and more than anybody. Neither is there reason to fear that
Moscow will take advantage of its rapprochement with its
Western neighbors to overthrow their social regimes. The revolution in Poland and Rumania would convert Hitler in reality
into a crusader of capitalist Europe in the East. This danger
hangs as heavy as a nightmare on the conscience of the Krem-

lin. If the very fact of the entrance of the Red troops into
Poland, independently of any plans, gives, in spite of everything, an impulsion to the revolutionary movement — and the
internal conditions in Poland, as well as in Rumania, are favorable enough for that — the Red Army, we can foretell with assurance, would play the role of subduer. The Kremlin would
take care in advance to have the most reliable troops in Poland
and Rumania. If they were, nevertheless, seized by the revolutionary movement, this would menace the Kremlin with the
same dangers as the Belvedere. One must be deprived of all
historical imagination in order to admit for a single instant
that in case of a revolutionary victory in Poland or in Germany, the Soviet masses will support patiently the terrible oppression of the Soviet bureaucracy. The Kremlin does not want
war or revolution; it does want order, tranquility, the status
quo, and at any cost. It is time to get accustomed to the idea
that the Kremlin has become a conservative factor in world
politics!

NOTES AND ACKNOWLEDGMENTS

1. "Phrases and Reality." **Socialist Appeal,** October 1, 1938, where it appeared under the title "New War Flows from Versailles Banditry." **Socialist Appeal** was then the newspaper of the Socialist Workers Party. This article was written eleven days before British Prime Minister Chamberlain and French Premier Daladier signed the Munich Pact with Hitler and Mussolini on September 30, 1938. The pact, which Chamberlain promised would bring "peace in our time," permitted Germany to annex the Sudetenland, a Bohemian border region of Czechoslovakia, under the pretext of defending the rights of its predominantly German population. It also represented the acquiescence of the Western powers in Hitler's plans to invade and conquer Czechoslovakia, which he did in March 1939. In Spain the International Brigades were fighting their final campaign before withdrawing from Spain in November under the onslaught of Franco's fascist forces, which also completed their victory in March. In the midst of the threatening war crisis, thirty delegates from eleven countries had met in Paris on September 3 to found the Fourth International.

2. **Neville Chamberlain** (1869-1940) was Conservative prime minister of Britain from 1937 until May 1940, when he resigned after failing to receive a vote of confidence in Parliament for his prosecution of the war.

3. **Leon Jouhaux** (1870-1954) was general secretary of the CGT (General Confederation of Labor), the chief union federation in France. He was a reformist, social patriot, and class collaborationist. **John L. Lewis** (1880-1969) was president of the United Mine Workers of America from 1920 until his death. He headed the minority in the AFL executive council in the mid-thirties which favored industrial unionism, and he was the principal founder of the CIO in 1935 and its main leader until 1940, when he resigned. Although he spoke sharply against the drive toward war, he backed President Roosevelt's "neutrality" measures, which were a smokescreen for the war drive.

4. **Adolph Hitler** (1889-1945) was appointed chancellor of Germany in January 1933 and, at the head of the National Socialist (Nazi) Party, led Germany into World War II.

5. **The Versailles treaty** was imposed by the victors in World War I. It was based on heavy reparations payments by the defeated countries to the victors.

6. **The Entente,** or alliance, between France, Russia, Britain, and

371

Serbia went to war against Austria-Hungary and Germany in August 1914, thus beginning World War I. The new Soviet government withdrew from the Entente after the October Revolution. **The Second International** was organized in 1889 as a loose association of national Social Democratic and labor parties, uniting both revolutionary and reformist elements; its strongest and most authoritative section was the German Social Democracy. Its progressive role had ended by 1914, when its major sections violated the most elementary socialist principles and supported their own imperialist governments in World War I. It fell apart during the war, but was revived as a completely reformist organization in 1923.

7. After the breakup of Austria-Hungary at the end of World War I, the Versailles treaty and the treaty of Saint-Germain (1919) left **Austria** truncated and forbade any political or economic union with Germany. Austria was deprived of raw materials, food, and markets, and in the immediate postwar period suffered widespread starvation and epidemics of influenza, followed by currency inflation, chronic unemployment, and financial scandals. The growth of fascism was rapid after 1932, and in March 1938 Hitler's troops occupied the country. It was fully incorporated into Germany in 1940. It regained its independent status after World War II. **The Saar** is an industrial and coal-mining region between Germany and France. The Versailles treaty made it an autonomous territory administered by France, and subjected its coal fields to French exploitation. In a 1935 plebiscite sponsored by the League of Nations, 90 percent of the votes were for reunion with Germany. The Saar was restored to German control, but after World War II it was again placed under French military occupation; today it has an autonomous government under French jurisdiction.

8. **The Third (or Communist) International — the Comintern —** was organized under Lenin's leadership as the revolutionary successor to the Second International. Trotsky regarded the theses of the Comintern's first four congresses, held between 1919 and 1922, as the programmatic cornerstones of the Left Opposition and the Fourth International. Stalin dissolved the Comintern in 1943 as a gesture of goodwill to his imperialist allies.

9. **Bonapartism** was a central concept in Trotsky's writings during the 1930s. He used the term to describe a dictatorship, or a regime with certain features of a dictatorship, during periods when class rule is not secure; it is based on the military, the police, and the state bureaucracy, rather than on parliamentary parties or a mass movement. Trotsky saw two types — bourgeois and Soviet. His most extensive writings on bourgeois Bonapartism are found in **The Struggle Against Fascism in Germany** (Pathfinder Press, 1970). His views on Soviet Bonapartism reached their final form in his essay, "The Workers' State, Thermidor and Bonapartism," reprinted in **Writings 34-35**. **Joseph Stalin** (1879-1953) became a Social Democrat in 1898, joined the Bolshevik faction in 1904, was coopted to

its Central Committee in 1912, and was elected to it for the first time in 1917. After the February revolution and before Lenin returned and reoriented the Bolsheviks toward winning power, he favored a conciliatory attitude to the Provisional Government. He was commissar of nationalities in the first Soviet government, and became general secretary of the Communist Party in 1922. Lenin called in 1923 for his removal from the post of general secretary because he was using it to bureaucratize the party and state apparatuses. After Lenin's death in 1924, Stalin gradually eliminated his major opponents, starting with Trotsky, until he became virtual dictator of the party and the Soviet Union in the 1930s. The chief concepts associated with his name are "socialism in one country," "social fascism," and "peaceful coexistence."

10. **Benito Mussolini** (1883-1945), the founder of Italian fascism, had been a member of the antiwar wing of the Socialist Party in 1914. He organized the fascist movement in 1919, became dictator in 1922, and set the pattern of repression on which the German Nazis modeled their regime. He was overthrown in 1943; then he ruled over only a part of Italy until his execution by partisans.

11. **Maxim Litvinov** (1876-1951), an Old Bolshevik, was people's commissar for foreign affairs, 1930-39; ambassador to the United States, 1941-43; and deputy commissar for foreign affairs, 1943-46. Stalin used him to personify "collective security" when he sought alliances with democratic imperialists and shelved him during the period of the Stalin-Hitler pact and the cold war.

12. The Stalinists in **Spain** supported the People's Front in order to prevent a socialist transformation of Spain; at that time Stalin was anxious to prove his loyalty to the bourgeois democracies so that they would include him in their diplomatic and military pacts. The People's Front permitted the bourgeoisie to stay in power during the crisis of the revolution and the Civil War (1936-39) and assured victory to Franco's fascist troops.

13. On Stalin's orders, several outstanding Red Army generals were charged with treason in May 1937 and were executed. Their executions opened a purge that affected 25,000 officers and decapitated the Red Army on the eve of the war. After Stalin's death, many of the generals were exonerated. For a full description of the Stalinist policies of the Soviet government, see Trotsky's **Revolution Betrayed** (Pathfinder Press, 1972).

14. **GPU** was one of the abbreviated names for the Soviet political police; other names were Cheka, NKVD, MVD, KGB, etc., but GPU is often used in their place.

15. **Francisco Franco** (1892-   ) organized the Spanish army based in Morocco and with military aid from Nazi Germany and Italy overthrew the Spanish Republican government. His victory was to become complete in March 1939.

16. **Vicente Lombardo Toledano** (1893-1968), a Stalinist, was also head of the Mexican Confederation of Workers, the major trade

union in Mexico. He was an active participant in the slander campaign carried out by the Mexican Stalinists against Trotsky, which was designed to prepare public opinion for his assassination.

17. The Left Opposition (Bolshevik-Leninists or "Trotskyists") was formed in 1923 as a faction of the Russian Communist Party, and the International Left Opposition was formed in 1930 as a faction of the Comintern, with the aim of returning it to revolutionary principles. After the German Communist Party allowed Hitler to take power without lifting a finger, and the Comintern as a whole failed even to discuss the defeat, Trotsky decided that the Comintern was dead as a revolutionary movement, and that a new international had to be formed. The founding conference of the **Fourth International** was held in Paris on September 3, 1938 (see **Documents of the Fourth International: The Formative Years** [**1933-40**]).

18. "The Totalitarian 'Right of Asylum.'" **Biulleten Oppozitsii** (Bulletin of the Opposition), no. 70, October 1938. Unsigned. Translated by John Fairlie for the first edition of **Writings 37-38**. **Biulleten Oppozitsii** was the Russian-language organ of the Soviet section of the Fourth International; it was being published at this time in Paris, and was edited by Trotsky from the start of his last exile until his death.

19. **Futuro** was the official magazine of the Mexican Confederation of Labor, and was under the control of the Stalinists.

20. **The CTM** is the Mexican Confederation of Workers, the major trade union federation in Mexico. It was organized in 1936 with government support. Throughout the thirties it was controlled by the Stalinists.

21. "The Assassination of Rudolf Klement." **Lutte Ouvriere**, September 30, 1938. Translated for this volume from the French by Russell Block. **Lutte Ouvriere** was the newspaper of the POI (Internationalist Workers Party, the French section of the Fourth International). **Rudolf Klement** had been Trotsky's secretary in Turkey and France, and was secretary of the committee preparing the founding conference of the Fourth International in 1938. He was kidnaped and murdered by the GPU in Paris shortly before the conference was held (see **Writings 37-38**, 2nd ed.).

22. **Jeanne Martin des Pallieres** was the second wife of Trotsky's elder son, Leon Sedov. She belonged to a group that had split from the French section of the Fourth International, the PCI (Internationalist Communist Party), called the **"La Commune"** group after the name of its newspaper.

23. **Pierre Naville** (1904-   ) was a founder of the French Communist League and of **La Verite**. He opposed the entry of the Trotskyists into the French Socialist Party in 1934, although he and his group later joined. In 1938 he also opposed entry into the PSOP (Workers and Peasants Socialist Party). He is the author of a

memoir, **Trotsky vivant** (1962). **Jean Rous** (1908-   ) was a leader
of the POI and had been the delegate of the International Secretariat
in Spain in 1936. Both Naville and Rous left the Fourth International during the war and joined a series of centrist groups.

24. **Leon Sedov** (1906-1938), Trotsky's elder son, joined the Left
Opposition and accompanied his parents in their last exile. He was
Trotsky's closest collaborator and co-editor of the Russian **Biulleten
Oppozitsii**. He lived in Germany from 1931 to 1933, and then in
Paris, until his death at the hands of the GPU. **Writings 37-38** (2nd
ed.) includes an evaluation of his life and death.

25. "Fight Imperialism to Fight Fascism." **Socialist Appeal,** October
8, 1938, where it carried the subhead "A Statement to a Cuban
Paper." The paper was **El Pais** (The Nation).

26. **Edouard Daladier** (1884-1970), a Radical Socialist, was
French premier from 1933 until 1934, when he was ousted during
an attempted fascist coup d'etat. He was minister of war under Leon
Blum. Later he became premier again, and signed the Munich Pact
with Hitler. **Franklin D. Roosevelt** (1882-1945) was Democratic president of the U. S. from 1933 until his death.

27. Between 1934 and 1940, the Mexican government redistributed
about 25 million acres of land to poor or landless peasants; this
was more than double the amount previously expropriated from
wealthy Mexican landowners. However, an estimated 1880 million
acres remained concentrated in the hands of about 1000 native and
imperialist landowners. **General Saturnino Cedillo** was a right-wing
army officer who led an unsuccessful uprising against the Mexican
government in May 1938 and was killed the following January by
government troops.

28. **Manuel Azana y Diaz** (1880-1940) was prime minister of the
Spanish Republican government in June 1931 and again in 1936.
He was president of the Republic from May 1936 until his resigna-
tion in Paris in 1939.

29. "After the Collapse of Czechoslovakia, Stalin Will Seek Accord
with Hitler." This article was written as a postscript to "Phrases and
Reality," and was dated September 22, 1938. But when it appeared in
Socialist Appeal, October 8, 1938 (under the title "After Munich,
Stalin Will Seek Accord with Hitler"), it was not identified as a postscript and was undated. The first edition of **Writings 38-39** also
omitted the postscript designation and mistakenly dated the article
October 7, 1938. Eleven months after Trotsky wrote this article, the
pact between Stalin and Hitler was made public.

30. "Anti-Imperialist Struggle Is Key to Liberation." **Socialist Appeal,** November 5, 1938. **Mateo Fossa** (1904-1973) was a revolutionary trade union leader who played a major role in the development of Argentine Trotskyism. In 1938 he was delegated by the Com-

mittee for Trade Union Freedom to attend the September congress of Latin American trade unions in Mexico, but the Stalinists excluded him as a Trotskyist.

31. **The Amsterdam International** was the popular name of the Social Democratic-dominated International Federation of Trade Unions, with headquarters in Amsterdam. **The People's Front** (or Popular Front) was a governmental coalition of the Communist and Socialist parties with bourgeois parties around a program of liberal capitalism. The Comintern adopted its People's Front policy at its Seventh Congress in 1935.

32. In March 1938, the Mexican government nationalized foreign-owned oil properties. In retaliation, an embargo on Mexican oil was imposed by the British and U. S. governments and by the oil companies that owned the tankers for shipping oil abroad. At the same time, they initiated a slander campaign designed to create a public sentiment in the U. S. that would facilitate U. S. government intervention in Mexico (see **Writings 37-38**, 2nd ed.). In 1941 the Mexican and U. S. governments reached an agreement for indemnification of U. S. oil companies; in 1947 a similar agreement was concluded with the British companies.

33. **APRA** (American Popular Revolutionary Alliance) was founded in 1924 by the Peruvian Haya de la Torre (see note 109). At its peak APRA movements existed in Cuba, Mexico, Peru, Chile, Costa Rica, Haiti, and Argentina. Aprismo was the first movement to urge the economic and political unification of Latin America against imperialist domination. A populist movement, its five-point program was: action against Yankee imperialism; the unity of Latin America; industrialization and land reform; the internationalization of the Panama Canal; and world solidarity of all peoples and oppressed classes. APRA later degenerated into a liberal, anti-Communist, pro-capitalist reform party.

34. **The "World Congress Against War and Fascism"** took place in Mexico on September 12, 1938. Its Stalinist sponsors attempted to recruit the international labor movement to the defense of the "democratic" imperialists against the fascist countries in the coming war and the delegates were handpicked accordingly. However, Mexican, Puerto Rican, and Peruvian delegates argued that the Allied governments shared responsiblity for the coming war.

35. **Getulio Vargas** (1883-1954) held power in Brazil from 1930 to 1945, and quickly declared strikes illegal, closed down labor publications, and arrested union leaders. His 1937 constitution denied workers as a class all rights. He took power again in 1950.

36. "Problems of the American Party." From the personal archives of James P. Cannon, then a member of the International Executive Committee of the Fourth International and the national secretary of the Socialist Workers Party, the U. S. section of the Fourth Inter-

national. The "meeting in Europe" he had just returned from was the founding conference of the Fourth International, held in Paris on September 3. This letter and several others in this volume were written in English.

37. **The referendum on the labor party.** From 1931 to 1938, the Communist League of America and its successors had opposed calling for a labor party, while recognizing that revolutionaries should work in any labor party that might be formed. Trotsky agreed with this position in a 1932 article, "The Labor Party Question in the United States," reprinted in **Writings 32**, and it had been reaffirmed at the founding conference of the SWP in January 1938. Less than three months later, in a discussion in Mexico, Trotsky persuaded the SWP's leaders that they should now change their policy and advocate a labor party (see **The Transitional Program for Socialist Revolution** [Pathfinder Press, 1973]). A discussion of the new proposal was opened in the SWP's internal bulletins and branch meetings, and to a lesser extent in the columns of the **New International**. But instead of following the usual procedure of having this important political issue resolved by a national convention, the SWP leaders decided to settle it through a referendum vote of the membership. Trotsky thought the referendum arrangement was "not a very happy invention" because it took so long and wasted time that he felt should have been used working to build labor party sentiment among the workers. The **Socialist Appeal** of October 1, 1938, reported that at the end of a three-month discussion a decisive majority of the SWP membership had adopted a resolution, which was printed in that issue, favoring the new proposal.

38. The full text of the article "Discussion with a CIO Organizer," September 29, 1938, is in **Leon Trotsky on the Trade Unions** (Pathfinder Press, 1972).

39. **The National Committee** is the leading committee of the Socialist Workers Party, elected by its national convention.

40. For a fuller discussion of Trotsky's views on the labor party slogan see **The Transitional Program for Socialist Revolution**.

41. **Socialist Appeal** was the weekly newspaper of the SWP; it was later renamed **The Militant.**

42. **The New International** was the magazine of the SWP until April 1940, when it was taken over by Max Shachtman and his followers, who had split from the SWP to form their own organization. The SWP then began publishing **Fourth International**, whose name was later changed to **International Socialist Review**.

43. **The patriotic, imperialist turn of the CP.** In the wake of the Munich Pact, the Soviet government stepped up its efforts to conclude a military alliance with the "democracies." For this purpose, Communist parties around the world adopted an uncritical stance towards the Allied governments. They used their influence within the working-class movement to support the imperialists' war aims and to assure them "class peace" in exchange for such a military pact. In the

U. S. Earl Browder, the CP's secretary, volunteered the information that in the event of war, American Communists would defend the U. S.

44. The House Un-American Activities Committee (HUAC) was headed at this time by Martin **Dies** (1901-1972), a Texas Democrat. The committee was hated by radicals and liberals because it served as a forum to "expose" radical and liberal groups and demand that they be outlawed. After World War II, HUAC began to subpoena witnesses and violate their First and Fifth Amendment rights; in the thirties, however, it relied primarily on voluntary testimony. In August 1938 it opened an "investigation" of the CP.

45. **Mossaiye J. Olgin** (1874-1939) in 1921 joined what was to become the American Communist Party. He was the first editor of the party's Jewish newspaper **Freiheit** (Freedom). He wrote the official anti-Trotskyist manual, **Trotskyism: Counter-Revolution in Disguise** (1935).

46. "What Is the Meaning of the Struggle Against 'Trotskyism'?" Published by the Mexican section of the Fourth International in 1938 and translated for this volume from the Spanish by Will Reissner.

47. **Hernan Laborde** was the chief leader of the Mexican CP until early 1940, when he was purged in a reorganization of the party that was related to preparations for the Trotsky assassination.

48. From 1936 to 1938 Stalin conducted three big **Moscow confession show trials,** in which most of the leaders of the Russian Revolution were accused of plotting to restore capitalism. The main defendants in the proceedings, in absentia, were Trotsky and his son Leon Sedov. Through these trials, Stalin consolidated his personal rule over the Soviet Union.

49. **The Commission of Inquiry into the Charges Made Against Leon Trotsky in the Moscow Trials** was called the Dewey Commission after its chairman, John Dewey (1859-1952), the noted American philosopher and educator. The Commission conducted hearings in Mexico, April 10-17, 1937. The summary of its findings was published in **Not Guilty** (Monad Press, 1972). The transcript of the Commission's proceedings was published in **The Case of Leon Trotsky** (Merit Publishers, 1968).

50. **Andrei Vyshinsky** (1883-1954) joined the Social Democracy in 1902 but remained a Menshevik until 1920. He received international notoriety as the prosecuting attorney in the Moscow trials and was Soviet foreign minister, 1949-53.

51. **Joseph Goebbels** (1897-1945) was the Nazi minister for propaganda and national enlightenment (from 1933) and a member of Hitler's cabinet council (from 1938). He committed suicide upon Germany's defeat.

52. **General Lazaro Cardenas** (1895-1970) was president of Mexico from 1934 to 1940. His administration was marked by plans for the redistribution of the land, industrial and transportation development, renewal of struggle with the Roman Catholic church, and, in 1938,

expropriations of foreign-owned oil properties. His was the only government in the world that would grant Trotsky asylum in the last years of his life.

53. **El Popular** was the newspaper of the CTM, edited by Lombardo Toledano. **Dr. Atl** was Gerardo Murillo, painter and teacher of Diego Rivera. Formerly a revolutionary, by the late thirties he had become a fascist sympathizer.

54. **Rudolf Hess** (1894-   ) joined the German Nazis in 1921. He was head of the political section of the Nazi party from 1932, and was a member of Hitler's cabinet council from 1934. In 1941, he flew to Scotland where he was held as a prisoner of war; in 1946 he was sentenced to life imprisonment by the Nuremburg war crimes tribunal.

55. **Erwin Wolf**, a Czech, served as Trotsky's secretary in Norway. He was kidnaped and killed by the GPU in Spain in 1937 (see **Writings 36-37**). **Ignace Reiss** was the pseudonym of Ignace Poretsky, a GPU agent who broke with Stalin in the summer of 1937 and joined the Fourth Internationalists. He was murdered by GPU agents near Lausanne, Switzerland, on September 4, 1937 (see **Writings 36-37**). He is the subject of a memoir by his widow, Elizabeth K. Poretsky, entitled **Our Own People** (1970).

56. "A Fresh Lesson." **New International**, December 1938.

57. **The February Revolution** in Russia in 1917 overthrew the czar and established the bourgeois Provisional Government, which held power until the October Revolution brought the soviets, led by the Bolsheviks, to power. **Nicholas II** (1868-1918) was the last of the Russian czars. He took the throne in 1894 and abdicated in March 1917. He was held prisoner by the Bolsheviks and later executed, along with his family. (See page 106 for Trotsky's discussion of his execution.)

58. **Pavel Miliukov** (1859-1943), a leader of the liberal Constitutional Democrats (Cadets), was minister of foreign affairs in the Russian Provisional Government, March-May 1917, and an outstanding enemy of the Bolshevik Revolution. **Alexander F. Kerensky** (1882-1970) was the leader of one wing of the Russian Social Revolutionary Party. He became vice-chairman of the Petrograd Soviet, then bolted from its discipline to become minister of justice in the Provisional Government in March 1917. In May he took the post of minister of war and navy, which he continued to hold when he became premier; later he appointed himself commander-in-chief as well. He fled Petrograd when the Bolsheviks came to power. In spite of its pacifist verbiage and declarations of nonintervention, the Provisional Government pursued an imperialist policy of seizing and annexing foreign territory, and attempted to abide by the terms of the czar's secret treaties with the Allied powers. These treaties were later disowned, and then published, by the Bolsheviks.

59. **Erich F. Ludendorff** (1865-1937) was one of the top German generals in World War I.

60. **Woodrow Wilson** (1856-1924) was Democratic president of the United States from 1913 to 1921. Although he was the inspirer of the League of Nations, he was unable to get U. S. participation approved by the Senate. **The League of Nations**, which Lenin referred to as the "thieves' kitchen," was created by the Versailles Peace Conference in 1919, ostensibly as a form of world government that would prevent future wars through cooperation. However, its complete powerlessness became clear when its resolutions were unable to stop the Japanese invasion of China, the Italian invasion of Ethiopia, and other links in the chain of events that led to World War II.

61. **Karl Kautsky** (1854-1938) was regarded as the outstanding Marxist theoretician until World War I, when he abandoned internationalism and opposed the October Revolution. Trotsky's obituary on Kautsky begins on page 98.

62. Wilson outlined his **"fourteen points"** for a peace settlement in a message to Congress in January 1918. Idealistic in tone, the fourteen points were chiefly designed to demagogically identify the Allies with the most popular demands of the new Soviet government — for an end to secret treaties and colonial annexations — and thus to rally dwindling popular support for the Allied governments' prosecution of the war. The major tenets of the fourteen points cut across the imperialists' purpose for waging the war, and so were ignored by them at the Versailles Conference, except for the fourteenth, which provided the framework for the League of Nations. **Herbert Hoover** (1874-1964) was Republican president of the U. S. from 1929 to 1933. After World War I, he was the head of the American Relief Association (**ARA**), which provided medicine and supplies to famine- and disease-ridden areas of Europe. Its main role was to serve the counterrevolutionary forces in the Russian civil war. **The New Deal** was the program of reforms adopted by President Roosevelt, in an attempt to alleviate the worst conditions of the Depression and buy off the militancy of American workers. The first **Neutrality Act** was passed by the U. S. Congress in August 1935, applying a mandatory arms embargo to both sides in the event of a European war. In November 1939 the arms embargo was lifted and replaced with "cash and carry" provisions allowing the Allies to buy war goods. By December 1940 the British could no longer pay for war supplies, and Lend-Lease went into effect, committing the economic resources of the U. S. to the defeat of Germany.

63. **Weimar** was the small town where the government of the German Republic was organized in 1919. The Weimar Republic lasted until Hitler assumed full power in 1933.

64. **The Napoleonic wars** raged from 1803 to 1815, but the subjection of Prussia was accomplished in 1806, when Napoleon defeated the Prussian army at Jena and marched into Berlin. **The Versailles peace of 1871** was signed at the end of the Franco-Prussian War. Its terms included French payment of an indemnity and cession of Alsace and part of Lorraine to Germany.

65. **Otto von Bismarck** (1815-1898) was head of the Prussian government from 1862, and the first chancellor of the German empire. His career was a long campaign to unify Germany under Prussia and the Hohenzollerns.

66. As the German defeat in World War I became clear, a German naval mutiny turned into a revolutionary movement. On November 8, 1918, the Bavarian Socialist Republic was proclaimed in Munich. In Berlin, workers and soldiers organized soviets, and a delegation of Social Democrats demanded that the chancellor surrender the government to the workers. The German empire fell the next day. Hindenburg and Kaiser Wilhelm II fled to Holland, and a provisional government was established in Berlin consisting of three Social Democrats and three members of the Independent Social Democratic Party. It was this government that murdered leading revolutionists and prevented the revolution from going beyond the establishment of a liberal bourgeois democracy.

67. **Hohenzollern** was the name of the ruling family of Prussia and Germany until 1918.

68. **The British Labour Party** was founded in 1906 and is affiliated to the Second International. It developed out of the Labour Representation Committee, which had been constituted in 1899 to secure the election of labour members to Parliament.

69. **Clement Attlee** (1883-1967) was the leader of the British Labour Party from 1935, and was in Winston Churchill's cabinet from 1940 to 1945. In 1945 the Labour Party won the elections, and Attlee became prime minister. **Sir Walter Citrine** (1887-   ) was the general secretary of the British Trades Union Congress from 1926 to 1946. For his services to British capitalism he was knighted in 1935, and was made a baronet in 1946.

70. **Edouard Benes** (1884-1948) became president of Czechoslovakia in 1935 and resigned in October 1938 when the Germans occupied the Sudetenland. He was succeeded by **General Jan Syrovy**, who formed a new cabinet and carried through the transition from a unified Czechoslovakia to a federated state, ceding the Sudetenland to Germany and other areas to Poland and Hungary. Benes was reelected president in 1946.

71. **Vladimir Ilyich Lenin** (1870-1924) restored Marxism as the theory and practice of revolution in the imperialist epoch after it had been debased by the opportunists, revisionists, and fatalists of the Second International. He initiated the Bolshevik tendency, which was the first to build the kind of party needed to lead a working class revolution. He led the first victorious workers' revolution in 1917, and served as the first head of state of the Soviet government. He founded the Communist International and helped to elaborate its principles, strategy, and tactics. He prepared a fight against the bureaucratization of the Russian Communist Party and the Soviet state, but died before he could carry it out.

72. **Paul von Hindenburg** (1847-1934) was president of Germany

from 1925 until his death. Although he ran as an opponent of the
Nazis when he defeated Hitler at the polls in 1932, he appointed
Hitler chancellor in 1933.

73. **"Socialism in one country"** was Stalin's theory, introduced into
the communist movement for the first time in 1924, that a socialist
society could be achieved inside the borders of a single country. Later,
when it was incorporated into the program and tactics of the Comintern, it became the ideological cover for the abandonment of revolutionary internationalism and was used to justify the conversion of
the Communist parties throughout the world into docile pawns of
the Kremlin's foreign policy. A comprehensive critique by Trotsky
is in his 1928 book **The Third International After Lenin** (Pathfinder
Press, 1970).

74. **Earl Browder** (1891-1973) became general secretary of the
Communist Party of the United States by Stalin's directive in 1930
and was similarly deposed in 1945 and expelled from the party in
1946. He was the party's presidential candidate in 1936 and 1940.

75. The International Bureau of Revolutionary Socialist Parties
(the **"London Bureau"**) was established in 1935 but its forerunner,
the International Labor Community (IAG), dated back to 1932.
It was a loose association of centrist parties not affiliated to either
the Second or the Third International but opposed to the formation
of a Fourth International. Among its members were the SAP (Socialist Workers Party) of Germany, the Independent Labour Party
of Great Britain, the Spanish POUM (Workers Party of Marxist Unification), and the French PSOP (Workers and Peasants Socialist
Party). The unification Trotsky refers to took place at a conference
in Paris in February 1938. **Fenner Brockway** (1890-   ) was an
opponent of the Fourth International and secretary of the London
Bureau. He was also a leader of the British ILP. **Jacob Walcher**
(1887-   ) was a founder of the German CP but was expelled
in 1929 as a supporter of the Brandlerite Communist Right Opposition (KPO). He left the KPO in 1932 and joined the SAP. After World
War II he rejoined the CP, holding various governmental posts in
East Germany. **Heinrich Brandler** (1881-1967) was a founder of
the German CP and its principal leader when it failed to take advantage of the revolutionary crisis of 1923. He was made a scapegoat by the Kremlin and removed from the party leadership in 1924.
He formed the KPO, which aligned itself with Bukharin's Right Opposition in the USSR, and was expelled from the CP in 1929. The
KPO continued as an independent organization until World War II.
Henricus Sneevliet (1883-1942) was a founder of the CPs of Holland
and Indonesia. He had been secretary of the Colonial Commission
of the Comintern at its Second Congress, and was for a time the
Comintern's representative in China. After leaving the CP in 1927,
he formed the Revolutionary Socialist Party, which fused with other
revolutionary elements and in 1935 became the Revolutionary So-

cialist Workers Party. From 1933 his group adhered to the international Trotskyist movement although it also maintained its membership in the London Bureau. Because of differences on the POUM and on trade union policy, the RSAP broke with the Trotskyist movement in 1938, but remained in the London Bureau. In 1942 Sneevliet was arrested by the Nazis and shot. **Marceau Pivert** (1895-1958) had been a leader of a left-wing tendency in the French Socialist Party in 1935. He served as an aide of Leon Blum in the 1936 People's Front government, but when his group was ordered dissolved in 1937 he left the Socialist Party and in 1938 founded the PSOP, which was affiliated with the London Bureau. After World War II he returned to the Socialist Party.

76. **The POUM** (Workers Party of Marxist Unification) was founded in Spain in 1935, when the Spanish Left Opposition broke with Trotsky and merged with the centrist Workers and Peasants Bloc. Trotsky severed all relations with them when they joined the Spanish People's Front government.

77. **Jean Jaures** (1859-1914), a prominent French socialist and orator, was assassinated on July 31, 1914. **Karl Liebknecht** (1871-1919) was a left-wing Social Democrat who led the opposition to World War I within the German party. He formed the Spartacus League with **Rosa Luxemburg** (1871-1919), an outstanding leader of the Marxist movement and a prominent opponent of revisionism and opportunism before World War I. They were both jailed for antiwar activity at the outbreak of the war, but were freed by the November 1918 uprising and organized the German Communist Party. In January 1919 they were assassinated by officers of the Social Democratic government.

78. "To Our Friends and Readers." **Clave,** November 1938. Unsigned. Translated for this volume from the Spanish by Russell Block. **Clave** was the theoretical review of the Spanish-speaking sections of the Fourth International. When Cardenas granted Trotsky a visa to enter Mexico, he asked Trotsky to pledge not to interfere in Mexico's domestic affairs. Trotsky agreed, and according to Isaac Deutscher (**Prophet Outcast,** p. 358), he "strictly observ[ed] his pledge, [and] never ventured to state any opinion on Mexican politics even in private. . . ." However, Trotsky did make sure that his views on Mexican affairs found expression, by writing editorially or with pen names in the press of his cothinkers. This explains the large number of articles in this volume that were originally unsigned or signed with pen names, and could not be positively identified as Trotsky's until their original manuscripts were examined in the Trotsky Archives at the Harvard College Library.

79. **Juan Negrin Lopez** (1889-1956) became the final premier of the Spanish Republic in May 1937, resigning in exile in France after the Civil War.

80. "The Problem of a New International." **Clave,** November 1938. Unsigned. Translated for this volume from the Spanish by Russell Block.

81. **Diego Rivera** (1886-1957) was the noted Mexican painter whose murals were removed from Rockefeller Center in New York because of their Communist content. A founder of the Mexican CP and a member of its Central Committee since 1922, he left the CP in 1927 over the expulsion of the Left Opposition. He was Trotsky's host in Mexico at first, but Trotsky was forced to break from him publicly in 1939 over the issues of dual unionism, the class nature of the Soviet state, and the presidential campaign of 1940, in which Rivera supported the candidacy of a right-wing general, Juan Andreu Almazan.

82. "Tasks of the Trade Union Movement in Latin America." Unsigned. By permission of the Harvard College Library. Translated for this volume from the Russian by Marilyn Vogt. This article was apparently intended for circulation as a petition and for publication, but it is not known who signed it or whether it was published.

83. **The Pan-American Trade Union Congress** was held in Mexico September 6-8, 1938, and was attended by delegates from most Latin American countries, as well as by John L. Lewis from the U.S., Leon Jouhaux from France, and Gonzales Pena, the Spanish minister of justice. It resulted in the formation of the **Confederation of Latin American Workers** (CTAL), with headquarters in Mexico and Lombardo Toledano as president.

84. **The Casa del Pueblo** was a bakers' union headquarters that served as a revolutionary trade union center in Mexico City. The Regional Confederation of Mexican Workers **(CROM)** was formed in 1918 as a moderate and opportunist organization that affiliated with the Amsterdam International. Unlike most other Mexican union federations, it never fell under Stalinist influence. By 1938 it had declined in size and importance. The General Confederation of Labor **(CGT)** was formed in 1921 and became the most powerful labor federation in Mexico until it was displaced by the CTM in the mid-thirties. It defined itself as an anarchist group rather than a political organization; it belonged simultaneously to the AIT (the Anarchist International) and the PRM (Mexican Revolutionary Party, Mexico's ruling party).

85. "The Founding of the Fourth International." **Socialist Appeal,** November 5, 1938. Trotsky presented this speech evaluating the founding conference of the Fourth International in a recording made on October 18, 1938; it was played at a New York mass meeting ten days later in celebration of the founding of the Fourth International and the tenth anniversary of the American Trotskyist movement.

86. **Max Shachtman** (1903-1972) and **Martin Abern** (1898-1949)

were leaders in the American CP and cofounders of the American Trotskyist movement. In 1940 they split from the Socialist Workers Party because of differences over the defense of the Soviet Union, and formed the Workers Party. In 1958 Shachtman joined the Socialist Party.

87. **The Sixth Congress of the Comintern** was held in 1928, after a lapse of four years since its Fifth Congress. Trotsky was in exile in Alma Ata at that time and could not attend the congress. However, his "Draft Program of the Communist International — A Critique of Fundamentals" (in **The Third International After Lenin**) was circulated in censored form and fell into the hands of foreign delegates, including James P. Cannon from the American Communist Party; this was the first programmatic document of the Left Opposition many foreign Communists would see and most of the first cadres of the International Left Opposition were won at that time.

88. "To the Editors of the **Biulleten Oppozitsii, Lutte Ouvriere,** and **Quatrieme Internationale.**" Biulleten Oppozitsii, no. 72, December 1938. Translated by John Fairlie for the first edition of **Writings 37-38.** Lutte Ouvriere was the newspaper of the POI (Internationalist Workers Party, the French section of the Fourth International). **Quatrieme Internationale** was then the theoretical review of the POI.

89. **La Commune** was the newspaper of the PCI (Internationalist Communist Party). Its leader, Raymond Molinier, had been denied readmission to the Fourth International by its founding conference in September 1938. During the Second World War the Molinier group was accepted back into the French section.

90. **La Verite** was then the theoretical review of the PCI.

91. "A False View." **Biulleten Oppozitsii,** no. 72, December 1938. Signed "The Editor." Translated by John Fairlie for the first edition of **Writings 37-38.**

92. "Two Agents of 'Democratic' Imperialism." By permission of the Harvard College Library. Translated for this volume from the Russian by Marilyn Vogt. This article also appeared in **Hoy** (Today, a Mexico City magazine), November 4, 1938, under the title "Jouhaux and Toledano."

93. **Karl Marx** (1818-1883) was, along with Engels, the founder of scientific socialism and the leader of the First International, 1864-76.

94. "American Prospects." From the personal archives of James P. Cannon.

95. The article is "A Fresh Lesson"; the recording is "On the Founding of the Fourth International."

96. At this time, Trotsky was writing his biography of Stalin; he did not live to complete it, but it was published posthumously

in a heavily edited form by Harper and Brothers despite the protests of his widow, Natalia Sedova.

97. Part of Trotsky's papers remained in Europe when he went to Mexico in 1937. They were now being reassembled, and were to be transferred to Harvard University shortly before his assassination in 1940. **John Glenner** was the pen name of Jan Frankel, who was one of Trotsky's secretaries. He was a Czech and was a witness at the Dewey Commission hearings.

98. "A Few Words on Breton." An excerpt from a letter to Gerard Rosenthal, Trotsky's French attorney. From **Trotsky vivant,** by Pierre Naville. Translated for this volume from the French by Russell Block. **Andre Breton** (1896-1966) was a French poet, essayist, and critic; he was a member of the Dadaists and a founder of the surrealist movement. He joined the CP in the twenties but broke with it in 1935, insisting on the need of artists to be free of political controls. In 1938 he and Diego Rivera formed the International Federation of Independent Revolutionary Art (FIARI) to resist totalitarian encroachments on literature and the arts.

99. Breton's literary magazine was **La Revolution Surrealiste. The "bloc"** is FIARI.

100. "Letter to Andre Breton." **Arsenal: Surrealist Subversion** (Chicago), Autumn 1970. Translated by Louise Hudson.

101. **The manifesto,** "Towards a Free Revolutionary Art," was published in the Autumn 1938 **Partisan Review** over the signatures of Diego Rivera and Andre Breton, although Trotsky was its chief author. Its full text is in **Leon Trotsky on Literature and Art** (Pathfinder Press, 1970).

102. "'Peace in Our Time'?" By permission of the Harvard College Library. Translated for this volume from the Russian by Marilyn Vogt. This article also appeared in **Hoy,** November 19, 1938, where it was entitled "A 'New Era of Peace'?"

103. **General Franz Xaver von Epp** (1868-1947) led the anti-Communist campaign in Munich in 1919. Between 1919 and 1923 he organized the Nazi Storm Troops and was one of its leaders. He was governor of Bavaria from 1933 to 1945.

104. **Prince Fumimaro Konoye** (1891-1945) was Japanese premier (1937-41) and foreign minister (1938).

105. Trotsky here is paraphrasing two lines from Pushkin's 1829 poem "The Hero," much quoted in Russian literary and political tradition. The intent of the lines was to express a hope, against all likelihood, that a tale of merciful behavior by a stern ruler might actually be true (a veiled reference to Czar Nicholas I, who had condemned Pushkin's friends, the Decembrists). For if it was not true, the merciful "hero" would only be a tyrant. The trusting poet

would like to believe the more favorable alternative. The reader is left to understand how unlikely that is. — Translator.

106. "Karl Kautsky." **The New International,** February 1939.

107. **Frederick Engels** (1820-1895), with Marx, was the founder of scientific socialism and the leader of the First International. In his last years, he was also the outstanding figure in the young Second International. Trotsky's essay "Engels's Letters to Kautsky," written October 15, 1935, is in his book **Political Portraits** (Pathfinder Press, 1975).

108. **The Independent Social Democratic Party of Germany** (USPD) was composed of centrists who had been in a minority in the Social Democratic Party. The majority of the USPD fused with the German CP in 1920. The minority continued as an independent organization adhering to the **Two-and-a-Half International,** or International Association of Socialist Parties, until 1922, when it returned to the Socialist Party. In 1923 the Two-and-a-Half International reunited with the Second International.

109. "Haya de la Torre and Democracy." **New International,** February 1939, where it was subtitled "A Program of Militant Struggle or of Adaptation to American Imperialism?" Signed "Diego Rivera." Translated by Bernard Ross. **Victor Raul Haya de la Torre** (1895-) founded APRA (see note 34) in 1924 and in 1931 ran for president of Peru; although he polled a majority of the votes, the election was fixed against him and he was imprisoned by his victorious opponent. During the Second World War Haya's support for the Allied imperialist governments was rewarded by legalization of APRA, but in 1948 a military coup again sent APRA underground and Haya into asylum in the Colombian Embassy in Lima, from where he eventually escaped Peru. Haya also won the 1962 elections in Peru, but another military coup prevented him from taking office.

110. "In Defense of Asylum." **Socialist Appeal,** November 19, 1938.

111. "Terrorism and the Murders of Rasputin and Nicholas II." By permission of the Harvard College Library. Translated for this volume from the Spanish by Naomi Allen. A more detailed account of the execution of the czar's family is in **Trotsky's Diary in Exile, 1935** (Harvard University Press, 1958), in the entries for April 9 and 10. **Grigory Rasputin** (1871-1916), a monk from a family of poor peasants, gained such ascendancy over the czar and czarina that he became a major influence in court politics. His ignorance and debauchery were legendary. He was assassinated by a group of desperate Russian noblemen in an effort to rid the royal family of his influence.

112. **White Guards,** or Whites, was the name given the Russian counterrevolutionary forces after the October Revolution.

113. **Ferdinand Maximilian Joseph** (1832-1867) became emperor of Mexico in 1864, after France had partially conquered the country. When the United States demanded that the French withdraw their army, Napoleon III complied; Maximilian was defeated by the Mexican forces under Juarez and was court-martialed and shot.

114. "The Twenty-First Anniversary." **Biulleten Oppozitsii,** no. 73, January 1939. Unsigned. Translated by John Fairlie for the first edition of **Writings 37-38.**

115. **The Provisional Government** established by the February revolution included the liberal bourgeois Constitutional Democratic Party (see note 120). Also in it were the **Mensheviks,** a moderate socialist party which believed that the working class must unite with the liberal bourgeoisie to overthrow czarism and establish a democratic republic. The Mensheviks were formed after a split in the Russian Social Democratic Labor Party in 1903, and remained in the Second International. **The Social Revolutionary Party** was founded in Russia in 1900, emerging in 1901-02 as the political expression of all the earlier populist currents; it had the largest share of influence among the peasantry prior to the revolution of 1917.

116. Newly arrived from exile in Switzerland, Lenin appeared on the final day of the **March Conference** of the Bolsheviks. He presented his **Theses** of April 4, 1917, "On the Tasks of the Proletariat in the Present Revolution," which precipitated a crisis in the Bolshevik Party. He condemned the Provisional Government, called for an end to the war, and defined the task of the Bolsheviks as preparing the Soviets to take full power and establish a workers' state. Lenin's attempt to reorient the Bolsheviks away from support to the bourgeois Provisional Government and toward the perspective of organizing a struggle for power by the proletariat and poor peasantry, was initially opposed by virtually the entire Bolshevik leadership.

117. **Iraklii Tsereteli** (1882-1959), a Menshevik leader who supported the war, held ministerial positions March-August 1917.

118. **Defensism** was a term applied to those who after February 1917 supported the Provisional Government's policy of national defense, or pursuit of the war. Lenin proposed a policy of revolutionary defeatism toward what remained an imperialist war being waged by the bourgeois Provisional Government.

119. **Black Hundreds** was the popular name for the Association of the Russian People and the Association to Combat Revolution. These were gangs of reactionaries and "patriotic" hoodlums that existed up through the Russian civil war. They were organized with the czarist government's clandestine backing, and specialized in carrying out anti-Semitic pogroms and terrorizing radicals.

120. The Russian Constitutional Democrats, called **Cadets,** were the liberal party favoring a constitutional monarchy in Russia or even ultimately a republic. It was a party of progressive landlords, middle bourgeois, and bourgeois intellectuals.

121. **The Jacobins** were the most radical political faction in the Great French Revolution and dominated French politics from the overthrow of the Gironde in 1791 until the month of **Thermidor** 1794, when they were defeated by a reactionary wing in the revolution, which did not go so far, however, as to restore the feudal regime. Trotsky used the term "Thermidor" as a historical analogy to designate seizure of power by the conservative Stalinist bureaucracy within the framework of nationalized property relations.

122. **Gregory Zinoviev** (1883-1936) and **Leon Kamenev** (1883-1936) helped Stalin initiate the crusade against Trotskyism in 1923, but they blocked with the Left Opposition from 1926 until they were expelled from the party in 1927. They capitulated, were readmitted, but were expelled again in 1932. They repented again, but became victims of the first big Moscow show trial and were executed. Zinoviev was the first president of the Comintern (1919-26). **Alexei Rykov** (1881-1938) succeeded Lenin as chairman of the Council of People's Commissars. With **Nikolai Bukharin** (1888-1938) he led the Right Opposition in the party. When it was expelled in 1929 they both capitulated, but they were made defendants in the third Moscow trial in March 1938 and were executed. Bukharin succeeded Zinoviev as head of the Comintern (1926-29). **Karl Radek** (1885-1939), **Georgi Pyatakov** (1890-1937), and **Leonid Serebryakov** (1890-1937) were outstanding leaders of the Bolshevik Party. All of them capitulated quickly after they were expelled in 1927 for membership in the Left Opposition. They were given posts in the party and government but were victims of the second Moscow trial. **Grigory Sokolnikov** (1888-1939) filled diplomatic and military posts after the revolution. For a short time in 1925 he supported the Zinovievist opposition on the issue of the party regime. For that he was made a victim of the second Moscow trial. **Ivan N. Smirnov** (1881-1936) had played a leading role in the civil war. He was expelled from the party in 1927 as a Left Oppositionist, but capitulated in 1929 and was reinstated in the party. He was arrested in 1933 and executed after the first Moscow trial. Among the Red Army generals charged with treason and executed in May 1937 were **Mikhail Tukhachevsky** (1893-1937), **Nikolai Muralov** (1877-1937), **Iona Yakir** (1896-1937), and **I. P. Uborevich**. **Ian Gamarnik** (1894-1937) committed suicide at the prospect of arrest. Others who perished in the Red Army purge were **S. D. Mrachkovsky** (1883-1936), **Alexander Yegorov** (1886-1941), **V. K. Bluecher** (1889-1938).

123. During June and July 1936 a massive strike wave broke out in France, involving up to seven million workers, many on sitdown strikes. In 1935 the French Communist Party had endorsed and participated in the formation of the People's Front coalition with the bourgeois Radical Party and the Socialist Party. The People's Front followed the policy of containing the mass workers' struggles.

124. **The "third period,"** according to the schema proclaimed by the Stalinists in 1928, was the final period of capitalism, the period

of its immediately impending demise and replacement by soviets. Flowing from this, the Comintern's tactics during the next six years were marked by ultraleftism and sectarianism, including refusing to join the mass labor unions in the capitalist countries and building smaller "red" unions instead, as well as refusing to build united fronts with other working class organizations. The Stalinists abandoned this policy in 1934, and the following year adopted the People's Front policy.

125. "A Contribution to Centrist Literature." **Clave**, December 1938. Signed "L. Amago." By permission of the Harvard College Library. Translated for this volume from the French by Russell Block. This was a review of a booklet by Rodrigo Garcia Trevino, a leader of the CTM who led a group in a break with the Stalinist union leadership. He was the author of several books about Mexico. **Centrism** is the term used by Trotsky for tendencies in the radical movement that stand or vacillate between reformism, which is the position of the labor bureaucracy and the labor aristocracy, and Marxism, which represents the historic interests of the working class. Since a centrist tendency has no independent social base, it must be evaluated in terms of its origin, its internal dynamic, and the direction in which it is going or being pushed by events.

126. Marx and Engels wrote the **Communist Manifesto** in 1847. In **1848** struggles for bourgeois democratic rights, national independence, and constitutional reforms took place throughout Europe.

127. **Imperialism: The Highest Stage of Capitalism**, by V. I. Lenin, was written in 1916.

128. **The Chinese revolution of 1925-27** was crushed because the Chinese Communists, under orders from Moscow, entered the bourgeois Kuomintang (Nationalist Party) and subordinated the revolution to the preservation of this coalition, which could not permit a social transformation of China. Trotsky publicly initiated the "enormous volume of critical work" on the Stalinist degeneration of the Third International in 1923 with the formation of the Left Opposition.

129. **Jozef Pilsudski** (1867-1935), a Polish nationalist, organized his own army to fight against Russia during World War I, and was a leader of the counterrevolutionary interventionist forces during the Russian civil war. He moved his troops into Warsaw in May 1926 and became virtual dictator of Poland until his death. **The defeat of the Austrian Social Democracy** occurred in February 1934, when the Austrian workers staged a general strike against governmental repression but were crushed after a heroic armed struggle. After this defeat the Austrian Social Democracy, once the most powerful in the world, was outlawed.

130. On January 28, 1937, **El Universal** printed a letter from Trotsky to **Luis Cabrera**, a wealthy right-wing lawyer retained by

the oil companies and landlords of Yucatan, praising Cabrera's stand on the Moscow trials. Cabrera's article, "El Carnaval Sangriento" (The Bloody Circus), had been printed in **El Universal** on January 25, 1937. The full text of Trotsky's letter is in **Writings 36-37**.

131. See several of Trotsky's articles between March and July 1933 in **Writings 32-33**.

132. "Toward a Revolutionary Youth Organization." By permission of the Harvard College Library. An uncorrected stenogram of a discussion with Nathan Gould, national secretary of the Young People's Socialist League (YPSL), shortly before the YPSL held a national convention in Chicago at the end of November 1938. For security reasons the pseudonym "Crux" was used for Trotsky in the stenogram. The YPSL had been the youth group of the Socialist Party, but a majority of its members had supported the left wing that had been expelled from the SP in the summer of 1937, and shifted their affiliation to the Socialist Workers Party when it was founded at the start of 1938. The convention the YPSL was about to hold was its first since it had adhered to the SWP. (For a letter Trotsky wrote to the convention in June 1938, see **Writings 37-38,** 2nd ed.) In 1940 most of the YPSL, including Gould, joined Shachtman in splitting from the SWP.

133. "The Death Agony of Capitalism and the Tasks of the Fourth International," also known as the **Transitional Program,** is the basic programmatic document adopted at the founding conference of the Fourth International in September 1938. Its full text is in **The Transitional Program for Socialist Revolution.** The "minimum program" of the Social Democracy consisted of a list of immediate demands that did not transcend the limits of bourgeois democracy. As the Social Democracy became dominated by reformists, it limited itself to struggles for its minimum program. Its "maximum program"—socialism—bore no relation to these struggles and was viewed as an abstract goal relegated to the future.

134. **Frank P. Hague** (1876-1956) was Democratic mayor of Jersey City, New Jersey, from 1917 to 1947. In the thirties his notoriously corrupt administration used governmental power and police violence, in cooperation with hired company thugs, to prevent CIO unions from organizing. Picketing was forbidden, and distributors of union leaflets were jailed or run out of town.

135. After 1933, the radicalization began to take the form of emerging left wings in the old Social Democratic parties. Trotsky proposed the temporary entry of the International Communist League into the Socialist parties to link up with the new youthful revolutionaries. This was known as the French turn because it was first applied in France in 1934. The American Trotskyists in the Workers Party joined the Socialist Party in 1936; expelled with other left-wingers in 1937, they founded the SWP on New Year's Day 1938.

136. **Challenge of Youth** was the newspaper of the YPSL.

137. "The Individual in History." **International Socialist Review,** Winter 1964, where this excerpt of a letter was translated by William F. Warde (George Novack) in a review of Pierre Naville's memoir, **Trotsky vivant.**

138. **Boris Souvarine** (1893-   ) was a founder of the French Communist Party and was one of the first serious biographers of Stalin. He was repelled by Stalinism in the twenties and was the only foreign delegate to the thirteenth congress of the Russian CP to defend Trotsky against the Stalinist slanders. He was expelled from the French party shortly thereafter. In the thirties he turned against Leninism. For Trotsky he was a prototype of the cynicism and defeatism that characterized the renegades from Bolshevism.

139. **The Girondists** were moderate bourgeois republicans during the French Revolution. They wanted to overthrow the old regime but feared the city poor and the peasant masses who were capable of doing it; they therefore wavered between the revolution and the counterrevolution, finally going over to the latter.

140. **Georges Danton** (1759-1794), a leader of the right wing of the Jacobins, was minister of justice from 1792, and was guillotined less than a year after the Girondists.

141. **Maximilien Robespierre** (1758-1794) became the leader of the Jacobins and was effective head of state from 1793. He was overthrown by the counterrevolution of the Ninth of Thermidor and guillotined.

142. "Stalin vs. Stalin." **Hoy,** December 3, 1938. By permission of the Harvard College Library. Translated for this volume from the French by Michael Baumann.

143. The official **History of the Communist Party of the Soviet Union (Bolsheviks),** called the "Short Course," was edited by a commission of the Central Committee of the CPSU and published by International Publishers, New York, 1939.

144. **Kliment Voroshilov** (1881-1969) was an early supporter of Stalin, a member of the Politbureau of the CPSU from 1926, president of the Revolutionary Military Council, and people's commissar of defense. **Vyacheslav Molotov** (1890-   ), an Old Bolshevik, was an editor of **Pravda** prior to the October Revolution. Elected to the Russian party's Central Committee in 1920, he aligned himself with Stalin. He was president of the Council of People's Commissars from 1930 to 1941; in 1939 he became minister of foreign affairs. He was eliminated from the leadership in 1957 when he opposed the Khrushchev "de-Stalinization" campaign. **Felix Dzerzhinsky** (1877-1926) was a founder of the Social Democratic Party of Poland and Lithuania. In 1906 he was elected to the Bolshevik Central Committee. After the revolution he became chairman of the All-Russian Extraordinary Commission for Combating Counterrevolution and Sabotage (Cheka). He was also commissar for internal affairs. **G.K. Ordzhonikidze** (1886-1937), an organizer of the Stalin faction, was later put in charge of heavy industry. Although he remained

a faithful Stalinist, the circumstances around his death are still not publicly known. **Sergei Kirov** (1886-1934) was a member of the Central Committee from 1923 and was party secretary in Leningrad from 1926. His assassination signaled the start of the purges that culminated in the Moscow trials and the extermination of the entire remaining leadership of the Russian Revolution. **Lazar Kaganovich** (1893-   ) was commissar of heavy industry (1938-39) and a member of the Central Committee from 1939. He was removed from all his posts as an "antiparty element" when Khrushchev took over the Soviet leadership in the 1950s. **Valerian Kuibyshev** (1888-1935) held a variety of posts before becoming chairman of the Supreme Council of National Economy in 1926. Although he was a dedicated Stalinist, he met with a mysterious death. **Mikhail Frunze** (1885-1925) held several important military posts during the civil war and in 1925 replaced Trotsky as chairman of the Military Revolutionary Council of the Republic. **Emelyan Yaroslavsky** (1878-1943) was a top Stalinist specialist in the campaign against Trotskyism and was part of the team that brought charges against Trotsky and demanded his expulsion from the party. He fell from favor in 1932-33 when he failed to keep up with the tempo demanded by Stalin in rewriting Soviet history.

145. **Andrei Zhdanov** (1896-1948), an ally of Stalin from 1923, replaced the assassinated Kirov as secretary of the Leningrad party committee in 1935. He was a member of the Politbureau from 1939, but died under mysterious circumstances. **Nicholas Yezhov**, the successor to Yagoda as head of the GPU, disappeared after the third Moscow trial.

146. The reference is to **Vladimir Antonov-Ovseenko** (1884-1938), who played a prominent role in the October Revolution, participating in the taking of the Winter Palace. He was in the Left Opposition from 1923 to 1927, but recanted in 1928. During the Spanish Civil War he was Russian Consul-General in Barcelona; he was made a scapegoat for the defeat of Stalinist policy in Spain and disappeared. **Nikolai Podvoisky** (1880-1948) was the chairman of the Petrograd Military Revolutionary Committee during the October Revolution, and later worked in the Commissariat of War.

147. **Ulrich von Hutten** (1488-1523), German humanist and poet, was a theoretician for elements of the nobility who wanted to reform the empire by eliminating princes and secularizing church property.

148. "Reply to Father Coughlin's Charges." By permission of the Harvard College Library. On November 28, 1938, the **New York Times** carried a front-page article on an anti-Semitic address by **Father Charles E. Coughlin,** a Catholic priest, whose protofascist career began with a local radio program in Detroit in the twenties. During the Depression he became a national spokesman for the incipient fascist movement in the U.S., the leader of the "National Union for Social Justice," and a vocal admirer of Nazi Germany. His anti-

labor, red-baiting, and anti-Semitic policies found backing among high capitalist and Catholic circles. In his speech, Coughlin charged that a "Jacob Schiff," as well as several other American Jews, were directors of the "work of destruction" being carried on in Russia. He also charged that the same Jacob Schiff had given money to Trotsky in 1917. **Times** reporter Frank Kluckhohn telephoned Trotsky and Trotsky's statement, printed in the **Times,** was read to him in reply to his question "Can you ask Trotsky if he ever got any money from Jacob Schiff in 1917 as alleged by Coughlin?"

149. "For an Independent Youth Movement." A letter to Rose Karsner (1890-1968), a leader of the Socialist Workers Party. She was Cannon's companion and close political collaborator from 1924. A founder of the American CP, she helped to organize the International Labor Defense and was its assistant secretary. In 1928 she was expelled from the CP for Trotskyism and became a founder of the first U.S. Trotskyist organization. The remainder of her life was linked to that movement. After World War II, she organized and was secretary of the American Committee for European Workers' Relief.

150. **Harold R. Isaacs** (1910-   ) was the author of **The Tragedy of the Chinese Revolution** (1938), to which Trotsky contributed a preface. Subsequent editions, which Isaacs revised after he rejected Marxism, omitted this preface.

151. The Tenth National Convention of the YPSL was held in Chicago November 24-27, 1938.

152. "On the Murder of Rudolf Klement." **Biulleten Oppozitsii,** no. 73, January 1939. Translated by George Saunders for the first edition of **Writings 38-39.**

153. "Open Letter to Senator Allen." By permission of the Harvard College Library. Translated for this volume from the Russian by Marilyn Vogt. This article was also printed in **Hoy,** December 17, 1938. **U.S. Senator Henry J. Allen** (Republican) was the former governor of Kansas.

154. **The Committee on Cultural Relations with Latin America** was headed by Professor Hubert Herring, the author of **A History of Latin America.** Trotsky met with this committee again on July 23, 1939; the full text of that interview is in **Writings 39-40.**

155. **Oliver Cromwell** (1599-1658) organized a parliamentary army to defeat the royalist forces of King Charles I. In 1653 Cromwell assumed the title Lord Protector of the Commonwealth. To Trotsky, Cromwell was a symbol of the revolutionary militancy of the youthful bourgeoisie, and Chamberlain a symbol of its senile decay.

156. **William Thomas Manning** (1866-1949) was Episcopalian bishop of New York (1921-46).

157. "Victor Serge and the Fourth International." **Biulleten Oppozitsii,** no. 73, January 1939. Signed "The Editor." Translated by George Saunders for the first edition of **Writings 38-39.** Victor Serge (1890-1947) was born in Belgium of Russian parents and became an anarchist in his youth, for which he was sentenced to five years in prison. After the Bolshevik revolution, he moved to the Soviet Union and worked for the Comintern. Arrested as an Oppositionist and then freed in 1928, he was rearrested in 1933. Thanks to a campaign by intellectuals in France, he was released and allowed to leave the USSR in 1936. He soon developed differences with the Fourth Internationalist movement and left it. He wrote several important historical works, including **The Year One of the Russian Revolution** and **From Lenin to Stalin** (Pathfinder Press, 1973).

158. **Georges Vereecken** had been the representative of a sectarian tendency in the Belgian section of the Trotskyist movement. He broke with Trotsky when the Belgian section entered the Belgian Socialist Party, rejoined later, and again split on the eve of the founding conference to form his own group.

159. "Problems of the Mexican Section." By permission of the Harvard College Library. Translated for this volume from the Russian by Marilyn Vogt. **Luciano Galicia** was the leader of the LCI (Internationalist Communist League, the Mexican section of the Trotskyist movement), which was organized in 1930. The organization pursued a sectarian policy in the trade unions and issued irresponsible and adventuristic slogans. A fact-finding delegation consisting of Cannon, Shachtman, and V.R. Dunne from the United States was sent to Mexico by the Latin American Department of the Fourth Internationalist movement, but a few days before its arrival Galicia dissolved the group. He subsequently reconstituted it, and the founding conference mandated the International Subsecretariat to reorganize the Mexican section on the basis of acceptance of the decisions of the founding conference and the discipline of the Fourth International. In January 1939 Galicia denounced the "totalitarian regime and centrist line of the leaders of the so-called Fourth International proclaimed at its September conference," and the organization split; later that year the Mexican section was reorganized under the name POI (Internationalist Workers Party). Galicia later rejoined the Fourth International.

160. **Paul Eiffel** led a small split-off from the Revolutionary Workers League (see note 161) in 1936. He advocated sabotage of the Loyalist struggle against Franco and the Chinese nationalist struggle against Japan. Trotsky refers to him and to the others cited here as models of cynical organizational maneuvering and unprincipled politics.

161. **Hugo Oehler** led a sectarian faction in the Workers Party of the United States that opposed on principle the WPUS's entry into

the Socialist Party, which was proposed as a way of reaching the growing left wing in that party. He and his group were expelled in 1935 for violating party discipline, and formed the Revolutionary Workers League.

162. **Ferdinand Freiligrath** (1810-1876) was a German poet whose works included lyric and political poems, patriotic war songs, and translations from Victor Hugo, Shakespeare, etc.

163. **Maxim Gorky** (1868-1936), the Russian writer of popular short stories, novels, and plays, was hostile to the October Revolution in 1917, but later gave support to the new government until he left the country in 1921, ostensibly for reasons of health. When he returned in 1932, he gave general support to Stalin's policies.

164. "A Revolutionary Name for a Revolutionary Youth Group." From the personal archives of James P. Cannon. Signed "Joe Hansen."

165. "For a Systematic Political Campaign." From the personal archives of James P. Cannon. Signed "Hansen."

166. "A Political Dialogue." Translated from the German for the British periodical **Workers Fight**, September 1939; revised in accord with the Russian by George Saunders for the first edition of **Writings 38-39**. Signed "L. T."

167. When the February Revolution broke out, Lenin was in Zurich. In order to get back to Russia, he had to travel through Germany, with which Russia was still at war. The German government consented to convey Lenin and twenty-nine other emigres back to Russia in a train with a sealed car. The German government was represented in these negotiations by Erich F. Ludendorff (see note 60), who undoubtedly agreed to transport Lenin back to Russia in the hope that he would add to the instability of Russia's already-disintegrating military position. Opponents of the Bolsheviks later charged that this trip through Germany was evidence that the Bolsheviks were agents of the German government.

168. "Answers to the Lies of the **New York Daily News**." **Daily News**, January 8, 1939. In a series of articles by Fred Pasley, the **Daily News** opened a campaign of attack on the Mexican government for its policy of expropriations. Editorially, the **News** had charged that Trotsky was the real power behind President Cardenas. In December, **News** reporter Pasley sent a list of questions which Trotsky agreed to answer if the **News** would publish the answers in full. The entire article also appeared in **Socialist Appeal**, January 14, 1939, accompanied by the postscript that is included here.

169. **Albert Goldman** (1897-1960) was a leader of the SWP and Trotsky's U. S. lawyer. He was defense counsel as well as one of the eighteen defendants convicted in the 1941 Minneapolis labor trial, the first use of the Smith Act. He left the SWP in 1946. On Novem-

ber 11, 1938, in a letter to Goldman now in the Trotsky Archives at Harvard, Trotsky had asserted that the Stalinists, in their effort to get him expelled from Mexico, were behind the slander campaign in the U. S., and he inquired about the possibility of suing the **Daily News** for libel.

170. "Lenin and Imperialist War." **Fourth International**, January 1942. When this was published in **Fourth International** it was mistakenly dated February 1939, and about four paragraphs were omitted. The first edition of **Writings 38-39** kept the error and the omissions; the full text appears here in English for the first time, with the missing sections translated for this volume from **Biulleten Oppozitsii**, no. 74, February 1939, by Marilyn Vogt. In another translation a shortened version of this article appears in Trotsky's biography of Stalin.

171. **Georgi Dimitrov** (1882-1949), a Bulgarian Communist who had moved to Germany, attracted world attention in 1933 when the Nazis imprisoned and tried him and others on charges of having set the Reichstag on fire. He defended himself courageously at the trial and was acquitted. He became a Soviet citizen, served as executive secretary of the Comintern from 1934 to 1943, and acted as the chief proponent of the People's Front policy adopted at the Comintern's Seventh Congress in 1935. He was premier of Bulgaria, 1946-49.

172. **Alexander G. Shlyapnikov** (1883-193?), an Old Bolshevik, was a member of the Central Committee from 1915 and was the first commissar of labor in the Soviet government. He was a leader of the Workers' Opposition, a syndicalist tendency in the Bolshevik Party that opposed the New Economic Policy and called for giving state power to the trade unions. He was expelled from the party, recanted, was readmitted, and was again expelled in 1927.

173. "To the Pillory!" **Clave**, January 1939. Unsigned. Translated for this volume from the Spanish by Ellen Fischer. The CGT's congress was in December 1938.

174. **Julio Ramirez** was the head of the CGT.

175. **The approaching election campaign** was for the presidential election, which was held in September 1940.

176. "One More Lesson on the Lima Conference." **Clave**, January 1939. Unsigned. Translated for this volume from the Spanish by Ellen Fischer. **The Eighth Pan-American Conference** was held in Lima, Peru, December 9-27, 1938. The U. S. government attempted to use the conference to enlist the Latin American peoples as pawns of U. S. imperialism in the approaching war and to establish unchallenged U. S. hegemony in Latin America, but the "Declaration of Lima" that was adopted was a compromise between the representatives of U. S. and British capitalism.

177. **Cordell Hull** (1871-1955) was U. S. secretary of state from 1933 to 1944. His speciality was negotiating reciprocal trade agreements with Latin American countries.

178. "To the Readers of **Clave**." **Clave**, February 1939. Unsigned. Translated for this volume from the Spanish by Russell Block.

179. " **Clave** and the Election Campaign." **Clave**, March 1939. Unsigned. Translated for this volume from the Spanish by Russell Block.

180. "A Proposed Biography." A letter to Enrique Espinoza. **Babel**, January-April 1941. Translated for this volume from the French by Russell Block. **Enrique Espinoza** was an Argentine writer and publisher of the review **Babel.**

181. "Jouhaux and Toledano." **Clave**, February 1939. Unsigned. Translated for this volume from the Spanish by Russell Block.

182. "Stalin, Skoblin, and Company." **Biulleten Oppozitsii**, no. 74, February 1939. Unsigned. Translated for this volume by Iain Fraser. **General Eugene Skoblin** was a GPU agent functioning in the White Guard emigre circles in France.

183. **Anton W. Turkul** (d. 1958) was a former czarist general.

184. Trotsky and his family were forcibly exiled from the Soviet Union by Stalin's order in February 1929, and lived in Turkey until July 1933. **Jakob Blumkin** (1899-1929) had been a Left Social Revolutionary terrorist who became a Communist and a GPU official. He was the first Russian supporter of the Left Opposition to visit Trotsky in exile in Turkey. Bringing back a letter from Trotsky to the Opposition, he was betrayed to the GPU and shot in December 1929, the first Oppositionist to be directly executed by the Stalinists.

185. **The trial of Nadja Plevitskaya**, Skoblin's wife, was held in Paris in December 1938. She was found guilty of complicity with her husband in the kidnaping of the White Guard leader General Eugene Miller, and was sentenced to twenty years' imprisonment.

186. **General Eugene Miller** had been named chief of the Union of Czarist Army Veterans — a White Guard organization — in January 1930, when the current chief had disappeared in Paris, presumably abducted by the Soviet secret police. Miller was in turn kidnaped by Skoblin on September 22, 1937. He left a note implicating Skoblin in the kidnaping, but Skoblin escaped, leaving his wife behind to stand trial. Miller was put aboard a Soviet ship that sailed immediately from le Havre with no other cargo.

187. **Henry Yagoda** (1891-1938) was the head of the Soviet secret police. In 1938 Yagoda, who had supervised the organization of the 1936 Moscow trial, was himself made a defendant and executed.

188. The full text of Trotsky's December 1931 article, "The White Guard Preparation of a Terrorist Attack Against Comrade Trotsky," is in **Writings 30-31.**

189. "Ignorance Is Not a Revolutionary Instrument." Translated from the February 1939 **Clave** for **The New International**, March 1939, where it had the title "Clarity or Confusion?" Signed "**Clave.**" According to Isaac Deutscher's **Prophet Outcast** (p. 445) this article was written for **Trinchera Aprista**; but the version in **Clave** is merely subtitled "About a Scandalous Article in **Trinchera Aprista.**"

190. **Guillermo Vegas Leon** was a writer for **El Popular**, the official newspaper of the CTM.

191. **Oscar Raimundo Benavides** (1876-1945) was president of Peru from 1933 to 1939.

192. **The Kuomintang** of China was the bourgeois nationalist party founded by Sun Yat-sen in 1911 and led after 1926 by Chiang Kai-shek. The Communists entered the party on the orders of the Comintern leadership in 1923.

193. **The Good Neighbor Policy**, proclaimed by U.S. president Franklin Roosevelt, stated that the U.S. would no longer resort to armed interventions in Latin America and the Caribbean, but would rather function as a "good neighbor."

194. **The CIO** (Congress of Industrial Organizations) began as a committee within the American Federation of Labor, a conservative craft union federation. The AFL leaders refused to respond to the demand for powerful new unions to organize radicalizing workers on an industry-wide basis; they expelled the CIO unions in 1938, forcing them to establish their own national organization. The AFL and CIO merged in 1955.

195. **William Green** (1873-1952) was the conservative president of the American Federation of Labor.

196. "For Grynszpan: Against Fascist Pogrom Gangs and Stalinist Scoundrels." **Socialist Appeal**, February 14, 1939. **Herschel Grynszpan**, a 17-year-old Polish Jew, shot and killed a Nazi official in the German embassy in Paris on November 7, 1938. His trial was postponed indefinitely when France and Germany declared war in 1939. After the occupation of France, he was transferred to a concentration camp in Germany; his subsequent fate is not known.

197. "Intellectual Ex-Radicals and World Reaction." **Socialist Appeal**, February 17, 1939. Unsigned. To dissociate himself from the current of intellectuals then fleeing from Marxism, Trotsky sent the following letter on March 6 to the **Modern Quarterly** (previously the **Modern Monthly**), edited by V.F. Calverton: "Gentlemen: I disagree completely with the general tendency of your review and therefore ask that you remove my name from your list of contributors. Sincerely yours, Leon Trotsky." The letter was published in **Socialist Appeal**, April 11, 1939, but not in **Modern Quarterly**.

198. **Georg Wilhelm Friedrich Hegel** (1770-1831), the most eminent German philosopher of the first half of the nineteenth century, developed the system of dialectics that Marx later adapted to historical materialism.

199. "Krupskaya's Death." **New International**, April 1939. Signed "L. T." **Nadezhda K. Krupskaya** (1869-1939) was an Old Bolshevik and the companion of Lenin. She played a central role in the underground and emigre organization of the Russian Social Democracy. After the revolution she worked in the Commissariat of Education. She adhered to the United Opposition for a brief time in 1926.

200. **Lavrenty P. Beria** (1899-1953) became chief of the GPU in 1938 when Yezhov was ousted, and became a member of the Political Bureau in 1946. After Stalin's death, he was accused of having been a British agent since 1919, and was executed.

201. "The Betrayers of India." **Clave**, March 1939. By permission of the Harvard College Library. Translated for this volume from the Russian by Marilyn Vogt.

202. **Sherman Stanley** was a member of the SWP who left with the Burnham-Shachtman group in 1940. His article in the March 1939 **Clave** was entitled "Will India Agree to Being Federalized?"

203. "What Lies Behind Stalin Bid for Agreement with Hitler?" **Socialist Appeal**, March 28, 1939. Signed "L. T."

204. **Brest-Litovsk** was a town on the Russo-Polish border where a treaty ending hostilities between Russia and Germany was signed in March 1918. The terms were exceedingly unfavorable to the new Soviet government, and there were sharp differences among its leaders about whether to accept them until Lenin's proposal to do so was adopted. The November 1918 revolution in Germany and the German defeat in the war enabled the Soviet government to recover most of the territory lost through the treaty.

205. **Chiang Kai-shek** (1887-   ) was the right-wing military leader of the Kuomintang during the Chinese revolution of 1925-27. The Stalinists hailed him as a great revolutionary until April 1927, when he conducted a bloody massacre of the Shanghai Communists and trade unionists. He ruled China until overthrown by the Chinese Communist Party in 1949. **Sun Yat-sen** (1866-1925), a revolutionary democrat, was the founder of the Kuomintang. After his death, **Sun Yat-senism**, which praised class "peace," became canonized as the ideology of the Kuomintang.

206. When Moscow sought the friendship of the Polish government, it ordered the Polish CP to support the Warsaw government. When it met resistance, it dissolved the CP in the summer of 1938, denounced its leaders as fascists, and annihilated them.

207. **The Radical (or Radical Socialist) Party of France,** neither radical nor socialist, was the principal capitalist party of France between World Wars I and II, comparable to the Democratic Party in the United States.

208. On February 20, 1939, the Socialist Workers Party sponsored an anti-Nazi demonstration at Madison Square Garden, where the American fascists were holding a rally. Fifty thousand workers turned

out to picket, and another 50,000 watched. Neither the Socialist Party nor the Communist Party had agreed to cosponsor the demonstration.

209. "Once Again on the 'Crisis of Marxism.'" **The New International,** May 1939. Signed "T."

210. **Harold Ickes** (1874-1952) was U.S. secretary of the interior from 1933 to 1946 in the Roosevelt-Truman administration. The expression **sixty families** comes from Ferdinand Lundberg's 1937 book **America's Sixty Families.** The book, a sensation when it appeared, documented the existence of an economic oligarchy in the U. S. headed by sixty families of immense wealth. The author brought the work up to date in 1968 with **The Rich and the Super-Rich.**

211. **Leon Blum** (1872-1950) was the head of the French Socialist Party in the thirties and premier of the first People's Front government in 1936.

212. "A Step Toward Social Patriotism." **The New International,** July 1939. Signed "Editorial Board, **Biulleten Oppozitsii.**" This article was written in reply to a letter from a group of Palestinian Bolshevik-Leninists who cited the danger of a pacifist deviation in the ranks of the Fourth International and argued that defeatism was not an adequate revolutionary policy in a war against fascism.

213. Trotsky's article "Germany and the USSR" is in English in **The Struggle Against Fascism in Germany.**

214. "'Learn to Work in the Stalin Manner.'" **The New International,** May 1939. Signed "Alpha."

215. "Stalin's Capitulation." **Socialist Appeal,** April 7, 1939. Signed "L. T." This article is Trotsky's initial evaluation of the eighteenth congress of the Communist Party of the Soviet Union, which took place March 10-21, 1939. The congress marked Stalin's final consolidation of his supremacy within the party; he was thus able to deplore the excesses of the great purge trials of the preceding decade. The effects of the purge itself can be gauged by the fact that less than 2 percent of the rank-and-file delegates at the seventeenth congress in 1934 were still around to hold that position in 1939. At the congress, Stalin sought to demonstrate to the Allied governments through Manuilsky's report the value of an alliance with the Kremlin; he proclaimed the Comintern's decision not to demand freedom for the colonies belonging to "democratic" governments, and called upon the colonial peoples to support their master countries in a war against fascism. At the same time, however, Stalin was anxious to make overtures to Hitler as well, because the camp of the Allied powers, a few months after the Munich conference and at the very moment of Hitler's invasion of Czechoslovakia, hardly looked like the stronger of the two. When Stalin made his address

at the opening of the congress on March 10 (published in **The Essential Stalin** [Anchor Books, 1972]), he denounced Nazi aggression
and called for an "antifascist coalition"; but he also, in passing, put
out feelers toward a rapprochement with Germany. In this article,
written the very day that the report of Stalin's speech reached the
West, Trotsky seized on the latter aspect of the speech, an aspect
that was belittled by Western diplomats and observers until it ma-
terialized in the Stalin-Hitler pact in August.

216. **Alexander Nevski** (1220?-1263), a legendary Russian saint
and hero, defeated the Swedes (1240) in a great battle near the site
of present-day Leningrad, on the Neva river (whence his name
Nevski). He also defeated the Livonian knights (1242). In his honor
Peter the Great founded the Order of Alexander Nevski in 1725.

217. "On Mexico's Second Six Year Plan." Translated for this volume from the French by Russell Block, by permission of the Harvard College Library. The first Six Year Plan was adopted by the
Mexican congress in 1934. It was designed to establish a "cooperative economic system tending toward socialism," and included an
extensive public works program, a labor code fixing minimum wages
and regulating hours, some land distribution, and aid to local co-
operatives for purchasing machinery and stock. Discussion on the
second Six Year Plan began in February 1939. The plan was drafted
by the ruling Mexican Revolutionary Party (PRM) and was considered the platform for its candidate in the September 1940 presidential elections, Manuel Avila Camacho. It included plans for
further expropriations and nationalizations, women's suffrage, compulsory military training, economic independence for Mexico, and
improvements in the standard of living of the Mexican masses. In
February, while it was still in the discussion stage, it was endorsed
by the congress of the CTM. The PRM adopted the plan that November, at the same time that it formally nominated Camacho. When
the final draft, much modified, was published in February 1940,
it included guarantees to private capital investors and the pledge
to "cooperate with other countries that favor a democratic form of
government."

218. **Emiliano Zapata** (1877?-1919) was a Mexican revolutionist with a radical agrarian program.

219. "A Proposal from Shanghai." From the personal papers of
Charles Curtiss. Signed "V.T. O'Brien." F., a foreigner living in
Shanghai, had submitted a proposal to smuggle Chen Tu-hsiu out
of China. Chen (1879-1942), referred to in Trotsky's reply as "C.,"
had been a founder of the Chinese CP and of the Left Opposition.
For his revolutionary activity he was imprisoned by the Kuomintang police from 1932 until 1937. Broken in health, he withdrew
from politics and settled in a village near Chungking, where Chiang

Kai-shek's government was located. Despite this, the Chinese Stalinists launched a slander campaign accusing him of being an agent of Japan. F. and others feared that this was part of the GPU's political preparation for his assassination (Leon Sedov and Rudolf Klement had both been murdered by the GPU in the preceding year). F.'s proposal to quietly take Chen out of the country to a place where he might be better protected was intended to avoid a request for a legal exit, which would have alerted Kuomintang authorities to Chen's intention of leaving China. F. felt that a legal exit was practically out of the question and that the "other method" would be made more difficult by any effort along that line. As his letter shows, Trotsky preferred the legal method, if it proved possible, with simultaneous "preparations for the other version." It turned out to be impossible to communicate with Chen across military lines and contact with him was lost. Chen was moving further away from Marxism in the meantime, and was completely isolated by the time of his death in 1942.

220. **Juan O'Gorman** was a revolutionary Mexican artist.

221. "Only Revolution Can End War." **Socialist Appeal,** April 4, 1939. These answers to questions of Sybil Vincent, correspondent for the Labour Party's paper, the **Daily Herald** (London), also appeared, after some delay, in the **Daily Herald,** May 27, 1939.

222. **Francisco Largo Caballero** (1869-1946) was a leader of the left wing of the Spanish Socialist Party. He was premier from September 1936 until May 1937. **Jose Garcia Oliver** (1901-   ) was a right-wing Spanish Anarchist leader who collaborated with the Stalinists to crush the revolutionary wing of the Loyalists. He was minister of justice in the Largo Caballero government.

223. **The revolution of 1905** in Russia grew out of discontent over the Russo-Japanese War and czarist despotism. On "Bloody Sunday," January 9, 1905, czarist troops fired on a peaceful march of Petersburg workers bearing a petition to the czar for democratic rights, and killed hundreds of them. Massive strikes ensued throughout Russia, marking the beginning of the revolution, which culminated in the formation of the Petersburg Soviet of Workers' Deputies in October. It was crushed by the czar in December. See Trotsky's **1905** (Random House, 1972).

224. "Our Work in the Communist Party." By permission of the Harvard College Library. A rough stenographic draft, not checked by the participants, of a discussion Trotsky held with a delegation from the Socialist Workers Party. For security reasons pseudonyms were used in the stenogram, but are replaced in the present text for participants who have been identified. Trotsky was identified as Crux. SWP members who participated were Charles Cornell, Vaughan T. O'Brien, and Sol Lankin. Others were "Gray" and "Guy." The "letter to

Trotsky" that he quotes was from Joseph Hansen, another of Trotsky's secretaries, who was in New York at the time.

225. **Terence Phelan** was Sherry Mangan (1904-1961), an American writer and journalist who had been a Trotskyist from 1934. He was active in France during the German occupation until he was expelled by the Petain government. He served on the European Secretariat in the last years of the war and then on the International Secretariat.

226. **The Nation** was then a liberal magazine strongly influenced by Stalinism.

227. **The Daily Worker** was the newspaper of the Communist Party, predecessor of the **Daily World.**

228. **The Old Guard** was the right-wing formation in the Socialist Party that split away in 1936 to form the Social Democratic Federation. **Norman Thomas** (1884-1968), Socialist Party candidate for president six times, presided over the decline of the SP after the right wing left and the Trotskyist-led left wing was expelled.

229. **Dimitri Manuilsky** (1883-1952), like Trotsky, had been a member of the independent Marxist group that fused with the Bolshevik Party in 1917. He supported the Stalin faction in the 1920s and served as secretary of the Comintern from 1931 to 1943.

230. **Jay Lovestone** had been a leader of the American Communist Party in the twenties, but was expelled in 1929 shortly after the downfall of his international ally, Bukharin. The Lovestoneites maintained an organization until the beginning of World War II, when they dissolved. Lovestone later became cold-war adviser on foreign affairs for AFL-CIO President George Meany.

231. **Jimmy Higgins** was an expression for a hard-working rank-and-file socialist who carries out the routine and dull but indispensable daily work of an organization. The expression was made famous by Upton Sinclair's 1919 novel by that name.

232. The Communist League of America **(CLA)** was formed by the first American Trotskyists shortly after they were expelled from the Communist Party in 1928. They retained that name until 1934, when they merged with the American Workers Party of A.J. Muste to form the Workers Party. In 1938, after the Trotskyists were expelled from the Socialist Party, they took their present name, Socialist Workers Party.

233. "Two Statements on Family Matters." "Deposition to the Court." From **La Verite,** May 5, 1939, in a special supplement devoted to Trotsky's efforts to gain legal custody of his only surviving grandchild, Vsievolod Volkov ("Sieva"). Translated for this volume from the French by Russell Block. **La Verite** was at this time the newspaper of the former members of the PCI (Internationalist Communist Party, the "Molinier group"), after they had dissolved their organization to enter the PSOP in December 1938. Because the child had been living with Jeanne Martin, a member of the PCI, the mem-

bers of that group sought to make factional use of Trotsky's attempt to regain custody of his grandchild. When she refused to relinquish him, Trotsky was forced to resort to legal measures. Sieva was finally brought to Mexico in March 1939 by Alfred and Marguerite Thevenet Rosmer.

234. "The 'Kidnaping' of Trotsky's Grandson." **L'Heure,** March 27, 1939. Translated for this volume from the French by Naomi Allen. A section of this statement to the press was also published in **Paris-Soir,** March 27, 1939.

235. "Fighting Against the Stream." **Internal Bulletin,** Socialist Workers Party, vol. II, no. 4, December 20, 1939, where it had the title "The Fourth International in Europe." This was the rough, uncorrected transcript of the first of two discussions on the Fourth International held in early April 1939. In this initial form, Trotsky was identified as Crux. C.L.R. James (1901-   ), who participated in the discussion under the name of Johnson, is the West Indian author of **The Black Jacobins** and **World Revolution.** He later left the Fourth Internationalist movement. When this transcript was reprinted in **Fourth International,** May 1941, the final three paragraphs were omitted, as well as the entire introductory statement by James. It appears here in its entirety for the first time in public form.

236. **C.** is James P. Cannon. **S.** is Max Shachtman. **Blasco** is Pietro Tresso (1893-1943), an Italian Communist who joined the Left Opposition in 1930 as an exile from Mussolini's Italy living in France. Under the name Julian, he was elected to the International Executive Committee at the founding conference of the Fourth International. Imprisoned during World War II, he was freed by partisans and then, apparently, assassinated by Stalinists.

237. **Reg Groves** was a founder of the British Left Opposition in the early thirties and was the British delegate to the conference of the International Left Opposition in Paris in February 1933. Shortly after that the British group split over the perspective of joining the Independent Labour Party, with Groves's group rejecting entry. Groves himself joined the Labour Party and became a trade union official. **The Marxist Group** was formed in late 1934 by the section that did enter the ILP.

238. **The Lee Group** came into existence in 1938 as a result of purely personal grievances and had no discernible political program. Millie Lee was a South African and a former member of the CP.

239. **Harry Wicks** was a leader of the old Communist League. **Charles Sumner** was the head of the Revolutionary Socialist League in 1938. He was also a secretary at the founding conference in 1938. **Henry Sara** was a Left Oppositionist who at first went with the majority, refusing to enter the ILP, and then withdrew from politics.

240. **The Militant** was the name of both the predecessor and the successor of **Socialist Appeal.**

241. The Independent Labour Party **(ILP)** was founded in 1893 by Keir Hardie and Ramsay MacDonald. The party played a major role in the founding of the Labour Party, to which it was affiliated and in which it usually held a position on the left. At the outbreak of World War I, the ILP at first adopted an antiwar position, but later supported the British war role. The ILP left the Second International when the Comintern was formed, but did not join the Comintern. When it returned to the Second International, its left wing split to join the Communist Party. Briefly attracted by the Stalinists, and then by other centrists, the ILP left the Labour Party in 1931 but returned in 1939. As early as September 1933, Trotsky urged the British Trotskyists to enter the ILP in order to win over the growing left wing there (see **Writings 33-34**).

242. **James Maxton** (1885-1946) was the principal leader of the Independent Labour Party in the thirties. His pacifism led him to hail Chamberlain's role at Munich.

243. This resolution, entitled "The International Bureau for Socialist Unity ('London Bureau') and the Fourth International," was adopted by the first International Conference for the Fourth International, held in Geneva in July 1936. Its full text is in **Documents of the Fourth International.**

244. **Mikhail Borodin** (1884-1953) was the senior Comintern military and diplomatic adviser to the Chinese nationalist government in the mid-twenties. His chief assignment was to prevent the Chinese Communists from withdrawing from the Kuomintang and conducting an independent policy against Chiang Kai-shek. He was withdrawn from China in July 1927, after the left Kuomintang had expelled the Communists from its ranks.

245. On April 12, 1927, three weeks after the victorious uprising of the Shanghai workers, Chiang Kai-shek ordered a massacre in which tens of thousands of Shanghai Communists and workers were slaughtered.

246. The conference in Zimmerwald, Switzerland, in September 1915, was designed to reassemble the antiwar and internationalist currents that had survived the debacle of the Second International. Although most of the participants were centrists, it proved to be a step in the direction of a new International. The Zimmerwald manifesto against the war, written by Trotsky, is in **Leon Trotsky Speaks** (Pathfinder Press, 1972).

247. **Max Eastman** (1883-1969) was an early sympathizer of the Left Opposition and a translator of several of Trotsky's books. His rejection of dialectical materialism in the 1920s was followed by his rejection of socialism in the 1930s. He became an anti-Communist and an editor of **Reader's Digest.**

248. "On the History of the Left Opposition." **Internal Bulletin,** Socialist Workers Party, vol. II, no. 7, January 1940. A rough, uncorrected transcript made by C. L. R. James of the second of two discussions on the Fourth International held in early April 1939. As in the first transcript, Trotsky was called Crux and James was called Johnson. Another participant was Otto Schuessler, a German who had been Trotsky's secretary in Turkey, and who used the name Oskar Fischer. This was mainly a discussion of James's book **World Revolution** (Pioneer Publishers, 1937).

249. A revolutionary situation developed in Germany in 1923, due to a severe economic crisis and the French invasion of the Ruhr. A majority of the German working class turned toward support of the Communist Party. But the CP leadership vacillated, missed an exceptionally favorable opportunity to conduct a struggle for power, and permitted the German capitalists to recover their balance before the year ended. The Kremlin's responsibility for this wasted opportunity was one of the factors that led to the formation of the Russian Left Opposition at the end of 1923.

250. **Pavel Dybenko** (1889-1938) was an Old Bolshevik who occupied several posts in the Red Army during the civil war. He was purged while in command of the Leningrad Military District. It is not possible to say just which interview Trotsky is referring to here.

251. In 1926 Trotsky presided over a special commission, consisting of Chicherin, Dzerzhinsky, and Voroshilov, which was to prepare recommendations for the Politbureau on the line that Soviet diplomacy should pursue in China. **Grigory V. Chicherin** (1872-1936) had been in the czarist diplomatic service until 1904, but resigned out of sympathy with revolutionary agitation. He became a Bolshevik in 1918, and succeeded Trotsky as people's commissar of foreign affairs, 1918-30.

252. **The New Economic Policy** (NEP) was initiated in 1921 to replace the policy of "Military Communism," which prevailed during the civil war and led to drastic declines in agricultural and industrial production. To revive the economy after the civil war, the NEP was adopted as a temporary measure allowing a limited growth of free trade inside the Soviet Union and foreign concessions alongside the nationalized and state-controlled sections of the economy. The NEP stimulated the growth of a class of wealthy peasants and of a commercial bourgeoisie (NEPmen), and produced a long series of political and economic concessions to private farming and trade.

253. After the Shanghai and Wuhan massacres, Stalin switched to an ultraleft course, urging the Chinese Communists to make an attempt to seize power. In December 1927 they staged an insurrection in Canton.

254. **Mikhail Tomsky** (1886-1936), an Old Bolshevik, was always in the right wing of the party and opposed the Bolshevik insurrec-

tion. He was head of the Soviet trade unions and a member of the Politbureau until he joined the right-wing fight against Stalin led by Bukharin. He committed suicide during the first Moscow trial.

255. Before his death, Lenin prepared a fight against the bureaucratization of the Russian Communist Party and the Soviet state, but he died before he could carry it out. His notes of the last week of December 1922 and the first week of January 1923 (or, more specifically, his letter of December 25 and postscript of January 4), written shortly before his last stroke, which led to his death, are known as his **testament.** In the letter of December 25 Lenin said of Bukharin: "He has never learned, and I think never has fully understood, the dialectic." In the postscript he called for the removal of Stalin from the post of general secretary. The testament is reprinted in **Lenin's Fight Against Stalinism** (Pathfinder Press, 1974).

256. When Bukharin became convinced of the failure of revolution in the West, he turned all his hopes on the Russian peasantry as the only reliable ally of the workers. His famous appeal **"enrich yourselves!"** was addressed to the peasants, and was accompanied by a policy of economic concessions designed to strengthen the peasantry as a way of increasing the national wealth as a whole. He also argued that the peasants' needs should determine the pace of the nation's advance toward socialism; therefore, it would be very slow, or **"socialism at a snail's pace."**

257. Beginning in 1930, Trotsky warned that despite the ultraleft "third period" rhetoric employed by the German CP leadership, there was a serious danger that it might capitulate to the Nazis when a showdown came. In 1932 the Stalinists characterized such warnings as "Trotskyite slander." In 1933 the CP allowed itself and the German working class movement to be destroyed without firing a single shot. Between his appointment as chancellor on January 30 and the Reichstag elections he held on March 5, Hitler moved boldly and swiftly to establish Nazi supremacy. Constitutional rights were suspended, the CP press was banned, thousands of Communists and Socialists were arrested, and their candidates were prevented from campaigning. The Nazis got 44 percent of the vote, giving them and their Nationalist coalition partners a clear majority and the "legal" pretext for demanding that the Reichstag grant Hitler total dictatorial power (granted later that month). Much more significant, in Trotsky's opinion, was the fact that the once-powerful German workers' movement proved incapable of promoting any struggle to preserve its own existence.

258. **J. R. Campbell** was one of the British delegates to the Sixth Congress of the Comintern in 1928, which adopted the theory of **"social fascism,"** a brainchild of Stalin. It held that Social Democracy and fascism were not opposites but twins. Since the Social Democrats were only a variety of fascist, and since just about everyone but the Stalinists was some kind of fascist, then it was impermissible for the Stalinists to engage in united fronts with any other tendency against

the real fascists. No theory was or could have been more helpful to Hitler in the years leading up to his winning power in Germany. The Stalinists finally dropped the theory in 1934, and were soon wooing not only the Social Democrats but also capitalist politicians like Roosevelt and Daladier.

259. On April 4, 5, and 11, 1939, Trotsky held a series of three discussions with C. L. R. James and others on the nature of Negro oppression in the U. S. and the tasks it presented to revolutionaries. These discussions are reprinted in **Leon Trotsky on Black Nationalism and Self-Determination** (Pathfinder Press, 1972).

260. **Old Bolsheviks** were those who joined the party prior to 1917, that is, members of the party's "Old Guard."

261. The Marxist theory of **permanent revolution** elaborated by Trotsky states, among other things, that in order to accomplish and consolidate even bourgeois democratic tasks such as land reform in an underdeveloped country, the revolution must go beyond the limits of a democratic revolution into a socialist one, which sets up a workers' and peasants' government. Such a revolution will therefore not take place in "stages" (first a stage of capitalist development to be followed at some time in the future by a socialist revolution), but will be continuous or "permanent," passing swiftly to a post-capitalist stage. For a full exposition of the theory, see **The Permanent Revolution and Results and Prospects,** by Leon Trotsky (Pathfinder Press, 1972).

262. The German Stalinists developed agitation for the "national liberation" of Germany in order to compete with the Nazis as champions of German nationalism in opposition to the oppressive Versailles treaty. Only the Nazis benefited from this competition. In the summer of 1931, the Nazis demanded a referendum to dissolve the Prussian Landtag, which would mean ousting the Social Democratic government of the state that had a majority of Germany's population. The German Stalinists initially sided with the Social Democrats against the fascists, but on orders from Moscow they abruptly reversed their position and supported the fascist referendum campaign. The Prussian workers revolted against this stupidity and refused to vote, so that the fascists received less than half of the twenty-five million votes needed to ratify the plebiscite. This incident is often referred to as the **Red Referendum. Hermann Remmele** (1880-1937) was a leader of the German CP during the years when the Nazis rose to power. He fled to the Soviet Union in 1933 and was executed by the GPU in 1937.

263. **Walter Duranty** (1884-1957) was a **New York Times** correspondent in Moscow for many years, and supported the Stalinists against the Opposition.

264. **Marcel Cachin** (1869-1958) was a leader of the French CP who came from a parliamentary background in the Socialist Party. Without the memorandum which James submitted, and which served as the basis for part of the discussion, it is impossible to know

whether by "the slogan of Blum-Cachin" Trotsky means the 1934 slogan for a united front between the SP (led by Blum) and the CP (led by Cachin), or the 1936 slogan for a workers' government.

265. "The Diego Rivera Affair." The thirteen letters and statements in this section were written between October 1938 and April 1939. They are presented together in order to provide a clear picture of the evolution of the famous artist away from revolutionary Marxism and the Fourth International, an evolution shared by many intellectuals in the period immediately preceding the outbreak of World War II. The editors wish to express their gratitude to Charles Curtiss, who was the representative of the Pan-American Committee and the International Secretariat in Mexico during this period, for providing this material from his personal papers.

266. **The resolution** on the Mexican question endorsed the recommendations of the PAC regarding the reorganization of the Mexican section. The final paragraph, dealing with Rivera, states that "in view of the difficulties that have arisen in the past with this comrade in the internal relationships of the Mexican section, he shall not form part of the reconstituted organization, but his work and activity for the Fourth International shall remain under the direct control of the International Secretariat." The full text is in **Documents of the Fourth International.**

267. This is a reference to the fact-finding commission from the United States (see note 159). **V.R. Dunne** (1890-1970) was one of the eighteen prisoners in the Minneapolis labor case. A founding member of the Trotskyist movement in the U.S., Dunne was a leader in the Minneapolis truck drivers' strikes. He remained active in the SWP until his death.

268. This resolution and several other conference documents were published in English in **Socialist Appeal,** October 22, 1938. Its full text may be found in **Documents of the Fourth International.**

269. **The Pan-American Committee** was organized to help prepare the founding conference of the Fourth International, and was assigned the task of coordinating the International's work in Latin America and the Far East after the conference. Its statement of November 8, 1938, explaining the meaning of the decision concerning Diego Rivera, was published in the November 12, 1938, **Socialist Appeal.**

270. **Octavio Fernandez** was the managing editor of **Clave** and a leader of the Mexican section before it was reorganized.

271. **C.** is Charles Curtiss (1908-   ), a member of the SWP National Committee and the representative of the International Secretariat of the Fourth International assigned to work in Mexico. He left the SWP in 1951 and joined the Socialist Party. **The Bureau** is the Pan-American Committee, which was also called the All-American and Pacific Bureau.

272. Rivera's article, "On the Intrinsic Nature and Functions of

Art," was published in the December 1938 **Clave** in the "Open Forum" section of the magazine. It was subtitled "A Letter from Diego Rivera and Juan O'Gorman." The short article Trotsky refers to at the end of the letter was not printed in **Clave.**

273. "A Necessary Statement" was translated for this volume from the French by Michael Baumann.

274. **The IS** (International Secretariat) was a subcommittee of the International Executive Committee of the Fourth International.

275. In November 1938, the frescos of the revolutionary painter Juan O'Gorman at the main passenger terminal of Mexico City's Central Airport were ordered destroyed by the Mexican government because they pictured Hitler and Mussolini in an uncomplimentary way. The destruction occasioned protests by several prominent Mexican and North American artists and writers, who saw in it a dangerous parallel to the book-burnings and inquisitions against artists in Nazi Germany. For Trotsky's comments on the event, see his letter on page 292.

276. **A.Z.** was Adolfo Zamora, Trotsky's lawyer while he was in Mexico. He and **Ferrel** (Jose Ferrel) were both members of the editorial board of **Clave.**

277. **Cr.** was Crux, a Trotsky pseudonym.

278. Rivera prepared a report on the December congress of the CGT, the congress at which Julio Ramirez, secretary-general of the CGT, formalized the organization's turn from "anarcho-syndicalism" to support of the liberal bourgeois PRM (Mexican Revolutionary Party, Mexico's ruling party). In the form in which he prepared it, the article was not printed.

279. "The Source of the Problem" was translated for this volume from the French by Naomi Allen.

280. **Van** was Jean van Heijenoort, who had served as one of Trotsky's secretaries in all four countries of his last exile. He rejected Marxism after the war and became a professor of philosophy. Rivera submitted his **resignation** from the Fourth International on January 7, 1939.

281. **James Burnham** (1905-   ) was then a leader of the SWP. He broke with the SWP in 1940 over the class nature of the Soviet state, and later became a propagandist for McCarthyism and other ultraright movements, and an editor of the right-wing **National Review. Joseph Carter** was also a leader of the SWP. **Yvan Craipeau** (1912-   ) was a Bolshevik-Leninist leader in the French Socialist Youth and a Fourth Internationalist during World War II. He was a leader of the tendency in the POI that favored entry into the PSOP (see note 303). He left the Trotskyist movement in 1948 to join various centrist groups. Trotsky's **discussions on the character of the Soviet state** with Burnham and Carter ("Not a Workers' and Not a Bourgeois State?") and with Craipeau ("Once Again: The USSR and Its Defense") are in **Writings 37-38.**

282. **Frida Kahlo de Rivera** (1910-1954), an artist in her own

right, exhibited her work in New York in November-December 1938.

283. Van Heijenoort wrote to Breton on January 11, 1939, in an attempt to set the record straight.

284. "Clave's Statement on Rivera's Resignation" was published in **Clave,** March 1939, along with Rivera's letter of resignation from the editorial board, written January 7, the same day he resigned from the Fourth International. When it appeared in **Clave** it bore the signatures of Jose Ferrel and Adolfo Zamora. The original manuscript was also signed by F. Zamora and Crux (Trotsky).

285. It was Rivera's intercession on Trotsky's behalf that convinced President Cardenas to allow Trotsky into Mexico. The Trotskys lived in Frida Kahlo's house from the time they arrived in Mexico until Rivera's split with the Fourth International. In early May 1939 they left the Rivera home on the Avenida Londres and moved into a house on the Avenida Viena.

286. For Trotsky's evaluation of the **Revolutionary Workers and Peasants Party** see "Statement of the Pan-American Committee" on page 295.

287. Andre Breton arrived in Coyoacan in February 1938, and returned to France in August. Trotsky's June 18, 1938, letter to **Partisan Review,** "Art and Politics," is reprinted in **Leon Trotsky on Literature and Art.**

288. **Antonio Hidalgo** was a high government official, a friend of Diego Rivera. **General Francisco Mujica** was secretary of communications and public works in Cardenas's cabinet. He had helped secure Trotsky's admission to Mexico. In January 1939 he declared his candidacy in the presidential elections, and Rivera supported him until he withdrew from the race later that year.

289. The report of the International Secretariat on the **Molinier** group was published in the October 22, 1938, **Socialist Appeal,** on the same page as the statement on the Mexican question. Its full text is in **Documents of the Fourth International.**

290. **Bertram Wolfe** (1896-   ), a Lovestoneite, was an apologist for the Moscow trials until late 1937, when he changed his position. (Trotsky's article on that occasion, "Bertram Wolfe on the Moscow Trials," is in **Writings 37-38.**) He collaborated with Rivera on a book entitled **Portrait of Mexico** (1927) and wrote a biography, **The Fabulous Life of Diego Rivera.** He is also the author of **Three Who Made a Revolution,** about Lenin, Trotsky, and Stalin.

291. The statement of the Pan-American Committee, written by Trotsky, was published in part in the April 18, 1939, **Socialist Appeal.** It begins on page 295 of this volume.

292. **Transitional slogans** are demands that cannot be granted under capitalism or can be granted only partially, but are designed to bridge the gap between the present level of consciousness of the masses and the needs of the socialist revolution, by drawing the masses into action around them. Trotsky's thinking on transitional slogans is developed in **The Transitional Program for Socialist Revolution.**

293. "More on Our Work in the Communist Party." From the personal archives of James P. Cannon. Signed "V. T. O'Brien."

294. This refers to the hesitations or disagreements of some SWP leaders when Trotsky first proposed, in the discussion preceding the writing of the transitional program, that the SWP should advocate the formation of workers' defense guards to fight the fascists.

295. "Greetings to Carlo Tresca." **Socialist Appeal,** April 21, 1939. **Carlo Tresca** (1878-1943) was a well-known Italian-American anarchist and editor of **Il Martello** (The Hammer). He was also a member of the Dewey Commission. His birthday and the fortieth anniversary of his participation in the working class movement were celebrated in New York City with a banquet in his honor.

296. "The Ukrainian Question." **Socialist Appeal,** May 9, 1939, where it was entitled "The Problem of the Ukraine." The policy it presents is further amplified in **Writings 39-40.**

297. In the summer of 1922, disagreements arose in the Bolshevik Party over the manner in which Moscow controlled the non-Russian republics of the Soviet Federation. Stalin was in the process of drafting a new constitution which was much more centralistic than its 1918 predecessor, and which would curtail the rights of the non-Russian nationalities and transform the Soviet Federation of republics into a Soviet Union, a step that was vigorously opposed by the Georgians and Ukrainians. Lenin supported Stalin at this time; it was not until December 1922, after Lenin had received the report of an independent fact-finding commission he had sent to Georgia, that he changed his opinion on the Georgian events, arguing that the rights of the Georgians, Ukrainians, and other non-Russian nationalities took precedence over the needs of administrative centralization that Stalin evoked. Lenin expressed his opinions in the article "On the National Question and 'Autonomization,'" in his **Collected Works,** vol. 36. It is contained in **Lenin's Fight Against Stalinism.**

298. **Taras Shevchenko** (1814-1861) was a Ukrainian poet who became known as the father of Ukrainian nationalist literature. He founded an organization to promote social equality, abolition of slavery, etc. He remains a symbol of the aspirations and goals of the Ukrainian people. **Kobzar** was the title of his first book of verse (published 1840), and is generally regarded as one of the greatest achievements of Ukrainian literature. The title is taken from the name of an ancient Ukrainian stringed instrument and symbolizes the distinct Ukrainian heritage.

299. **Pavel P. Skoropadsky** (1873-1945), a general in the czarist army, was for a short time in 1918 the Ukrainian puppet governor established in power when German troops occupied the Ukraine and dissolved the Ukrainian Rada. His regime fell after the defeat of Germany in World War I. **Simon V. Petlura** (1877-1926) was a right-wing Social Democrat before the revolution. In June 1917 he became

secretary-general for military affairs in the Ukrainian Rada. He allied himself with Poland in the Soviet-Polish war of 1920.

300. "Letter to Emrys Hughes." **Forward**, August 31, 1940. **Emrys Hughes** (1894-1969), a Welshman, was a left Labourite and editor (1936-41) of the Scottish **Forward**, one of the few public journals that would print Trotsky's writings during the Moscow trials. From 1924 to 1946 he played a leading part in local politics in a Scottish mining area, and from 1947 until his death he represented this area in Parliament where he became known as an uncompromising pacifist whose ideal was international socialism. Among his writings are **Keir Hardie** (a biography, 1950), and many pamphlets. Trotsky's letter to Hughes authorizing him to make use of his articles freely is in **Writings 37-38**.

301. "The Crisis in the French Section." The five letters in this section were written between December 1938 and July 1939. They are presented together in order to minimize duplication of notes and explanations, and to provide the greatest possible continuity for the reader. All five letters are from the personal archives of James P. Cannon. The POI (Internationalist Workers Party, French section of the Fourth International) was at this time engaged in a paralyzing struggle over whether or not its members should enter a new centrist party, the PSOP (Workers and Peasants Socialist Party), which had been formed in June 1938 when Marceau Pivert led his Gauche Revolutionnaire out of the Socialist Party. Trotsky's writings on the PSOP will be found in **Leon Trotsky on France** (Pathfinder Press, 1974).

302. **The internal crisis** refers to the general disarray produced on the French left by the Munich accords. The patriotic fervor accompanying the preparations for war had repercussions in virtually every political formation, producing pacifist sentiment as well as sentiment in support of the French government.

303. Cannon did go to Paris in the beginning of 1939.

304. **Alfred Rosmer** (1877-1964) had been a friend of Trotsky since World War I, and was a member of the Left Opposition until 1930, when he resigned because of political and organizational differences with the majority. He and Trotsky became personally reconciled in 1936.

305. When Cannon returned to the United States in April 1939, he made a report on the French situation to a New York membership meeting. He reported that the PSOP had welcomed members of the POI joining their party; however, because they had only recently had their founding congress (June 1938) and because they were significantly larger than the POI, they resisted the idea of a joint congress or a formal fusion of the two groups. It was disagreement over whether to join individually or to insist on a formal fusion that split the POI into a minority, led by Rous, which was willing to join individually, and a majority, led by Boitel, which insisted on

organizational guarantees as a pretext for refusing to join. The minority walked out of the POI's February 1939 congress and announced its intention of joining the PSOP.

306. A reference to Mathias Corvin and Fred Zeller. Zeller had been a leader of the Socialist Youth in France and International Youth Secretary of the International Communist League; later he became a leading Freemason. They were expelled from the French party in November 1937 for illicit dealings with the Stalinists, and sought to rejoin for some time thereafter.

307. Albert Goldman was sent to France in early May, and gave all the support he could to the grouping headed by Rous and Craipeau.

308. "Letter to the International Secretariat" was translated for this volume from the French by Naomi Allen.

309. In July 1939 the discord in the POI produced a split, with the minority staying in the PSOP and the majority leaving the Fourth International. The two groups were reunited during the war.

310. **Boitel** was Joannes Bardin, one of the POI leaders opposed to entering the PSOP.

311. "On Laborde and Trotskyists in General." **Clave**, May 1939. Unsigned. Translated for this volume from the Spanish by Russell Block.

312. **La Voz de Mexico** was the official publication of the Mexican CP.

313. "The Bonapartist Philosophy of the State." **New International,** June 1939.

314. **Nikolai V. Krylenko** (1885-1940), an Old Bolshevik, was commander in chief for a brief time in 1917 and became public prosecutor in 1918. He was people's commissar of justice of the Russian Republic in 1931 and of the Siberian Republic in 1936, from which post he was removed in 1937 during the purges. He was posthumously rehabilitated. **Yevgeny B. Pashukanis** (1891-1938?) joined the Bolsheviks before 1917 and worked in the People's Commissariat of Justice. He became the most prominent Soviet jurist and deputy people's commissar of justice in the Russian Republic. He disappeared during the purges. The chief Marxist writings on the nature of the state are in Lenin's book **The State and Revolution** (1917).

315. **The Political Bureau** (Politbureau) was the ruling body of the Russian CP, although ostensibly it was subordinate to the Central Committee. The first Political Bureau, elected in 1919, consisted of Kamenev, Krestinsky, Lenin, Stalin, and Trotsky. In 1939 its members were Andreyev, Kaganovich, Kalinin, Khrushchev, Mikoyan, Molotov, Stalin, and Zhdanov.

316. The **Stakhanovist** movement was a special system of speedup

in production named after a coal miner, Aleksei Stakhanov, who reportedly exceeded his quota sixteen-fold by sheer effort. The system was introduced in the Soviet Union in 1935, and led to great wage disparities and widespread discontent among the masses of workers. For his reward Stakhanov was made a full member of the CP and a deputy to the Supreme Soviet of the USSR.

317. "Nationalized Industry and Workers' Management." **Fourth International,** August 1946. Unsigned. Translated from the French by Duncan Ferguson. The date of this article, which was not on the manuscript, was tentatively identified as May or June 1938 when it was printed in **Fourth International.** However, an examination of the original at the Trotsky Archives at Harvard supplied the correct date of May 12, 1939. Trotsky wrote this article after the Cardenas government expropriated the oil industry and the railroads and placed a large degree of responsibility for managing them on the unions. An official of the CTM, Rodrigo Garcia Trevino, in opposition to the Stalinists at the time, sought Trotsky's opinion on the attitude the unions should take toward involvement in management. Trotsky agreed to write a memorandum, and several days later gave this article to Trevino. Whether Trevino used Trotsky's arguments in the debate within the CTM is not known. He kept the article secret until 1946.

318. "A Graphic History of Bolshevism." **New International,** August 1939. The tables were compiled by the editorial board of the **Biulleten Oppozitsii.**

319. **The "triumvirate"** was formed to carry on a crusade against "Trotskyism" in 1923, and was continued after Lenin's death in January 1924. Zinoviev and Kamenev broke with Stalin in 1925 and collaborated with the Left Opposition in the United Opposition in 1926-27.

320. **The Right Opposition** group in the Soviet Union was headed by Bukharin, Rykov, and Tomsky. Its program was based upon concessions to the wealthy peasants at the expense of the industrial workers and poor peasants, and upon an extension of the NEP and the free market, in the hope of averting a famine.

321. **Semyon M. Budenny** (1883-1973) joined the Bolsheviks in 1919. He won fame in the civil war as a cavalry commander, and was one of the few leading military figures to escape execution or imprisonment in the Stalinist purges.

322. **Boris M. Shaposhnikov** (1882-1945), a general in the czarist army, joined the Red Army in May 1918. He held various high military posts and in 1940 was made a marshal of the Soviet Union.

323. **Mikhail Kalinin** (1875-1946) joined the Russian Social Democracy in 1898. He succeeded Sverdlov as president of the Soviet Central Executive Committee and was a member of the Political Bureau from 1925.

324. **Andrei Andreyev** (1895-   ) joined the Bolsheviks in 1914. For his loyalty to the Stalinists in the trade union apparatus he was elevated to the Organization Bureau in the 1920s and to the Politbureau in 1932. **Anastas Mikoyan** (1895-   ) became a Bolshevik in 1915. He was elected to the Central Committee in 1923 and became a candidate member of the Politbureau in 1935. He was one of the few Old Bolsheviks to survive the purges and made his career representing the Soviet government in foreign trade negotiations.

325. "Ten Years." **New International,** August 1939, where it had the title "Ten Years of the Russian Bulletin." Signed "Editorial Board."

326. "Soviet Plutarchs." **Biulleten Oppozitsii,** no. 77-78, May-July 1939. Signed "A." Translated by John Fairlie for the first edition of **Writings 37-38.**
327. **Gad** is the Russian term for a reptile, a loathsome creature, a "skunk." — Translator.
328. **Plut** is the Russian term for a rogue or swindler. Trotsky is making a play on words with the expression "arch-pluts," or arch-rogues. — Translator.

329. "Toward a Balance Sheet of the Purges." **Biulleten Oppozitsii,** no. 77-78, May-July 1939. Signed "M.N." Translated by John Fairlie for the first edition of **Writings 37-38.** In another translation, it appeared in **Socialist Appeal,** June 30, 1939.

330. "1917-1939." **Biulleten Oppozitsii,** no. 77-78, May-July 1939. Unsigned. Translated by John Fairlie for the first edition of **Writings 37-38.**
331. **Yakov M. Sverdlov** (1885-1919), after 1917, was the chairman of the Central Executive Committee of the Congress of Soviets, and secretary of the Central Committee of the Bolshevik Party. He was also the first president of the Russian Soviet Republic. For Trotsky's obituary, see **Political Portraits** (Pathfinder Press, 1974).

332. "For a Courageous Reorientation." From the personal archives of James P. Cannon. This letter was partly quoted in Trotsky's **In Defense of Marxism**, in "From a Scratch to the Danger of Gangrene," p. 113.
333. At its congress in late May 1939, the PSOP voted to approve Pivert's motion to adhere to the **International Marxist Center**, which was a reorganization of the London Bureau (see note 75) initiated by the American Jay Lovestone, the Spaniard Julian Gorkin, and the Frenchman Michel Collinet. The motion carried the proviso that the London Bureau should invite the Fourth International to its conference in September. Trotsky speaks of a "repetition of the experi-

ment of direct contact with the centrists" because in 1933 the International Left Opposition (the predecessor of the Fourth International) had proposed joint collaboration to build a new international with the parties that later took the name London Bureau.

334. "The Riddle of the USSR." **International Socialist Review**, June 1971. Translated from the Russian by John Fairlie. This article was written for the bourgeois press.

335. **The Conservative Party,** or Tories, emerged in Britain in the eighteenth century from the old royalist party of the English civil war, the Cavaliers. Formerly the party of the aristocracy, it exists in Britain today as the party of the current ruling class, the bourgeoisie.

336. **William Strang,** a diplomat of the British Foreign Office, flew to Moscow in June 1939 to negotiate a military treaty with the Soviet Union. It was the failure of these negotiations that led in August to the Stalin-Hitler pact.

337. **The Italo-German Alliance** was signed on May 22, 1939. **The Aland Islands,** in the Baltic Sea between Finland and Sweden, were the scene of political maneuvers in the months preceding the war. In May 1939, Russia blocked Finland from fortifying the islands, whose chief value is their strategic position. They were later used by the Soviet Union to defeat Finland in the Soviet-Finnish war of 1939-40.

338. **"Collective security"** was the concept behind the League of Nations that was expected to prevent future wars. Member states of the League had the obligation under its Article 16 to invoke sanctions against acts of aggression by other states.

339. **Walter Krivitsky** (1889-1941) defected from the Soviet military intelligence service in 1937 while in Paris, and revealed numerous secrets of Soviet intelligence. He was the author of **In Stalin's Secret Service** (1939). He died under mysterious circumstances six months after the assassination of Trotsky.

340. **Berchtesgaden,** a resort in the Bavarian Alps, was the unofficial capital of the Third Reich and Hitler's private retreat.

341. In the British press, this appeared as the approximately equivalent proverb "getting other people to pull the chestnuts out of the fire for them." — Translator.

342. Germany demanded the return of the Polish free city of Gdansk (**Danzig**), and a strip of land across Polish territory to connect Germany proper with East Prussia. This was the pretext used for the invasion of Poland in September 1939. Hitler actually struck at the East (Poland) before he struck at the West (France), but he had allayed Russian fears by concluding the nonaggression pact with the Soviet Union first.

343. "The Kremlin in World Politics." **New International**, October 1942.

344. **The Treaty of Rapallo** (April 1922) made the German government the first in the world to extend diplomatic recognition to the USSR. In addition, it canceled all prewar debts and all war claims between the two governments. Germany, which was then laboring under the Versailles system, was accorded most-favored-nation status and significant trade concessions in return for its technological assistance to the young Soviet government.

345. **Friedrich Ebert** (1871-1925) was a leader of the right wing of the German Social Democracy. As chancellor, he presided with Scheidemann over the crushing of the November 1918 revolution, executing Rosa Luxemburg, Karl Liebknecht, and other German revolutionists. He was president of the Weimar Republic from 1919 to 1925.

346. **Anthony Eden** (1897-   ), as secretary of state for foreign affairs in the Chamberlain government, followed a policy of rapprochement with the Soviet Union. He was forced to resign when he came into conflict with Chamberlain's appeasement policy after the Munich conference. When World War II broke out, he was brought back into the cabinet as foreign secretary.

347. **Colonel Jozef Beck** (1894-1944) was Polish minister of foreign affairs from 1932 to 1939.

348. **The English Liberals** were a coalition of reformers that emerged from the Whigs in the mid-nineteenth century.

349. **The New York Times** published the full text of the letter, translated from the French, along with photostats of the first and last pages of the four-page original. An accompanying interview with Luis Araquistain testified to the authenticity of the letter. **Araquistain** (1886-1959) had been editor of the Spanish Socialist Party's newspaper **Claridad** before he became ambassador to France in September 1936.

INDEX

OTHER WRITINGS OF 1938-39

In addition to the material in the present volume, the following writings by Trotsky during the period covered here have been published:

Leon Trotsky on the Trade Unions. 1969. Includes "Discussion with a CIO Organizer" (September 29, 1938).

The Spanish Revolution (1931-39). 1973. Includes "Traitors in the Role of Accusers" (October 22, 1938), "The Tragedy of Spain" (February 1939), "Spain, Stalin, and Yezhov," "Mysteries of Imperialism" and "Once Again on the Causes of the Defeat in Spain" (all three dated March 4, 1939), and "Their Friend Miaja" (March 24, 1939).

Leon Trotsky on China. 1975. Includes Trotsky's review of The Tragedy of the Chinese Revolution, by Harold R. Isaacs (October 23, 1938).

Leon Trotsky on France. 1974. Includes "SOS" (December 8, 1938), "The Decisive Hour" (December 14, 1938), "Where Is the PSOP Going?" (December 22, 1938), "Letter to a Friend in France" (February 14, 1939), "Centrism and the Fourth International" (March 10, 1939), "'Trotskyism' and the PSOP" (July 15, 1939), and "Letter to the Editors of Juin 36" (July 23, 1939).

Leon Trotsky on the Jewish Question. 1970. Includes "Appeal to American Jews Menaced by Fascism and Anti-Semitism" (December 22, 1938).

Leon Trotsky on Literature and Art. 1970. Includes "The Independence of the Artist: A Letter to Andre Breton" (December 22, 1938).

Leon Trotsky on Black Nationalism and Self-Determination. 1970. Includes transcripts of three discussions with C. L. R. James and others (April 4, 5, and 11, 1939).

Their Morals and Ours: Marxist versus Liberal Views on Morality. 1966. Includes "Moralists and Sycophants Against Marxism" (June 9, 1939).

Marxism in Our Time. 1970. A slightly shortened version of this essay, dated April 18, 1939, was used as the introduction to The Living Thoughts of Karl Marx (1939).

Finally, Trotsky was working at this time on his biography of Stalin, about which a cautionary note appears in the 1939-40 volume.